FIVE GREAT
GERMAN SHORT STORIES

FIVE GREAT GERMAN SHORT STORIES

FÜNF DEUTSCHE MEISTERERZÄHLUNGEN

A DUAL-LANGUAGE BOOK

Edited and Translated by

STANLEY APPELBAUM

DOVER PUBLICATIONS, INC.
NEW YORK

Copyright © 1993 by Dover Publications, Inc.
All rights reserved under Pan American and International Copyright Conventions.

Five Great German Short Stories / Fünf deutsche Meistererzählungen, first published by Dover Publications, Inc., in 1993, consists of a new selection of German stories, reprinted from standard German texts (see the individual story introductions for details of first publication in German), accompanied by new English translations prepared specially for the present edition, with new introductory matter.

Manufactured in the United States of America
Dover Publications, Inc., 31 East 2nd Street, Mineola, N.Y. 11501

Library of Congress Cataloging-in-Publication Data

Five great German short stories = Fünf deutsche Meistererzählungen : a dual-language book / edited and translated by Stanley Appelbaum.
    p.   cm.
    Contents: Das Erdbeben in Chili / Heinrich von Kleist — Der Sandmann / E.T.A. Hoffmann — Leutnant Gustl / Arthur Schnitzler — Tristan / Thomas Mann — Das Urteil / Franz Kafka.
    ISBN 0-486-27619-8
    1. Short stories, German—Translations into English. 2. German fiction—Translations into English. 3. Short stories, English—Translations from German. 4. English fiction—Translations from German. I. Appelbaum, Stanley. II. Title: Fünf deutsche Meistererzählungen.
PT1327.F58   1993
863'.0108—dc20   92-42992
                                                  CIP

CONTENTS

FOREWORD

ARTISTIC PROSE NARRATIVE in German lagged far behind poetry and drama throughout the medieval and Renaissance periods. Germany had its *Nibelungenlied* and *Parzival*, minnesingers and mastersingers, philosophers and theologians, but no *Decameron*, *Heptameron*, *Gargantua*, *Morte Darthur*, *Conde Lucanor* or *Lazarillo de Tormes*. Some important novels appeared in Germany in the seventeenth and eighteenth centuries, particularly Grimmelshausen's *Simplicissimus* (1668–9) and several by Goethe, but it was not until about 1800 that the short story made a widespread appearance, following the lead of prototypes by Schiller and Goethe.[1] Amid the turmoil of the Napoleonic wars and the fervor of the new Romantic movement, short stories were soon being written in all parts of German-speaking Europe. In the hands of such writers as Novalis, Tieck, Brentano, Kleist and Hoffmann, the short story quickly established itself as one of the most expressive and characteristic genres in German literature.

The remainder of the nineteenth century—passing through such literary trends as the Biedermeier (the peaceful, domesticated, bourgeois era from 1815 to 1848), "poetic realism," regionalism, social consciousness, naturalism and symbolism—has been seen as the golden age of the German short story, which was consecrated by writers such as Büchner; Eichendorff; Droste-Hülshoff; the Austrians Grillparzer and Stifter; the three Swiss authors Meyer, Gotthelf and Keller; Storm; and Hauptmann—many of whom are still not sufficiently well known outside their homelands.

Two towering figures at the turn of the present century (and beyond) were Thomas Mann and the Austrian Arthur Schnitzler. In their work, nineteenth-century thought is subjected to searching reevaluations and the storyteller's art becomes even more complex

---

[1] There are a number of German designations for story or short story, variously defined by critics. They include *Erzählung, Novelle, Geschichte, Kurzgeschichte* (this last applies to the very short, anecdotal story typical of such English-language writers as Saki and O'Henry), as well as several more specific appellations (e.g., *Märchen*, "fairy tale").

and self-conscious. In the early decades of the century Kafka's baleful comet portends the anguish of contemporary man.

Through the remainder of this century—obedient to the sometimes transient modes of expressionism, surrealism, existentialism, the absurd and so on, but still appreciative of and nurtured by their forerunners' accomplishments—such writers as Hesse, Stefan Zweig, Huch, Bachmann, Böll and Handke (to single out just a very few great names) have maintained the preeminence of the German-language short story.

Clearly, dozens of first-class anthologies could be based on this wealth of material. For the present volume, necessarily limited to a handful of stories, the overriding criterion for inclusion was that each story should be a recognized pinnacle in the oeuvre of an internationally venerated author.

Kleist, with his spirit of revolt, and Hoffmann, with his matchless imagination, represent the northern (Prussian) branch of high Romanticism (with Hoffmann's career blending into early Biedermeier both chronologically and in subject matter). The cream of turn-of-the-century artistry is represented by Schnitzler, dissecting Viennese gaiety with a surgeon's scalpel, and Mann, preoccupied with the Germanic love/death complex and the artist's role in society. Finally, Kafka probes the alienation, absurdity and guilt we have all become heir to.

The stories are arranged in the sequence of their first appearance, not by their authors' birth dates. A complete standard German text is supplied for each, the only alteration from the original consisting in the additional paragraphing that has been introduced in the first three stories, for greater convenience in reading and in comparing the German with the facing English versions. (Additional paragraphing has been a common procedure in English translations of these stories.)

The translations, prepared specially for the present volume, are absolutely complete and as literal as possible without denaturing the English. It is hoped that the English versions are readable in their own right, but close adherence to the German was a major consideration. Every attempt has been made to reflect the nuances of the author's intentions.

The brief introductions to the individual stories keep biographical data (easily obtainable in encyclopedias) to a minimum, concentrating instead on a discussion of the story itself and, to some extent, on the characteristics of the author's German style. For four of these stories, extensive English-language analyses by literary historians and critics are available elsewhere; unfortunately, "Lieutenant

Gustl," for all its significance, is still the least accessible to English readers.

The succinct footnotes, all by the present editor and translator, identify historical references or discuss textual problems.

Among those who made helpful suggestions, Shane Weller above all, as well as Alan Weissman, deserve special thanks.

FIVE GREAT
GERMAN SHORT STORIES

KLEIST
AND
"THE EARTHQUAKE IN CHILE"

HEINRICH VON KLEIST—in his plays, stories and poems, the first great German literary rebel against eighteenth-century rationalism and the aging Goethe's classicism—was born in Frankfurt an der Oder in 1777. The son of a Prussian officer and nobleman, he himself was trained for the army and saw action as a youth, but his preference was for philosophical and scientific studies. He traveled in the German lands and in France and Switzerland, meeting influential literary figures and nurturing boundless ambitions as an author, but remaining unsettled, unattached and subject to nervous fits. His major works were all planned and written within one decade. From 1804 to 1807 he was in government financial service in Berlin and Königsberg (the later Kaliningrad). Between 1808 and 1811 he was an editor of the literary journal *Phöbus* and the newspaper *Berliner Abendblätter*. In 1811—his patriotism thwarted by Napoleon's successes, his talents largely unrecognized and his income dried up—he killed himself after shooting an incurably ill female friend. His major plays, including *Der zerbrochene Krug* (The Broken Pitcher), *Penthesilea* and *Der Prinz von Homburg*, were still unproduced, or had been given only very inadequate productions.

"The Earthquake in Chile," inspired by a historical disaster, was probably the earliest written of Kleist's eight stories, the first high point of German short-story writing after the pioneering work of Schiller and Goethe. Written in Königsberg and finished by the fall of 1806, it was first published by the eminent Johann Friedrich Cotta in Stuttgart, in issues of his *Morgenblatt für gebildete Stände* dating from the 10th to the 15th of September 1807. (Its title in the magazine was "Jeronimo und Josephe. Eine Szene aus dem Erdbeben zu Chili, vom Jahr 1647" [Jerónimo and Josefa. A Scene from the Earthquake in Chile in the Year 1647].) Kleist then included it in the first volume of his *Erzählungen,* published by Georg Andreas Reimer, Berlin, 1810 (the volume was censored in Vienna for its antiestablishment tendencies). There is no known source for the plot, but Kleist is believed to have incorporated descriptions by Kant and others of the Lisbon earthquake of 1755.

As in so many of Kleist's works, the principal characters of "The Earthquake in Chile" are strong-willed individuals, pitted against authority by the urgency of their personal drives and their vision

of a better social order. Upheavals in nature and the external world accompany and reflect their own seething minds. Magnanimous thoughts and deeds are powerless against entrenched reactionary beliefs at all levels of society.

Kleist's writing is as volcanic as his subject matter. The narrative progresses with such lapidary rapidity that it almost seems like the précis of a story; note the amount of information conveyed by the opening sentence alone. There are only a couple of seeming pauses for reflective description, but even these chiefly serve to motivate the characters or act as a foil for the human emotions in the foreground: the beautiful night in the forest reconciles Jerónimo and Josefa to life and encourages them to plan for the future; the awesome splendor of the church in readiness for the Te Deum celebration provides a telling contrast to the savagery soon to be unleashed.

Also volcanic, from a different point of view, are the slag and scoria of Kleist's style, one of the least polished in the front rank of German literature. His hot haste leads him to awkward repetitions of words, ambiguous placement of dependent clauses and tics of sentence construction: in this brief story, at least eight sentences share the general pattern "scarcely did X occur when Y occurred." But these are forgivable flaws in a style otherwise admirable for clarity and directness of expression, and emulated by such later masters as Kafka.

In the present translation, all Christian names have been regularized into their correct Spanish form (the German original offers a babel of forms), and additional paragraphing has been liberally introduced for convenience of reading and comparing the languages. The German original story is divided into no more than three paragraphs, the second commencing at the words "Als sie erwachten" (page 14), and the third at "Inzwischen war" (page 20).

DAS ERDBEBEN IN CHILI

In St. Jago, der Hauptstadt des Königreichs Chili, stand gerade in dem Augenblicke der großen Erderschütterung vom Jahre 1647, bei welcher viele tausend Menschen ihren Untergang fanden, ein junger, auf ein Verbrechen angeklagter Spanier namens Jeronimo Rugera an einem Pfeiler des Gefängnisses, in welches man ihn eingesperrt hatte, und wollte sich erhenken. Don Henrico Asteron, einer der reichsten Edelleute der Stadt, hatte ihn ohngefähr ein Jahr zuvor aus seinem Hause, wo er als Lehrer angestellt war, entfernt, weil er sich mit Donna Josephe, seiner einzigen Tochter, in einem zärtlichen Einverständnis befunden hatte. Eine geheime Bestellung, die dem alten Don, nachdem er die Tochter nachdrücklich gewarnt hatte, durch die hämische Aufmerksamkeit seines stolzen Sohnes verraten worden war, entrüstete ihn dergestalt, daß er sie in dem Karmeliter-Kloster unsrer lieben Frauen vom Berge daselbst unterbrachte. Durch einen glücklichen Zufall hatte Jeronimo hier die Verbindung von neuem anzuknüpfen gewußt und in einer verschwiegenen Nacht den Klostergarten zum Schauplatze seines vollen Glückes gemacht.

Es war am Fronleichnamsfeste, und die feierliche Prozession der Nonnen, welchen die Novizen folgten, nahm eben ihren Anfang, als die unglückliche Josephe bei dem Anklange der Glocken in Mutterwehen auf den Stufen der Kathedrale niedersank. Dieser Vorfall machte außerordentliches Aufsehn; man brachte die junge Sünderin ohne Rücksicht auf ihren Zustand sogleich in ein Gefängnis, und kaum war sie aus den Wochen erstanden, als ihr schon auf Befehl des Erzbischofs der geschärfteste Prozeß gemacht ward.

Man sprach in der Stadt mit einer so großen Erbitterung von diesem Skandal, und die Zungen fielen so scharf über das ganze Kloster her, in welchem er sich zugetragen hatte, daß weder die Fürbitte der Familie Asteron noch auch sogar der Wunsch der Äbtissin selbst, welche das junge Mädchen wegen ihres sonst untadelhaften Betragens liebgewonnen hatte, die Strenge, mit welcher das klösterliche Gesetz sie bedrohte, mildern konnte. Alles, was gesche-

THE EARTHQUAKE IN CHILE

In Santiago, the capital of the kingdom of Chile,[1] at the very moment of the great earthquake of the year 1647, in which many thousands of people perished, a young Spaniard accused of a crime, Jerónimo Rugera by name, was standing by a pillar of the prison in which he had been confined and was about to hang himself. About a year previously, Don Enrique Asterón, one of the richest noblemen in the city, had dismissed him from his house, where he was employed as a tutor, because Jerónimo and Doña Josefa, Asterón's only daughter, had fallen in love. A secret tryst, which had been revealed to the old Don—after he had expressly warned his daughter—by the malicious vigilance of his haughty son, so infuriated him that he placed her in the Carmelite convent of Our Lady of the Mountain in that city. Here, through a lucky accident, Jerónimo had been able to resume the relationship and, one night, had secretly made the convent garden the scene of his highest bliss.

It was Corpus Christi day, and the solemn procession of the nuns, whom the novices followed, was just setting out when the unfortunate Josefa sank down on the cathedral steps in labor pains as the bells began to ring. This incident created an unusual sensation; the young sinner, with no regard to her condition, was immediately thrown in prison, and scarcely had she arisen from childbed when, by order of the archbishop, she was subjected to the most harrowing trial.

This scandal was discussed in the city with so much animosity, and people's tongues dealt so harshly with the entire convent in which it had taken place, that neither the intercession of the Asterón family nor even the request of the abbess herself—who had grown fond of the young girl because of her otherwise irreproachable conduct—was able to palliate the severity with which the monastic laws threatened her. All that could be done was

---

[1] Chile was never a kingdom; in 1647, when an earthquake did occur, it was a Spanish colony, part of the viceroyalty of Peru; the viceroy resided in Lima.

hen konnte, war, daß der Feuertod, zu dem sie verurteilt wurde,
zur großen Entrüstung der Matronen und Jungfrauen von St. Jago
durch einen Machtspruch des Vizekönigs in eine Enthauptung ver-
wandelt ward. Man vermietete in den Straßen, durch welche der
Hinrichtungszug gehen sollte, die Fenster, man trug die Dächer
der Häuser ab, und die frommen Töchter der Stadt luden ihre
Freundinnen ein, um dem Schauspiele, das der göttlichen Rache
gegeben wurde, an ihrer schwesterlichen Seite beizuwohnen.

Jeronimo, der inzwischen auch in ein Gefängnis gesetzt worden
war, wollte die Besinnung verlieren, als er diese ungeheure Wendung der Dinge erfuhr. Vergebens sann er auf Rettung: überall,
wohin ihn auch der Fittich der vermessensten Gedanken trug, stieß
er auf Riegel und Mauern, und ein Versuch, die Gitterfenster zu
durchfeilen, zog ihm, da er entdeckt ward, eine nur noch engere
Einsperrung zu. Er warf sich vor dem Bildnisse der heiligen Mutter
Gottes nieder und betete mit unendlicher Inbrunst zu ihr als der
einzigen, von der ihm jetzt noch Rettung kommen könnte.

Doch der gefürchtete Tag erschien und mit ihm in seiner Brust
die Überzeugung von der völligen Hoffnungslosigkeit seiner Lage.
Die Glocken, welche Josephen zum Richtplatze begleiteten, ertön-
ten, und Verzweiflung bemächtigte sich seiner Seele. Das Leben
schien ihm verhaßt, und er beschloß, sich durch einen Strick, den
ihm der Zufall gelassen hatte, den Tod zu geben. Eben stand er,
wie schon gesagt, an einem Wandpfeiler und befestigte den Strick,
der ihn dieser jammervollen Welt entreißen sollte, an eine Eisen-
klammer, die an dem Gesimse derselben eingefugt war, als plötzlich
der größte Teil der Stadt mit einem Gekrache, als ob das Firmament
einstürzte, versank und alles, was Leben atmete, unter seinen Trümmern begrub.

Jeronimo Rugera war starr vor Entsetzen; und gleich, als ob sein
ganzes Bewußtsein zerschmettert worden wäre, hielt er sich jetzt an
dem Pfeiler, an welchem er hatte sterben wollen, um nicht umzufal-
len. Der Boden wankte unter seinen Füßen, alle Wände des Gefängnisses rissen, der ganze Bau neigte sich, nach der Straße zu
einzustürzen, und nur der seinem langsamen Fall begegnende Fall
des gegenüberstehenden Gebäudes verhinderte durch eine zufäl-
lige Wölbung die gänzliche Zubodenstreckung desselben.

Zitternd, mit sträubenden Haaren und Knien, die unter ihm bre-
chen wollten, glitt Jeronimo über den schiefgesenkten Fußboden
hinweg der Öffnung zu, die der Zusammenschlag beider Häuser
in die vordere Wand des Gefängnisses eingerissen hatte. Kaum

to have the death by fire, to which she had been condemned, commuted to beheading by decree of the viceroy, much to the indignation of the matrons and maidens
of Santiago. In the streets along which the execution
procession would pass, windows were rented, the roofs of
the houses were leveled, and the pious daughters of the
city invited their girl friends to attend the spectacle offered to divine vengeance at their sisterly side.

Jerónimo, who meanwhile had also been clapped in
prison, thought he would go out of his mind when he
heard about this horrible turn of events. In vain did he
ponder ways of rescuing her: wherever the wings of even
the most unbridled notions carried him, he came up
against bolts and walls; and an attempt to file through
the window grating only gained him a still more cramped
dungeon when he was discovered. He flung himself down
before the image of the Mother of God, and prayed to her
with tremendous ardor, believing her to be the only one
from whom salvation could still come.

But the dreaded day arrived, and with it, in his heart, a
conviction of the total hopelessness of his situation. The
bells that accompanied Josefa to her place of execution
rang out, and despair took hold of his soul. Life seemed
hateful to him, and he decided to kill himself with a rope
that had been left to him by chance. He was just standing,
as mentioned above, by a wall pillar and was securing the
rope that was to snatch him from this world of sorrow to
an iron clamp that was inserted into the pillar molding,
when suddenly the greater part of the city sank with a
roar as if the sky were falling, and buried all living things
beneath its ruins.

Jerónimo Rugera was rigid with terror; and, as if all his
presence of mind had been wiped out, he now held on to
the pillar on which he had intended to die, in order not
to fall over. The ground shook beneath his feet, all the
walls of the prison were cleft, the whole structure threatened to collapse onto the street, and only the subsidence
of the building opposite, occurring at the same time as
the prison was slowly falling apart, prevented its complete
leveling with the ground by creating an accidental sup-
porting vault.

Trembling, his hair on end, and with knees about to
buckle under him, Jerónimo slid across the now tilted
floor toward the opening that the collision of the two
buildings had torn in the front wall of the prison. Scarcely

befand er sich im Freien, als die ganze schon erschütterte Straße
auf eine zweite Bewegung der Erde völlig zusammenfiel. Besin-
nungslos, wie er sich aus diesem allgemeinen Verderben retten
würde, eilte er über Schutt und Gebälk hinweg, indessen der Tod
von allen Seiten Angriffe auf ihn machte, nach einem der nächsten
Tore der Stadt.

Hier stürzte noch ein Haus zusammen und jagte ihn, die Trümmer weit umherschleudernd, in eine Nebenstraße; hier leckte die
Flamme schon, in Dampfwolken blitzend, aus allen Giebeln und
trieb ihn schreckenvoll in eine andere; hier wälzte sich, aus seinem
Gestade gehoben, der Mapochofluß an ihn heran und riß ihn brül-
lend in eine dritte. Hier lag ein Haufen Erschlagener, hier ächzte
noch eine Stimme unter dem Schutte, hier schrien Leute von brennenden Dächern herab, hier kämpften Menschen und Tiere mit
den Wellen, hier war ein mutiger Retter bemüht, zu helfen; hier
stand ein anderer, bleich wie der Tod, und streckte sprachlos zit-
ternde Hände zum Himmel.

Als Jeronimo das Tor erreicht und einen Hügel jenseits desselben bestiegen hatte, sank er ohnmächtig auf demselben nieder.
Er mochte wohl eine Viertelstunde in der tiefsten Bewußtlosigkeit
gelegen haben, als er endlich wieder erwachte und sich mit nach
der Stadt gekehrtem Rücken halb auf dem Erdboden erhob. Er
befühlte sich Stirn und Brust, unwissend, was er aus seinem Zustande machen sollte, und ein unsägliches Wonnegefühl ergriff ihn,
als ein Westwind vom Meere her sein wiederkehrendes Leben an-
wehte, und sein Auge sich nach allen Richtungen über die blühende
Gegend von St. Jago hinwandte. Nur die verstörten Menschenhau-
fen, die sich überall blicken ließen, beklemmten sein Herz; er begriff nicht, was ihn und sie hierhergeführt haben konnte, und erst,
da er sich umkehrte und die Stadt hinter sich versunken sah, erinnerte er sich des schrecklichen Augenblicks, den er erlebt hatte. Er
senkte sich so tief, daß seine Stirn den Boden berührte, Gott für
seine wunderbare Errettung zu danken; und gleich, als ob der eine
entsetzliche Eindruck, der sich seinem Gemüt eingeprägt hatte, alle
früheren daraus verdrängt hätte, weinte er vor Lust, daß er sich
des lieblichen Lebens voll bunter Erscheinungen noch erfreue.

Drauf, als er eines Ringes an seiner Hand gewahrte, erinnerte er
sich plötzlich auch Josephens; und mit ihr seines Gefängnisses, der
Glocken, die er dort gehört hatte, und des Augenblicks, der dem
Einsturze desselben vorangegangen war. Tiefe Schwermut erfüllte
wieder seine Brust; sein Gebet fing ihn zu reuen an, und fürchterlich schien ihm das Wesen, das über den Wolken waltet. Er mischte

was he out in the open when a second earth tremor caused the entire street, already badly shaken, to cave in altogether. Unable to think how he could escape from this universal destruction, he hastened away over debris and timbers toward one of the nearest city gates, while death attacked him from all sides.

Here yet another house collapsed and, flinging its ruins far and wide, forced him into a side street; here flames were already shooting out of every gable, flashing in clouds of smoke, driving him in terror into another street; here the Mapocho River, shifting from its bed, rolled toward him, sweeping him with a roar into a third street. Here lay a heap of corpses, here a voice was still groaning beneath the debris, here people were shouting from burning rooftops, here humans and animals were struggling with the waves, here a courageous rescuer was making an effort to help; here stood another man, pale as death, speechlessly extending his trembling hands toward heaven.

When Jerónimo reached the gate and had ascended a hill outside it, he fell down there in a faint. He had probably lain there completely unconscious for a quarter of an hour when he finally awoke again and partly raised himself from the ground, his back turned toward the city. He felt his forehead and chest, not knowing what to make of his condition, and an immense feeling of bliss came over him when a westerly breeze from the sea quickened his recovering senses, and his eyes roved in all directions over the flourishing countryside of Santiago. Only the clusters of agitated people that were everywhere to be seen saddened his heart; he could not comprehend what had brought him and them to this place, and only when he turned around and saw the city in ruins behind him, did he recall the fearful moment he had lived through. He bowed his head so low that his forehead touched the ground, in order to thank God for his miraculous rescue; and, as if the one terrible impression that had been stamped on his mind had driven all earlier ones from it, he wept for happiness because he still enjoyed the charms of life with all its manifold phenomena.

Then, noticing a ring on his finger, he suddenly recalled Josefa as well; and, along with her, his prison, the bells he had heard there, and the moment preceding its collapse. Deep melancholy filled his heart again; he began to regret having prayed, and the Being that rules above the clouds

sich unter das Volk, das überall, mit Rettung des Eigentums beschäftigt, aus den Toren stürzte, und wagte schüchtern nach der Tochter Asterons, und ob die Hinrichtung an ihr vollzogen worden sei, zu fragen; doch niemand war, der ihm umständliche Auskunft gab. Eine Frau, die auf einem fast zur Erde gedrückten Nacken eine ungeheure Last von Gerätschaften und zwei Kinder, an der Brust hängend, trug, sagte im Vorbeigehen, als ob sie es selbst angesehen hätte: daß sie enthauptet worden sei.

Jeronimo kehrte sich um; und da er, wenn er die Zeit berechnete, selbst an ihrer Vollendung nicht zweifeln konnte, so setzte er sich in einem einsamen Walde nieder und überließ sich seinem vollen Schmerz. Er wünschte, daß die zerstörende Gewalt der Natur von neuem über ihn einbrechen möchte. Er begriff nicht, warum er dem Tode, den seine jammervolle Seele suchte, in jenen Augenblicken, da er ihm freiwillig von allen Seiten rettend erschien, entflohen sei. Er nahm sich fest vor, nicht zu wanken, wenn auch jetzt die Eichen entwurzelt werden und ihre Wipfeln über ihn zusammenstürzen sollten.

Darauf nun, da er sich ausgeweint hatte, und ihm mitten unter den heißesten Tränen die Hoffnung wieder erschienen war, stand er auf und durchstreifte nach allen Richtungen das Feld. Jeden Berggipfel, auf dem sich die Menschen versammelt hatten, besuchte er; auf allen Wegen, wo sich der Strom der Flucht noch bewegte, begegnete er ihnen; wo nur irgendein weibliches Gewand im Winde flatterte, da trug ihn sein zitternder Fuß hin: doch keines deckte die geliebte Tochter Asterons.

Die Sonne neigte sich und mit ihr seine Hoffnung schon wieder zum Untergange, als er den Rand eines Felsens betrat und sich ihm die Aussicht in ein weites, nur von wenigen Menschen besuchtes Tal eröffnete. Er durchlief, unschlüssig, was er tun sollte, die einzelnen Gruppen derselben und wollte sich schon wieder wenden, als er plötzlich an einer Quelle, die die Schlucht bewässerte, ein junges Weib erblickte, beschäftigt, ein Kind in ihren Fluten zu reinigen. Und das Herz hüpfte ihm bei diesem Anblick: er sprang voll Ahnung über die Gesteine herab und rief:»O Mutter Gottes, du Heilige!« und erkannte Josephen, als sie sich bei dem Geräusche schüchtern umsah.

Mit welcher Seligkeit umarmten sie sich, die Unglücklichen, die ein Wunder des Himmels gerettet hatte! Josephe war auf ihrem Gang zum Tode dem Richtplatze schon ganz nahe gewesen, als durch den krachenden Einsturz der Gebäude plötzlich der ganze Hinrichtungszug auseinandergesprengt ward. Ihre ersten entsetzensvollen Schritte trugen sie hierauf dem nächsten Tore zu; doch

seemed fearsome to him. He mingled with the people who were dashing out of the gates on all sides, busy saving their belongings, and timidly risked asking about Asterón's daughter and whether her execution had been carried out; but no one was able to give him detailed information. A woman bent over almost to the ground under an enormous load of utensils she was carrying on her shoulders and two children who were clutching her bosom, said as she passed by—speaking as if she had been an eyewitness—that Josefa had been beheaded.

Jerónimo turned aside; and, since, on calculating the time elapsed, he himself had no doubts that the execution had taken place, he sat down in a lonely wood and abandoned himself fully to his grief. He wished that the destructive power of nature would come down upon him again. He could not comprehend why he had escaped death, which his miserable soul now sought, at the time when it was offering itself to him freely on all sides. He resolved firmly not to waver even if the oaks were now uprooted and their tops were to tumble down upon him.

So, after he had wept his fill and, in the midst of his hottest tears, hope had returned to him, he arose and walked back and forth over the area in all directions. He visited every hilltop on which people had gathered; he met them on every path on which the stream of refugees still flowed; his trembling feet bore him wherever a women's garment fluttered in the breeze, but no garment clad the beloved daughter of Asterón.

The sun was again setting, and with it his hope, when he stepped to the edge of a cliff and obtained a view of a broad valley to which very few people had come. Undecided what he should do, he hurried from one to another of the individual groups, and was about to turn away again when he suddenly saw, by a brook that watered the valley, a young woman busy bathing a child in its stream. And his heart leaped at that sight: full of presentiment, he sprang down over the rocks, shouting "O Holy Mother of God!" and recognized Josefa when she timidly looked about on hearing the sound.

With what rapture they embraced, that unfortunate pair whom a miracle of heaven had saved! On her march to death, Josefa had already been quite close to the place of execution when suddenly the entire procession had been scattered by the resounding collapse of the buildings. Then her first terrified steps brought her to the nearest

die Besinnung kehrte ihr bald wieder, und sie wandte sich, um nach
dem Kloster zu eilen, wo ihr kleiner hilfloser Knabe zurückgeblie-
ben war.

Sie fand das ganze Kloster schon in Flammen, und die Äbtissin,
die ihr in jenen Augenblicken, die ihre letzten sein sollten, Sorge
für den Säugling angelobt hatte, schrie eben, vor den Pforten ste-
hend, nach Hilfe, um ihn zu retten. Josephe stürzte sich uner-
schrocken durch den Dampf, der ihr entgegenqualmte, in das von
allen Seiten schon zusammenfallende Gebäude, und gleich, als ob
alle Engel des Himmels sie umschirmten, trat sie mit ihm unbeschä-
digt wieder aus dem Portal hervor. Sie wollte der Äbtissin, welche
die Hände über ihr Haupt zusammenschlug, eben in die Arme
sinken, als diese mit fast allen ihren Klosterfrauen von einem herab-
fallenden Giebel des Hauses auf eine schmähliche Art erschlagen
ward.

Josephe bebte bei diesem entsetzlichen Anblicke zurück; sie
drückte der Äbtissin flüchtig die Augen zu und floh, ganz von
Schrecken erfüllt, den teuern Knaben, den ihr der Himmel wieder
geschenkt hatte, dem Verderben zu entreißen. Sie hatte noch wenig
Schritte getan, als ihr auch schon die Leiche des Erzbischofs begegnete, die man soeben zerschmettert aus dem Schutt der Kathedrale
hervorgezogen hatte. Der Palast des Vizekönigs war versunken, der
Gerichtshof, in welchem ihr das Urteil gesprochen worden war,
stand in Flammen, und an die Stelle, wo sich ihr väterliches Haus
befunden hatte, war ein See getreten und kochte rötliche Dämpfe
aus. Josephe raffte alle ihre Kräfte zusammen, sich zu halten.

Sie schritt, den Jammer von ihrer Brust entfernend, mutig mit
ihrer Beute von Straße zu Straße und war schon dem Tore nahe,
als sie auch das Gefängnis, in welchem Jeronimo geseufzt hatte, in
Trümmern sah. Bei diesem Anblicke wankte sie und wollte besin-
nungslos an einer Ecke niedersinken; doch in demselben Augenblick jagte sie der Sturz eines Gebäudes hinter ihr, das die Erschütte-
rungen schon ganz aufgelöst hatten, durch das Entsetzen gestärkt,
wieder auf; sie küßte das Kind, drückte sich die Tränen aus den
Augen und erreichte, nicht mehr auf die Greuel, die sie umringten,
achtend, das Tor.

Als sie sich im Freien sah, schloß sie bald, daß nicht jeder, der
ein zertrümmertes Gebäude bewohnt hatte, unter ihm notwendig
müsse zerschmettert worden sein. An dem nächsten Scheidewege
stand sie still und harrte, ob nicht einer, der ihr nach dem kleinen
Philipp der liebste auf der Welt war, noch erscheinen würde. Sie
ging, weil niemand kam und das Gewühl der Menschen anwuchs,
weiter und kehrte sich wieder um und harrte wieder; und schlich,

gate; but she soon recovered her presence of mind and turned back in haste to the convent, where her helpless little boy had been left behind.

She found the entire convent already in flames; the abbess, who in those moments which were to have been Josefa's last, had promised to care for the infant, was standing in front of the gates calling for help to save him. Josefa, undaunted by the smoke that billowed toward her, dashed into the building, which was already collapsing all around her, and, as if all the angels in heaven were protecting her, carried him out through the entrance again, unharmed. She was just about to sink into the arms of the abbess, who clasped her hands together over her head, when the abbess, together with almost all her nuns, was ignominiously killed by a falling gable of the building.

At this horrible sight Josefa stepped back, trembling; she hastily closed the abbess' eyes and, filled with terror, ran off to save from destruction her dear boy, whom heaven had restored to her. She had taken only a few more steps when she came across the crushed corpse of the archbishop as well, which had just been pulled out of the debris of the cathedral. The viceroy's palace had disappeared, the court in which her sentence had been pronounced was in flames, and on the spot where her father's house had stood there was a boiling lake emitting reddish vapors. Josefa summoned up all her strength in order to go on.

Banishing sorrow from her heart, she courageously proceeded from street to street with her prize and was already near the gate, when she also saw lying in ruins the prison in which Jerónimo had languished. At that sight she tottered and thought she would faint away at a street corner; but at the same moment the collapse of a building behind her, which the tremors had already totally shaken apart, frightened her into renewed vigor and propelled her forward; she kissed the child, squeezed the tears from her eyes and, no longer heeding the horrors that surrounded her, reached the gate.

When she found herself outside, she soon realized that not everyone who had lived in a ruined building had necessarily been crushed beneath it. At the next crossroads she stopped and waited to see whether the one who, after little Felipe, was dearest to her in the world, might still appear. She went on, since no one came and the crowd of people grew, and turned around again and waited again;

viel Tränen vergießend, in ein dunkles, von Pinien beschattetes Tal, um seiner Seele, die sie entflohen glaubte, nachzubeten; und fand ihn hier, diesen Geliebten, im Tale und Seligkeit, als ob es das Tal von Eden gewesen wäre.

Dies alles erzählte sie jetzt voll Rührung dem Jeronimo und reichte ihm, da sie vollendet hatte, den Knaben zum Küssen dar.—Jeronimo nahm ihn und hätschelte ihn in unsäglicher Vaterfreude und verschloß ihm, da er das fremde Antlitz anweinte, mit Liebkosungen ohne Ende den Mund.

Indessen war die schönste Nacht herabgestiegen voll wundermilden Duftes, so silberglänzend und still, wie nur ein Dichter davon träumen mag. Überall längs der Talquelle hatten sich im Schimmer des Mondscheins Menschen niedergelassen und bereiteten sich sanfte Lager von Moos und Laub, um von einem so qualvollen Tage auszuruhen. Und weil die Armen immer noch jammerten: dieser, daß er sein Haus, jener, daß er Weib und Kind, und der dritte, daß er alles verloren habe, so schlichen Jeronimo und Josephe in ein dichteres Gebüsch, um durch das heimliche Gejauchz ihrer Seelen niemand zu betrüben. Sie fanden einen prachtvollen Granatapfelbaum, der seine Zweige voll duftender Früchte weit ausbreitete; und die Nachtigall flötete im Wipfel ihr wollüstiges Lied.

Hier ließ sich Jeronimo am Stamme nieder, und Josephe in seinem, Philipp in Josephens Schoß, saßen sie, von seinem Mantel bedeckt, und ruhten. Der Baumschatten zog mit seinen verstreuten Lichtern über sie hinweg, und der Mond erblaßte schon wieder vor der Morgenröte, ehe sie einschliefen. Denn Unendliches hatten sie zu schwatzen, vom Klostergarten und den Gefängnissen und was sie umeinander gelitten hätten; und waren sehr gerührt, wenn sie dachten, wieviel Elend über die Welt kommen mußte, damit sie glücklich würden!

Sie beschlossen, sobald die Erderschütterungen aufgehört haben würden, nach La Concepción zu gehen, wo Josephe eine vertraute Freundin hatte, sich mit einem kleinen Vorschuß, den sie von ihr zu erhalten hoffte, von dort nach Spanien einzuschiffen, wo Jeronimos mütterliche Verwandten wohnten, und daselbst ihr glückliches Leben zu beschließen. Hierauf unter vielen Küssen schliefen sie ein.

Als sie erwachten, stand die Sonne schon hoch am Himmel, und

and, shedding many tears, she stole into a dark, pine-shaded valley to pray for his soul, which she thought had departed; and found him here in the valley, that beloved man, and found bliss, as if it had been the valley of Eden.

She now told Jerónimo all this with great emotion, and, when she had finished, held the boy out for him to kiss. Jerónimo took him, dandled him with immense paternal joy and, when the child started to cry on seeing a strange face, stopped his mouth with endless kisses and caresses.

Meanwhile, a most beautiful night had fallen, full of wonderfully soft fragrance, as silvery-bright and calm as only poets dream of. Everywhere along the brook in the valley people had settled down in the glimmer of the moonlight and were preparing soft beds of moss and leaves to rest upon after such a painful day. And because the poor people were still lamenting—one because he had lost his house, another because he had lost wife and child, and a third because he had lost everything—Jerónimo and Josefa stole into a denser thicket so as not to sadden anyone with the secret rejoicing of their souls. They found a splendid pomegranate tree with wide-spreading branches full of aromatic fruit; and the nightingale sang its song of delight[2] in the top of the tree.

Here Jerónimo sat down by the tree trunk and, with Josefa in his lap and Felipe in hers, they sat, covered by his cloak, and rested. The shadow of the tree, with its scattering of light, moved over them, and the moon was already growing pale again in anticipation of dawn before they fell asleep. For they had an infinite number of things to talk about, the convent garden, and the prisons, and what they had gone through for each other; and they were very moved when they thought of how much misery had to come upon the world for them to be happy!

They decided to go to Concepción, where Josefa had an intimate woman friend, as soon as the earth tremors ended; with a small loan that she hoped to receive from her they would take ship for Spain, where Jerónimo's maternal relatives lived, and remain happily there to the end of their days. Then, exchanging many kisses, they fell asleep.

When they awoke the sun was already high in the sky,

---

[2] In the German of this era, *Wollust* could denote any pleasure, whereas it has now been narrowed semantically to erotic lust (out of place in this scene of repose and reconciliation to life).

sie bemerkten in ihrer Nähe mehrere Familien, beschäftigt, sich am Feuer ein kleines Morgenbrot zu bereiten. Jeronimo dachte eben auch, wie er Nahrung für die Seinigen herbeischaffen sollte, als ein junger wohlgekleideter Mann mit einem Kinde auf dem Arm zu Josephen trat und sie mit Bescheidenheit fragte: ob sie diesem armen Wurme, dessen Mutter dort unter den Bäumen beschädigt liege, nicht auf kurze Zeit ihre Brust reichen wolle.

Josephe war ein wenig verwirrt, als sie in ihm einen Bekannten erblickte; doch da er, indem er ihre Verwirrung falsch deutete, fortfuhr: »Es ist nur auf wenige Augenblicke, Donna Josephe, und dieses Kind hat seit jener Stunde, die uns alle unglücklich gemacht hat, nichts genossen«, so sagte sie: »Ich schwieg—aus einem andern Grunde, Don Fernando; in diesen schrecklichen Zeiten weigert sich niemand, von dem, was er besitzen mag, mitzuteilen«, und nahm den kleinen Fremdling, indem sie ihr eigenes Kind dem Vater gab, und legte ihn an ihre Brust.

Don Fernando war sehr dankbar für diese Güte und fragte: ob sie sich nicht mit ihm zu jener Gesellschaft verfügen wollten, wo eben jetzt beim Feuer ein kleines Frühstück bereitet werde. Josephe antwortete, daß sie dies Anerbieten mit Vergnügen annehmen würde, und folgte ihm, da auch Jeronimo nichts einzuwenden hatte, zu seiner Familie, wo sie auf das innigste und zärtlichste von Don Fernandos Schwägerinnen, die sie als sehr würdige junge Damen kannte, empfangen ward.

Donna Elvire, Don Fernandos Gemahlin, welche schwer an den Füßen verwundet auf der Erde lag, zog Josephen, da sie ihren abgehärmten Knaben an der Brust derselben sah, mit vieler Freundlichkeit zu sich nieder. Auch Don Pedro, sein Schwiegervater, der an der Schulter verwundet war, nickte ihr liebreich mit dem Haupte zu.

In Jeronimos und Josephens Brust regten sich Gedanken von seltsamer Art. Wenn sie sich mit so vieler Vertraulichkeit und Güte behandelt sahen, so wußten sie nicht, was sie von der Vergangenheit denken sollten, vom Richtplatze, von dem Gefängnisse und der Glocke; und ob sie bloß davon geträumt hätten. Es war, als ob die Gemüter seit dem fürchterlichen Schlage, der sie durchdröhnt hatte, alle versöhnt wären. Sie konnten in der Erinnerung gar nicht weiter, als bis auf ihn zurückgehen.

Nur Donna Elisabeth, welche bei einer Freundin auf das Schauspiel des gestrigen Morgens eingeladen worden war, die Einladung aber nicht angenommen hatte, ruhte zuweilen mit träumerischem Blick auf Josephen; doch der Bericht, der über irgendein neues gräßliches Unglück erstattet ward, riß ihre der Gegenwart kaum entflohene Seele schon wieder in dieselbe zurück. Man erzählte, wie die Stadt gleich nach der ersten Haupterschütterung von Wei-

and they noticed several families near them busy preparing a small breakfast by the fire. Jerónimo, too, was just thinking how he could procure food for his own family, when a well-dressed young man with a child in his arms came over to Josefa and discreetly asked her whether she would not briefly nurse the poor infant whose mother was lying injured under the trees there.

Josefa was a little confused when she recognized him as an acquaintance; but when, misinterpreting her confusion, he continued, "It would be just for a few minutes, Doña Josefa, and this child has had no nourishment since the moment that was calamitous for us all," she replied: "My silence—was for a different reason, Don Fernando; in these terrible times no one refuses to give a share of whatever he possesses." She took the little stranger, giving her own child to his father, and laid him to her breast.

Don Fernando was very grateful for this kindness and asked whether they did not wish to accompany him to that group of people who were just preparing a small breakfast by the fire. Josefa replied that she would accept that invitation with pleasure, and, since Jerónimo had no objection either, she followed Don Fernando to his family and was received most heartily and tenderly by his two sisters-in-law, whom she knew to be very respectable young ladies.

When Doña Elvira, Don Fernando's wife, who was lying on the ground with severe foot wounds, saw her hungry child at Josefa's breast, she drew her down toward herself with great friendliness. Don Pedro, too, Fernando's father-in-law, who was wounded in the shoulder, nodded to her kindly.

Thoughts of a strange kind stirred in the hearts of Jerónimo and Josefa. If they found themselves treated with so much familiarity and goodness, they did not know in what light to consider the past, the place of execution, the prison and the bell; had they merely dreamed all that? It was as if all minds were reconciled since the fearsome blow that had stunned them. They could go no farther back in their memory than to the catastrophe.

Only Doña Isabel, who had been invited to stay with a lady friend in order to see the previous morning's spectacle, but had not accepted the invitation, let her dreamy gaze occasionally rest on Josefa; but an account that was made of some ghastly new misfortune jerked her mind back into the present, from which it had barely escaped. It was reported that right after the first main tremor the

bern ganz voll gewesen, die vor den Augen aller Männer niederge-
kommen seien; wie die Mönche darin mit dem Kruzifix in der
Hand umhergelaufen wären und geschrien hätten: das Ende der
Welt sei da! wie man einer Wache, die auf Befehl des Vizekönigs
verlangte, eine Kirche zu räumen, geantwortet hätte: es gäbe keinen Vizekönig von Chili mehr; wie der Vizekönig in den schrecklichsten Augenblicken hätte müssen Galgen aufrichten lassen, um
der Dieberei Einhalt zu tun; und wie ein Unschuldiger, der sich
von hinten durch ein brennendes Haus gerettet, von dem Besitzer
aus Übereilung ergriffen und sogleich auch aufgeknüpft worden
wäre.

Donna Elvire, bei deren Verletzungen Josephe viel beschäftigt
war, hatte in einem Augenblick, da gerade die Erzählungen sich
am lebhaftesten kreuzten, Gelegenheit genommen, sie zu fragen,
wie es denn ihr an diesem fürchterlichen Tage ergangen sei. Und
da Josephe ihr mit beklemmtem Herzen einige Hauptzüge davon
angab, so ward ihr die Wollust, Tränen in die Augen dieser Dame
treten zu sehen; Donna Elvire ergriff ihr Hand und drückte sie
und winkte ihr, zu schweigen.

Josephe dünkte sich unter den Seligen. Ein Gefühl, das sie nicht
unterdrücken konnte, nannte den verfloßnen Tag, soviel Elend er
auch über die Welt gebracht hatte, eine Wohltat, wie der Himmel
noch keine über sie verhängt hatte. Und in der Tat schien mitten
in diesen gräßlichen Augenblicken, in welchen alle irdischen Güter
der Menschen zugrunde gingen und die ganze Natur verschüttet
zu werden drohte, der menschliche Geist selbst wie eine schöne
Blume aufzugehen.

Auf den Feldern, so weit das Auge reichte, sah man Menschen
von allen Ständen durcheinanderliegen, Fürsten und Bettler, Matronen und Bäuerinnen, Staatsbeamte und Tagelöhner, Kloster-
herren und Klosterfrauen: einander bemitleiden, sich wechselsei-
tig Hilfe reichen, von dem, was sie zur Erhaltung ihres Lebens
gerettet haben mochten, freudig mitteilen, als ob das allgemeine
Unglück alles, was ihm entronnen war, zu einer Familie gemacht
hätte.

Statt der nichtssagenden Unterhaltungen, zu welchen sonst die
Welt an den Teetischen den Stoff hergegeben hatte, erzählte man
jetzt Beispiele von ungeheuren Taten: Menschen, die man sonst in
der Gesellschaft wenig geachtet hatte, hatten Römergröße gezeigt;
Beispiele zu Haufen von Unerschrockenheit, von freudiger Ver-
achtung der Gefahr, von Selbstverleugnung und der göttlichen
Aufopferung, von ungesäumter Wegwerfung des Lebens, als ob es
dem nichtswürdigsten Gute gleich auf dem nächsten Schritte schon
wiedergefunden würde. Ja, da nicht einer war, für den nicht an

city had been full of women who went into labor in the sight of all the men; that the monks had run about, crucifixes in their hands, shouting that the end of the world was at hand; that a guard who had requested the evacuation of a church by order of the viceroy received the reply that there was no longer any viceroy of Chile; that at the most fearful moments the viceroy had been compelled to have gallows erected to put a halt to looting; and that an innocent man who had entered a burning house from the back to save himself had been seized by the overhasty owner and immediately hanged.

Doña Elvira, to whose wounds Josefa was busily attending, had at one point—just when these stories were arriving most quickly, each interrupting the other—taken the opportunity to ask her how *she* had fared on that terrible day. And when, with anguished heart, Josefa recounted some of the main features of her story, she was delighted to see tears well up in that lady's eyes; Doña Elvira seized her hand and squeezed it and gestured to her to be silent.

Josefa counted herself among the blessed. With a feeling she could not suppress, she began to consider the previous day—despite all the misery it had brought to the world—a benefaction greater than any yet vouchsafed her by heaven. And, indeed, in the midst of these awful moments, in which all the earthly goods of man were destroyed and all of nature was threatened with burial, the human spirit itself seemed to open out like a beautiful flower.

In the fields, as far as the eye could reach, people of all ranks could be seen mingled together, princes and beggars, matrons and peasant women, bureaucrats and day laborers, monks and nuns. They sympathized with one another, assisted one another and cheerfully shared whatever they had been able to save to keep themselves alive, as if the universal calamity had made a single family of all who had escaped it.

Instead of the usual meaningless tea-table chitchat based on mundane events, now they narrated examples of extraordinary feats: people who had normally been of low esteem in society had shown greatness worthy of ancient Romans; there were examples in plenty of fearlessness, of cheerful disregard of danger, of self-denial and godlike self-sacrifice, of the unhesitating casting away of one's own life as if, like the most worthless possession, it might be recovered the next minute. Yes, since there was

diesem Tage etwas Rührendes geschehen wäre oder der nicht selbst
etwas Großmütiges getan hätte, so war der Schmerz in jeder Men-
schenbrust mit so viel süßer Lust vermischt, daß sich, wie sie meinte,
gar nicht angeben ließ, ob die Summe des allgemeinen Wohlseins
nicht von der einen Seite um ebensoviel gewachsen war, als sie von
der anderen abgenommen hatte.

Jeronimo nahm Josephen, nachdem sich beide in diesen Betrach-
tungen stillschweigend erschöpft hatten, beim Arm und führte sie
mit unaussprechlicher Heiterkeit unter den schattigen Lauben des
Granatwaldes auf und nieder. Er sagte ihr, daß er bei dieser Stimmung der Gemüter und dem Umsturz aller Verhältnisse seinen
Entschluß, sich nach Europa einzuschiffen, aufgebe; daß er vor
dem Vizekönig, der sich seiner Sache immer günstig gezeigt, falls
er noch am Leben sei, einen Fußfall wagen würde; und daß er
Hoffnung habe (wobei er ihr einen Kuß aufdrückte), mit ihr in
Chili zurückzubleiben.

Josephe antwortete, daß ähnliche Gedanken in ihr aufgestiegen
wären; daß auch sie nicht mehr, falls ihr Vater nur noch am Leben
sei, ihn zu versöhnen zweifle; daß sie aber statt des Fußfalles lieber
nach La Concepción zu gehen und von dort aus schriftlich das
Versöhnungsgeschäft mit dem Vizekönig zu betreiben rate, wo man
auf jeden Fall in der Nähe des Hafens wäre und für den besten,
wenn das Geschäft die erwünschte Wendung nähme, ja leicht wieder nach St. Jago zurückkehren könnte. Nach einer kurzen Überle-
gung gab Jeronimo der Klugheit dieser Maßregel seinen Beifall,
führte sie noch ein wenig, die heitern Momente der Zukunft über-
fliegend, in den Gängen umher und kehrte mit ihr zur Gesellschaft
zurück.

Inzwischen war der Nachmittag herangekommen, und die Gemüter der herumschwärmenden Flüchtlinge hatten sich, da die
Erdstöße nachließen, nur kaum wieder ein wenig beruhigt, als sich
schon die Nachricht verbreitete, daß in der Dominikanerkirche,
der einzigen, welche das Erdbeben verschont hatte, eine feierliche
Messe von dem Prälaten des Klosters selbst gelesen werden würde,
den Himmel um Verhütung fernern Unglücks anzuflehen. Das
Volk brach schon aus allen Gegenden auf und eilte in Strömen zur
Stadt.

In Don Fernandos Gesellschaft ward die Frage aufgeworfen, ob
man nicht auch an dieser Feierlichkeit teilnehmen und sich dem
allgemeinen Zuge anschließen solle. Donna Elisabeth erinnerte mit
einiger Beklemmung, was für ein Unheil gestern in der Kirche

no one who had not had some emotional experience on that day, or who had not himself done something magnanimous, the sorrow in every heart was mingled with so much sweet pleasure that Josefa felt it could not be determined whether the sum of universal welfare had not increased on the one hand just as much as it had been diminished on the other.

Jerónimo took Josefa by the arm, after the two of them had silently dwelt on these thoughts for as long as they wished, and led her to and fro beneath the leafy shade of the pomegranate grove with enormous cheerfulness. He told her that, in view of this general frame of mind and this revolution in the entire social order, he was abandoning his decision to take ship for Europe; that he would risk prostrating himself before the viceroy (should he still be alive), who had always favored his cause; and that he had hopes—and here he kissed her—of remaining in Chile with her.

Josefa replied that similar thoughts had occurred to her; that, were her father only still alive, she too no longer doubted she could be reconciled with him; but that, instead of the personal petition to the viceroy, she advised going to Concepción and corresponding with the viceroy from there with the aim of reconciliation; in Concepción they would be close to the harbor in any case, and in the best case—if the affair should take the desired turn—they could easily return to Santiago. After considering the wisdom of these measures briefly, Jerónimo gave them his approval, walked around with her a little more on the forest paths, speaking about the happy times they would have in the future, and returned to their group with her.

Meanwhile it had become afternoon, and the minds of the refugees who were roving about had barely become a little calmer again—now that the tremors were abating—when the news spread that in the Dominican church, the only one spared by the earthquake, a solemn Mass would be read by the prior of the monastery himself, to beseech heaven to prevent further disaster. People were already starting out all over the countryside and hastening to the city in throngs.

In Don Fernando's party the question was raised whether or not to participate in this solemnity and join the general procession. Doña Isabel, with some anguish, reminded them what a calamity had occurred in the

vorgefallen sei; daß solche Dankfeste ja wiederholt werden würden und daß man sich der Empfindung alsdann, weil die Gefahr schon mehr vorüber wäre, mit desto größerer Heiterkeit und Ruhe überlassen könnte.

Josephe äußerte, indem sie mit einiger Begeisterung sogleich aufstand, daß sie den Drang, ihr Antlitz vor dem Schöpfer in den Staub zu legen, niemals lebhafter empfunden habe als eben jetzt, wo er seine unbegreifliche und erhabene Macht so entwickle. Donna Elvire erklärte sich mit Lebhaftigkeit für Josephens Meinung. Sie bestand darauf, daß man die Messe hören sollte, und rief Don Fernando auf, die Gesellschaft zu führen, worauf sich alles, Donna Elisabeth auch, von den Sitzen erhob.

Da man jedoch letztere mit heftig arbeitender Brust die kleinen Anstalten zum Aufbruch zaudernd betreiben sah und sie auf die Frage, was ihr fehle, antwortete: sie wisse nicht, welch eine unglückliche Ahnung in ihr sei, so beruhigte sie Donna Elvire und forderte sie auf, bei ihr und ihrem kranken Vater zurückzubleiben. Josephe sagte:»So werden Sie mir wohl, Donna Elisabeth, diesen kleinen Liebling abnehmen, der sich ¢chon wieder, wie Sie sehen, bei mir eingefunden hat.«—»Sehr gern«, antwortete Donna Elisabeth und machte Anstalten, ihn zu ergreifen; doch da dieser über das Unrecht, das ihm geschah, kläglich schrie und auf keine Art darein willigte, so sagte Josephe lächelnd, daß sie ihn nur behalten wolle und küßte ihn wieder still.

Hierauf bot Don Fernando, dem die ganze Würdigkeit und Anmut ihres Betragens sehr gefiel, ihr den Arm; Jeronimo, welcher den kleinen Philipp trug, führte Donna Constanzen; die übrigen Mitglieder, die sich bei der Gesellschaft eingefunden hatten, folgten; und in dieser Ordnung ging der Zug nach der Stadt.

Sie waren kaum fünfzig Schritte gegangen, als man Donna Elisabeth, welche inzwischen heftig und heimlich mit Donna Elvire gesprochen hatte,»Don Fernando!« rufen hörte und dem Zuge mit unruhigen Tritten nacheilen sah. Don Fernando hielt und kehrte sich um, harrte ihrer, ohne Josephen loszulassen und fragte, da sie, gleich als ob sie auf sein Entgegenkommen wartete, in einiger Ferne stehenblieb, was sie wolle.

Donna Elisabeth näherte sich ihm hierauf, obschon, wie es schien, mit Widerwillen und raunte ihm doch so, daß Josephe es nicht hören konnte, einige Worte ins Ohr.—»Nun?« fragte Don Fernando,»und das Unglück, das daraus entstehen kann?« Donna

church the day before; she remarked that thanksgiving celebrations like this one would be repeated, and that at a later date, when the danger would be clearly past, they could give vent to their feelings all the more cheerfully and calmly.

Josefa, standing up quickly with a degree of enthusiasm, stated that she had never felt a livelier urge to lay her face in the dust before her Creator than she did right then, when He was thus manifesting His incomprehensible and lofty power. Doña Elvira declared with vivacity that she shared Josefa's opinion. She insisted upon hearing the Mass, and called upon Don Fernando to lead their group; whereupon everyone stood up, including Doña Isabel.

But when Isabel, her breast heaving violently, lagged back upon observing their little preparations for departure and, on being asked what was wrong with her, replied that she had a strange foreboding of disaster, Doña Elvira calmed her and invited her to stay behind with her and her wounded father. Josefa said: "In that case, Doña Isabel, perhaps you would take my little darling, who, as you see, is with me once again." "Very gladly," answered Doña Isabel, and made as if to take hold of him; but when he screamed lamentably over the injustice being done him and would in no way consent to it, Josefa said with a smile that she would keep him, and she kissed him until he was quiet again.

Then Don Fernando, who was very pleased with all the dignity and grace of her demeanor, offered her his arm; Jerónimo, who carried little Felipe, escorted Doña Constancia; the other people who had become members of the group followed; and in this order they proceeded to the city.

They had scarcely gone fifty paces when Doña Isabel, who had meanwhile been engaged in vehement secret conversation with Doña Elvira, was heard to call: "Don Fernando!" and was seen hastening toward the walking group with agitated steps. Don Fernando halted and turned around; he tarried for her without releasing his hold on Josefa and—when she stopped at some distance as if waiting for him to meet her partway—he asked her what she wished.

Then Doña Isabel approached him, although with reluctance as it seemed, and murmured a few words in his ear, too low for Josefa to hear. "Well," asked Don Fernando, "and what calamity can arise from that?" Doña

Elisabeth fuhr fort, ihm mit verstörtem Gesicht ins Ohr zu zischeln. Don Fernando stieg eine Röte des Unwillens ins Gesicht; er antwortete: es wäre gut! Donna Elvire möchte sich beruhigen; und führte seine Dame weiter.

Als sie in der Kirche der Dominikaner ankamen, ließ sich die Orgel schon mit musikalischer Pracht hören, und eine unermeßliche Menschenmenge wogte darin. Das Gedränge erstreckte sich bis weit vor den Portalen auf den Vorplatz der Kirche hinaus, und an den Wänden hoch in den Rahmen der Gemälde hingen Knaben und hielten mit erwartungsvollen Blicken ihre Mützen in der Hand. Von allen Kronleuchtern strahlte es herab, die Pfeiler warfen bei der einbrechenden Dämmerung geheimnisvolle Schatten, die große von gefärbtem Glas gearbeitete Rose in der Kirche äußerstem Hintergrunde glühte wie die Abendsonne selbst, die sie erleuchtete, und Stille herrschte, da die Orgel jetzt schwieg, in der ganzen Versammlung, als hätte keiner einen Laut in der Brust. Niemals schlug aus einem christlichen Dom eine solche Flamme der Inbrunst gen Himmel wie heute aus dem Dominikanerdom zu St. Jago; und keine menschliche Brust gab wärmere Glut dazu her als Jeronimos und Josephens!

Die Feierlichkeit fing mit einer Predigt an, die der ältesten Chorherren einer, mit dem Festschmuck angetan, von der Kanzel hielt. Er begann gleich mit Lob, Preis und Dank, seine zitternden, vom Chorhemde weit umflossenen Hände hoch gen Himmel erhebend, daß noch Menschen seien auf diesem in Trümmer zerfallenden Teile der Welt, fähig, zu Gott empor zu stammeln. Er schilderte, was auf den Wink des Allmächtigen geschehen war; das Weltgericht kann nicht entsetzlicher sein; und als er das gestrige Erdbeben gleichwohl, auf einen Riß, den der Dom erhalten hatte, hinzeigend, einen bloßen Vorboten davon nannte, lief ein Schauder über die ganze Versammlung.

Hierauf kam er im Flusse priesterlicher Beredsamkeit auf das Sittenverderbnis der Stadt; Greuel, wie Sodom und Gomorra sie nicht sahen, strafte er an ihr; und nur der unendlichen Langmut Gottes schrieb er es zu, daß sie noch nicht gänzlich vom Erdboden vertilgt worden sei. Aber wie dem Dolche gleich fuhr es durch die von dieser Predigt schon ganz zerrissenen Herzen unserer beiden Unglücklichen, als der Chorherr bei dieser Gelegenheit umständlich des Frevels erwähnte, der in dem Klostergarten der Karmeliterinnen verübt worden war; die Schonung, die er bei der Welt gefunden hatte, gottlos nannte und in einer von Verwünschungen

Isabel continued to whisper in his ear with a haggard expression on her face. Don Fernando's face grew red with displeasure; he replied: "All right! Please tell Doña Elvira to calm down," and continued to escort Josefa onward.

When they arrived at the Dominican church, they could already hear the musical splendor of the organ, and a countless number of people were surging inside. Outside the doors the crowd stretched far out over the forecourt of the church, and high up on the walls, in the frames of the paintings, boys were perched, holding their caps in their hands with an expectant gaze. Light poured down from all the chandeliers; the pillars cast mysterious shadows in the twilight that was falling; the great stained-glass rose window at the far back of the church glowed like the very evening sun that illuminated it; and, now that the organ had fallen silent, silence reigned in the whole congregation as if no one had a word to say. Never did a flame of ardor leap up to heaven from a Christian church as on that day from the Dominican church in Santiago; and no human heart added a warmer glow to the whole than Jerónimo's and Josefa's!

The celebration began with a sermon spoken from the pulpit by the oldest prebendary, dressed in ceremonial robes. Raising to heaven his trembling hands, which were encircled by his surplice, he began immediately with praise, glorification and thanks that in that part of the world, which was falling into ruins, there were still people able to stammer their thanks to God. He described what had occurred at the beck of the Almighty; the Last Judgment could not be more awesome; and when, pointing to a crack that the church had sustained, he called the previous day's earthquake merely a foretaste, as it were, a shudder ran through the entire congregation.

Next, in the flow of his sacerdotal eloquence, he turned to the moral depravity of the city; he castigated the city for abominations unknown to Sodom and Gomorrah; and he ascribed it only to the infinite forbearance of God that Santiago had not yet been totally wiped out by the earthquake. But the hearts of our two unfortunates, already deeply wounded by this sermon, were stabbed as by a dagger when the prebendary took this opportunity to mention circumstantially the sin that had been committed in the Carmelites' convent garden; he termed the indulgence it had received from society "godless" and, in a parentheti-

erfüllten Seitenwendung die Seelen der Täter, wörtlich genannt, allen Fürsten der Hölle übergab!

Donna Constanze rief, indem sie an Jeronimos Armen zuckte: »Don Fernando!« Doch dieser antwortete so nachdrücklich und doch so heimlich, wie sich beides verbinden ließ: »Sie schweigen, Donna, Sie rühren auch den Augapfel nicht und tun, als ob Sie in eine Ohnmacht versänken, worauf wir die Kirche verlassen.« Doch ehe Donna Constanze diese sinnreich zur Rettung erfundene Maßregel noch ausgeführt hatte, rief schon eine Stimme, des Chorherrn Predigt laut unterbrechend, aus: »Weichet fern hinweg, ihr Bürger von St. Jago, hier stehen diese gottlosen Menschen!« Und als eine andere Stimme schreckenvoll, indessen sich ein weiter Kreis des Entsetzens um sie bildete, fragte: »Wo?«—»Hier!« versetzte ein Dritter und zog, heiliger Ruchlosigkeit voll, Josephen bei den Haaren nieder, daß sie mit Don Fernandos Sohne zu Boden getaumelt wäre, wenn dieser sie nicht gehalten hätte.

»Seid ihr wahnsinnig?« rief der Jüngling und schlug den Arm um Josephen: »Ich bin Don Fernando Ormez, Sohn des Kommandanten der Stadt, den ihr alle kennt.«—»Don Fernando Ormez?« rief dicht vor ihn hingestellt, ein Schuhflicker, der für Josephen gearbeitet hatte und diese wenigstens so genau kannte als ihr kleinen Füße. »Wer ist der Vater zu diesem Kinde?« wandte er sich mit frechem Trotz zur Tochter Asterons.

Don Fernando erblaßte bei dieser Frage. Er sah bald den Jeronimo schüchtern an, bald überflog er die Versammlung, ob nicht einer sei, der ihn kenne. Josephe rief, von entsetzlichen Verhältnissen gedrängt: »Dies ist nicht mein Kind, Meister Pedrillo, wie Er glaubt«, indem sie in unendlicher Angst der Seele auf Don Fernando blickte; »dieser junge Herr ist Don Fernando Ormez, Sohn des Kommandanten der Stadt, den ihr alle kennt!« Der Schuster fragte: »Wer von euch, ihr Bürger, kennt diesen jungen Mann?« Und mehrere der Umstehenden wiederholten: »Wer kennt den Jeronimo Rugera? Der trete vor!«

Nun traf es sich, daß in demselben Augenblicke der kleine Juan, durch den Tumult erschreckt, von Josephens Brust weg Don Fernando in die Arme strebte. Hierauf: »Er ist der Vater!« schrie eine Stimme; und: »Er ist Jeronimo Rugera!« eine andere; und: »Sie sind die gotteslästerlichen Menschen!« eine dritte; und »Steinigt sie! steinigt sie!« die ganze im Tempel Jesu versammelte Christenheit!

cal passage filled with curses, consigned the souls of the perpetrators, mentioned by name, to all the princes of hell!

Doña Constancia, tugging Jerónimo's arm, cried out: "Don Fernando!" But the latter replied, as forcefully as was consonant with his secret tones: "Doña, be silent, don't move a muscle, and pretend to faint; then we will leave the church." But before Doña Constancia had taken these ingeniously conceived measures for escape, a voice, loudly interrupting the prebendary's sermon, was already exclaiming: "Stand well back, citizens of Santiago, here are these godless people!" And when another voice fearfully asked "Where?"—while a wide circle of horror formed around them—"Here!" replied a third and, with vileness prompted by religion, dragged Josefa down by the hair so that she would have reeled to the floor with Don Fernando's son if the Don had not been holding onto her.

"Are you insane?" shouted the young man, putting his arm around Josefa: "I am Don Fernando Ormez, son of the commandant of the city, whom you all know." "Don Fernando Ormez?" shouted a cobbler, standing directly in front of him; this cobbler had done work for Josefa and knew her at least as well as he knew her dainty feet. "Who is the father of this child?" he said, turning with insolent defiance toward Asterón's daughter.

Don Fernando turned pale at that question. Now he looked timidly at Jerónimo, now he glanced quickly over the congregation to see if there was anyone who knew him. Josefa, urged on by the frightening situation, cried out: "This is not my child as you think, Master Pedrillo," and, looking at Don Fernando in extreme anguish of soul, "this young gentleman is Don Fernando Ormez, son of the commandant of the city, whom you all know." The cobbler asked: "Citizens, who among you knows this young man?" And several of those standing near repeated: "Who can recognize Jerónimo Rugera? Let him step forth!"

Now, it happened that at the same moment little Juan, frightened by the uproar, strained to leave Josefa's breast for Don Fernando's arms. Whereupon, "He *is* the father!" a voice shouted; a second voice called, "He *is* Jerónimo Rugera!"; a third, "They *are* the blasphemous people!"; and "Stone them! Stone them!" cried all the Christians assembled in the temple of Jesus!

Drauf jetzt Jeronimo: »Halt! Ihr Unmenschlichen! Wenn ihr den
Jeronimo Rugera sucht: hier ist er! Befreit jenen Mann, welcher
unschuldig ist!«—Der wütende Haufen, durch die Äußerung Jeronimos verwirrt, stutzte; mehrere Hände ließen Don Fernando los;
und da in demselben Augenblick ein Marineoffizier von bedeuten-
dem Rang herbeieilte und, indem er sich durch den Tumult
drängte, fragte: »Don Fernando Ormez! Was ist Euch widerfah-
ren?«, so antwortete dieser, nun völlig befreit, mit wahrer helden-
mütiger Besonnenheit: »Ja, sehn Sie, Don Alonzo, die Mord-
knechte! Ich wäre verloren gewesen, wenn dieser würdige Mann
sich nicht, die rasende Menge zu beruhigen, für Jeronimo Rugera
ausgegeben hätte. Verhaften Sie ihn, wenn Sie die Güte haben wollen, nebst dieser jungen Dame zu ihrer beiderseitigen Sicherheit;
und diesen Nichtswürdigen«, indem er Meister Pedrillo ergriff,
»der den ganzen Aufruhr angezettelt hat!«
     Der Schuster rief: »Don Alonzo Onoreja, ich frage Euch auf Euer
Gewissen, ist dieses Mädchen nicht Josephe Asteron?« Da nun Don
Alonzo, welcher Josephen sehr genau kannte, mit der Antwort zau-
derte und mehrere Stimmen, dadurch von neuem zur Wut ent-
flammt, riefen: »Sie ist's, sie ist's!« und: »Bringt sie zu Tode!«, so
setzte Josephe den kleinen Philipp, den Jeronimo bisher getragen
hatte, samt dem kleinen Juan auf Don Fernandos Arm und sprach:
»Gehn Sie, Don Fernando, retten Sie Ihre beiden Kinder und überlassen Sie uns unserm Schicksale!«
     Don Fernando nahm die beiden Kinder und sagte, er wolle eher
umkommen, als zugeben, daß seiner Gesellschaft etwas zuleide ge-
schehe. Er bot Josephen, nachdem er sich den Degen des Marineof-
fiziers ausgebeten hatte, den Arm und forderte das hintere Paar
auf, ihm zu folgen. Sie kamen auch wirklich, indem man ihnen bei
solchen Anstalten mit hinlänglicher Ehrerbietigkeit Platz machte,
aus der Kirche heraus und glaubten sich gerettet.
     Doch kaum waren sie auf den von Menschen gleichfalls erfüllten
Vorplatz derselben getreten, als eine Stimme aus dem rasenden
Haufen, der sie verfolgt hatte, rief: »Dies ist Jeronimo Rugera,
ihr Bürger, denn ich bin sein eigner Vater!« und ihn an Donna
Constanzens Seite mit einem ungeheuren Keulenschlag zu Boden
streckte. »Jesus Maria!« rief Donna Constanze und floh zu ihrem
Schwager; doch »Klostermetze!« erscholl es schon mit einem zwei-
ten Keulenschlage von einer andern Seite, der sie leblos neben Jero-
nimo niederwarf.
     »Ungeheuer!« rief ein Unbekannter, »dies war Donna Constanze
Xares!«—»Warum belogen sie uns!« antwortete der Schuster;
»Sucht die rechte auf und bringt sie um!« Don Fernando, als er

Then Jerónimo said, "Stop, you inhuman people! If you seek Jerónimo Rugera, he is here! Release that man, who is innocent!" The furious mob, confused by Jerónimo's statement, hesitated; several hands loosed their grip on Don Fernando; and when at the same moment a naval officer of high rank rushed over and, pushing through the press of people, asked, "Don Fernando Ormez, what has happened to you?," Don Fernando, now completely free, answered with truly heroic self-possession: "Just look at these assassins, Don Alonzo! I would have been lost if this estimable man had not pretended to be Jerónimo Rugera to pacify the raging crowd. Be so good as to take him as well as this young lady into custody for the protection of both; and," seizing Master Pedrillo: "Arrest this scoundrel, who instigated the whole uproar!"

The cobbler shouted: "Don Alonzo Onoreja, I ask you on your conscience, is this girl not Josefa Asterón?" When Don Alonzo, who knew Josefa very well, hesitated to answer, and several bystanders, in whom this kindled new rage, called: "It is she, it is she!" and "Death to her!," Josefa placed little Felipe, whom Jerónimo had been carrying up to then, in Don Fernando's arms together with little Juan, and said: "Go, Don Fernando, save your two children and leave us to our fate!"

Don Fernando took the two children and said that he would rather be killed than allow harm to befall his party. After requesting the naval officer's sword, he offered Josefa his arm and invited the couple behind him to follow him. The crowd, impressed by this procedure, made way for them with a sufficient show of respect, and they actually managed to leave the church, thinking they were safe.

But scarcely had they stepped into the forecourt, which was just as crowded with people, when a man from the frenzied throng that had dogged their steps called: "Citizens, this is Jerónimo Rugera, for I am his own father!" and knocked him to the ground at Doña Constancia's side with a mighty cudgel blow. "Jesus and Mary!" shouted Doña Constancia, fleeing to her brother-in-law; but there were already cries of "Convent whore!" and from another side came a second cudgel blow that laid her lifeless alongside Jerónimo.

"Monsters!" shouted an unidentified man, "that was Doña Constancia Xares!" "Why did they lie to us?" replied the cobbler; "find the right woman and kill her!" When

Constanzens Leichnam erblickte, glühte vor Zorn; er zog und
schwang das Schwert und hieb, daß er ihn gespalten hätte, den
fanatischen Mordknecht, der diese Greuel veranlaßte, wenn derselbe nicht durch eine Wendung dem wütenden Schlag entwichen
wäre.

Doch da er die Menge, die auf ihn eindrang, nicht überwältigen
könnte:»Leben Sie wohl, Don Fernando mit den Kinder!« rief
Josephe—und:»Hier mordet mich, ihr blutdürstenden Tiger!«
und stürzte sich freiwillig unter sie, um dem Kampf ein Ende zu
machen. Meister Pedrillo schlug sie mit der Keule nieder. Drauf,
ganz mit ihrem Blute bespritzt:»Schickt ihr den Bastard zur Hölle
nach!« rief er und drang mit noch ungesättigter Mordlust von
neuem vor.

Don Fernando, dieser göttliche Held, stand jetzt den Rücken an
die Kirche gelehnt; in der Linken hielt er die Kinder, in der Rechten das Schwert. Mit jedem Hieb wetterstrahlte er einen zu Boden;
ein Löwe wehrt sich nicht besser. Sieben Bluthunde lagen tot
vor ihm, der Fürst der satanischen Rotte selbst war verwundet.
Doch Meister Pedrillo ruhte nicht eher, als bis er der Kinder
eines bei den Beinen von seiner Brust gerissen und, hochher im
Kreise geschwungen, an eines Kirchpfeilers Eck zerschmettert
hatte.

Hierauf ward es still, und alles entfernte sich. Don Fernando,
als er seinen kleinen Juan vor sich liegen sah mit aus dem Hirne
vorquellendem Mark, hob voll namenlosen Schmerzes seine Augen
gen Himmel. Der Marineoffizier fand sich wieder bei ihm
ein, suchte ihn zu trösten und versicherte ihn, daß seine Untätig-
keit bei diesem Unglück, obschon durch mehrere Umstände ge-
rechtfertigt, ihn reue; doch Fernando sagte, daß ihm nichts vorzu-
werfen sei und bat ihn nur, die Leichname jetzt fortschaffen zu
helfen.

Man trug sie alle bei der Finsternis der einbrechenden Nacht in
Don Alonzos Wohnung, wohin Don Fernando ihnen, viel über das
Antlitz des kleinen Philipp weinend, folgte. Er übernachtete auch
bei Don Alonzo und säumte lange unter falschen Vorspiegelungen,
seine Gemahlin von dem ganzen Umfang des Unglücks zu unter-
richten; einmal, weil sie krank war und dann, weil er auch nicht
wußte, wie sie sein Verhalten bei dieser Begebenheit beurteilen
würde; doch kurze Zeit nachher, durch einen Besuch zufällig von
allem, was geschehen war, benachrichtigt, weinte diese treffliche
Dame im stillen ihren mütterlichen Schmerz aus und fiel ihm mit
dem Rest einer erglänzenden Träne eines Morgens um den Hals

Don Fernando caught sight of Constancia's body, he burned with anger; he drew the sword, swung it and aimed a stroke at the fanatical assassin who had caused these abominations, a furious stroke that would have cut him in two had he not eluded it by a twist of his body.

But when she saw that the Don could not overpower the mob crowding in on him, Josefa cried: "Farewell, Don Fernando, you and the children!" and "Here, murder me, you bloodthirsty tigers!" and voluntarily threw herself into their midst, to put an end to the combat. Master Pedrillo felled her with his cudgel. Then, spattered all over with her blood, he cried: "Send her bastard to hell after her!" and, his blood lust still unsated, pushed forward again.

Don Fernando, that godlike hero, now stood with his back leaning on the church; with his left hand he held the children, in his right hand the sword. With every flash of his weapon an opponent fell to the ground; a lion does not defend itself better. Seven ravenous dogs lay dead before him, even the prince of the satanic horde was wounded. But Master Pedrillo could not rest until he had pulled one of the children away from his bosom by the legs and, swinging it through the air in a circle, had shattered it against the corner of a church pillar.

Then all became quiet and everyone withdrew. Don Fernando, seeing little Juan lying before him with his brains oozing out, raised his eyes to heaven in inexpressible sorrow. The naval officer rejoined him, attempted to console him and assured him that he regretted his lack of participation in those unhappy events, although it was excusable because of the circumstances; but Don Fernando said that he was not at all to blame and merely asked him to help carry away the bodies now.

In the darkness of the night that was falling they were all brought to Don Alonzo's residence; Don Fernando followed them there, shedding many tears on little Felipe's face. He spent the night at Don Alonzo's, too, and, misrepresenting the true situation to his wife, hesitated a long time before informing her of the whole extent of the tragedy—for one thing, because she was ill, and another, because he did not know how she would judge his conduct during those events. But shortly afterward, happening to be apprised by a visitor of all that had occurred, that excellent lady quietly wept her fill over her maternal sorrow and, one morning, with the last tears still glistening in

und küßte ihn. Don Fernando und Donna Elvire nahmen hierauf den kleinen Fremdling zum Pflegesohn an; und wenn Don Fernando Philippen mit Juan verglich und wie er beide erworben hatte, so war es ihm fast, als müßte er sich freuen.

her eyes, fell about his neck and kissed him. Then Don Fernando and Doña Elvira adopted the little stranger as their own son; and when Don Fernando compared Felipe to Juan and thought of how he had acquired both, he felt almost as if he should rejoice.

HOFFMANN
AND
"THE SANDMAN"

FREQUENTLY UNDERRATED in the past by critics for whom fantasy and terror were intrinsically inferior genres, Hoffmann has also been called the greatest German Romantic story writer. His professional career also included extensive musical activity (as composer, conductor and critic) and artistic endeavor (set design, cartooning); these other interests are evident in his stories.

Ernst Theodor Wilhelm Hoffmann (he himself later substituted Amadeus for Wilhelm in honor of Mozart) was born in Königsberg in 1776. Like his father, he studied law. From 1800 to 1806 he was in Prussian government service in various parts of partitioned Poland; it was in cosmopolitan Warsaw that he became acquainted with the progressive German literature of the day. After Napoleon conquered Poland, Hoffmann resided in Berlin, Bamberg, Dresden and Leipzig, gradually shifting his main interest from music to literature. Clerking for a high court, with plenty of time for writing and socializing, he remained in Berlin from 1814 until his early death in 1822, which was at least partially due to a drinking problem. His legacy of dozens of brilliant stories includes "Der goldne Topf" (The Golden Pot), "Prinzessin Brambilla," "Meister Floh" (Master Flea) and "Das Fräulein von Scuderi."

"The Sandman" was written in 1815–16 and first appeared in 1816 in the first volume of the *Nachtstücke* (Night Pieces), published in Berlin by Reimer, who had earlier brought out Kleist's *Erzählungen.*

Hoffmann's best stories feature an interference between normal earthly events and their close counterparts on other planes of existence. In "The Sandman," for instance, Coppelius resembles the owl in the nanny's cautionary tale. This kind of ambiguity is well maintained throughout "The Sandman": *almost* all the strangeness and horror can be imputed to Nathanael's mental distortion of unexceptional occurrences (a condition perhaps resulting from his severe childhood illness after he was caught spying on his father), but Hoffmann leaves enough deliberate loopholes to nurture doubt.

A peerless storyteller, smooth and jovial, Hoffmann chooses his words deftly and rarely presents syntactic difficulties. In "The Sandman" he uses an unorthodox variety of narrative approaches

to serve his purposes: letters, straight narration and apparently ingenuous addresses to the reader. Like a musician he uses specific motifs that recur ever more hauntingly (eyes, circle of fire, etc.). His characters often have significant names: Clara, of course, represents clear vision and clear thought; Coppelius/Coppola has been associated with the Italian word *coppo,* one meaning of which is eye socket.

Quiet humor and irony pervade Hoffmann's stories. "The Sandman" also contains biting satire on social gatherings, learned pontificators and courting couples; in subtle fashion, the satire reaches its height in an interlude that immediately precedes the suspenseful climax.

A long series of explicit or implicit contrasts, woven into the fabric of the story (reality/imagination; organism/mechanism; clear sight/lack of vision; deathly chill/living warmth; . . .), mirror the fundamental plot element: the dichotomy in Nathanael's mind and character.

No first-time reader is likely to observe the few flaws in the plotting: Nathanael's sisters disappear totally from the story after their scene of mourning; Lothar and Clara have never heard the full story of Nathanael's father even though they have lived in his house and the incident was the talk of the neighborhood; . . . .

Hoffmann quickly became internationally famous and imitated; in France alone, plot elements from "The Sandman" were used in Offenbach's opera *Les Contes d'Hoffmann* and Delibes's ballet *Coppélia*—both charming works, but diluted and trivialized versions of Hoffmann's ideas. In the twentieth century the story has been subjected to various types of analysis. Taking it as a bald case history of insanity, Freud identified Nathanael's fear for his eyes as a castration complex. At least one critic, more sympathetic to literary nuances, sees the story as an allegory of the artist's place in society; Nathanael comes to grief by trying to transfer poetry to real life, and Clara is more of a stumbling block than a helpmate.

The present translator has introduced additional paragraphing for the convenience of the reader.

DER SANDMANN

NATHANAEL AN LOTHAR

Gewiß seid Ihr alle voll Unruhe, daß ich so lange—lange nicht geschrieben. Mutter zürnt wohl, und Clara mag glauben, ich lebe hier in Saus und Braus und vergesse mein holdes Engelsbild, so tief mir in Herz und Sinn eingeprägt, ganz und gar. —Dem ist aber nicht so; täglich und stündlich gedenke ich Eurer aller und in süßen Träumen geht meines holden Clärchens freundliche Gestalt vorüber und lächelt mich mit ihren hellen Augen so anmutig an, wie sie wohl pflegte, wenn ich zu Euch hineintrat.

Ach wie vermochte ich denn Euch zu schreiben, in der zerrissenen Stimmung des Geistes, die mir bisher alle Gedanken verstörte!—Etwas Entsetzliches ist in mein Leben getreten!—Dunkle Ahnungen eines gräßlichen mir drohenden Geschicks breiten sich wie schwarze Wolkenschatten über mich aus, undurchdringlich jedem freundlichen Sonnenstrahl. —Nun soll ich Dir sagen, was mir widerfuhr. Ich muß es, das sehe ich ein, aber nur es denkend, lacht es wie toll aus mir heraus.

Ach mein herzlieber Lothar! wie fange ich es denn an, Dich nur einigermaßen empfinden zu lassen, daß das, was mir vor einigen Tagen geschah, denn wirklich mein Leben so feindlich zerstören konnte! Wärst Du nur hier, so könntest Du selbst schauen; aber jetzt hältst Du mich gewiß für einen aberwitzigen Geisterseher. —Kurz und gut, das Entsetzliche, was mir geschah, dessen tödlichen Eindruck zu vermeiden ich mich vergebens bemühe, besteht in nichts anderm, als daß vor einigen Tagen, nämlich am 30. Oktober mittags um 12 Uhr, ein Wetterglashändler in meine Stube trat und mir seine Ware anbot. Ich kaufte nichts und drohte, ihn die Treppe herabzuwerfen, worauf er aber von selbst fortging.

Du ahnest, daß nur ganz eigne, tief in mein Leben eingreifende Beziehungen diesem Vorfall Bedeutung geben können, ja, daß wohl die Person jenes unglückseligen Krämers gar feindlich auf mich wirken muß. So ist es in der Tat. Mit aller Kraft fasse ich mich zusammen, um ruhig und geduldig Dir aus meiner frühern Jugendzeit so viel zu erzählen, daß Deinem regen Sinn alles klar und deutlich in leuchtenden Bildern aufgehen wird. Indem ich

THE SANDMAN

You must certainly all be quite anxious at my not having written for so very, very long. Mother is surely vexed, and Clara must think I am leading a riotous life here, totally forgetting the image of my beloved angel, which is so deeply imprinted on my heart and mind. It is not so; daily and hourly I remember you all, and in my sweet dreams the genial figure of my lovely Clara goes by, smiling at me with her bright eyes as graciously as she did when I lived among you in person.

Oh, how *could* I write to you in the distracted state of mind that has troubled all my thoughts until now! Something terrible has entered my life! Dark forebodings of a ghastly fate that threatens me are looming over me like black clouds, casting shadows that no kind sunbeam can penetrate. Now I shall tell you what has befallen me. I must do so, I realize, but when I merely think of it, mad laughter bursts from me.

Oh, my very dear Lothar, how shall I begin to persuade you even partially that the events of a few days ago have really had the power to destroy my life with such hostility! If you were only here, you could see for yourself; but, as it is, you will certainly think me a foolish visionary. To be brief, the terrible thing that happened to me, the fatal impression of which I am striving in vain to avoid, is simply that, a few days ago, at twelve noon on October 30th, to be precise, a barometer vendor walked into my room and offered me his wares. I bought nothing and threatened to throw him down the stairs, whereupon he left voluntarily.

You surely realize that only very special associations, deeply rooted in my life, could make that incident significant; moreover, that it must be the wretched merchant himself who is producing this hostile effect on me. And such is the case. I am concentrating with all my might so that, calmly and patiently, I can tell you enough about my youthful days for everything to be revealed clearly and distinctly, in glowing images, to your lively intelligence.

37

anfangen will, höre ich Dich lachen und Clara sagen: »Das sind ja
rechte Kindereien!«—Lacht, ich bitte Euch, lacht mich recht herzlich aus!—ich bitt Euch sehr!—Aber Gott im Himmel! die Haare
sträuben sich mir und es ist, als flehe ich Euch an, mich auszula-
chen, in wahnsinniger Verzweiflung, wie Franz Moor den Daniel.
—Nun fort zur Sache!

Außer dem Mittagsessen sahen wir, ich und mein Geschwister,
tagüber den Vater wenig. Er mochte mit seinem Dienst viel beschäftigt sein. Nach dem Abendessen, das alter Sitte gemäß schon um
sieben Uhr aufgetragen wurde, gingen wir alle, die Mutter mit uns,
in des Vaters Arbeitszimmer und setzten uns um einen runden
Tisch. Der Vater rauchte Tabak und trank ein großes Glas Bier
dazu. Oft erzählte er uns viele wunderbare Geschichten und geriet
darüber so in Eifer, daß ihm die Pfeife immer ausging, die ich, ihm
brennend Papier hinhaltend, wieder anzünden mußte, welches mir
denn ein Hauptspaß war. Oft gab er uns aber Bilderbücher in die
Hände, saß stumm und starr in seinem Lehnstuhl und blies starke
Dampfwolken von sich, daß wir alle wie im Nebel schwammen. An
solchen Abenden war die Mutter sehr traurig und kaum schlug die
Uhr neun, so sprach sie: »Nun Kinder!—zu Bette! zu Bette! der
Sandmann kommt, ich merk es schon.«

Wirklich hörte ich dann jedesmal etwas schweren langsamen
Tritts die Treppe heraufpoltern; das mußte der Sandmann sein.
Einmal war mir jenes dumpfe Treten und Poltern besonders grau-
lich; ich frug die Mutter, indem sie uns fortführte: »Ei Mama! wer
ist denn der böse Sandmann, der uns immer von Papa fort-
treibt?—wie sieht er denn aus?«—»Es gibt keinen Sandmann, mein
liebes Kind«, erwiderte die Mutter: »wenn ich sage, der Sandmann
kommt, so will das nur heißen, ihr seid schläfrig und könnt die
Augen nicht offen behalten, als hätte man euch Sand hineinge-
streut.«

Der Mutter Antwort befriedigte mich nicht, ja in meinem kindischen Gemüt entfaltete sich deutlich der Gedanke, daß die Mutter
den Sandmann uns verleugne, damit wir uns vor ihm nicht fürchten sollten, ich hörte ihn ja immer die Treppe heraufkommen. Voll
Neugierde, Näheres von diesem Sandmann und seiner Beziehung
auf uns Kinder zu erfahren, frug ich endlich die alte Frau, die
meine jüngste Schwester wartete: was denn das für ein Mann sei,
der Sandmann? »Ei Thanelchen«, erwiderte diese, »weißt du das

As I am about to begin, I can hear you laugh and say to Clara: "But this is really childish!"—Laugh, I ask of you both, have a hearty laugh at my expense!—I want you to!—But God in heaven! My hair is standing on end and I feel as if I were imploring you to laugh at me, in mad despair, as Franz Moor implored Daniel.[1]—Now to the subject!

Except at noon meals, my sisters[2] and I saw little of our father during the day. He must have been very busy with his official duties. After dinner, which in traditional fashion was served early, at seven, we would all go, we and Mother, to Father's study and sit down at a round table. Father would smoke and also drink a large glass of beer. Often he told us many amazing stories, becoming so enthusiastic as he did so that his pipe always went out and I would have to hold out a burning spill and light it for him again, which was a real treat for me. But often he handed us picture books, sat in his armchair mute and rigid, and emitted huge clouds of smoke until we all seemed to be lost in a fog. On such evenings Mother was very sad, and scarcely would the clock strike nine when she would say: "Now, children!—to bed, to bed! The sandman is coming, I can tell."

On each occasion I would then really hear something lumbering up the stairs with a slow, heavy tread; it had to be the sandman. Once, that hollow, rumbling step was especially frightening to me; I asked Mother as she led us away: "Oh, Mama! who *is* the evil sandman that always chases us away from Papa? What does he look like?" "There is no sandman, dear," Mother replied; "when I say the sandman is coming, it only means that you are all sleepy and can't keep your eyes open, as if someone had scattered sand in them."

Mother's answer did not satisfy me; indeed, the idea developed distinctly in my childish mind that Mother was denying the existence of the sandman so that we should not be afraid of him—I *did* always hear him coming up the stairs. Full of curiosity to learn details about this sandman and his relation to us children, I finally asked the old woman who took care of my youngest sister what kind of man the sandman was. "Ah, Natty," she replied, "don't

---

[1] Characters in Schiller's play *Die Räuber* (The Robbers).

[2] *Geschwister* means siblings, brothers *and* sisters, but only sisters are mentioned later on.

noch nicht? Das ist ein böser Mann, der kommt zu den Kindern, wenn sie nicht zu Bett gehen wollen und wirft ihnen Händevoll Sand in die Augen, daß sie blutig zum Kopf herausspringen, die wirft er dann in den Sack und trägt sie in den Halbmond zur Atzung für seine Kinderchen; die sitzen dort im Nest und haben krumme Schnäbel, wie die Eulen, damit picken sie der unartigen Menschenkindlein Augen auf.«

Gräßlich malte sich nun im Innern mir das Bild des grausamen Sandmanns aus; sowie es abends die Treppe heraufpolterte, zitterte ich vor Angst und Entsetzen. Nichts als den unter Tränen hergestotterten Ruf: »Der Sandmann! der Sandmann!« konnte die Mutter aus mir herausbringen. Ich lief darauf in das Schlafzimmer, und wohl die ganze Nacht über quälte mich die fürchterliche Erscheinung des Sandmanns.

Schon alt genug war ich geworden, um einzusehen, daß das mit dem Sandmann und seinem Kindernest im Halbmonde, so wie es mir die Wartefrau erzählt hatte, wohl nicht ganz seine Richtigkeit haben könne; indessen blieb mir der Sandmann ein fürchterliches Gespenst, und Grauen—Entsetzen ergriff mich, wenn ich ihn nicht allein die Treppe heraufkommen, sondern auch meines Vaters Stubentür heftig aufreißen und hineintreten hörte. Manchmal blieb er lange weg, dann kam er öfter hintereinander. Jahrelang dauerte das, und nicht gewöhnen konnte ich mich an den unheimlichen Spuk, nicht bleicher wurde in mir das Bild des grausigen Sandmanns. Sein Umgang mit dem Vater fing an meine Fantasie immer mehr und mehr zu beschäftigen: den Vater darum zu befragen hielt mich eine unüberwindliche Scheu zurück, aber selbst—selbst das Geheimnis zu erforschen, den fabelhaften Sandmann zu sehen, dazu keimte mit den Jahren immer mehr die Lust in mir empor.

Der Sandmann hatte mich auf die Bahn des Wunderbaren, Abenteuerlichen gebracht, das so schon leicht im kindlichen Gemüt sich einnistet. Nichts war mir lieber, als schauerliche Geschichten von Kobolten, Hexen, Däumlingen usw. zu hören oder zu lesen; aber obenan stand immer der Sandmann, den ich in den seltsamsten, abscheulichsten Gestalten überall auf Tische, Schränke und Wände mit Kreide, Kohle, hinzeichnete.

Als ich zehn Jahre alt geworden, wies mich die Mutter aus der Kinderstube in ein Kämmerchen, das auf dem Korridor unfern von meines Vaters Zimmer lag. Noch immer mußten wir uns, wenn auf den Schlag neun Uhr sich jener Unbekannte im Hause hören ließ, schnell entfernen. In meinem Kämmerchen vernahm ich, wie er bei dem Vater hineintrat und bald darauf war es mir dann,

you know that yet? He is an evil man who comes to children when they refuse to go to bed and throws handfuls of sand in their eyes, so that they pop out of their heads all bloody; then he throws the eyes into his sack and carries them to the half moon as food for his little children; they sit there in their nest and have curved beaks like owls, with which they peck up the eyes of the naughty human children."

Now my mind painted a grisly picture of the cruel sandman; as soon as there was lumbering on the stairs in the evening, I trembled with fear and terror. Mother could get nothing out of me but the stammering cry "The sandman! the sandman!" accompanied by tears. Then I would run into our bedroom and the fearsome apparition of the sandman might torture me all night long.

I had already grown old enough to realize that the story of the sandman and his children's nest on the half moon, as the nurse had told it to me, could not be strictly correct; nevertheless the sandman continued to be a frightful ghost for me, and dread—horror—took hold of me when I not only heard him coming up the stairs but also heard him yank open the door to Father's room violently and walk in. Sometimes he stayed away for a long time, then he would make frequent visits. This lasted for years, and I could not grow accustomed to the uncanny specter; the image of the terrible sandman did not fade from my mind. His association with Father began to occupy my imagination increasingly: an unconquerable shyness prevented me from asking Father about it, but with the years there constantly grew within me the urge to investigate the mystery myself—to see the fabulous sandman with my own eyes.

The sandman had led me onto the trail of the unusual and the adventurous, which take root so naturally in a child's mind. I liked nothing better than to hear or read scary stories about goblins, witches, Tom Thumbs and so on; but at the head of the list was always the sandman, whom I would draw with chalk or charcoal everywhere, on tables, cupboards and walls, in the oddest and most repulsive shapes.

When I was ten years old, Mother moved me out of the nursery into a little bedroom on the corridor not far from Father's room. We still had to withdraw briskly whenever, at the stroke of nine, that unknown man could be heard in the house. In my little bedroom I heard him step into

als verbreite sich im Hause ein feiner seltsam riechender Dampf. Immer höher mit der Neugierde wuchs der Mut, auf irgend eine Weise des Sandmanns Bekanntschaft zu machen. Oft schlich ich schnell aus dem Kämmerchen auf den Korridor, wenn die Mutter vorübergegangen, aber nichts konnte ich erlauschen, denn immer war der Sandmann schon zur Türe hinein, wenn ich den Platz erreicht hatte, wo er mir sichtbar werden mußte. Endlich von unwiderstehlichem Drange getrieben, beschloß ich, im Zimmer des Vaters selbst mich zu verbergen und den Sandmann zu erwarten.

An des Vaters Schweigen, an der Mutter Traurigkeit merkte ich eines Abends, daß der Sandmann kommen werde; ich schützte daher große Müdigkeit vor, verließ schon vor neun Uhr das Zimmer und verbarg mich dicht neben der Türe in einen Schlupfwinkel. Die Haustür knarrte, durch den Flur ging es, langsamen, schweren, dröhnenden Schrittes nach der Treppe. Die Mutter eilte mit dem Geschwister mir vorüber.

Leise—leise öffnete ich des Vaters Stubentür. Er saß, wie gewöhnlich, stumm und starr den Rücken der Türe zugekehrt, er bemerkte mich nicht, schnell war ich hinein und hinter der Gardine, die einem gleich neben der Türe stehenden offenen Schrank, worin meines Vaters Kleider hingen, vorgezogen war. —Näher—immer näher dröhnten die Tritte—es hustete und scharrte und brummte seltsam draußen. Das Herz bebte mir vor Angst und Erwartung. —Dicht, dicht vor der Türe ein scharfer Tritt—ein heftiger Schlag auf die Klinke, die Tür springt rasselnd auf!—Mit Gewalt mich ermannend gucke ich behutsam hervor. Der Sandmann steht mitten in der Stube vor meinem Vater, der helle Schein der Lichter brennt ihm ins Gesicht!—Der Sandmann, der fürchterliche Sandmann ist der alte Advokat Coppelius, der manchmal bei uns zu Mittage ißt!

Aber die gräßlichste Gestalt hätte mir nicht tieferes Entsetzen erregen können, als eben dieser Coppelius. —Denke Dir einen großen breitschultrigen Mann mit einem unförmlich dicken Kopf, erdgelbem Gesicht, buschigten grauen Augenbrauen, unter denen ein Paar grünliche Katzenaugen stechend hervorfunkeln, großer, starker über die Oberlippe gezogener Nase. Das schiefe Maul verzieht sich oft zum hämischen Lachen; dann werden auf den Backen ein paar dunkelrote Flecke sichtbar und ein seltsam zischender Ton fährt durch die zusammengekniffenen Zähne. Coppelius erschien immer in einem altmodisch zugeschnittenen aschgrauen Rocke, eben solcher Weste und gleichen Beinkleidern, aber dazu schwarze

Father's room, and shortly afterward it seemed to me as if a thin vapor with a peculiar smell were spreading through the house. My bold wish to meet the sandman face to face by one means or another grew as my curiosity grew. Often I would quickly sneak out of my room into the corridor after Mother had passed by, but I could hear nothing, for the sandman was always inside Father's door by the time I reached a spot where I could catch sight of him. Finally, impelled by an irresistible urge, I determined to hide in Father's room and wait for the sandman.

One evening I could tell from Father's silence and Mother's sadness that the sandman was going to come; therefore I pretended to be very tired, left the sitting room before nine and hid in a recess very close to Father's door. The street door creaked, and I heard slow, heavy thudding steps crossing the vestibule and approaching the stairs. Mother hastened past me with my sisters.

Quietly, oh so quietly, I opened Father's door. He was sitting as usual, mute and rigid, with his back to the door; he did not notice me; in a trice I was inside, hiding behind the curtain that was drawn in front of the open cabinet in which Father kept his clothes; this cabinet stood right beside the door. Closer and closer thudded the footsteps—outside there was a strange coughing and scraping and rumbling. My heart quaked with fear and expectancy. Right in front of the door a loud step—a violent blow on the handle, and the door flew open with a clatter!—Mustering my courage with all my might, I peeped out cautiously. The sandman was standing in front of Father in the middle of the room, the bright glow from the candles blazing on his face! The sandman, the terrible sandman, was old lawyer Coppelius, who sometimes took his midday meal with us!

But the most ghastly shape could not have aroused deeper horror in me than this very Coppelius did. Picture to yourself a tall, broad-shouldered man with a heavy, shapeless head, a face yellow as ocher, bushy gray eyebrows beneath which two greenish cat's eyes gleamed piercingly, and a large, prominent nose hanging down over his upper lip. His crooked mouth was frequently twisted into a malicious smile; then two dark red patches would appear on his cheeks and a peculiar hissing sound would escape through his clenched teeth. Coppelius always went abroad in an ash-gray frock coat of an old-fashioned cut, with waistcoat and trousers to match, but

Strümpfe und Schuhe mit kleinen Steinschnallen. Die kleine Perücke reichte kaum bis über den Kopfwirbel heraus, die Kleblocken standen hoch über den großen roten Ohren und ein breiter verschlossener Haarbeutel starrte von dem Nacken weg, so daß man die silberne Schnalle sah, die die gefältelte Halsbinde schloß.

Die ganze Figur war überhaupt widrig und abscheulich; aber vor allem waren uns Kindern seine großen knotigten, haarigten Fäuste zuwider, so daß wir, was er damit berührte, nicht mehr mochten. Das hatte er bemerkt und nun war es seine Freude, irgend ein Stückchen Kuchen, oder eine süße Frucht, die uns die gute Mutter heimlich auf den Teller gelegt, unter diesem, oder jenem Vorwande zu berühren, daß wir, helle Tränen in den Augen, die Näscherei, der wir uns erfreuen sollten, nicht mehr genießen mochten vor Ekel und Abscheu. Ebenso machte er es, wenn uns an Feiertagen der Vater ein klein Gläschen süßen Weins eingeschenkt hatte. Dann fuhr er schnell mit der Faust herüber, oder brachte wohl gar das Glas an die blauen Lippen und lachte recht teuflisch, wenn wir unsern Ärger nur leise schluchzend äußern durften.

Er pflegte uns nur immer die kleinen Bestien zu nennen; wir durften, war er zugegen, keinen Laut von uns geben und verwünschten den häßlichen, feindlichen Mann, der uns recht mit Bedacht und Absicht auch die kleinste Freude verdarb. Die Mutter schien ebenso, wie wir, den widerwärtigen Coppelius zu hassen; denn sowie er sich zeigte, war ihr Frohsinn, ihr heiteres unbefangenes Wesen umgewandelt in traurigen, düstern Ernst. Der Vater betrug sich gegen ihn, als sei er ein höheres Wesen, dessen Unarten man dulden und das man auf jede Weise bei guter Laune erhalten müsse. Er durfte nur leise andeuten und Lieblingsgerichte wurden gekocht und seltene Weine kredenzt.

Als ich nun diesen Coppelius sah, ging es grausig und entsetzlich in meiner Seele auf, daß ja niemand anders, als er, der Sandmann sein könne, aber der Sandmann war mir nicht mehr jener Popanz aus dem Ammenmärchen, der dem Eulennest im Halbmonde Kinderaugen zur Atzung holt—nein!—ein häßlicher gespenstischer Unhold, der überall, wo er einschreitet, Jammer—Not—zeitliches, ewiges Verderben bringt.

Ich war fest gezaubert. Auf die Gefahr entdeckt, und, wie ich deutlich dachte, hart gestraft zu werden, blieb ich stehen, den Kopf lauschend durch die Gardine hervorgestreckt. Mein Vater empfing den Coppelius feierlich. »Auf!—zum Werk«, rief dieser mit heise-

with black stockings and shoes that had little buckles set with stones. His small wig scarcely extended past the crown of his head, two plastered-down locks of hair rode high above his large red ears, and a wide tiewig stood out stiffly from the nape of his neck, so that you could see the silver buckle that fastened his pleated neckcloth.

In short, his whole appearance was repellent and loathsome; but we children especially detested his large, knotty, hairy hands, so much so that we had no further use for anything he touched with them. He had observed this and now it gave him pleasure, under one pretext or another, to touch some piece of cake or sweet fruit that dear Mother had secretly put on our plates, so that bright tears came to our eyes, and disgust and repulsion kept us from enjoying the tidbit placed there for our delight. He did the same when on special occasions Father had poured us a little glass of sweet wine. Then he would pass his hand quickly over the glass, or would even raise the glass to his blue lips; and he would laugh like a real devil when we could do no more than vent our vexation with quiet sobs.

His only name for us was "the little beasts"; if he was there, we were not allowed to make a sound, and we cursed the ugly, hateful man who deliberately and intentionally spoiled even our slightest pleasures. Mother seemed to hate the repulsive Coppelius as much as we did; for as soon as he appeared, her cheerfulness and her merry, easygoing nature were changed into sad, dreary gravity. Father behaved toward him as if Coppelius were a higher being whose shortcomings had to be indulged and whose good temper had to be preserved at all costs. The slightest hint from the lawyer, and his favorite dishes were cooked and rare wines served.

So, when I saw this Coppelius, it became clear in my mind, to my fear and horror, that no one but he could be the sandman; for me, however, the sandman was no longer that bogeyman out of an old wives' tale who brought children's eyes as food to the owls' nest on the half moon—no!—but an ugly, spectral monster who brings sorrow—distress—temporal and eternal perdition everywhere he appears.

I was completely spellbound. At the risk of being discovered and, as I firmly believed, severely punished, I remained there listening, with my head poking through the curtain. Father greeted Coppelius ceremoniously. "Come—let us begin!" called the latter in a hoarse, snarl-

rer, schnarrender Stimme und warf den Rock ab. Der Vater zog
still und finster seinen Schlafrock aus und beide kleideten sich in
lange schwarze Kittel. Wo sie *die* hernahmen, hatte ich übersehen.
Der Vater öffnete die Flügeltür eines Wandschranks; aber ich sah,
daß das, was ich solange dafür gehalten, kein Wandschrank, sondern vielmehr eine schwarze Höhlung war, in der ein kleiner Herd
stand.

Coppelius trat hinzu und eine blaue Flamme knisterte auf dem
Herde empor. Allerlei seltsames Geräte stand umher. Ach
Gott!—wie sich nun mein alter Vater zum Feuer herabbückte, da
sah er ganz anders aus. Ein gräßlicher krampfhafter Schmerz
schien seine sanften ehrlichen Züge zum häßlichen widerwärtigen
Teufelsbilde verzogen zu haben. Er sah dem Coppelius ähnlich.
Dieser schwang die glutrote Zange und holte damit hellblinkende
Massen aus dem dicken Qualm, die er dann emsig hämmerte.
Mir war es als würden Menschengesichter ringsumher sichtbar,
aber ohne Augen—scheußliche, tiefe schwarze Höhlen statt ihrer.
»Augen her, Augen her!« rief Coppelius mit dumpfer dröhnender
Stimme. Ich kreischte auf von wildem Entsetzen gewaltig erfaßt
und stürzte aus meinem Versteck heraus auf den Boden. Da ergriff
mich Coppelius, »kleine Bestie!—kleine Bestie!« meckerte er zähn-
fletschend!—riß mich auf und warf mich auf den Herd, daß die
Flamme mein Haar zu sengen begann: »Nun haben wir Augen—Augen—ein schön Paar Kinderaugen.« So flüsterte Coppelius, und griff mit den Fäusten glutrote Körner aus der Flamme,
die er mir in die Augen streuen wollte. Da hob mein Vater flehend
die Hände empor und rief: »Meister! Meister! laß meinem Nathanael die Augen—laß sie ihm!« Coppelius lachte gellend auf und
rief: »Mag denn der Junge die Augen behalten und sein Pensum
flennen in der Welt; aber nun wollen wir doch den Mechanismus
der Hände und der Füße recht observieren.«
Und damit faßte er mich gewaltig, daß die Gelenke knackten,
und schrob mir die Hände ab und die Füße und setzte sie bald hier,
bald dort wieder ein. »'s steht doch überall nicht recht! 's gut so
wie es war!—Der Alte hat's verstanden!« So zischte und lispelte
Coppelius; aber alles um mich her wurde schwarz und finster, ein
jäher Krampf durchzuckte Nerv und Gebein—ich fühlte nichts
mehr.

Ein sanfter warmer Hauch glitt über mein Gesicht, ich erwachte
wie aus dem Todesschlaf, die Mutter hatte sich über mich hingebeugt. »Ist der Sandmann noch da?« stammelte ich. »Nein, mein

ing voice, and threw off his coat. Silently and gloomily Father pulled off his robe and the two of them put on long, black smocks. I failed to notice where *they* came from. Father opened the folding door of a wall closet; but I saw that what I had imagined all along was a closet, was actually a dark opening in which a small stove stood.

Coppelius went over to it, and a blue flame crackled upward on the stove. Round about stood all kinds of strange equipment. God! when my old father now stooped down over the fire, he looked altogether different. A ghastly, convulsive pain seemed to have twisted his gentle, honest features into an ugly, repellent devil's face. He looked like Coppelius. The latter wielded red-hot pincers, with which he drew brightly gleaming lumps out of the thick smoke; he then busily hammered the lumps.

It seemed to me as if human faces were visible all around, but without eyes—with hideous deep, black cavities instead. "Bring some eyes, bring some eyes!" Coppelius called in hollow, rumbling tones. In the violent throes of wild terror, I screamed and dashed out of my hiding-place onto the floor. Then Coppelius seized me—"Little beast! little beast!" he piped, gnashing his teeth—ripped me open and threw me onto the stove so that the flame began to singe my hair. "Now we have eyes—eyes—a nice pair of child's eyes," Coppelius whispered, and with his fists he snatched red-hot grains out of the flame, and was about to strew them in my eyes. Then Father raised his hands beseechingly, shouting: "Master! Master! let my Nathanael keep his eyes—let him keep them!" Coppelius laughed shrilly and shouted: "So then, let the boy keep his eyes and do his share of blubbering in the world; but now we still want to examine the mechanism of his hands and feet."

Whereupon he grabbed hold of me so hard that my joints cracked, and unscrewed my hands and feet, putting them back in various places. "They aren't right anywhere! They're best the way they were!—The old man knew what he was doing!" said Coppelius, hissing and murmuring; but everything around me grew black and dark; a sudden convulsion shot through my nerves and bones—I felt nothing more.

A gentle, warm breath passed over my face; I awoke as if from the sleep of death; Mother was bending over me. "Is the sandman still here?" I stammered. "No, dear, he

liebes Kind, der ist lange, lange fort, der tut dir keinen Schaden!«—So sprach die Mutter und küßte und herzte den wiederge-
wonnenen Liebling.

Was soll ich Dich ermüden, mein herzlieber Lothar! was soll ich
so weitläuftig einzelnes hererzählen, da noch so vieles zu sagen
übrig bleibt? Genug!—ich war bei der Lauscherei entdeckt, und
von Coppelius gemißhandelt worden. Angst und Schrecken hatten
mir ein hitziges Fieber zugezogen, an dem ich mehrere Wochen
krank lag.»Ist der Sandmann noch da?«—Das war mein erstes
gesundes Wort und das Zeichen meiner Genesung, meiner
Rettung.

Nur noch den schrecklichsten Moment meiner Jugendjahre darf
ich Dir erzählen; dann wirst Du überzeugt sein, daß es nicht meiner
Augen Blödigkeit ist, wenn mir nun alles farblos erscheint, sondern, daß ein dunkles Verhängnis wirklich einen trüben Wolken-
schleier über mein Leben gehängt hat, den ich vielleicht nur ster-
bend zerreiße.

Coppelius ließ sich nicht mehr sehen, es hieß, er habe die Stadt
verlassen.

Ein Jahr mochte vergangen sein, als wir der alten unveränderten
Sitte gemäß abends an dem runden Tische saßen. Der Vater war
sehr heiter und erzählte viel Ergötzliches von den Reisen, die er in
seiner Jugend gemacht. Da hörten wir, als es neune schlug, plötzlich
die Haustür in den Angeln knarren und langsame eisenschwere
Schritte dröhnten durch den Hausflur die Treppe herauf.»Das ist
Coppelius«, sagte meine Mutter erblassend. »Ja!—es ist Coppelius«, wiederholte der Vater mit matter gebrochener Stimme. Die
Tränen stürzten der Mutter aus den Augen. »Aber Vater, Vater!«
rief sie, »muß es denn so sein?«—»Zum letzten Male!« erwiderte
dieser, »zum letzten Male kommt er zu mir, ich verspreche es dir.
Geh nur, geh mit den Kindern!—Geht—geht zu Bette! Gute
Nacht!«

Mir war es, als sei ich in schweren kalten Stein eingepreßt
—mein Atem stockte!—Die Mutter ergriff mich beim Arm als ich
unbeweglich stehen blieb: »Komm Nathanael, komme nur!«—Ich
ließ mich fortführen, ich trat in meine Kammer. »Sei ruhig, sei
ruhig, lege dich ins Bette!—schlafe—schlafe«, rief mir die Mutter
nach; aber von unbeschreiblicher innerer Angst und Unruhe gequält, konnte ich kein Auge zutun. Der verhaßte abscheuliche Coppelius stand vor mir mit funkelnden Augen und lachte mich hämisch an, vergebens trachtete ich sein Bild los zu werden.

Es mochte wohl schon Mitternacht sein, als ein entsetzlicher
Schlag geschah, wie wenn ein Geschütz losgefeuert würde. Das
ganze Haus erdröhnte, es rasselte und rauschte bei meiner Türe
vorüber, die Haustüre wurde klirrend zugeworfen. »Das ist Coppe-

left long, long ago, he won't hurt you!" said Mother, and she kissed and caressed the darling boy she had regained.

Why should I tire you out, my dear Lothar? Why should I go on so long with details when so much still remains to be told? Enough! I was discovered at my eavesdropping and roughly handled by Coppelius. Fear and terror had brought on a raging fever, which kept me in bed for several weeks. "Is the sandman still here?" That was the first thing I said upon feeling better; it was the sign of my recovery, of my salvation.

The only other thing I shall tell you about is the most frightful moment of my youth; then you will be convinced that it is not a weakness in my eyes if everything now seems colorless to me, but that a dark fate has really drawn a dismal veil of cloud over my life, which I shall perhaps rend only when I die.

Coppelius did not show up any more; he was said to have left the city.

About a year had gone by, when one evening we were sitting at the round table in accordance with our old, unaltered custom. Father was very jolly and told many enjoyable stories about the journeys he had made in his youth. Then, at the stroke of nine, we suddenly heard the street door creaking on its hinges, and slow steps, heavy as iron, thudded across the vestibule and up the stairs. "It's Coppelius," said Mother, turning pale. "Yes, it's Coppelius!" repeated Father in a feeble, cracked voice. Tears streamed from Mother's eyes. "But Father, Father!" she cried, "must it be?"—"For the last time!" he replied, "he is visiting me for the last time, I promise you. Go, go and take the children!—Go—go to bed! Good night!"

I felt as if I had been squeezed flat into a heavy, cold stone slab—I couldn't breathe!—Mother seized me by the arm as I stood there motionless: "Come, Nathanael, come!"—I allowed myself to be led away, I entered my bedroom. "Be calm, be calm, go to bed!—sleep—sleep," Mother called after me; but, tormented by indescribable fear and anxiety of mind, I could not close my eyes. The hateful, abhorrent Coppelius stood before me with gleaming eyes and smiled at me maliciously; in vain did I attempt to rid myself of his image.

It must have been around midnight when there was a terrible explosion as if a cannon had been fired. The whole house echoed, a rattling and a swishing noise went past my door, the street door was slammed shut with a

lius!« rief ich entsetzt und sprang aus dem Bette. Da kreischte es auf in schneidendem trostlosen Jammer, fort stürzte ich nach des Vaters Zimmer, die Türe stand offen, erstickender Dampf quoll mir entgegen, das Dienstmädchen schrie:»Ach, der Herr!—der Herr!«

Vor dem dampfenden Herde auf dem Boden lag mein Vater tot mit schwarz verbranntem gräßlich verzerrtem Gesicht, um ihn herum heulten und winselten die Schwestern—die Mutter ohnmächtig daneben!—»Coppelius, verruchter Satan, du hast den Vater erschlagen!«—So schrie ich auf; mir vergingen die Sinne. Als man zwei Tage darauf meinen Vater in den Sarg legte, waren seine Gesichtszüge wieder mild und sanft geworden, wie sie im Leben waren. Tröstend ging es in meiner Seele auf, daß sein Bund mit dem teuflischen Coppelius ihn nicht ins ewige Verderben gestürzt haben könne.

Die Explosion hatte die Nachbarn geweckt, der Vorfall wurde ruchtbar und kam vor die Obrigkeit, welche den Coppelius zur Verantwortung vorfordern wollte. Der war aber spurlos vom Orte verschwunden.

Wenn ich Dir nun sage, mein herzlieber Freund! daß jener Wetterglashändler eben der verruchte Coppelius war, so wirst Du mir es nicht verargen, daß ich die feindliche Erscheinung als schweres Unheil bringend deute. Er war anders gekleidet, aber Coppelius' Figur und Gesichtszüge sind zu tief in mein Innerstes eingeprägt, als daß hier ein Irrtum möglich sein sollte. Zudem hat Coppelius nicht einmal seinen Namen geändert. Er gibt sich hier, wie ich höre, für einen piemontesischen Mechanikus aus, und nennt sich Giuseppe Coppola.

Ich bin entschlossen es mit ihm aufzunehmen und des Vaters Tod zu rächen, mag es denn nun gehen wie es will.

Der Mutter erzähle nichts von dem Erscheinen des gräßlichen Unholds—Grüße meine liebe holde Clara, ich schreibe ihr in ruhigerer Gemütsstimmung. Lebe wohl etc. etc.

CLARA AN NATHANAEL

Wahr ist es, daß Du recht lange mir nicht geschrieben hast, aber dennoch glaube ich, daß Du mich in Sinn und Gedanken trägst. Denn meiner gedachtest Du wohl recht lebhaft, als Du Deinen letzten Brief an Bruder Lothar absenden wolltest und die Aufschrift, statt an ihn an mich richtetest. Freudig erbrach ich den Brief und wurde den Irrtum erst bei den Worten inne:»Ach mein herzlieber Lothar!«—Nun hätte ich nicht weiter lesen, sondern den Brief dem

bang. "That's Coppelius!" I cried in terror and jumped out of bed. Then there was a scream of harrowing, inconsolable sorrow. I dashed over to Father's room; the door was open; suffocating smoke poured out at me; the servant girl yelled: "Oh, the master, the master!"

On the floor in front of the smoking stove lay Father, dead, his face hideously contorted and burned black; around him my sisters were howling and whimpering—Mother in a faint beside them! "Coppelius, you villainous devil, you have killed Father!" I shouted, and lost consciousness. When Father was placed in his coffin two days later, his features had become kind and gentle again, as they had been in life. The consoling thought flashed upon my soul that his covenant with the fiendish Coppelius could not have doomed him to eternal perdition.

The explosion had awakened our neighbors; the incident got abroad and came to the notice of the authorities, who wanted to summon Coppelius as the party responsible. But he had vanished without a trace.

If I now tell you, my dear friend, that that barometer vendor was none other than the villainous Coppelius, you will not blame me for interpreting his hateful reappearance as a forecast of great disaster. He wore different clothes, but Coppelius' form and features are too deeply imprinted on my mind for a mistake to be possible in this case. Besides, Coppelius has not even changed his name. As I hear, he now claims to be a Piedmontese inventor of mechanical contrivances, and calls himself Giuseppe Coppola.

I am determined to confront him and avenge Father's death, no matter what may result.

Tell Mother nothing about the reappearance of the horrible monster.—Give my regards to lovely, dear Clara; I shall write to her when my mood is calmer. Farewell, . . .

LETTER FROM CLARA TO NATHANAEL

It is true that you have not written to me for a very long time, but I believe all the same that I am in your mind and thoughts. For you must have been thinking of me quite actively when you intended to send your last letter to my brother Lothar and addressed it to me instead of to him. I opened the letter joyfully and learned of my mistake only at the words "Oh, my very dear Lothar." Now, I

Bruder geben sollen. Aber, hast Du mir auch sonst manchmal in kindischer Neckerei vorgeworfen, ich hätte solch ruhiges, weiblich besonnenes Gemüt, daß ich wie jene Frau, drohe das Haus den Einsturz, noch vor schneller Flucht ganz geschwinde einen falschen Kniff in der Fenstergardine glattstreichen würde, so darf ich doch wohl kaum versichern, daß Deines Briefes Anfang mich tief erschütterte. Ich konnte kaum atmen, es flimmerte mir vor den Augen.

Ach, mein herzgeliebter Nathanael! was konnte so Entsetzliches in Dein Leben getreten sein! Trennung von Dir, Dich niemals wiedersehen, der Gedanke durchfuhr meine Brust wie ein glühender Dolchstich. —Ich las und las!—Deine Schilderung des widerwärtigen Coppelius ist gräßlich. Erst jetzt vernahm ich, wie Dein guter alter Vater solch entsetzlichen, gewaltsamen Todes starb. Bruder Lothar, dem ich sein Eigentum zustellte, suchte mich zu beruhigen, aber es gelang ihm schlecht. Der fatale Wetterglashändler Giuseppe Coppola verfolgte mich auf Schritt und Tritt und beinahe schäme ich mich, es zu gestehen, daß er selbst meinen gesunden, sonst so ruhigen Schlaf in allerlei wunderlichen Traumgebilden zerstören konnte. Doch bald, schon den andern Tag, hatte sich alles anders in mir gestaltet. Sei mir nur nicht böse, mein Inniggeliebter, wenn Lothar Dir etwa sagen möchte, daß ich trotz Deiner seltsamen Ahnung, Coppelius werde Dir etwas Böses antun, ganz heitern unbefangenen Sinnes bin, wie immer.

Geradeheraus will ich es Dir nur gestehen, daß, wie ich meine, alles Entsetzliche und Schreckliche, wovon Du sprichst, nur in Deinem Innern vorging, die wahre wirkliche Außenwelt aber daran wohl wenig teilhatte. Widerwärtig genug mag der alte Coppelius gewesen sein, aber daß er Kinder haßte, das brachte in Euch Kindern wahren Abscheu gegen ihn hervor.

Natürlich verknüpfte sich nun in Deinem kindischen Gemüt der schreckliche Sandmann aus dem Ammenmärchen mit dem alten Coppelius, der Dir, glaubtest Du auch nicht an den Sandmann, ein gespenstischer, Kindern vorzüglich gefährlicher, Unhold blieb. Das unheimliche Treiben mit Deinem Vater zur Nachtzeit war wohl nichts anders, als daß beide insgeheim alchymistische Versuche machten, womit die Mutter nicht zufrieden sein konnte, da gewiß viel Geld unnütz verschleudert und obendrein, wie es immer mit solchen Laboranten der Fall sein soll, des Vaters Gemüt ganz von

ought not to have read on, but ought to have given the letter to my brother. But, even though you often teased me as a child for having such a femininely calm and collected nature that I would behave like the woman in the story and, if my house were about to cave in, before dashing out I would quickly smooth out a wrinkle in the window curtains—I scarcely need to assure you that the beginning of your letter affected me deeply. I could scarcely breathe, I saw spots before my eyes.

Oh, my beloved Nathanael, what could have come into your life that was so dreadful? Being parted from you, never seeing you again: that thought pierced my heart like the thrust of a red-hot dagger. I went on reading! Your description of the repellent Coppelius is horrible. Only now have I learned that your kind old father died such a terrible, violent death. My brother Lothar, to whom I handed over what belonged to him, tried to calm me down, but did not succeed very well. The nasty barometer vendor Giuseppe Coppola dogged my every step, and I am almost ashamed to confess that he was able to disturb even *my* healthy slumbers, usually so peaceful, by turning up in all sorts of odd dream shapes. But soon, even by the next day, I was looking at everything differently. Don't be angry with me, darling, if Lothar should tell you that, despite your strange foreboding that Coppelius will do you some harm, my mind is quite cheerful and at ease, as always.

I will only confess to you quite openly that, as I believe, all the horror and terror of which you speak has only occurred in your mind, and the external world of reality has had little share in it. Old Coppelius may have been repulsive enough, but it was his hatred of children that caused you children to have such a real aversion to him.

Naturally an association was formed in your young mind between the horrible sandman in the old wives' tale and old Coppelius, who, even when you no longer believed in the sandman, remained in your mind as a ghostly monster especially dangerous to children. His eerie nighttime activities with your father were surely nothing but experiments in alchemy, which the two of them carried on secretly and which could not fail to upset your mother, not only because a lot of money must have been squandered to no purpose but also, as is always the case with researchers of that sort, your father's mind was completely

dem trügerischen Drange nach hoher Weisheit erfüllt, der Familie abwendig gemacht wurde.

Der Vater hat wohl gewiß durch eigne Unvorsichtigkeit seinen Tod herbeigeführt, und Coppelius ist nicht schuld daran: Glaubst Du, daß ich den erfahrnen Nachbar Apotheker gestern frug, ob wohl bei chemischen Versuchen eine solche augenblicklich tötende Explosion möglich sei? Der sagte:»Ei allerdings« und beschrieb mir nach seiner Art gar weitläuftig und umständlich, wie das zugehen könne, und nannte dabei so viel sonderbar klingende Namen, die ich gar nicht zu behalten vermochte. —Nun wirst Du wohl unwillig werden über Deine Clara, Du wirst sagen:»In dies kalte Gemüt dringt kein Strahl des Geheimnisvollen, das den Menschen oft mit unsichtbaren Armen umfaßt; sie erschaut nur die bunte Oberfläche der Welt und freut sich, wie das kindische Kind über die gold-gleißende Frucht, in deren Innern tödliches Gift verborgen.«

Ach mein herzgeliebter Nathanael! glaubst Du denn nicht, daß auch in heitern—unbefangenen—sorglosen Gemütern die Ah-nung wohnen könne von einer dunklen Macht, die feindlich uns in unserm eignen Selbst zu verderben strebt?—Aber verzeih es mir, wenn ich einfältig Mädchen mich unterfange, auf irgend eine Weise Dir anzudeuten, was ich eigentlich von solchem Kampfe im Innern glaube. —Ich finde wohl gar am Ende nicht die rechten Worte und Du lachst mich aus, nicht, weil ich was Dummes meine, sondern weil ich mich so ungeschickt anstelle, es zu sagen.

Gibt es eine dunkle Macht, die so recht feindlich und verräterisch einen Faden in unser Inneres legt, woran sie uns dann festpackt und fortzieht auf einem gefahrvollen verderblichen Wege, den wir sonst nicht betreten haben würden—gibt es eine solche Macht, so muß sie in uns sich, wie wir selbst gestalten, ja unser Selbst werden; denn nur *so* glauben wir an sie und räumen ihr den Platz ein, dessen sie bedarf, um jenes geheime Werk zu vollbringen. Haben wir fe-sten, durch das heitre Leben gestärkten, Sinn genug, um fremdes feindliches Einwirken als solches stets zu erkennen und den Weg, in den uns Neigung und Beruf geschoben, ruhigen Schrittes zu verfolgen, so geht wohl jene unheimliche Macht unter in dem ver-geblichen Ringen nach der Gestaltung, die unser eignes Spiegelbild sein sollte.

Es ist auch gewiß, fügt Lothar hinzu, daß die dunkle psychische Macht, haben wir uns durch uns selbst ihr hingegeben, oft fremde Gestalten, die die Außenwelt uns in den Weg wirft, in unser Inneres hineinzieht, so, daß wir selbst nur den Geist entzünden, der, wie

filled with the illusory thirst for higher wisdom and was estranged from his family.

Your father almost certainly brought about his death through his own carelessness, and Coppelius is not to blame for it. Would you believe that yesterday I asked our neighbor, an experienced apothecary, whether in the course of chemical experiments such an explosion causing instant death was possible? He said, "Oh, to be sure!" and in his own manner he described to me at great length and in detail how it could happen, reeling off many, many strange-sounding terms that I was quite unable to remember. Now you will become annoyed with your Clara, you will say: "Her cold spirit is impervious to any ray of the mysteries that often embrace man with invisible arms; she sees only the motley surface of the world and is like the innocent child who rejoices over the glittering golden fruit inside of which deadly poison is concealed."

Oh, my beloved Nathanael! don't you believe that even cheerful—easygoing—carefree minds can shelter the presentiment of a dark power that is hostilely striving to destroy us within ourselves?—But forgive me if I, a simple girl, presume to give you some indication of what I really think about such inward struggles.—I may not find the right words and you will laugh at me, not because my thoughts are foolish but because I am so awkward in the way I state them.

If there *is* a dark power that so very hostilely and treacherously implants a thread within us by which it then seizes us and drags us off along a dangerous path to perdition, on which we would otherwise not have set foot—if there *is* such a power, it must take shape within us like ourselves—it must become our selves; for only in that manner could we believe in it and give it the space it needs in order to accomplish that secret activity. If our mind, strengthened by a cheerful life, is firm enough always to recognize outside hostile influences for what they are, and to pursue with calm steps the path onto which our inclinations and vocations have led us, that uncanny power will surely perish in its useless struggle to assume a shape that would be our own mirror image.

It is also certain, Lothar adds, that the dark mental power, if through our own doing we have surrendered to it, often calls into our mind the shapes of other people who cross our path in the external world. So that it is we ourselves who generate the spirit that, in our strange

wir in wunderlicher Täuschung glauben, aus jener Gestalt spricht. Es ist das Phantom unseres eigenen Ichs, dessen innige Verwandtschaft und dessen tief Einwirkung auf unser Gemüt uns in die Hölle wirft, oder in den Himmel verzückt. Du merkst, mein herzlieber Nathanael! daß wir, ich und Bruder Lothar uns recht über die Materie von dunklen Mächten und Gewalten ausgesprochen haben, die mir nun, nachdem ich nicht ohne Mühe das Hauptsächlichste aufgeschrieben, ordentlich tiefsinnig vorkommt. Lothars letzte Worte verstehe ich nicht ganz, ich ahne nur, was er meint, und doch ist es mir, als sei alles sehr wahr. Ich bitte Dich, schlage Dir den häßlichen Advokaten Coppelius und den Wetterglasmann Giuseppe Coppola ganz aus dem Sinn. Sei überzeugt, daß diese fremden Gestalten nichts über Dich vermögen; nur der Glaube an ihre feindliche Gewalt kann sie Dir in der Tat feindlich machen.

Spräche nicht aus jeder Zeile Deines Briefes die tiefste Aufregung Deines Gemüts, schmerzte mich nicht Dein Zustand recht in innerster Seele, wahrhaftig, ich könnte über den Advokaten Sandmann und den Wetterglashändler Coppelius scherzen. Sei heiter—heiter!—Ich habe mir vorgenommen, bei Dir zu erscheinen, wie Dein Schutzgeist, und den häßlichen Coppola, sollte er es sich etwa beikommen lassen, Dir im Traum beschwerlich zu fallen, mit lautem Lachen fortzubannen. Ganz und gar nicht fürchte ich mich vor ihm und vor seinen garstigen Fäusten, er soll mir weder als Advokat eine Näscherei, noch als Sandmann die Augen verderben.

Ewig, mein herzinnigstgeliebter Nathanael etc. etc. etc.

NATHANAEL AN LOTHAR

Sehr unlieb ist es mir, daß Clara neulich den Brief an Dich aus, freilich durch meine Zerstreutheit veranlaßtem, Irrtum erbrach und las. Sie hat mir einen sehr tiefsinnigen philosophischen Brief geschrieben, worin sie ausführlich beweiset, daß Coppelius und Coppola nur in meinem Innern existieren und Phantome meines Ichs sind, die augenblicklich zerstäuben, wenn ich sie als solche erkenne. In der Tat, man sollte gar nicht glauben, daß der Geist, der aus solch hellen holdlächelnden Kindesaugen, oft wie ein lieblicher süßer Traum, hervorleuchtet, so gar verständig, so magistermäßig distinguieren könne. Sie beruft sich auf Dich. Ihr habt über mich gesprochen. Du liesest ihr wohl logische Kollegia, damit sie alles fein sichten und sondern lerne. —Laß das bleiben!

delusion, we imagine is speaking from that shape. It is the phantom of our own ego, whose inner affinity and whose profound influence on our mind casts us into hell or transports us to heaven.

You can see, darling Nathanael, that my brother Lothar and I have had a long discussion on the subject of dark forces and powers, and now that I have set down the chief results, not without an effort, I believe that our discussion really went to the root of the matter. I don't fully understand Lothar's last words, I merely sense what he means, and yet I feel it is all very true. I beseech you to drive the ugly lawyer Coppelius and the barometer man Giuseppe Coppola from your mind completely. Be convinced that these strange shapes have no power over you; only the belief in their hostile power can make them hostile to you in reality.

If every line of your letter did not testify to a most profound agitation of mind, your condition would not grieve me deep down in my heart—to tell the truth, I could joke about lawyer Sandman and barometer vendor Coppelius. Be cheerful—cheerful!—I have resolved to appear before you as your guardian angel and, should the ugly Coppola take a notion to trouble you in your dreams, to exorcise him with hearty laughter. I am not at all afraid of him or of his nasty hands; he will not spoil my tidbits as a lawyer or my eyes as the sandman.

Eternally yours, my most dearly beloved Nathanael, . . .

LETTER FROM NATHANAEL TO LOTHAR

I find it very unpleasant that Clara recently opened and read my letter to you—through an error caused by my own distractedness, to be sure. She has written me a very profound philosophical letter in which she proves in detail that Coppelius and Coppola exist only in my mind and are phantoms of my ego who will turn to dust at once if I recognize them for what they are. Really, I would not have imagined that the spirit that shines from such bright, sweetly smiling, childlike eyes, often like a lovely, sweet dream, was capable of furnishing such rational proofs, like a professor. She quotes you as an authority. The two of you have discussed me. You probably gave her lectures on logic for her to be able to sift and distinguish everything so subtly. Let that go!

Übrigens ist es wohl gewiß, daß der Wetterglashändler Giuseppe Coppola keinesweges der alte Advokat Coppelius ist. Ich höre bei dem erst neuerdings angekommenen Professor der Physik, der, wie jener berühmte Naturforscher, Spalanzani heißt und italienischer Abkunft ist, Kollegia. Der kennt den Coppola schon seit vielen Jahren und überdem hört man es auch seiner Aussprache an, daß er wirklich Piemonteser ist. Coppelius war ein Deutscher, aber wie mich dünkt, kein ehrlicher.

Ganz beruhigt bin ich nicht. Haltet Ihr, Du und Clara, mich immerhin für einen düstern Träumer, aber nicht los kann ich den Eindruck werden, den Coppelius' verfluchtes Gesicht auf mich macht. Ich bin froh, daß er fort ist aus der Stadt, wie mir Spalanzani sagt. Dieser Professor ist ein wunderlicher Kauz. Ein kleiner rundlicher Mann, das Gesicht mit starken Backenknochen, feiner Nase, aufgeworfenen Lippen, kleinen stechenden Augen. Doch besser, als in jeder Beschreibung, siehst Du ihn, wenn Du den Cagliostro, wie er von Chodowiecki in irgend einem Berlinischen Taschenkalender steht, anschauest. —So sieht Spalanzani aus.

Neulich steige ich die Treppe herauf und nehme wahr, daß die sonst einer Glastüre dicht vorgezogene Gardine zur Seite einen kleinen Spalt läßt. Selbst weiß ich nicht, wie ich dazu kam, neugierig durchzublicken. Ein hohes, sehr schlank im reinsten Ebenmaß gewachsenes, herrlich gekleidetes Frauenzimmer saß im Zimmer vor einem kleinen Tisch, auf den sie beide Ärme, die Hände zusammengefaltet, gelegt hatte. Sie saß der Türe gegenüber, so, daß ich ihr engelschönes Gesicht ganz erblickte. Sie schien mich nicht zu bemerken, und überhaupt hatten ihre Augen etwas Starres, beinahe möcht ich sagen, keine Sehkraft, es war mir so, als schliefe sie mit offnen Augen.

Mir wurde ganz unheimlich und deshalb schlich ich leise fort ins Auditorium, das daneben gelegen. Nachher erfuhr ich, daß die Gestalt, die ich gesehen, Spalanzanis Tochter, Olimpia war, die er sonderbarer und schlechter Weise einsperrt, so, daß durchaus kein Mensch in ihre Nähe kommen darf. —Am Ende hat es eine Bewandtnis mit ihr, sie ist vielleicht blödsinnig oder sonst.

Weshalb schreibe ich Dir aber das alles? Besser und ausführlicher

Anyway, it is fairly certain that the barometer vendor Giuseppe Coppola is not at all the same man as old lawyer Coppelius. I am attending lectures given by a newly arrived professor of physics, who is named Spalanzani, like the famous physiologist,[3] and is of Italian descent. He has known Coppola for many years and, besides, one can tell from his speech that he really is a Piedmontese. Coppelius was a German, but, as I believe, not a respectable one.

My mind is not completely at ease. You and Clara can go on thinking of me as a gloomy dreamer, but I cannot rid myself of the impression which Coppelius' accursed face makes on me. I am glad that he is out of town, as Spalanzani tells me. This professor is an odd character. A short, roly-poly man, a face with prominent cheekbones, a thin nose, turned-up lips and small, piercing eyes. But you will picture him better than in any description if you look at Chodowiecki's engraving of Cagliostro[4] in one edition of the *Berlin Pocket Calendar*. That is how Spalanzani looks.

Lately I went upstairs at his place and noticed that the curtain that is usually drawn tightly over a glass door was open a little at one side. I myself don't know what made me look through it like a busybody. A tall, very slender, perfectly proportioned, splendidly dressed woman was sitting in the room by a little table, on which she was resting both arms, her hands clasped. She sat opposite the door so that I had a full view of her angelically beautiful face. She seemed not to notice me and, besides, her eyes had a certain rigidity—I might always say, no power of vision—it seemed to me as if she were sleeping with open eyes.

An uncanny feeling came over me, and so I stole away quietly into the auditorium, which was adjoining. Later I heard that the figure I had seen was that of Spalanzani's daughter Olimpia, who he keeps locked up in a strange and unbecoming manner so that no one at all can come near her. Perhaps there is something peculiar about her; maybe she is simpleminded or something.

But why am I writing to you about all this? I could have

---

[3] Lazzaro Spallanzani (1729–1799).

[4] Daniel Chodowiecki (1726–1801), foremost German printmaker of his day. Alessandro, conte di Cagliostro (Giuseppe Balsamo, 1743–1795), high-society charlatan who claimed to predict the future and who peddled an elixir of longevity.

hätte ich Dir das mündlich erzählen können. Wisse nämlich, daß ich über vierzehn Tage bei Euch bin. Ich muß mein süßes liebes Engelsbild, meine Clara, wiedersehen. Weggehaucht wird dann die Verstimmung sein, die sich (ich muß das gestehen) nach dem fatalen verständigen Briefe meiner bemeistern wollte. Deshalb schreibe ich auch heute nicht an sie.

   Tausend Grüße etc. etc. etc.

Seltsamer und wunderlicher kann nichts erfunden werden, als dasjenige ist, was sich mit meinem armen Freunde, dem jungen Studenten Nathanael, zugetragen, und was ich dir, günstiger Leser! zu erzählen unternommen. Hast du, Geneigtester! wohl jemals etwas erlebt, das deine Brust, Sinn und Gedanken ganz und gar erfüllte, alles andere daraus verdrängend? Es gärte und kochte in dir, zur siedenden Glut entzündet sprang das Blut durch die Adern und färbte höher deine Wangen. Dein Blick war so seltsam als wolle er Gestalten, keinem andern Auge sichtbar, im leeren Raum erfassen und die Rede zerfloß in dunkle Seufzer. Da frugen dich die Freunde: »Wie ist Ihnen, Verehrter?—Was haben Sie, Teurer?« Und nun wolltest du das innere Gebilde mit allen glühenden Farben und Schatten und Lichtern aussprechen und mühtest dich ab, Worte zu finden, um nur anzufangen. Aber es war dir, als müßtest du nun gleich im ersten Wort alles Wunderbare, Herrliche, Entsetzliche, Lustige, Grauenhafte, das sich zugetragen, recht zusammengreifen, so daß es, wie ein elektrischer Schlag, alle treffe. Doch jedes Wort, alles was Rede vermag, schien dir farblos und frostig und tot. Du suchst und suchst, und stotterst und stammelst, und die nüchternen Fragen der Freunde schlagen, wie eisige Windeshauche, hinein in deine innere Glut, bis die verlöschen will.
   Hattest du aber, wie ein kecker Maler, erst mit einigen verwegenen Strichen, den Umriß deines innern Bildes hingeworfen, so trugst du mit leichter Mühe immer glühender und glühender die Farben auf und das lebendige Gewühl mannigfacher Gestalten riß die Freunde fort und sie sahen, wie du, sich selbst mitten im Bilde, das aus deinem Gemüt hervorgegangen!—Mich hat, wie ich es dir, geneigter Leser! gestehen muß, eigentlich niemand nach der Geschichte des jungen Nathanael gefragt; du weißt ja aber wohl, daß ich zu dem wunderlichen Geschlechte der Autoren gehöre, denen, tragen sie etwas so in sich, wie ich es vorhin beschrieben, so zumute wird, als frage jeder, der in ihre Nähe kommt und nebenher

told it to you in person more skillfully and in more detail. For I want you to know: I shall be visiting you in two weeks. I must see my dear, sweet angel, my Clara, again. Then that bad mood will disappear which (I must confess) has taken hold of me since reading that awful letter with its "good common sense." For that reason, I am not writing to her today either.

Best regards, . . .

No one can conceive anything more strange and singular than that which befell my poor friend, the young student Nathanael, and which I have undertaken to narrate to you, kind reader. Have you, gentle reader, ever had an experience that completely occupied your heart, mind and thoughts, driving out all else? There was a simmering and a boiling inside you; heated to a seething incandescence, your blood raced through your veins and lent higher color to your cheeks. Your gaze was peculiar, as if it wished to grasp shapes in empty space that were visible to no other eyes, and your speech dissolved into gloomy sighs. Then your acquaintances asked you: "How are you feeling, sir?—What's wrong with you, my friend?" And then you wanted to describe your inner vision with all its glowing colors and shadows and lights, and struggled to find words even to begin. But you felt compelled to gather together all the wondrous, splendid, horrible, comic and frightening occurrences in your very first utterance so that it might affect everyone like an electric shock. Every word, however, everything that human speech is capable of, seemed to you colorless, glacial and dead. You try and try, you stutter and stammer, and your friends' sober questions blow upon your inward flame like icy blasts of wind until it almost goes out.

But if, like a daring painter, you had begun to sketch the outline of your inner vision with a few bold strokes, it would not have been difficult to lay on warmer and warmer colors, and your friends would have been swept away by the lively throng of manifold images. They would have found themselves, like you, in the midst of the picture that emanated from your mind!—I must confess to you, gentle reader, that no one actually asked me for the story of young Nathanael; but you are well aware that I belong to that eccentric species known as authors, who—if they carry inside themselves something of the sort I previously described—feel as if everyone who comes near

auch wohl noch die ganze Welt: »Was ist es denn? Erzählen Sie Liebster?«

So trieb es mich denn gar gewaltig, von Nathanaels verhängnisvollem Leben zu dir zu sprechen. Das Wunderbare, Seltsame davon erfüllte meine ganze Seele, aber eben deshalb und weil ich dich, o mein Leser! gleich geneigt machen mußte, Wunderliches zu ertragen, welches nichts Geringes ist, quälte ich mich ab, Nathanaels Geschichte, bedeutend—originell, ergreifend, anzufangen: »Es war einmal«—der schönste Anfang jeder Erzählung, zu nüchtern!—»In der kleinen Provinzialstadt S. lebte«—etwas besser, wenigstens ausholend zum Klimax. —Oder gleich medias in res: »›Scher er sich zum Teufel‹, rief, Wut und Entsetzen im wilden Blick, der Student Nathanael, als der Wetterglashändler Giuseppe Coppola«—Das hatte ich in der Tat schon aufgeschrieben, als ich in dem wilden Blick des Studenten Nathanael etwas Possierliches zu verspüren glaubte; die Geschichte ist aber gar nicht spaßhaft.

Mir kam keine Rede in den Sinn, die nur im mindesten etwas von dem Farbenglanz des innern Bildes abzuspiegeln schien. Ich beschloß gar nicht anzufangen. Nimm, geneigter Leser! die drei Briefe, welche Freund Lothar mir gütigst mitteilte, für den Umriß des Gebildes, in das ich nun erzählend immer mehr und mehr Farbe hineinzutragen mich bemühen werde. Vielleicht gelingt es mir, manche Gestalt, wie ein guter Porträtmaler, so aufzufassen, daß du es ähnlich findest, ohne das Original zu kennen, ja daß es dir ist, als hättest du die Person recht oft schon mit leibhaftigen Augen gesehen. Vielleicht wirst du, o mein Leser! dann glauben, daß nichts wunderlicher und toller sei, als das wirkliche Leben und daß dieses der Dichter doch nur, wie in eines matt geschliffnen Spiegels dunklem Widerschein, auffassen könne.

Damit klarer werde, was gleich anfangs zu wissen nötig, ist jenen Briefen noch hinzuzufügen, daß bald darauf, als Nathanaels Vater gestorben, Clara und Lothar, Kinder eines weitläuftigen Verwandten, der ebenfalls gestorben und sie verwaist nachgelassen, von Nathanaels Mutter ins Haus genommen wurden. Clara und Nathanael faßten eine heftige Zuneigung zueinander, wogegen kein Mensch auf Erden etwas einzuwenden hatte; sie waren daher Verlobte, als Nathanael den Ort verließ um seine Studien in G.— fortzusetzen.

them, and the whole world to boot, were asking: "But what is it? Tell me, my good fellow."

Thus I had a powerful urge to tell you the story of Nathanael's disastrous life. Its odd and strange aspects filled my entire soul, but for that very reason, and because, reader, I had to make you immediately predisposed to put up with oddities, which is no easy task, I racked my brains trying to begin Nathanael's story in a significant, original, gripping way. "Once upon a time," the finest beginning for any story, was too matter-of-fact! "In the small provincial town of S. there lived"—a little better, at least capable of leading to a climax.—Or to plunge *medias in res:*[5] "'Go to the devil,' shouted the student Nathanael, with rage and fear in his wild gaze, when the barometer vendor Giuseppe Coppola"—In fact, I had already written that down, when I thought I detected something comic in the student Nathanael's wild gaze; but the story is not at all humorous.

I could think of no phrase that seemed in the least to reflect some of the glowing colors of my inner vision. I decided not to begin at all. Gentle reader, accept the three letters (which my friend Lothar kindly made available to me) as the outline of the picture, to which I shall now, while narrating, strive to add more and more color. Perhaps, like a good portraitist, I shall succeed in depicting many a figure so well that you will find it a good likeness, without knowing the original—that you will in fact feel as if you had already seen the person quite often with your own eyes. Perhaps, reader, you will then believe that nothing is stranger and droller than real life, and that, after all, the poet can only conceive this life as a dark reflection in a frosted mirror.

In order to make clearer the information that is necessary from the outset, the following must be added to those letters: Immediately after Nathanael's father died, Clara and Lothar, children of a distant relative who had also died, leaving them orphans, were taken into the household by Nathanael's mother. Clara and Nathanael developed a strong affection for each other, to which no one on earth had any objections; therefore they were already engaged when Nathanael left town to continue his studies in G——. That is where we find him in his last letter,

---

[5] Latin for "right into the midst of events"; a quotation from Horace.

Da ist er nun in seinem letzten Brief und hört Kollegia bei dem berühmten Professor Physices, Spalanzani.

Nun könnte ich getrost in der Erzählung fortfahren; aber in dem Augenblick steht Claras Bild so lebendig mir vor Augen, daß ich nicht wegschauen kann, so wie es immer geschah, wenn sie mich holdlächelnd anblickte. —Für schön konnte Clara keinesweges gelten; das meinten alle, die sich von Amtswegen auf Schönheit verstehen. Doch lobten die Architekten die reinen Verhältnisse ihres Wuchses, die Maler fanden Nacken, Schultern und Brust beinahe zu keusch geformt, verliebten sich dagegen sämtlich in das wunderbare Magdalenenhaar und faselten überhaupt viel von Battonischem Kolorit. Einer von ihnen, ein wirklicher Fantast, verglich aber höchstseltsamer Weise Claras Augen mit einem See von Ruisdael, in dem sich des wolkenlosen Himmels reines Azur, Wald- und Blumenflur, der reichen Landschaft ganzes buntes, heitres Leben spiegelt.

Dichter und Meister gingen aber weiter und sprachen:»Was See—was Spiegel!—Können wir denn das Mädchen anschauen, ohne daß uns aus ihrem Blick wunderbare himmlische Gesänge und Klänge entgegenstrahlen, die in unser Innerstes dringen, daß da alles wach und rege wird? Singen wir selbst dann nichts wahrhaft Gescheutes, so ist überhaupt nicht viel an uns und das lesen wir denn auch deutlich in dem um Claras Lippen schwebenden feinen Lächeln, wenn wir uns unterfangen, ihr etwas vorzuquinkelieren, das so tun will als sei es Gesang, unerachtet nur einzelne Töne verworren durcheinander springen.«

Es war dem so. Clara hatte die lebenskräftige Fantasie des heitern unbefangenen, kindischen Kindes, ein tiefes weiblich zartes Gemüt, einen gar hellen scharf sichtenden Verstand. Die Nebler und Schwebler hatten bei ihr böses Spiel; denn ohne zu viel zu reden, was überhaupt in Claras schweigsamer Natur nicht lag, sagte ihnen der helle Blick, und jenes feine ironische Lächeln: Liebe Freunde! wie möget ihr mir denn zumuten, daß ich eure verfließende Schattengebilde für wahre Gestalten ansehen soll, mit Leben und Regung?—Clara wurde deshalb von vielen kalt, gefühllos, prosaisch

attending the lectures of the celebrated professor of physics Spalanzani.

Now I might continue my narrative confidently; but at the moment the image of Clara stands before my eyes with such distinctness that I cannot look away—as always happened when she looked at me with a sweet smile.—Clara could in no way be considered beautiful; that was the opinion of all professional judges of beauty. But architects praised the clean proportions of her figure, while painters found her neck, shoulders and bosom almost too chastely formed but, on the other hand, all were enamored with her marvelous hair, like the Magdalen's, and in general babbled a great deal about her Battoni coloring.[6] One of them, however, a real fantasist, compared Clara's eyes in the most peculiar fashion to a Ruysdael lake,[7] in which were reflected the pure azure of the cloudless sky, the tract of forest and flowers, and the whole variegated and merry life of the opulent landscape.

But poets and musicians went further and said: "What do you mean, lake! What do you mean, mirror!—Can we look at the girl without having miraculous heavenly voices and instruments beam at us from her eyes and penetrate our inmost recesses, awakening and stirring everything there? If we ourselves fail to sing anything noteworthy at such times, well, there's nothing special about us anyway, and we can also see that distinctly in the subtle smile playing about Clara's lips when we venture to entertain her with our jingles, which have pretensions to being noble song even though a few isolated notes are merely crisscrossing one another in confusion."

That was indeed the case. Clara had the healthy imagination of a jolly, unaffected, childlike child, a gentle, truly feminine spirit, and a very bright mind capable of subtle distinctions. People with clouded, unfocused thoughts were out of luck when dealing with her; because without her saying much—long speeches did not accord with her taciturn character, anyway—her bright glance and that subtle, ironic smile said to them: "Dear friends, how can you expect me to regard your transitory shadow-images as real figures endowed with life and motion?" Many people,

---

[6] Refers to the Italian portraitist Pompeo Battoni, or Batoni (1708–1787).

[7] Either Salomon (1602–1670) or his son Jacob (1628–1682) van Ruysdael, outstanding Dutch landscape painters.

gescholten; aber andere, die das Leben in klarer Tiefe aufgefaßt, liebten ungemein das gemütvolle, verständige, kindliche Mädchen, doch keiner so sehr, als Nathanael, der sich in Wissenschaft und Kunst kräftig und heiter bewegte. Clara hing an dem Geliebten mit ganzer Seele; die ersten Wolkenschatten zogen durch ihr Leben, als er sich von ihr trennte. Mit welchem Entzücken flog sie in seine Arme, als er nun, wie er im letzten Briefe an Lothar es verheißen, wirklich in seiner Vaterstadt ins Zimmer der Mutter eintrat. Es geschah so wie Nathanael geglaubt; denn in dem Augenblick, als er Clara widersah, dachte er weder an den Advokaten Coppelius, noch an Claras verständigen Brief, jede Verstimmung war verschwunden.

Recht hatte aber Nathanael doch, als er seinem Freunde Lothar schrieb, daß des widerwärtigen Wetterglashändlers Coppola Gestalt recht feindlich in sein Leben getreten sei. Alle fühlten das, da Nathanael gleich in den ersten Tagen in seinem ganzen Wesen durchaus verändert sich zeigte. Er versank in düstre Träumereien, und trieb es bald so seltsam, wie man es niemals von ihm gewohnt gewesen. Alles, das ganze Leben war ihm Traum und Ahnung geworden; immer sprach er davon, wie jeder Mensch, sich frei wähnend, nur dunklen Mächten zum grausamen Spiel diene, vergeblich lehne man sich dagegen auf, demütig müsse man sich dem fügen, was das Schicksal verhängt habe. Er ging so weit, zu behaupten, daß es töricht sei, wenn man glaube, in Kunst und Wissenschaft nach selbsttätiger Willkür zu schaffen; denn die Begeisterung, in der man nur zu schaffen fähig sei, komme nicht aus dem eignen Innern, sondern sei das Einwirken irgend eines außer uns selbst liegenden höheren Prinzips.

Der verständigen Clara war diese mystische Schwärmerei im höchsten Grade zuwider, doch schien es vergebens, sich auf Widerlegung einzulassen. Nur dann, wenn Nathanael bewies, daß Coppelius das böse Prinzip sei, was ihn in dem Augenblick erfaßt habe, als er hinter dem Vorhange lauschte, und daß dieser widerwärtige *Dämon* auf entsetzliche Weise ihr Liebesglück stören werde, da wurde Clara sehr ernst und sprach: »Ja Nathanael! du hast recht, Coppelius ist ein böses feindliches Prinzip, er kann Entsetzliches wirken, wie eine teuflische Macht, die sichtbarlich in das Leben trat, aber nur dann, wenn du ihn nicht aus Sinn und Gedanken verbannst. Solange du an ihn glaubst, *ist* er auch und wirkt, nur dein Glaube ist seine Macht.«

therefore, called Clara cold, unfeeling, prosaic; others, however, who had clearly comprehended the profundities of life, loved the affectionate, sensible, childlike girl extremely—but none as much as Nathanael, who moved about in the world of science and art with assurance and ease.

Clara doted on her sweetheart with all her soul; the first clouds passed over her life when he parted from her. With what rapture she flew into his arms when now, as he had promised in his last letter to Lothar, he actually stepped into his mother's room in his home town. It was just as Nathanael had thought; for as soon as he saw Clara again he stopped thinking about lawyer Coppelius or about Clara's common-sense letter; all his bad temper had vanished.

Nevertheless Nathanael was right when he wrote his friend Lothar that the figure of the repellent barometer vendor Coppola had entered his life in a truly hostile way. Everyone perceived his, for it was obvious even in the first few days that Nathanael's entire nature was altogether changed. He fell into gloomy reveries, and soon acted more strangely than anyone had grown accustomed to. Everything, all of life, had become dream and foreboding for him; he constantly spoke of how every person, under the delusion of acting freely, was merely being used in a cruel game by dark powers; of how pointless it was to rebel—one must humbly bow to the dictates of fate. He went so far as to assert that it was foolish for artists and scientists to believe they were creating things of their own free will; for the inspiration that alone makes creativity possible does not come from within a person but is the effect of some higher principle lying outside ourselves.

Sensible Clara found this mystical fanaticism repugnant in the highest degree, but it seemed to be useless to attempt to refute it. Only when Nathanael offered a proof that Coppelius was the evil principle, which had seized hold of him at the moment he was eavesdropping behind the curtain, and that this abhorrent *daimon* would interfere with their happiness in love in a frightful way, did Clara become very serious and say: "Yes, Nathanael, you are right, Coppelius is an evil, hostile principle; he can cause terrible things, like a fiendish power that has come visibly to life, but only if you fail to drive him out of your mind and thoughts. As long as you believe in him, he does both exist and act; his only power is your belief in him."

Nathanael, ganz erzürnt, daß Clara die Existenz des *Dämons* nur in seinem eignen Innern statuiere, wollte dann hervorrücken mit der ganzen mystischen Lehre von Teufeln und grausen Mächten, Clara brach aber verdrüßlich ab, indem sie irgend etwas Gleichgültiges dazwischen schob, zu Nathanaels nicht geringem Ärger. *Der* dachte, kalten unempfänglichen Gemütern verschließen sich solche tiefe Geheimnisse, ohne sich deutlich bewußt zu sein, daß er Clara eben zu solchen untergeordneten Naturen zähle, weshalb er nicht abließ mit Versuchen, sie in jene Geheimnisse einzuweihen.

Am frühen Morgen, wenn Clara das Frühstück bereiten half, stand er bei ihr und las ihr aus allerlei mystischen Büchern vor, daß Clara bat:»Aber lieber Nathanael, wenn ich *dich* nun das böse Prinzip schelten wollte, das feindlich auf meinen Kaffee wirkt?—Denn, wenn ich, wie du es willst, alles stehen und liegen lassen und dir, indem du liesest, in die Augen schauen soll, so läuft mir der Kaffee ins Feuer und ihr bekommt alle kein Frühstück!«—Nathanael klappte das Buch heftig zu und rannte voll Unmut fort in sein Zimmer.

Sonst hatte er eine besondere Stärke in anmutigen, lebendigen Erzählungen, die er aufschrieb, und die Clara mit dem innigsten Vergnügen anhörte, jetzt waren seine Dichtungen düster, unverständlich, gestaltlos, so daß, wenn Clara schonend es auch nicht sagte, er doch wohl fühlte, wie wenig sie davon angesprochen wurde. Nichts war für Clara tötender, als das Langweilige; in Blick und Rede sprach sich dann ihre nicht zu besiegende geistige Schläfrigkeit aus.

Nathanaels Dichtungen waren in der Tat sehr langweilig. Sein Verdruß über Claras kaltes prosaisches Gemüt stieg höher, Clara konnte ihren Unmut über Nathanaels dunkle, düstere, langweilige Mystik nicht überwinden, und so entfernten beide im Innern sich immer mehr voneinander, ohne es selbst zu bemerken.

Die Gestalt des häßlichen Coppelius war, wie Nathanael selbst es sich gestehen mußte, in seiner Fantasie erbleicht und es kostete ihm oft Mühe, ihn in seinen Dichtungen, wo er als grauser Schicksalspopanz auftrat, recht lebendig zu kolorieren. Es kam ihm endlich ein, jene düstre Ahnung, daß Coppelius sein Liebesglück stören werde, zum Gegenstande eines Gedichts zu machen. Er stellte sich und Clara dar, in treuer Liebe verbunden, aber dann und wann war es, als griffe eine schwarze Faust in ihr Leben und risse irgend eine Freude heraus, die ihnen aufgegangen. Endlich, als sie schon am Traualtar stehen, erscheint der entsetzliche Coppelius und berührt

Nathanael, very angry at Clara's affirmation that the *daimon* existed only in his own mind, was about to expatiate on the whole mystical doctrine of devils and fearful powers, but Clara interrupted him disagreeably by interposing some indifferent topic, to Nathanael's decided vexation. *He* thought that such deep mysteries were impenetrable to cold, unreceptive minds—without being clearly aware that he was thereby classifying Clara as just such a subordinate being. Therefore he did not leave off his attempts to initiate her into those mysteries.

Early in the morning, when Clara was helping prepare breakfast, he stood near her and read aloud to her from all sorts of mystical books, until Clara implored: "But, Nathanael, dear, what if I were now to call *you* the evil principle that is having a hostile influence on my coffee?—Because if I am to do as you wish and let everything go, and just gaze into your eyes while you read, my coffee will run over into the fire and none of you will get any breakfast!" Nathanael slammed the book shut and ran off to his room in great displeasure.

He had formerly been especially good at pleasant, lively stories, which he would write down, and which Clara would listen to with heartfelt enjoyment; now his writings were gloomy, incomprehensible and formless, so that, even though Clara spared him and did not say so, he still felt how little they appealed to her. Nothing was deadlier to Clara than to be bored; then her unconquerable mental somnolence was expressed in her looks and words.

Nathanael's productions were indeed very boring. His vexation over Clara's cold, prosaic spirit increased; Clara was unable to overcome her dislike of Nathanael's dark, gloomy, boring mysticism, and so the couple grew further and further apart from each other inwardly without noticing it.

As Nathanael had to confess even to himself, the figure of ugly Coppelius had faded in his imagination, and it was often an effort for him to give his portrait sufficiently lively colors in his tales, in which Coppelius appeared as a frightening bogeyman of destiny. He finally hit on the idea of making the gloomy foreboding of Coppelius' interference with his happiness in love the subject of a poem. He portrayed Clara and himself as joined in true love, but from time to time a dark hand seemed to encroach on their life and tear away some joy that had dawned for them. Finally, when they have reached the altar, the terri-

Claras holde Augen; *die* springen in Nathanaels Brust wie blutige
Funken sengend und brennend, Coppelius faßt ihn und wirft ihn
in einen flammenden Feuerkreis, der sich dreht mit der Schnellig-
keit des Sturmes und ihn sausend und brausend fortreißt. Es ist ein
Tosen, als wenn der Orkan grimmig hineinpeitscht in die schäumen-
den Meereswellen, die sich wie schwarze, weißhauptige Riesen em-
porbäumen in wütendem Kampfe. Aber durch dies wilde Tosen
hört er Claras Stimme: »Kannst du mich denn nicht erschauen?
Coppelius hat dich getäuscht, das waren ja nicht meine Augen, die
so in deiner Brust brannten, das waren ja glühende Tropfen deines
eignen Herzbluts—ich habe ja meine Augen, sieh mich doch
nur an!«—Nathanael denkt: Das ist Clara, und ich bin ihr eigen
ewiglich. —Da ist es, als faßt der Gedanke gewaltig in den
Feuerkreis hinein, daß er stehen bleibt, und im schwarzen Ab-
grund verrauscht dumpf das Getöse. Nathanael blickt in Claras
Augen; aber es ist der Tod, der mit Claras Augen ihn freundlich
anschaut.

Während Nathanael dies dichtete, war er sehr ruhig und beson-
nen, er feilte und besserte an jeder Zeile und da er sich dem metri-
schen Zwange unterworfen, ruhte er nicht, bis alles rein und wohl-
klingend sich fügte. Als er jedoch nun endlich fertig worden, und
das Gedicht für sich laut las, da faßte ihn Grausen und wildes Entsetzen und er schrie auf: »Wessen grauenvolle Stimme ist
das?«—Bald schien ihm jedoch das Ganze wieder nur eine
sehr gelungene Dichtung, und es war ihm, als müsse Claras kaltes
Gemüt dadurch entzündet werden, wiewohl er nicht deutlich
dachte, wozu denn Clara entzündet, und wozu es denn nun
eigentlich führen solle, sie mit den grauenvollen Bildern zu ängsti-
gen, die ein entsetzliches, ihre Liebe zerstörendes Geschick weis-
sagten.

Sie, Nathanael und Clara, saßen in der Mutter kleinem Garten,
Clara war sehr heiter, weil Nathanael sie seit drei Tagen, in denen
er an jener Dichtung schrieb, nicht mit seinen Träumen und Ahnungen geplagt hatte. Auch Nathanael sprach lebhaft und froh von
lustigen Dingen wie sonst, so, daß Clara sagte: »Nun erst habe ich
dich ganz wieder, siehst du es wohl, wie wir den häßlichen Coppelius vertrieben haben?« Da fiel dem Nathanael erst ein, daß er ja
die Dichtung in der Tasche trage, die er habe vorlesen wollen. Er
zog auch sogleich die Blätter hervor und fing an zu lesen: Clara,
etwas Langweiliges wie gewöhnlich vermutend und sich darein er-

ble Coppelius appears and touches Clara's lovely eyes, which start from her head and penetrate Nathanael's breast like bloody sparks, singeing and burning; Coppelius seizes him and throws him into a blazing circle of fire that spins with the swiftness of a storm and carries him off with a terrific roar. The tumult is like that of a hurricane furiously whipping up the foaming waves of the sea, which in their raging struggle rear up like dark, white-haired giants. But through this wild uproar he hears Clara's voice: "Can't you see me, then? Coppelius has deceived you, those were not my eyes that were burning so in your breast, they were red-hot drops of your own heart's blood—I still have my eyes, just look at me!"—Nathanael thinks: "That is Clara, and I belong to her eternally." Then that thought seems to reach into the circle of fire with great force, so that it comes to a halt, and the uproar sinks into the black abyss, dying away in hollow tones. Nathanael looks into Clara's eyes; but it is Death that looks at him amicably with Clara's eyes.

While Nathanael was writing this, he was very calm and self-possessed; he polished and improved every line and, since he had subjected himself to the constraints of meter, he did not rest until the entire construction was neat and euphonious. When he was finally done, however, and read the poem aloud to himself, he was seized by fear and wild terror and shouted out: "Whose awful voice is that?" But soon it all seemed to him once more to be merely a very successful piece of writing, and he felt that Clara's sober mind just *had* to be kindled by it—although he had no distinct idea to what purpose Clara was to be kindled, and where it was actually to lead if she *were* frightened by the gruesome images predicting a terrible fate destructive of their love.

They, Nathanael and Clara, were sitting in his mother's little garden; Clara was very jolly because in the three days during which he was working on that poem, Nathanael had not plagued her with his dreams and forebodings. Nathanael, too, was speaking in a lively, happy way about amusing things as in the past, so that Clara said: "Now for the first time I really have you back again completely; do you see how we have driven away ugly Coppelius?" Only then did Nathanael recall that the poem he had wanted to recite was in his pocket. He drew out the pages at once and began to read; Clara, assuming that it would be something dull as usual and resigning herself to the chore,

gebend, fing an, ruhig zu stricken. Aber so wie immer schwärzer und schwärzer das düstre Gewölk aufstieg, ließ sie den Strickstrumpf sinken und blickte starr dem Nathanael ins Auge. *Den* riß seine Dichtung unaufhaltsam fort, hochrot färbte seine Wangen die innere Glut, Tränen quollen ihm aus den Augen.

Endlich hatte er geschlossen, er stöhnte in tiefer Ermattung—er faßte Claras Hand und seufzte wie aufgelöst in trostlosem Jammer: »Ach!—Clara—Clara!«—Clara drückt ihn sanft an ihren Busen und sagte leise, aber sehr langsam und ernst: »Nathanael—mein herzlieber Nathanael!—wirf das tolle—unsinnige—wahnsinnige Märchen ins Feuer.« Da sprang Nathanael entrüstet auf und rief, Clara von sich stoßend: »Du lebloses, verdammtes Automat!« Er rannte fort, bittre Tränen vergoß die tief verletzte Clara: »Ach er hat mich niemals geliebt, denn er versteht mich nicht«, schluchzte sie laut.

Lothar trat in die Laube; Clara mußte ihm erzählen was vorgefallen; er liebte seine Schwester mit ganzer Seele, jedes Wort ihrer Anklage fiel wie ein Funke in sein Inneres, so, daß der Unmut, den er wider den träumerischen Nathanael lange im Herzen getragen, sich entzündete zum wilden Zorn. Er lief zu Nathanael, er warf ihm das unsinnige Betragen gegen die geliebte Schwester in harten Worten vor, die der aufbrausende Nathanael ebenso erwiderte. Ein fantastischer, wahnsinniger Geck wurde mit einem miserablen, gemeinen Alltagsmenschen erwidert. Der Zweikampf war unvermeidlich. Sie beschlossen, sich am folgenden Morgen hinter dem Garten nach dortiger akademischer Sitte mit scharfgeschliffenen Stoßrapieren zu schlagen.

Stumm und finster schlichen sie umher, Clara hatte den heftigen Streit gehört und gesehen, daß der Fechtmeister in der Dämmerung die Rapiere brachte. Sie ahnte was geschehen sollte. Auf dem Kampfplatz angekommen hatten Lothar und Nathanael soeben düsterschweigend die Röcke abgeworfen, blutdürstige Kampflust im brennenden Auge wollten sie gegeneinander ausfallen, als Clara durch die Gartentür herbeistürzte. Schluchzend rief sie laut: »Ihr wilden entsetzlichen Menschen!—stoßt mich nur gleich nieder, ehe ihr euch anfallt; denn wie soll ich denn länger leben auf der Welt, wenn der Geliebte den Bruder, oder wenn der Bruder den Geliebten ermordet hat!«

Lothar ließ die Waffe sinken und sah schweigend zur Erde nieder, aber in Nathanaels Innern ging in herzzerreißender Wehmut alle Liebe wieder auf, wie er sie jemals in der herrlichen Jugendzeit schönsten Tagen für die holde Clara empfunden. Das Mordgewehr

began to knit quietly. But, as the gloomy cloud bank rose and grew ever darker, she let the stocking she was knitting fall into her lap and looked into Nathanael's eyes fixedly. He was carried away uncontrollably by his poem; his inner warmth lent a bright red color to his cheeks, tears were pouring from his eyes.

Finally he finished, groaned with profound exhaustion, grasped Clara's hand and sighed as if reduced to inconsolable sorrow: "Ah!—Clara—Clara!" Clara pressed him gently to her bosom and said quietly, but very slowly and gravely: "Nathanael—my darling Nathanael!—throw that mad—senseless—insane tale into the fire." Then Nathanael leaped up in anger and, pushing Clara away from him, cried: "You damned lifeless automaton!" He ran off; Clara, deeply hurt, shed bitter tears. "Oh, he never loved me, because he doesn't understand me," she loudly sobbed.

Lothar entered the arbor; Clara had to tell him what had occurred; he loved his sister wholeheartedly; every word of her accusation burned him inwardly like a hot spark, so that the displeasure with the visionary Nathanael that he had long nurtured in his heart was kindled into raging anger. He ran to Nathanael and reproached him in severe terms for his senseless conduct toward his beloved sister; Nathanael, flaring up, replied in like fashion. "Fantasizing, insane ass!" was countered with "Wretched, vulgar philistine!" A duel was unavoidable. They decided to fight behind the garden the next morning, using sharp rapiers, in accordance with the local students' custom.

They stalked about silently and sternly; Clara had heard the violent quarrel and seen the fencing master deliver the rapiers at dawn. She guessed what was afoot. Lothar and Nathanael, after arriving at the scene of combat, had just thrown aside their coats in gloomy silence and were about to attack each other with bloodthirsty lust for battle in their blazing eyes, when Clara dashed up through the garden gate. Sobbing, she shouted loudly: "You wild, horrible men!—why not cut me down before attacking each other? For how am I to go on living in the world after my sweetheart has killed my brother or my brother has killed my sweetheart?"

Lothar let his weapon fall and looked down at the ground in silence, but in Nathanael's bosom, with heart-rending melancholy, all the love returned that he had ever felt for lovely Clara in the most beautiful days of their

entfiel seiner Hand, er stürzte zu Claras Füßen. »Kannst du mir
denn jemals verzeihen, du meine einzige, meine herzgeliebte
Clara!—Kannst du mir verzeihen, mein herzlieber Bruder Lothar!«—Lothar wurde gerührt von des Freundes tiefem Schmerz;
unter tausend Tränen umarmten sich die drei versöhnten Menschen und schwuren, nicht voneinander zu lassen in steter Liebe
und Treue.

Dem Nathanael war es zumute, als sei eine schwere Last, die ihn
zu Boden gedrückt, von ihm abgewälzt, ja als habe er, Widerstand
leistend der finstern Macht, die ihn befangen, sein ganzes Sein,
dem Vernichtung drohte, gerettet. Noch drei selige Tage verlebte
er bei den Lieben, dann kehrte er zurück nach G., wo er noch
ein Jahr zu bleiben, dann aber auf immer nach seiner Vaterstadt
zurückzukehren gedachte.

Der Mutter war alles, was sich auf Coppelius bezog, verschwiegen
worden; denn man wußte, daß sie nicht ohne Entsetzen an ihn
denken konnte, weil sie, wie Nathanael, ihm den Tod ihres Mannes
schuld gab.

Wie erstaunte Nathanael, als er in seine Wohnung wollte und sah,
daß das ganze Haus niedergebrannt war, so daß aus dem Schutt-
haufen nur die nackten Feuermauern hervorragten. Unerachtet
das Feuer in dem Laboratorium des Apothekers, der im untern
Stocke wohnte, ausgebrochen war, das Haus daher von unten herauf gebrannt hatte, so war es doch den kühnen, rüstigen Freunden
gelungen, noch zu rechter Zeit in Nathanaels im obern Stock gele-
genes Zimmer zu dringen, und Bücher, Manuskripte, Instrumente
zu retten. Alles hatten sie unversehrt in ein anderes Haus getragen,
und dort ein Zimmer in Beschlag genommen, welches Nathanael
nun sogleich bezog.

Nicht sonderlich achtete er darauf, daß er dem Professor Spalanzani gegenüber wohnte, und ebensowenig schien es ihm etwas Besonderes, als er bemerkte, daß er aus seinem Fenster gerade hinein
in das Zimmer blickte, wo oft Olimpia einsam saß, so, daß er ihre
Figur deutlich erkennen konnte, wiewohl die Züge des Gesichts
undeutlich und verworren blieben. Wohl fiel es ihm endlich auf,
daß Olimpia oft stundenlang in derselben Stellung, wie er sie einst
durch die Glastüre entdeckte, ohne irgend eine Beschäftigung an
einem kleine Tische saß und daß sie offenbar unverwandten Blickes
nach ihm herüberschaute; er mußte sich auch selbst gestehen, daß
er nie einen schöneren Wuchs gesehen; indessen, Clara im Herzen,

wonderful youth. The instrument of death dropped from his hand and he threw himself at Clara's feet. "Can you ever forgive me, my one and only, my dearly beloved Clara?—Can you forgive me, my dear brother Lothar?" Lothar was touched by his friend's deep grief; with a thousand tears the three reconciled people embraced, swearing never to falter in their constant love and fidelity to one another.

Nathanael felt as if a heavy load, which had bowed him to the ground, had been removed from him—as if, actively resisting the dark power that had enmeshed him, he had saved his whole existence from the annihilation that had threatened it. He spent three more rapturous days with his dear ones, then returned to G——, where he intended to stay another year and then go back to his home town for good.

His mother had not been informed of anything pertaining to Coppelius, because it was known that she could not think of him without terror, since she, like Nathanael, blamed him for her husband's death.

How amazed Nathanael was when he was nearly back at his lodgings and saw that the whole house had burnt to the ground, so that only the bare fireproof walls projected from the heap of debris! Even though the fire had broken out in the laboratory of the apothecary who lived on the lower floor, and the house had thus burned from the bottom up, Nathanael's brave, energetic friends had succeeded in forcing their way into his upper-floor room in time to save his books, manuscripts and scientific instruments. They had brought all this undamaged to another house and rented a room there, into which Nathanael now immediately moved.

He paid no special attention to the fact that he was living opposite Professor Spalanzani, nor did he think it noteworthy when he observed that from his window he could look into the very room in which Olimpia often sat alone, so that he could recognize her figure clearly although her features remained indistinct and blurred. He did finally take note that Olimpia often sat unoccupied for hours at a small table in the same position in which he had once discovered her through the glass door, and that she obviously gazed fixedly in his direction. He also had to admit to himself that he had never seen a finer figure. Meanwhile, with Clara in his heart, the stiff, rigid Olimpia re-

blieb ihm die steife, starre Olimpia höchst gleichgültig und nur
zuweilen sah er flüchtig über sein Kompendium herüber nach der
schönen Bildsäule, das war alles.

Eben schrieb er an Clara, als es leise an die Türe klopfte; sie
öffnete sich auf seinen Zuruf und Coppolas widerwärtiges Gesicht
sah hinein. Nathanael fühlte sich im Innersten erbeben; eingedenk
dessen, was ihm Spalanzani über den Landsmann Coppola gesagt
und was er auch rücksichts des Sandmanns Coppelius der Geliebten
so heilig versprochen, schämte er sich aber selbst seiner kindischen
Gespensterfurcht, nahm sich mit aller Gewalt zusammen und
sprach so sanft und gelassen, als möglich: »Ich kaufe kein Wetterglas, mein lieber Freund! gehen Sie nur!«

Da trat aber Coppola vollends in die Stube und sprach mit heiserem Ton, indem sich das weite Maul zum häßlichen Lachen verzog
und die kleinen Augen unter den grauen langen Wimpern stechend hervorfunkelten: »Ei, nix Wetterglas, nix Wetterglas!—hab
auch sköne Oke—sköne Oke!«—Entsetzt rief Nathanael: »Toller
Mensch, wie kannst du Augen haben?—Augen—Augen?—«
Aber in dem Augenblick hatte Coppola seine Wettergläser beiseite
gesetzt, griff in die weiten Rocktaschen und holte Lorgnetten und
Brillen heraus, die er auf den Tisch legte.

»Nu—Nu—Brill—Brill auf der Nas su setze, das sein meine
Oke—sköne Oke!«—Und damit holte er immer mehr und mehr
Brillen heraus, so, daß es auf dem ganzen Tisch seltsam zu flim-
mern und funkeln begann. Tausend Augen blickten und zuckten
krampfhaft und starrten auf zum Nathanael; aber er konnte nicht
wegschauen von dem Tisch, und immer mehr Brillen legte Coppola
hin, und immer wilder und wilder sprangen flammende Blicke
durcheinander und schossen ihre blutrote Strahlen in Nathanaels
Brust.

Übermannt von tollem Entsetzen schrie er auf: »Halt ein! halt
ein, fürchterlicher Mensch!«—Er hatte Coppola, der eben in die
Tasche griff, um noch mehr Brillen herauszubringen, unerachtet
schon der ganze Tische überdeckt war, beim Arm festgepackt. Coppola machte sich mit heiserem widrigen Lachen sanft los und mit
den Worten: »Ah!—nix für Sie—aber hier sköne Glas«—hatte er
alle Brillen zusammengerafft, eingesteckt und aus der Seitentasche
des Rocks eine Menge großer und kleiner Perspektive hervor-
geholt.

Sowie die Brillen fort waren, wurde Nathanael ganz ruhig und
an Clara denkend sah er wohl ein, daß der entsetzliche Spuk nur
aus seinem Innern hervorgegangen, sowie daß Coppola ein höchst
ehrlicher Mechanikus und Optikus, keineswegs aber Coppelii ver-

mained a matter of complete indifference to him, and only occasionally did he raise his eyes from his *Compendium* and glance fleetingly at the beautiful statue; that was all.

He was just writing to Clara when a quiet knock came at the door; at his reply it opened and Coppola's repugnant face looked in. Nathanael felt himself trembling deep within; however, recalling what Spalanzani had said about his compatriot Coppola and the solemn promise he had made to his beloved concerning the sandman Coppelius, he was ashamed at his own childish fear of spooks, summoned up his courage with all his might, and said, as gently and calmly as he could: "I'm not in the market for any barometers, my good man! That will be all!"

But then Coppola stepped completely into the room and, as his wide mouth twisted into an ugly smile and his small eyes gleamed piercingly below his long, gray lashes, he said hoarsely: "Oh, no barometro, no barometro!—Also have beau'ful eye—beau'ful eye!" Horrified, Nathanael cried: "Madman, how can you have eyes?—Eyes—Eyes?—" But by that time Coppola had laid aside his barometers and was now reaching into his wide coat pockets and pulling out lorgnettes and spectacles, which he placed on the table.

"Now—Now—Eyeglass—Eyeglass to put on nose, this are my eye—beau'ful eye!" And, saying that, he pulled out more and more pairs of spectacles, so that there was a strange glimmering and sparkling all over the table. A thousand eyes gazed and blinked convulsively and stared upward at Nathanael; but he could not look away from the table, and Coppola put down more and more spectacles, whose blazing glances crisscrossed ever more wildly, shooting their bloodred rays into Nathanael's breast.

Overcome by mad terror, he shouted out: "Stop, stop, you fearful man!" He had seized Coppola by the arm as the latter was reaching into his pocket to pull out even more spectacles although the whole table was already covered with them. With a hoarse, repellent laugh Coppola freed himself gently, and saying, "Ah! not'ing for you—but here beau'ful glass," he swept up and pocketed all the spectacles and pulled a number of large and small telescopes from the side pocket of his coat.

As soon as the spectacles were gone, Nathanael grew perfectly calm and, thinking of Clara, he realized that the terrible apparition had only been a figment of his imagination, and that Coppola might be a highly honorable me-

fluchter Doppeltgänger und Revenant sein könne. Zudem hatten alle Gläser, die Coppola nun auf den Tisch gelegt, gar nichts Besonderes, am wenigsten so etwas Gespenstisches wie die Brillen und, um alles wieder gutzumachen, beschloß Nathanael dem Coppola jetzt wirklich etwas abzukaufen.

Er ergriff ein kleines sehr sauber gearbeitetes Taschenperspektiv und sah, um es zu prüfen, durch das Fenster. Noch im Leben war ihm kein Glas vorgekommen, das die Gegenstände so rein, scharf und deutlich dicht vor die Augen rückte. Unwillkürlich sah er hinein in Spalanzanis Zimmer; Olimpia saß, wie gewöhnlich, vor dem kleinen Tisch, die Arme darauf gelegt, die Hände gefaltet.

Nun erschaute Nathanael erst Olimpias wunderschön geformtes Gesicht. Nur die Augen schienen ihm gar seltsam starr und tot. Doch wie er immer schärfer und schärfer durch das Glas hinschaute, war es, als gingen in Olimpias Augen feuchte Mondesstrahlen auf. Es schien, als wenn nun erst die Sehkraft entzündet würde; immer lebendiger und lebendiger flammten die Blicke. Nathanael lag wie festgezaubert im Fenster, immer fort und fort die himmlisch-schöne Olimpia betrachtend.

Ein Räuspern und Scharren weckte ihn, wie aus tiefem Traum. Coppola stand hinter ihm: »Tre Zechini—drei Dukat«—Nathanael hatte den Optikus rein vergessen, rasch zahlte er das Verlangte. »Nick so?—sköne Glas—sköne Glas!« frug Coppola mit seiner widerwärtigen heisern Stimme und dem hämischen Lächeln. »Ja, ja, ja!« erwiderte Nathanael verdrießlich. »Adieu, lieber Freund!«—Coppola verließ nicht ohne viele seltsame Seitenblicke auf Nathanael, das Zimmer. Er hörte ihn auf der Treppe laut lachen. »Nun ja«, meinte Nathanael, »er lacht mich aus, weil ich ihm das kleine Perspektiv gewiß viel zu teuer bezahlt habe—zu teuer bezahlt!«

Indem er diese Worte leise sprach, war es, als halle ein tiefer Todesseufzer grauenvoll durch das Zimmer, Nathanaels Atem stockte vor innerer Angst. —Er hatte ja aber selbst so aufgeseufzt, das merkte er wohl. »Clara«, sprach er zu sich selber, »hat wohl recht, daß sie mich für einen abgeschmackten Geisterseher hält; aber närrisch ist es doch—ach wohl mehr, als närrisch, daß mich der dumme Gedanke, ich hätte das Glas dem Coppola zu teuer bezahlt, noch jetzt so sonderbar ängstigt; den Grund davon sehe ich gar nicht ein.«

Jetzt setzte er sich hin, um den Brief an Clara zu enden, aber ein

chanician and optician, but could in no way be the accursed double and ghost of Coppelius. Moreover, none of the glasses that Coppola had now put on the table were at all peculiar, at least not as eerie as the spectacles, and in order to make amends Nathanael decided to make a real purchase from Coppola.

He picked up a small, very neatly made pocket telescope and, to test it, looked through the window. Never before in his life had he come across a glass that brought distant objects close to his eyes so clearly, sharply and distinctly. Involuntarily he looked into Spalanzani's room; Olimpia sat, as usual, by the little table, resting her arms on it, her hands clasped.

Now for the first time Nathanael espied Olimpia's magnificently formed face. Only her eyes seemed to him strangely rigid and dead. But as he looked through the glass more and more keenly, moist moonbeams appeared to radiate from Olimpia's eyes. It seemed that her power of vision had only now been ignited; her eyes shone with an ever livelier flame. Nathanael remained at the window as if magically bound to the spot, observing the divinely beautiful Olimpia uninterruptedly.

The sound of someone clearing his throat and scraping awoke him, as if from a profound dream. Coppola was standing behind him: "Tre zecchini—t'ree ducat." Nathanael had completely forgotten the optician; he quickly paid the desired sum. "Not so?—beau'ful glass—beau'ful glass!" asked Coppola with his repellent, hoarse voice and malicious smile. "Yes, yes, yes!" replied Nathanael with vexation; "adieu, dear friend!" Coppola left the room, not without many strange sidelong glances at Nathanael, who heard him laughing loudly on the stairs. "Of course," Nathanael thought, "he's laughing at me because I must have paid much too dearly for the little telescope—paid too dearly!"

As he said these words quietly, he seemed to hear a deep, deathly sigh echo eerily through the room; Nathanael could not catch his breath for the fear in his mind. But it was he alone who had heaved that sigh, he knew that clearly. "Clara," he said to himself, "is surely right to take me for a vulgar visionary; but it *is* foolish—ah, perhaps more than foolish—that the stupid thought of having paid Coppola too much for the glass continues to trouble me so strangely; I just cannot see the reason for it."

Now he sat down to complete his letter to Clara, but a

Blick durchs Fenster überzeugte ihn, daß Olimpia noch dasäße und im Augenblick, wie von unwiderstehlicher Gewalt getrieben, sprang er auf, ergriff Coppolas Perspektiv und konnte nicht los von Olimpias verführerischem Anblick, bis ihn Freund und Bruder Siegmund abrief ins Kollegium bei dem Professor Spalanzani.

Die Gardine vor dem verhängnisvollen Zimmer war dicht zugezogen, er konnte Olimpia ebensowenig hier, als die beiden folgenden Tage hindurch in ihrem Zimmer, entdecken, unerachtet er kaum das Fenster verließ und fortwährend durch Coppolas Perspektiv hinüberschaute. Am dritten Tage wurden sogar die Fenster verhängt. Ganz verzweifelt und getrieben von Sehnsucht und glühendem Verlangen lief er hinaus vors Tor. Olimpias Gestalt schwebte vor ihm her in den Lüften und trat aus dem Gebüsch, und guckte ihn an mit großen strahlenden Augen, aus dem hellen Bach. Claras Bild war ganz aus seinem Innern gewichen, er dachte nichts, als Olimpia und klagte ganz laut und weinerlich: »Ach du mein hoher herrlicher Liebesstern, bist du mir denn nur aufgegangen, um gleich wieder zu verschwinden, und mich zu lassen in finstrer hoffnungsloser Nacht?«

Als er zurückkehren wollte in seine Wohnung, wurde er in Spalanzanis Hause ein geräuschvolles Treiben gewahr. Die Türen standen offen, man trug allerlei Geräte hinein, die Fenster des ersten Stocks waren ausgehoben, geschäftige Mägde kehrten und stäubten mit großen Haarbesen hin- und herfahrend, inwendig klopften und hämmerten Tischler und Tapezierer. Nathanael blieb in vollem Erstaunen auf der Straße stehen; da trat Siegmund lachend zu ihm und sprach: »Nun, was sagst du zu unserem alten Spalanzani?« Nathanael versicherte, daß er gar nichts sagen könne, da er durchaus nichts vom Professor wisse, vielmehr mit großer Verwunderung wahrnehme, wie in dem stillen düstern Hause ein tolles Treiben und Wirtschaften losgegangen; da erfuhr er denn von Siegmund, daß Spalanzani morgen ein großes Fest geben wolle, Konzert und Ball, und daß die halbe Universität eingeladen sei. Allgemein verbreite man, daß Spalanzani seine Tochter Olimpia, die er so lange jedem menschlichen Auge recht ängstlich entzogen, zum erstenmal erscheinen lassen werde.

Nathanael fand eine Einladungskarte und ging mit hochklopfendem Herzen zur bestimmten Stunde, als schon die Wagen rollten

glance through the window convinced him that Olimpia was still sitting there, and at that very moment, as if compelled by an irresistible force, he leaped up, seized Coppola's telescope and could not tear himself away from the seductive sight of Olimpia until his friend and fellow student Siegmund came to fetch him for a lecture at Professor Spalanzani's.

The curtain in front of the fateful room was closely drawn; he was unable to detect Olimpia here, any more than he could find her in her room throughout the next two days, even though he scarcely left his window and constantly gazed in that direction through Coppola's glass. On the third day, the windows were even covered. In total despair, goaded by longing and hot desire, he ran out past the town gate. Olimpia's figure hovered in the air in front of him, stepped out from the bushes and peered out at him from the clear brook with large, radiant eyes. Clara's image had completely departed from his mind; he thought of nothing but Olimpia, and lamented loud and tearfully: "Oh, my lofty, splendid star of love, have you then risen in my sky only to vanish again at once and to leave me in dark, hopeless night?"

When he was about to return to his room, he became aware of noisy activity in Spalanzani's house. The doors were open; equipment of all sorts was being carried in; the first-floor windows had been removed; busy maids were sweeping and dusting back and forth with large bristle brooms; inside, carpenters and decorators were pounding and hammering. Nathanael stopped short in the street, quite astonished; then Siegmund walked over to him with a smile, saying: "Now, what do you say about our old Spalanzani?" Nathanael assured him that he could not say a thing since he knew nothing at all about the professor, but on the contrary was greatly amazed to perceive the frantic activity and hubbub that had broken out in the quiet, gloomy house; then he heard from Siegmund that Spalanzani intended to give an elaborate party the next day, with a recital and a dance, and that half of the university was invited. The news being spread abroad was that Spalanzani would allow his daughter Olimpia, whom he had anxiously concealed from all human eyes for so long, to make her first appearance there.

Nathanael found an invitation awaiting him, and with a strongly beating heart arrived at the professor's place at the appointed time, when the carriages were rolling up

und die Lichter in den geschmückten Sälen schimmerten, zum Professor. Die Gesellschaft war zahlreich und glänzend. Olimpia erschien sehr reich und geschmackvoll gekleidet. Man mußte ihr schöngeformtes Gesicht, ihren Wuchs bewundern. Der etwas seltsam eingebogene Rücken, die wespenartige Dünne des Leibes schien von zu starkem Einschnüren bewirkt zu sein. In Schritt und Stellung hatte sie etwas Abgemessenes und Steifes, das manchem unangenehm auffiel; man schrieb es dem Zwange zu, den ihr die Gesellschaft auflegte.

Das Konzert begann. Olimpia spielte den Flügel mit großer Fertigkeit und trug ebenso eine Bravour-Arie mit heller, beinahe schneidender Glasglockenstimme vor. Nathanael war ganz entzückt; er stand in der hintersten Reihe und konnte im blendenden Kerzenlicht Olimpias Züge nicht ganz erkennen. Ganz unvermerkt nahm er deshalb Coppolas Glas hervor und schaute hin nach der schönen Olimpia. Ach!—da wurde er gewahr, wie sie voll Sehnsucht nach ihm herübersah, wie jeder Ton erst deutlich aufging in dem Liebesblick, der zündend sein Inneres durchdrang. Die künstlichen Rouladen schienen dem Nathanael das Himmelsjauchzen des in Liebe verklärten Gemüts, und als nun endlich nach der Kadenz der lange Trillo recht schmetternd durch den Saal gellte, konnte er wie von glühenden Ärmen plötzlich erfaßt sich nicht mehr halten, er mußte vor Schmerz und Entzücken laut aufschreien: »Olimpia!«—Alle sahen sich um nach ihm, manche lachten. Der Domorganist schnitt aber noch ein finstreres Gesicht, als vorher und sagte bloß: »Nun nun!«

Das Konzert war zu Ende, der Ball fing an. »Mit ihr zu tanzen!—mit ihr!« das war nun dem Nathanael das Ziel aller Wünsche, alles Strebens; aber wie sich erheben zu dem Mut, sie, die Königin des Festes, aufzufordern? Doch!—er selbst wußte nicht wie es geschah, daß er, als schon der Tanz angefangen, dicht neben Olimpia stand, die noch nicht aufgefordert worden, und daß er, kaum vermögend einige Worte zu stammeln, ihre Hand ergriff. Eiskalt war Olimpias Hand, er fühlte sich durchbebt von grausigem Todesfrost, er starrte Olimpia ins Auge, das strahlte ihm voll Liebe und Sehnsucht entgegen und in dem Augenblick war es auch, als fingen an in der kalten Hand Pulse zu schlagen und des Lebensblutes Ströme zu glühen. Und auch in Nathanaels Innerm glühte höher

and the lights were glittering in the decorated rooms. The assembly was numerous and brilliant. Olimpia appeared in very costly and tasteful attire. It was impossible not to admire her beautifully shaped face and her figure. The somewhat strange bend in her back and the wasplike narrowness of her waist were seemingly the effect of excessive corseting. In her gait and stance she had a somewhat precise and stiff quality that many people found unpleasant; they ascribed it to the constraints laid on her by the formal occasion.

The recital began. Olimpia played the piano with great dexterity and, with equal skill, performed a bravura aria in a bright, almost cutting voice resembling musical glasses. Nathanael was totally enraptured; he stood in the back row and could not recognize Olimpia's features perfectly in the dazzling candlelight. Therefore, completely unnoticed, he pulled out Coppola's glass and directed it at the beautiful Olimpia. Ah!—then he became aware that she was looking at him in deep longing, that each note of hers only attained fully clarity when combined with that loving look which pierced and inflamed his heart. Her artificial roulades seemed to Nathanael the divine exultation of a spirit transfigured by love, and when now, finally, after the cadenza her long trill shrilled through the room with tremendous force, he seemed to be suddenly seized by glowing arms; he could no longer contain himself, but had to cry out loudly in pain and rapture: "Olimpia!" Everyone turned around to look at him; some laughed. But the cathedral organist's face became even gloomier than before, and he merely said: "Well, well!"

The recital was over, the dance began. "To dance with her!—with her!" That was now the goal of all Nathanael's wishes and efforts; but how was he to work up the courage to ask *her*, the queen of the ball, to dance with him? And yet!—he himself did not know how it came to pass that, with the dance already begun, he was standing right by Olimpia, who had not yet been invited to dance, and, barely able to stammer a few words, took her by the hand. Olimpia's hand was ice cold; he felt himself shaken by a fearful, deathly frost; he stared into Olimpia's eyes, which beamed at him full of love and longing, and at that very moment it seemed as if a pulse began to beat in that cold hand and warm lifeblood began to circulate. In Nathanael's heart, too, passion blazed higher; he embraced

auf die Liebeslust, er umschlang die schöne Olimpia und durchflog mit ihr die Reihen.

Er glaubte sonst recht taktmäßig getanzt zu haben, aber an der ganz eignen rhythmischen Festigkeit, womit Olimpia tanzte und die ihn oft ordentlich aus der Haltung brachte, merkte er bald, wie sehr ihm der Takt gemangelt. Er wollte jedoch mit keinem andern Frauenzimmer mehr tanzen und hätte jeden, der sich Olimpia näherte, um sie aufzufordern, nur gleich ermorden mögen. Doch nur zweimal geschah dies, zu seinem Erstaunen blieb darauf Olimpia bei jedem Tanz sitzen und er ermangelte nicht, immer wieder sie aufzuziehen.

Hätte Nathanael außer der schönen Olimpia noch etwas andres zu sehen vermocht, so wäre allerlei fataler Zank und Streit unvermeidlich gewesen; denn offenbar ging das halbleise, mühsam unterdrückte Gelächter, was sich in diesem und jenem Winkel unter den jungen Leuten erhob, auf die schöne Olimpia, die sie mit ganz kuriosen Blicken verfolgten, man konnte gar nicht wissen, warum?

Durch den Tanz und durch den reichlich genossenen Wein erhitzt, hatte Nathanael alle ihm sonst eigne Scheu abgelegt. Er saß neben Olimpia, ihre Hand in der seinigen und sprach hochentflammt und begeistert von seiner Liebe in Worten, die keiner verstand, weder er, noch Olimpia. Doch diese vielleicht; denn sie sah ihm unverrückt ins Auge und seufzte einmal übers andere: »Ach—Ach—Ach!«—worauf denn Nathanael also sprach: »O du herrliche, himmlische Frau!—du Strahl aus dem verheißenen Jenseits der Liebe—du tiefes Gemüt, in dem sich mein ganzes Sein spiegelt« und noch mehr dergleichen, aber Olimpia seufzte bloß immer wieder: »Ach, Ach!«

Der Professor Spalanzani ging einigemal bei den Glücklichen vorüber und lächelte sie ganz seltsam zufrieden an. Dem Nathanael schien es, unerachtet er sich in einer ganz andern Welt befand, mit einemmal, als würd es hienieden beim Professor Spalanzani merklich finster; er schaute um sich und wurde zu seinem nicht geringen Schreck gewahr, daß eben die zwei letzten Lichter in dem leeren Saal herniederbrennen und ausgehen wollten. Längst hatten Musik und Tanz aufgehört. »Trennung, Trennung«, schrie er ganz wild und verzweifelt, er küßte Olimpias Hand, er neigte sich zu ihrem Munde, eiskalte Lippen begegneten seinen glühenden!—So wie, als er Olimpias kalte Hand berührte, fühlte er sich von innerem Grausen erfaßt, die Legende von der toten Braut ging ihm plötzlich

the beautiful Olimpia and flew off with her through the ranks of dancers.

He usually thought that he kept very good time when dancing, but the unique rhythmic regularity with which Olimpia danced, and which often actually made him unsure of himself, soon showed him that he was missing every beat. Nevertheless, he no longer wished to dance with any other woman, and felt like killing every man who approached Olimpia to ask her to dance. But that happened only twice; to his amazement, Olimpia sat out every dance afterward and he did not fail to lead her out again and again.

If Nathanael had had eyes for anything else but the beautiful Olimpia, all sorts of unpleasant wrangles and quarrels would have been unavoidable; for obviously the muffled, difficultly suppressed laughter that was to be heard in this and that corner among the young guests was directed at the beautiful Olimpia, whom they pursued with most curious glances—it was impossible to say why.

Flushed by the dancing and the substantial amount of wine he had drunk, Nathanael had cast aside all his usual bashfulness. He sat next to Olimpia with her hand in his and, highly aroused and enthused, he spoke of his love in words that neither one understood, neither he nor Olimpia. But perhaps *she* did; for she looked fixedly into his eyes and sighed many times in succession: "Ah—Ah!—Ah!" Whereupon Nathanael said: "Oh, you splendid, divine woman!—You ray of light from the unattainable promised land of love—you profound spirit in which my entire being is reflected," and more of similar purport. But Olimpia merely sighed again and again: "Ah, ah!"

Professor Spalanzani walked past the happy couple several times, smiling at them with a quite strange satisfaction. It seemed to Nathanael all at once—even though he was in a totally different world—that it was now noticeably dark in this earthly home of Professor Spalanzani; he looked around, and to his considerable dismay, observed that the very last pair of candles in the empty ballroom were about to burn down and go out. The music and dancing had long ceased. "Parting, parting!" he shouted in wild despair; he kissed Olimpia's hand and bent down to kiss her on the mouth. Ice-cold lips met his burning ones! Just as when he had touched Olimpia's cold hand, he felt himself seized by inward terror; the legend of the dead

durch den Sinn; aber fest hatte ihn Olimpia an sich gedrückt, und in dem Kuß schienen die Lippen zum Leben zu erwarmen.

Der Professor Spalanzani schritt langsam durch den leeren Saal, seine Schritte klangen hohl wieder und seine Figur, von flackernden Schlagschatten umspielt, hatte ein grauliches gespenstisches Ansehen. »Liebst du mich—liebst du mich Olimpia?—Nur dies Wort!—Liebst du mich?« So flüsterte Nathanael, aber Olimpia seufzte, indem sie aufstand, nur: »Ach—Ach!«—»Ja du mein holder, herrlicher Liebesstern«, sprach Nathanael, »bist mir aufgegangen und wirst leuchten, wirst verklären mein Inneres immerdar!«—»Ach, ach!« replizierte Olimpia fortschreitend. Nathanael folgte ihr, sie standen vor dem Professor. »Sie haben sich außerordentlich lebhaft mit meiner Tochter unterhalten«, sprach dieser lächelnd: »Nun, nun, lieber Herr Nathanael, finden Sie Geschmack daran, mit dem blöden Mädchen zu konversieren, so sollen mir Ihre Besuche willkommen sein.«—Einen ganzen hellen strahlenden Himmel in der Brust schied Nathanael von dannen.

Spalanzanis Fest war der Gegenstand des Gesprächs in den folgenden Tagen. Unerachtet der Professor alles getan hatte, recht splendid zu erscheinen, so wußten doch die lustigen Köpfe von allerlei Unschicklichem und Sonderbarem zu erzählen, das sich begeben, und vorzüglich fiel man über die todstarre, stumme Olimpia her, der man, ihres schönen Äußern unerachtet, totalen Stumpfsinn andichten und darin die Ursache finden wollte, warum Spalanzani sie so lange verborgen gehalten.

Nathanael vernahm das nicht ohne innern Grimm, indessen schwieg er; denn, dachte er, würde es wohl verlohnen, diesen Burschen zu beweisen, daß eben ihr eigner Stumpfsinn es ist, der sie Olimpias tiefes herrliches Gemüt zu erkennen hindert? »Tu mir den Gefallen, Bruder«, sprach eines Tages Siegmund, »tu mir den Gefallen und sage, wie es dir gescheuten Kerl möglich war, dich in das Wachsgesicht, in die Holzpuppe da drüben zu vergaffen?« Nathanael wollte zornig auffahren, doch schnell besann er sich und erwiderte: »Sage *du* mir Siegmund, wie deinem, sonst alles Schöne klar auffassenden Blick, deinem regen Sinn, Olimpias himmlischer Liebreiz entgehen konnte? Doch eben deshalb habe ich, Dank sei

bride[8] suddenly passed through his mind; but Olimpia had clutched him to herself tightly and while they kissed her lips seemed to grow warm and alive.

Professor Spalanzani was striding slowly through the empty ballroom; his steps produced a hollow echo and his figure, with the wavering shadows from the waning light playing about it, had a fearsome, spectral appearance. "Do you love me—do you love me, Olimpia?—Just tell me that!—Do you love me?" Nathanael whispered, but, standing up, Olimpia only sighed: "Ah—Ah!" "Yes," said Nathanael, "you, my lovely, splendid star of love, have risen in my sky and there you will shine, you shall transfigure my heart forever!" "Ah, ah!" Olimpia replied as she walked away. Nathanael followed her; they now stood in front of the professor. "You have had an extraordinarily animated discussion with my daughter," said the latter, smiling. "Well, well, my dear Nathanael, if it is to your taste to converse with this witless girl, your calls will be agreeable to me." With all of bright, radiant heaven in his heart, Nathanael departed.

Spalanzani's party was the subject of conversation on the following days. Even though the professor had done all he could to make a really magnificent showing, waggish tongues were able to point to all sorts of social solecisms and eccentricities that had taken place, and an especially severe attack was made on the deathly-rigid, mute Olimpia, who, despite her beautiful exterior, was taxed with total mindlessness—which was now looked on as the reason that Spalanzani had kept her shut away so long.

Nathanael, hearing this, harbored considerable anger in his mind but kept silent; for, he thought, would it pay to prove to these roughnecks that it was precisely their own mindlessness that kept them from recognizing Olimpia's profound, splendid sensibilities? "Do me a favor, my friend," said Siegmund one day, "do me a favor and tell me how you, an intelligent fellow, could be smitten with that wax face, with that wooden doll?" Nathanael was about to flare up in a rage, but he quickly thought better of it and replied: "*You* tell me, Siegmund, how your clear sight, which usually appreciates fully all that is beautiful, how your lively mind, could fail to recognize Olimpia's divine charms? But for that very reason, thanks to destiny,

---

[8] A reference to Goethe's ballad "Die Braut von Korinth" (The Bride of Corinth).

es dem Geschick, dich nicht zum Nebenbuhler; denn sonst müßte einer von uns blutend fallen.«

Siegmund merkte wohl, wie es mit dem Freunde stand, lenkte geschickt ein, und fügte, nachdem er geäußert, daß in der Liebe niemals über den Gegenstand zu richten sei, hinzu: »Wunderlich ist es doch, daß viele von uns über Olimpia ziemlich gleich urteilen. Sie ist uns—nimm es nicht übel, Bruder!—auf seltsame Weise starr und seelenlos erschienen. Ihr Wuchs ist regelmäßig, so wie ihr Gesicht, das ist wahr!—Sie könnte für schön gelten, wenn ihr Blick nicht so ganz ohne Lebensstrahl, ich möchte sagen, ohne Sehkraft wäre. Ihr Schritt ist sonderbar abgemessen, jede Bewegung scheint durch den Gang eines aufgezogenen Räderwerks bedingt. Ihr Spiel, ihr Singen hat den unangenehm richtigen geistlosen Takt der singenden Maschine und ebenso ist ihr Tanz. Uns ist diese Olimpia ganz unheimlich geworden, wir mochten nichts mit ihr zu schaffen haben, es war uns als tue sie nur so wie ein lebendiges Wesen und doch habe es mit ihr eine eigne Bewandtnis.«

Nathanael gab sich dem bittern Gefühl, das ihn bei diesen Worten Siegmunds ergreifen wollte, durchaus nicht hin, er wurde Herr seines Unmuts und sagte bloß sehr ernst: »Wohl mag euch, ihr kalten prosaischen Menschen, Olimpia unheimlich sein. Nur dem poetischen Gemüt entfaltet sich das gleich organisierte!—Nur *mir* ging ihr Liebesblick auf und durchstrahlte Sinn und Gedanken, nur in Olimpias Liebe finde ich mein Selbst wieder. Euch mag es nicht recht sein, daß sie nicht in platter Konversation faselt, wie die andern flachen Gemüter. Sie spricht wenig Worte, das ist wahr; aber diese wenigen Worte erscheinen als echte Hieroglyphe der innern Welt voll Liebe und hoher Erkenntnis des geistigen Lebens in der Anschauung des ewigen Jenseits. Doch für alles das habt ihr keinen Sinn und alles sind verlorne Worte.«—»Behüte dich Gott, Herr Bruder«, sagte Siegmund sehr sanft, beinahe wehmütig, »aber mir scheint es, du seist auf bösem Wege. Auf mich kannst du rechnen, wenn alles—Nein, ich mag nichts weiter sagen!—« Dem Nathanael war es plötzlich, als meine der kalte prosaische Siegmund es sehr treu mit ihm, er schüttelte daher die ihm dargebotene Hand recht herzlich.

Nathanael hatte rein vergessen, daß es eine Clara in der Welt gebe, die er sonst geliebt;—die Mutter—Lothar—alle waren aus seinem Gedächtnis entschwunden, er lebte nur für Olimpia, bei der er täglich stundenlang saß und von seiner Liebe, von zum Leben

you aren't a rival; for otherwise one of us would have to die a bloody death."

Siegmund saw clearly how things stood with his friend, cleverly changed his tone and, after airing his view that in love no judgment should ever be made about the loved one, he added: "It *is* odd, though, that so many of us have practically the same opinion about Olimpia. Don't take it badly, my friend, but she impressed us as being unusually stiff and lifeless. Her figure is well-proportioned, and her face too, that's true! She could be called beautiful if her eyes weren't so completely devoid of the radiance of life—I might say, devoid of the power to see. Her walk is strangely precise; each movement seems to be controlled by the operation of a wind-up mechanism. Her playing and her singing have the unpleasantly accurate, soulless beat of a singing machine, and the same holds for her dancing. We all became quite uneasy about this Olimpia, we wanted nothing to do with her, we felt as if she were only pretending to be a living being but was really some sort of oddity."

Nathanael did not succumb to the bitter feelings that nearly overcame him at these words of Siegmund's; he mastered his displeasure and merely said, very gravely: "Olimpia may very well make you cold, prosaic people uneasy. Only to a poetic spirit can a similarly formed spirit reveal itself! It was only for *me* that her loving looks grew bright, filling my mind and thoughts with radiance; only in Olimpia's love do I find my own self again. You may think it wrong that she doesn't babble platitudes like other, shallow natures. She doesn't say much, it's true; but the few words she does speak are like genuine hieroglyphs of the inner world, full of love, full of the lofty knowledge of intellectual life in the contemplation of the eternity beyond this existence. But you and the others have no head for that and all I say is lost on you." "God protect you, friend," said Siegmund very softly, almost sadly, "but it seems to me you are on a fatal path. You can count on me if anything—No, I won't say any more!—" Nathanael suddenly felt that the cold, prosaic Siegmund was sincerely devoted to him, and he therefore shook the hand that Siegmund held out to him with real warmth.

Nathanael had completely forgotten the very existence of a Clara whom he once loved; his mother, Lothar, they were all gone from his memory. He lived only for Olimpia, with whom he sat for hours on end every day, spinning

erglühter Sympathie, von psychischer Wahlverwandtschaft fanta-
sierte, welches alles Olimpia mit großer Andacht anhörte. Aus dem
tiefsten Grunde des Schreibpults holte Nathanael alles hervor, was
er jemals geschrieben. Gedichte, Fantasien, Visionen, Romane, Erzählungen, das wurde täglich vermehrt mit allerlei ins Blaue flie-
genden Sonetten, Stanzen, Kanzonen, und das alles las er der Olimpia stundenlang hintereinander vor, ohne zu ermüden.
Aber auch noch nie hatte er eine solche herrliche Zuhörerin gehabt. Sie stickte und strickte nicht, sie sah nicht durchs Fenster, sie
fütterte keinen Vogel, sie spielte mit keinem Schoßhündchen, mit
keiner Lieblingskatze, sie drehte keine Papierschnitzchen, oder
sonst etwas in der Hand, sie durfte kein Gähnen durch einen leisen
erzwungenen Husten bezwingen—kurz!—stundenlang sah sie mit
starrem Blick unverwandt dem Geliebten ins Auge, ohne sich zu
rücken und zu bewegen und immer glühender, immer lebendiger
wurde dieser Blick. Nur wenn Nathanael endlich aufstand und
ihr die Hand, auch wohl den Mund küßte, sagte sie:»Ach,
Ach!«—dann aber:»Gute Nacht, mein Lieber!«
»O du herrliches, du tiefes Gemüt«, rief Nathanael auf seiner
Stube:»nur von dir, von dir allein werd ich ganz verstanden.« Er
erbebte vor innerm Entzücken, wenn er bedachte, welch wunderba-
rer Zusammenklang sich in seinem und Olimpias Gemüt täglich
mehr offenbare; denn es schien ihm, als habe Olimpia über seine
Werke, über seine Dichtergabe überhaupt recht tief aus seinem
Innern gesprochen, ja als habe die Stimme aus seinem Innern selbst
herausgetönt. Das mußte denn wohl auch sein; denn mehr Worte
als vorhin erwähnt, sprach Olimpia niemals.
Erinnerte sich aber auch Nathanael in hellen nüchternen Augenblicken, z. B. morgens gleich nach dem Erwachen, wirklich an Olimpias gänzliche Passivität und Wortkargheit, so sprach er doch:»Was
sind Worte—Worte!—Der Blick ihres himmlischen Auges sagt
mehr als jede Sprache hienieden. Vermag denn überhaupt ein
Kind des Himmels sich einzuschichten in den engen Kreis, den ein
klägliches irdisches Bedürfnis gezogen?«
Professor Spalanzani schien hocherfreut über das Verhältnis seiner Tochter mit Nathanael; er gab diesem allerlei unzweideutige
Zeichen seines Wohlwollens und als es Nathanael endlich wagte von
ferne auf eine Verbindung mit Olimpia anzuspielen, lächelte dieser

fantasies about his love, about the fondness that had been ignited into vibrant life, about the elective affinity of their minds—Olimpia listening to all this most attentively. From the very bottom of his desk Nathanael unearthed all that he had ever written. To his store of poems, fantasies, visions, novels and stories he added daily all sorts of chimerical sonnets, poems in regular stanzas and canzoni, all of which he read aloud to Olimpia for hours, one after another, without growing weary.

But, you see, he had never had such a marvelous listener. She neither embroidered nor knitted, she didn't look out the window, she didn't feed a bird, she didn't play with a lapdog or a favorite cat, she didn't twist shreds of paper or hold anything else in her hands, she didn't have to stifle a yawn by pretending to give a little cough—in short, for hours at a time she looked unblinkingly into her lover's eyes with a steady gaze, without fidgeting or moving, and her gaze grew more and more warm and animated. Only when Nathanael finally stood up and kissed her hand—and surely her lips too—did she say "Ah, ah!"—but then: "Good night, dear."

"Oh, you splendid, profound soul," cried Nathanael, back in his room: "only you, you alone, understand me completely." He trembled with inner rapture when he reflected on that wonderful harmony between his spirit and Olimpia's which was becoming more manifest with each passing day; for it seemed to him that everything Olimpia had said about his writings, about his poetic talent, was just what he himself would have said—in fact, it seemed as if the very voice had been his own. And that must really have been the case; for Olimpia never said a thing except the above-mentioned phrases.

But if Nathanael, in clear-sighted, sober moments—for instance, right after awakening in the morning—did actually recollect Olimpia's total passivity and parsimony of speech, he would nevertheless say: "What are words —words? The gaze of her divine eyes says more than any earthly language. Anyway, can a child of heaven find a place in that narrow circle in which our pitiful earthly necessities have confined us?"

Professor Spalanzani seemed overjoyed at his daughter's relationship with Nathanael; he gave him many unambiguous tokens of his approval, and when Nathanael finally dared to hint remotely at marriage with Olimpia,

mit dem ganzen Gesicht und meinte: er werde seiner Tochter völlig
freie Wahl lassen.

Ermutigt durch diese Worte, brennendes Verlangen im Herzen,
beschloß Nathanael, gleich am folgenden Tage Olimpia anzuflehen, daß sie das unumwunden in deutlichen Worten ausspreche,
was längst ihr holder Liebesblick ihm gesagt, daß sie sein eigen
immerdar sein wolle. Er suchte nach dem Ringe, den ihm beim
Abschiede die Mutter geschenkt, um ihn Olimpia als Symbol seiner
Hingebung, seines mit ihr aufkeimenden, blühenden Lebens dar-
zureichen. Claras, Lothars Briefe fielen ihm dabei in die Hände;
gleichgültig warf er sie beiseite, fand den Ring, steckte ihn ein und
rannte herüber zu Olimpia. Schon auf der Treppe, auf dem Flur,
vernahm er ein wunderliches Getöse; es schien aus Spalanzanis Stu-
dierzimmer herauszuschallen. —Ein Stampfen—ein Klirren—ein
Stoßen—Schlagen gegen die Tür, dazwischen Flüche und Verwünschungen.

Laß los—laß los—Infamer—Verruchter!—Darum Leib und
Leben daran gesetzt?—ha ha ha ha!—so haben wir nicht gewet-
tet—ich, ich hab die Augen gemacht—ich das Räderwerk—
dummer Teufel mit deinem Räderwerk—verfluchter Hund von
einfältigem Uhrmacher—fort mit dir—Satan—halt—Peipendre-
her—teuflische Bestie!—halt—fort—laß los!— Es waren Spalanzanis und des gräßlichen Coppelius Stimmen, die so durcheinander
schwirrten und tobten.

Hinein stürzte Nathanael von namenloser Angst ergriffen. Der
Professor hatte eine weibliche Figur bei den Schultern gepackt, der
Italiener Coppola bei den Füßen, die zerrten und zogen sie hin und
her, streitend in voller Wut um den Besitz. Voll tiefen Entsetzens
prallte Nathanael zurück, als er die Figur für Olimpia erkannte;
aufflammend in wildem Zorn wollte er den Wütenden die Geliebte
entreißen, aber in dem Augenblick wand Coppola sich mit Riesenkraft drehend die Figur dem Professor aus den Händen und versetzte ihm mit der Figur selbst einen fürchterlichen Schlag, daß er
rücklings über den Tisch, auf dem Phiolen, Retorten, Flaschen,
gläserne Zylinder standen, taumelte und hinstürzte; alles Gerät
klirrte in tausende Scherben zusammen. Nun warf Coppola die
Figur über die Schulter und rannte mit fürchterlich gellendem Gelächter rasch fort die Treppe herab, so daß die häßlich herunterhän-
genden Füße der Figur auf den Stufen hölzern klapperten und
dröhnten.

Spalanzani smiled all over his face and said that he would leave the choice completely to his daughter.

Encouraged by these words and with burning desire in his heart, Nathanael decided to beseech Olimpia on the very next day to say to him forthrightly in clear words what her beautiful, loving eyes had long told him: that she wished to be his forever. He looked for the ring that his mother had given him when he left home, so he could present it to Olimpia as a symbol of his devotion, of the new life that was budding and blossoming for him thanks to her. As he searched, he came across the letters from Clara and Lothar; he threw them aside with indifference, found the ring, put it in his pocket and hastened over to Olimpia. While still on the stairs, on the landing, he heard a peculiar noise, which seemed to come from Spalanzani's study: stamping, whirring, pushing, beating against the door—all mingled with curses and oaths.

"Let go—let go—rogue—villain!—Is it for this I spent my life and energy?—ha ha ha ha!—that wasn't our wager—I, I made the eyes—I, the mechanism—stupid fool, you and your mechanism—accursed dog, simple-minded clock maker—away with you—Satan—stop—swindler—devilish animal!—stop—away—let go!" The voices that were thus buzzing and raging confusedly were those of Spalanzani and the hideous Coppelius.

Nathanael burst in, gripped by inexpressible anguish. The professor had seized a feminine figure by the shoulders, while the Italian Coppola held it by the feet, as they tugged and pulled it back and forth, fighting rabidly over the possession of it. Full of profound terror, Nathanael lurched backward when he recognized the figure as Olimpia; flaring into wild anger, he was about to tear his beloved from the grip of the enraged pair, but at that very moment Coppola, writhing with the strength of a giant, twisted the figure out of the professor's hands and dealt him such a terrible blow with the figure itself that he staggered and fell backward onto the table, on which stood vials, retorts, bottles and glass cylinders; all this equipment shattered into a thousand tinkling pieces. Now Coppola threw the figure over his shoulder and, with a ghastly, shrill laugh, ran downstairs quickly, while the feet of the figure, hanging down in a most unsightly fashion, banged against the steps with a wooden sound.

Erstarrt stand Nathanael—nur zu deutlich hatte er gesehen, Olimpias toderbleichtes Wachsgesicht hatte keine Augen, statt ihrer schwarze Höhlen; sie war eine leblose Puppe. Spalanzani wälzte sich auf der Erde, Glasscherben hatten ihm Kopf, Brust und Arm zerschnitten, wie aus Springquellen strömte das Blut empor. Aber er raffte seine Kräfte zusammen. —»Ihm nach—ihm nach, was zauderst du?—Coppelius—Coppelius, mein bestes Automat hat er mir geraubt—Zwanzig Jahre daran gearbeitet—Leib und Leben daran gesetzt—das Räderwerk—Sprache—Gang—mein—die Augen—die Augen dir gestohlen. —Verdammter—Verfluchter—ihm nach—hol mir Olimpia—da hast du die Augen!—«

Nun sah Nathanael, wie ein Paar blutige Augen auf dem Boden liegend ihn anstarrten, die ergriff Spalanzani mit der unverletzten Hand und warf sie nach ihm, daß sie seine Brust trafen. —Da packte ihn der Wahnsinn mit glühenden Krallen und fuhr in sein Inneres hinein Sinn und Gedanken zerreißend. »Hui—hui—hui!—*Feuerkreis—Feuerkreis!* dreh dich *Feuerkreis*—lustig—lustig!—Holzpüppchen hui schön Holzpüppchen dreh dich—«

Damit warf er sich auf den Professor und drückte ihm die Kehle zu. Er hätte ihn erwürgt, aber das Getöse hatte viele Menschen herbeigelockt, die drangen ein, rissen den wütenden Nathanael auf und retteten so den Professor, der gleich verbunden wurde. Siegmund, so stark er war, vermochte nicht den Rasenden zu bändigen; der schrie mit fürchterlicher Stimme immerfort:»Holzpüppchen, dreh dich« und schlug um sich mit geballten Fäusten. Endlich gelang es der vereinten Kraft mehrerer, ihn zu überwältigen, indem sie ihn zu Boden warfen und banden. Seine Worte gingen unter in entsetzlichem tierischen Gebrüll. So in gräßlicher Raserei tobend wurde er nach dem Tollhause gebracht.

Ehe ich, günstiger Leser! dir zu erzählen fortfahre, was sich weiter mit dem unglücklichen Nathanael zugetragen, kann ich dir, solltest du einigen Anteil an dem geschickten Mechanikus und Automat-Fabrikanten Spalanzani nehmen, versichern, daß er von seinen Wunden völlig geheilt wurde. Er mußte indes die Universität verlassen, weil Nathanaels Geschichte Aufsehen erregt hatte und es allgemein für gänzlich unerlaubten Betrug gehalten wurde, vernünftigen Teezirkeln (Olimpia hatte sie mit Glück besucht) statt der lebendigen Person eine Holzpuppe einzuschwärzen.

Nathanael stood motionless—he had seen all too clearly that Olimpia's wax face, pale as death, had no eyes but black cavities in their place; she was a lifeless doll. Spalanzani was rolling on the ground; splinters of glass had cut his head, chest and one arm, and blood was gushing out as if from fountains. But he pulled himself together. "After him—after him, what are you waiting for?—Coppelius—Coppelius, he has stolen my best automaton—worked on it for twenty years—spent my life and energy on it—the mechanism—it talked—it walked—mine —the eyes—the eyes stolen from you.—Damn him —curse him—after him—get Olimpia back for me —here you have the eyes!—"

Now Nathanael saw a pair of bloody eyes lying on the floor and staring up at him; Spalanzani picked them up with his uninjured hand and threw them at him, hitting him on the chest with them. Then madness seized Nathanael with red-hot claws and penetrated him, lacerating his mind and thoughts. "Hey—hey—hey!—*Circle of fire—Circle of fire!* Turn, *circle of fire*—briskly— briskly!—Wooden doll, hey, pretty wooden doll— turn—"

Saying this, he threw himself upon the professor and squeezed his throat. He would have strangled him, but the racket had attracted many people; they forced their way in and pulled the furious Nathanael to his feet, thus saving the professor, who was immediately bandaged. Siegmund, strong as he was, could not control the madman, who continued to shout in frightening tones: "Wooden doll, turn," while he hit out all around him with clenched fists. Finally the combined strength of several men succeeded in subduing him; they threw him to the floor and tied him up. His words degenerated into a horrible, bestial roar. Thus, raging in hideous madness, he was brought to the insane asylum.

Gentle reader, before I go on to tell you what further befell the unfortunate Nathanael, I can assure you—should you feel some sympathy with the clever mechanician and constructor of automata Spalanzani—that he recovered completely from his injuries. He did have to leave the university because Nathanael's story had attracted attention, and it was generally held to be a totally inadmissible deception to smuggle a wooden doll instead of a living person into sensible tea parties (Olimpia had been a popular guest).

Juristen nannten es sogar einen feinen und um so härter zu be-
strafenden Betrug, als er gegen das Publikum gerichtet und so
schlau angelegt worden, daß kein Mensch (ganz kluge Studenten
ausgenommen) es gemerkt habe, unerachtet jetzt alle weise tun und
sich auf allerlei Tatsachen berufen wollten, die ihnen verdächtig
vorgekommen. Diese letzteren brachten aber eigentlich nichts Gescheutes zutage. Denn konnte z. B. wohl irgend jemanden verdächtig vorgekommen sein, daß nach der Aussage eines eleganten
Teeisten Olimpia gegen alle Sitte öfter genieset, als gegähnt
hatte? Ersteres, meinte der Elegant, sei das Selbstaufziehen des
verborgenen Triebwerks gewesen, merklich habe es dabei ge-
knarrt usw.

Der Professor der Poesie und Beredsamkeit nahm eine Prise,
klappte die Dose zu, räusperte sich und sprach feierlich:»Hochzuverehrende Herren und Damen! merken Sie denn nicht, wo der
Hase im Pfeffer liegt? Das Ganze ist eine Allegorie—eine fortge-
führte Metapher!—Sie verstehen mich!—Sapienti sat!«

Aber viele hochzuverehrende Herren beruhigten sich nicht
dabei; die Geschichte mit dem Automat hatte tief in ihrer Seele
Wurzel gefaßt und es schlich sich in der Tat abscheuliches Miß-
trauen gegen menschliche Figuren ein. Um nun ganz überzeugt
zu werden, daß man keine Holzpuppe liebe, wurde von mehrern
Liebhabern verlangt, daß die Geliebte etwas taktlos singe und tanze,
daß sie beim Vorlesen sticke, stricke, mit dem Möpschen spiele usw.
vor allen Dingen aber, daß sie nicht bloß höre, sondern auch
manchmal in *der* Art spreche, daß dies Sprechen wirklich ein Denken und Empfinden voraussetze. Das Liebesbündnis vieler wurde
fester und dabei anmutiger, andere dagegen gingen leise auseinander.»Man kann wahrhaftig nicht dafür stehen«, sagte dieser und
jener. In den Tees wurde unglaublich gegähnt und niemals genieset, um jedem Verdacht zu begegnen.

Spalanzani mußte, wie gesagt, fort, um der Kriminaluntersu-
chung wegen des der menschlichen Gesellschaft betrüglicherweise
eingeschobenen Automats zu entgehen. Coppola war auch verschwunden.

Nathanael erwachte wie aus schwerem, fürchterlichem Traum,
er schlug die Augen auf und fühlte wie ein unbeschreibliches Won-

Jurists even declared it to be a shrewd deception and one that was to be punished all the more severely because it was directed against the public, and so artfully planned that no one (except some very intelligent students) had been aware of it, even though everyone was now wise after the fact and spoke of all sorts of clues that had aroused their suspicions. But this latter group produced no evidence that would hold up. For—to take an example—could it have aroused anyone's suspicions if, according to the statement of an elegant habitué of tea parties, Olimpia, contrary to established custom, had sneezed more often than she had yawned? This dandy insisted that the sneezing was the automatic rewinding of the concealed mechanism; there was a noticeable whirring at the time, etc.

The professor of poetry and eloquence took a pinch of snuff, shut the snuffbox, cleared his throat and said solemnly: "Highly honored ladies and gentlemen, do you really fail to see where the difficulty lies? The whole thing is an allegory—an extended metaphor!—you understand me!—*Sapienti sat!*"[9]

But many highly honored gentlemen did not let things rest there; the story of the automaton had made a deep impression on them, and indeed terrible suspicions of humanoid figures gained currency. In order to be fully convinced he was not in love with some wooden doll, many a fiancé now insisted that his sweetheart should sing and dance somewhat off the beat; that, when being read to, she should embroider, knit, play with the little pug, etc.—but especially that she should not merely listen but also speak from time to time in a way that indicated she really possessed the capability to think and feel. The union between many couples became more solid and thus more enjoyable, but on the other hand others quietly broke up. "Really, one can't be sure about it," said this person and that. At tea parties there was an incredible amount of yawning but never any sneezing, to allay any suspicion.

Spalanzani, as mentioned above, had to leave town to avoid a police investigation concerning the automaton he had deceptively intruded upon human society. Coppola had vanished as well.

Nathanael awoke as from an oppressive, frightful dream; he opened his eyes and felt an indescribably raptu-

---

[9] Latin for "[A word] to the wise [is] sufficient."

negefühl mit sanfter himmlischer Wärme ihn durchströmte. Er lag in seinem Zimmer in des Vaters Hause auf dem Bette, Clara hatte sich über ihn hingebeugt und unfern standen die Mutter und Lothar. »Endlich, endlich, o mein herzlieber Nathanael—nun bist du genesen von schwerer Krankheit—nun bist du wieder mein!«—So sprach Clara recht aus tiefer Seele und faßte den Nathanael in ihre Arme. Aber dem quollen vor lauter Wehmut und Entzücken die hellen glühenden Tränen aus den Augen und er stöhnte tief auf: »Meine—meine Clara!«—Siegmund, der getreulich ausgeharrt bei dem Freunde in großer Not, trat herein. Nathanael reichte ihm die Hand: »Du treuer Bruder hast mich doch nicht verlassen.«

Jede Spur des Wahnsinns war verschwunden, bald erkräftigte sich Nathanael in der sorglichen Pflege der Mutter, der Geliebten, der Freunde. Das Glück war unterdessen in das Haus eingekehrt; denn ein alter karger Oheim, von dem niemand etwas gehofft, war gestorben und hatte der Mutter nebst einem nicht unbedeutenden Vermögen ein Gütchen in einer angenehmen Gegend unfern der Stadt hinterlassen. Dort wollten sie hinziehen, die Mutter, Nathanael mit seiner Clara, die er nun zu heiraten gedachte, und Lothar.

Nathanael war milder, kindlicher geworden, als er je gewesen und erkannte nun erst recht Claras himmlisch reines, herrliches Gemüt. Niemand erinnerte ihn auch nur durch den leisesten Anklang an die Vergangenheit. Nur, als Siegmund von ihm schied, sprach Nathanael: »Bei Gott Bruder! ich war auf schlimmem Wege, aber zu rechter Zeit leitete mich ein Engel auf den lichten Pfad!—Ach es war ja Clara!—« Siegmund ließ ihn nicht weiter reden, aus Besorgnis, tief verletzende Erinnerungen möchten ihm zu hell und flammend aufgehen.

Es war an der Zeit, daß die vier glücklichen Menschen nach dem Gütchen ziehen wollten. Zur Mittagsstunde gingen sie durch die Straßen der Stadt. Sie hatten manches eingekauft, der hohe Ratsturm warf seinen Riesenschatten über den Markt. »Ei!« sagte Clara: »steigen wir doch noch einmal herauf und schauen in das ferne Gebirge hinein!« Gesagt, getan! Beide, Nathanael und Clara, stiegen herauf, die Mutter ging mit der Dienstmagd nach Hause, und Lothar, nicht geneigt, die vielen Stufen zu erklettern, wollte unten warten. Da standen die beiden Liebenden Arm in Arm auf

rous sensation flow through him with gentle, divine
warmth. He was lying in bed in his room in his father's
house; Clara was bending over him, and his mother and
Lothar stood nearby. "Finally, finally, my beloved Nathanael—now you have recovered from a serious illness—now you are mine again!" said Clara from the bottom of her heart, taking Nathanael in her arms. But
bright, hot tears streamed from his eyes, purely from sadness and rapture; with a deep moan, he said: "My—my
Clara!" Siegmund, who had loyally remained with his
friend in his great distress, walked in. Nathanael gave him
his hand: "So you haven't abandoned me, my faithful
friend."

Every trace of madness had vanished, and Nathanael
soon regained his strength thanks to the loving care of
his mother, sweetheart and friends. Meanwhile happiness
had entered their home; for a stingy old uncle, from
whom no one had ever expected anything, had died, leaving Nathanael's mother a substantial fortune and a small
property in a pleasant area not far from town. To that
estate they now intended to move—Nathanael's mother;
he and his Clara, whom he now intended to marry; and
Lothar.

Nathanael had become more gentle and childlike than
he had ever been, and for the first time properly appreciated Clara's divinely pure and wonderful spirit. No one
made even the slightest reference that could remind him
of the past. But, when Siegmund was taking leave of him,
Nathanael said: "By God, friend! I was on the road to ruin,
but an angel led me onto the bright path in time!—Ah, it
was Clara, of course!—" Siegmund did not allow him to
continue, for fear that deeply wounding reminiscences
might come back to him with all too painful clarity.

It was about the time when the four happy people were
about to move to their small property. At midday they
were walking through the streets of the town. They had
made various purchases; the tall tower of the town hall
cast its gigantic shadow over the marketplace. "Ah!" said
Clara, "why don't we go up once more and enjoy the view
of the distant mountains?" The suggestion was acted upon
at once. The two, Nathanael and Clara, walked up; Nathanael's mother went home with the maid, and Lothar,
unwilling to climb all those steps, decided to wait below.
There stood the loving couple arm in arm on the highest

der höchsten Galerie des Turmes und schauten hinein in die dufti-
gen Waldungen, hinter denen das blaue Gebirge, wie eine Riesen-
stadt, sich erhob.

»Sieh doch den sonderbaren kleinen grauen Busch, der ordentlich auf uns los zu schreiten scheint«, frug Clara. —Nathanael faßte
mechanisch nach der Seitentasche; er fand Coppolas Perspektiv,
er schaute seitwärts—Clara stand vor dem Glase!—Da zuckte es
krampfhaft in seinen Pulsen und Adern—totenbleich starrte er
Clara an, aber bald glühten und sprühten Feuerströme durch die
rollenden Augen, gräßlich brüllte er auf, wie ein gehetztes Tier;
dann sprang er hoch in die Lüfte und grausig dazwischen lachend
schrie er in schneidendem Ton:»Holzpüppchen dreh dich—Holzpüppchen dreh dich«—und mit gewaltiger Kraft faßte er Clara
und wollte sie herabschleudern, aber Clara krallte sich in verzwei-
felnder Todesangst fest an das Geländer.

Lothar hörte den Rasenden toben, er hörte Claras Angstgeschrei,
gräßliche Ahnung durchflog ihn, er rannte herauf, die Tür der
zweiten Treppe war verschlossen—stärker hallte Claras Jammer-
geschrei. Unsinnig vor Wut und Angst stieß er gegen die Tür, die
endlich aufsprang—Matter und matter wurden nun Claras Laute:
»Hülfe—rettet—rettet—« so erstarb die Stimme in den Lüften.
»Sie ist hin—ermordet von dem Rasenden«, so schrie Lothar.

Auch die Tür zur Galerie war zugeschlagen. —Die Verzweiflung
gab ihm Riesenkraft, er sprengte die Tür aus den Angeln. Gott im
Himmel—Clara schwebte von dem rasenden Nathanael erfaßt
über der Galerie in den Lüften—nur mit einer Hand hatte sie noch
die Eisenstäbe umklammert. Rasch wie der Blitz erfaßte Lothar die
Schwester, zog sie hinein, und schlug im demselben Augenblick mit
geballter Faust dem Wütenden ins Gesicht, daß er zurückprallte
und die Todesbeute fallen ließ.

Lothar rannte herab, die ohnmächtige Schwester in den Armen.
—Sie war gerettet. —Nun raste Nathanael herum auf der Galerie
und sprang hoch in die Lüfte und schrie »*Feuerkreis* dreh
dich—*Feuerkreis* dreh dich«—Die Menschen liefen auf das wilde
Geschrei zusammen; unter ihnen ragte riesengroß der Advokat
Coppelius hervor, der eben in die Stadt gekommen und gerades
Weges nach dem Markt geschritten war. Man wollte herauf, um
sich des Rasenden zu bemächtigen, da lachte Coppelius sprechend:
»Ha ha—wartet nur, der kommt schon herunter von selbst«, und
schaute wie die übrigen hinauf. Nathanael blieb plötzlich wie erstarrt stehen, er bückte sich herab, wurde den Coppelius gewahr

gallery of the tower, gazing at the fragrant woodlands behind which the blue mountains rose like a city of giants.

"Just look at that strange little gray bush that actually seems to be walking toward us," said Clara. Nathanael reached automatically into his side pocket; he found Coppola's telescope, pointed it to one side—Clara was in front of the lens! There was a convulsive jerking in his pulse and veins—pale as death, he stared at Clara, but soon streams of fire glowed and sparkled in his rolling eyes, he roared hideously like a hunted beast; then he jumped high into the air and, punctuating his speech with gruesome laughter, he shouted in piercing tones: "Wooden doll, turn—wooden doll, turn"—and with tremendous force he seized Clara and tried to fling her down, but in desperate, mortal fear Clara tightly clutched the railing.

Lothar heard the madman raging, he heard Clara's scream of fright. A horrible foreboding came upon him; he dashed up. The door to the second flight was locked—Clara's sorrowful cry grew louder. Mindless with anger and fear, he hurled himself against the door, which finally flew open—Clara's voice was now growing weaker and weaker: "Help—save me—save me—" and her words died away in the air. "She's gone—murdered by that madman," Lothar screamed.

The door to the gallery was also tightly shut. His desperation lent him a giant's strength; he burst the door from its hinges. God in heaven—in the grasp of the mad Nathanael, Clara was suspended in the air above the gallery, still clinging to the iron bars with a single hand. Swift as lightning, Lothar seized his sister and drew her to safety; at the same moment he struck the madman in the face with his clenched fist, making him totter backward and release his hold on his prey.

Lothar ran downstairs, holding in his arms his sister, who had fainted. She was saved. Now Nathanael was running around the gallery in his madness, jumping high in the air and shouting: "*Circle of fire*, turn—*circle of fire*, turn!" Hearing the wild shouts, people assembled; towering like a giant among them was lawyer Coppelius, who had just come to town and had walked directly to the marketplace. There was talk of going up and subduing the madman, when Coppelius laughed and said: "Ha, ha—just wait and he'll soon come down on his own," and looked upward like the others. Nathanael suddenly stopped in his tracks as if frozen; he looked down, caught

und mit dem gellenden Schrei: »Ha! Sköne Oke—Sköne Oke«, sprang er über das Geländer.

Als Nathanael mit zerschmettertem Kopf auf dem Steinpflaster lag, war Coppelius im Gewühl verschwunden.

Nach mehreren Jahren will man in einer entfernten Gegend Clara gesehen haben, wie sie mit einem freundlichen Mann, Hand in Hand vor der Türe eines schönen Landhauses saß und vor ihr zwei muntre Knaben spielten. Es wäre daraus zu schließen, daß Clara das ruhige häusliche Glück noch fand, das ihrem heitern lebenslustigen Sinn zusagte und das ihr der im Innern zerrissene Nathanael niemals hätte gewähren können.

sight of Coppelius and, with the shrill cry: "Ha! Beau'ful eye—beau'ful eye," he jumped over the railing.

By the time Nathanael lay on the pavement with his head shattered, Coppelius had vanished into the crowd.

People say that they saw Clara several years later, in a distant region, sitting hand in hand with an amiable man in front of the door of a pretty country house, with two lively little boys playing near her. This would lead one to conclude that Clara was still able to find that peaceful domestic happiness which suited her cheerful, pleasure-loving temperament and which Nathanael, with the fundamental conflicts in his nature, would never have been able to offer her.

SCHNITZLER
AND
"LIEUTENANT GUSTL"

ARTHUR SCHNITZLER, possibly Austria's finest twentieth-century playwright, novelist and story writer, was born in Vienna in 1862, and rarely left that city except for vacations. The son of a Jewish doctor, he followed in the same profession, assisting his father in a clinic from 1888 to 1893, then, upon his father's death, setting up in private practice. He was especially interested in psychology and the new field of psychiatry, and corresponded with Freud, who admired his writing. Schnitzler, attracted to literature from childhood, started publishing in magazines in 1880. By the early 1890s he was an established, if controversial, playwright, and his first book appeared in 1895. His writing gradually became more important to him than his medical practice. Throughout his career he had trouble with anti-Semitism and with censorship, his social views being distressingly liberal and his recognition of sexuality too outspokenly realistic. (He certainly had himself in mind when portraying the doctor, the liberals and the Jews who irritate Lieutenant Gustl so badly in the story.) Schnitzler died in Vienna in 1931. Among his best-known plays are *Anatol, Reigen* (Hands Around; La Ronde; Merry-Go-Round), *Liebelei* (Flirtation; Light o' Love) and *Professor Bernhardi*. *Der Weg ins Freie* (The Road to the Open) is a particularly strong novel.

"Lieutenant Gustl" was first published in the Viennese *Neue freie Presse* on Christmas Day, 1900. It was published in book form in 1901 by S. Fischer in Berlin. Its unflattering depiction of the military (one of the sacrosanct branches of the establishment) created a public furore, and a court of honor (like the one in the story!) stripped Schnitzler of his reserve-officer status, depriving him of income from army medical attendance.

Aside from its intrinsic interest as an overview of an Austrian officer's existence, its masterful psychology, its refreshingly colloquial language and its evocation of Viennese life in the Belle Époque, "Lieutenant Gustl" is outstanding as perhaps the first important interior-monologue, or stream-of-consciousness, story in European literature, preceding *Ulysses* by some two decades. In this story, free association of ideas replaces chronological narration as the structuring factor, but by the end we know everything about Gustl's past and present, his satisfactions and his discontents. At the

beginning of the story he appears almost totally in a negative light (ignorant, prejudiced, cocky . . .), but the development reveals him as an unhappy victim of a crushingly authoritarian and regimented social order. (Schnitzler was to revert to the interior monologue in his famous story "Fräulein Else" in 1924. "Gustl" and "Else," in which the title characters do the "writing," are thus untypical of Schnitzler's German style, which is generally admired for its smoothness, lucidity and harmoniousness.)

It might be said that the second main character in the story after Gustl (which is a nickname for August, not for Gustav) is Vienna itself. Gustl's nocturnal peregrination through the Austrian capital has elements in common with Leopold Bloom's through Dublin; it would be possible to trace Gustl's exact path on a city plan—an old one, for many of the landmarks are gone. The Green Gate that he mentions was a famous old inn; Ronacher's was an important coffeehouse. There *was* a Horticultural Society actually concerned with gardening, which occasionally let rooms for balls, but the one in the story (quotation marks are intentionally used with the name to make the distinction) was a popular beer hall. The cosmopolitan nature of the Austro-Hungarian Empire is evident from the great variety of German, Magyar and Balkan proper names that occur in the story.

Finally, it should be noted that "Lieutenant Gustl" is a very difficult story linguistically; to present an English version alongside the German original is little short of foolhardy. It contains many Austrian forms and specifically Austrian words, including colloquialisms not found in dictionaries. Furthermore, to do full justice to its technical military and legal terms, and its varied allusions to the contemporary Viennese milieu, really calls for a lifetime's familiarity with the subject. The only previous English translation accessible for reference to the present translator was Richard L. Simon's, first published in 1926 as "None but the Brave." That version, besides containing a handful of outright mistakes and misapprehensions, simply omits many of the most troublesome passages. Nevertheless, it is a sturdy piece of work, and the present translator is grateful to it for a number of helpful hints. The translation in this volume, absolutely complete and as literal as possible, is offered as a tentative act of homage to this important literary work, which deserves to be more widely known. (Additional paragraphing has been introduced.)

LEUTNANT GUSTL

Wie lang' wird denn das noch dauern? Ich muß auf die Uhr schauen ... schickt sich wahrscheinlich nicht in einem so ernsten Konzert. Aber wer sieht's denn? Wenn's einer sieht, so paßt er gerade so wenig auf, wie ich, und vor dem brauch' ich mich nicht zu genieren ... Erst viertel auf zehn? ... Mir kommt vor, ich sitz' schon drei Stunden in dem Konzert. Ich bin's halt nicht gewohnt ... Was ist es denn eigentlich? Ich muß das Programm anschauen. .. Ja, richtig: Oratorium! Ich hab' gemeint: Messe. Solche Sachen gehören doch nur in die Kirche! Die Kirche hat auch das Gute, daß man jeden Augenblick fortgehen kann.—Wenn ich wenigstens einen Ecksitz hätt'!

Also Geduld, Geduld! Auch Oratorien nehmen ein End'! Vielleicht ist es sehr schön, und ich bin nur nicht in der Laune. Woher sollt' mir auch die Laune kommen? Wenn ich denke, daß ich hergekommen bin, um mich zu zerstreuen ... Hätt' ich die Karte lieber dem Benedek geschenkt, dem machen solche Sachen Spaß; er spielt ja selber Violine. Aber da wär' der Kopetzky beleidigt gewesen. Es war ja sehr lieb von ihm, wenigstens gut gemeint. Ein braver Kerl, der Kopetzky! Der einzige, auf den man sich verlassen kann ... Seine Schwester singt ja mit unter denen da oben. Mindestens hundert Jungfrauen, alle schwarz gekleidet; wie soll ich sie da herausfinden? Weil sie mitsingt, hat er auch das Billett gehabt, der Kopetzky ... Warum ist er denn nicht selber gegangen?

Sie singen übrigens sehr schön. Es ist sehr erhebend—sicher! Bravo! Bravo! ... Ja, applaudieren wir mit. Der neben mir klatscht wie verrückt. Ob's ihm wirklich so gut gefällt?—Das Mädel drüben in der Loge ist sehr hübsch. Sieht sie mich an oder den Herrn dort mit dem blonden Vollbart? ... Ah, ein Solo! Wer ist das? Alt: Fräulein Walker, Sopran: Fräulein Michalek ... das ist wahrscheinlich Sopran ... Lang' war ich schon nicht in der Oper. In der Oper unterhalt' ich mich immer, auch wenn's langweilig ist. Übermorgen könnt' ich eigentlich wieder hineingeh'n, zur ›Traviata‹. Ja, übermorgen bin ich vielleicht schon eine tote Leiche! Ah, Unsinn, das glaub' ich selber nicht! Warten S' nur, Herr Doktor, Ihnen wird's vergeh'n, solche Bemerkungen zu machen! Das Nasenspitzel hau' ich Ihnen herunter ...

LIEUTENANT GUSTL

How long is this going to last, anyhow? I must look at my watch . . . probably not polite at such a serious concert. But who's to see it? If someone sees it, then he's paying just as little attention as I am, and I don't have to bother on *his* account . . . Only a quarter to ten? I feel as if I'd been sitting at this concert for three hours now. I guess I'm not used to it . . . What is it, actually? I'll have to look at the program . . . Yes, that's it: oratorio. I thought it was a Mass. But surely things like that only belong in church! Also, the good thing about church is that you can leave any time. —If I at least had a corner seat!

Well, then, patience, patience! Even oratorios come to an end. Maybe it's very beautiful, and I'm just not in the mood. And why *should* I be in the mood? When I think that I came here to have a good time . . . I wish I'd given the ticket to Benedek instead, *he* gets a treat out of things like this; after all, he plays the violin himself. But then Kopetzky would have been insulted. Of course, it was very nice of him, at least he meant well. A good guy, Kopetzky! The only one you can rely on . . . Of course, his sister is one of the chorus singing up there. At least a hundred girls, all dressed in black; how could I pick her out? Because she's one of the singers, that's why he got the ticket, that Kopetzky . . . Then, why didn't he go himself?

By the way, they sing very nicely. It's very edifying—I'm sure! Bravo! Bravo! . . . Yes, let's join in the applause. That guy next to me is clapping like a lunatic. Does he really like it that much? —The girl in the box over there is really cute. Is she looking at me or at that man over there with the blonde beard? . . . Ah, a solo! Who is it? Alto: Miss Walker; soprano: Miss Michalek . . . this is probably the soprano . . . It's a long time since I was at the opera. At the opera I always have a good time, even if it's boring. Actually, the day after tomorrow I could go again, to *Traviata*. Yes, the day after tomorrow I may be dead and cold! Oh, nonsense, I don't believe that myself! Just wait, Doctor, you're going to lose your taste for making such remarks! I'm going to slice off the tip of your nose . . .

Wenn ich die in der Loge nur genau sehen könnt'! Ich möcht'
mir den Operngucker von dem Herrn neben mir ausleih'n, aber
der frißt mich ja auf, wenn ich ihn in seiner Andacht stör' . . . In
welcher Gegend die Schwester vom Kopetzky steht? Ob ich sie erkennen möcht'? Ich hab' sie ja nur zwei- oder dreimal gesehen, das
letztemal im Offizierskasino . . . Ob das lauter anständige Mädeln
sind, alle hundert? O jeh! . . . »Unter Mitwirkung des Singver-
eins«!—Singverein . . . komisch! Ich hab' mir darunter eigentlich
immer so was Ähnliches vorgestellt, wie die Wiener Tanzsängerin-
nen, das heißt, ich hab' schon gewußt, daß es was anderes ist! . .
Schöne Erinnerungen! Damals beim ›Grünen Tor‹ . . . Wie hat sie
nur geheißen? Und dann hat sie mir einmal eine Ansichtskarte aus
Belgrad geschickt . . . Auch eine schöne Gegend!—Der Kopetzky
hat's gut, der sitzt jetzt längst im Wirtshaus und raucht seine Virginia! . . .
    Was guckt mich denn der Kerl dort immer an? Mir scheint, der
merkt, daß ich mich langweil' und nicht herg'hör' . . . Ich möcht'
Ihnen raten, ein etwas weniger freches Gesicht zu machen, sonst
stell' ich Sie mir nachher im Foyer!—Schaut schon weg! . . . Daß
sie alle vor meinem Blick so eine Angst hab'n . . . »Du hast die
schönsten Augen, die mir je vorgekommen sind!« hat neulich die
Steffi gesagt . . . O Steffi, Steffi, Steffi!—Die Steffi ist eigentlich
schuld, daß ich dasitz' und mir stundenlang vorlamentieren lassen
muß.
    Ah, diese ewige Abschreiberei von der Steffi geht mir wirklich
schon auf die Nerven! Wie schön hätt' der heutige Abend sein
können. Ich hätt' große Lust, das Brieferl von der Steffi zu lesen.
Da hab' ich's ja. Aber wenn ich die Brieftasche herausnehm', frißt
mich der Kerl daneben auf!—Ich weiß ja, was drinsteht . . . sie
kann nicht kommen, weil sie mit »ihm« nachtmahlen gehen muß
. . . Ah, das war komisch vor acht Tagen, wie sie mit ihm in der
Gartenbaugesellschaft gewesen ist, und ich vis-à-vis mit'm Kopetzky; und sie hat mir immer die Zeichen gemacht mit den Au-
gerln, die verabredeten. Er hat nichts gemerkt—unglaublich! Muß
übrigens ein Jud' sein! Freilich, in einer Bank ist er, und der
schwarze Schnurrbart . . . Reserveleutnant soll er auch sein! Na, in
mein Regiment sollt' er nicht zur Waffenübung kommen! Überhaupt, daß sie noch immer so viel Juden zu Offizieren machen—da
pfeif' ich auf'n ganzen Antisemitismus! Neulich in der Gesellschaft,
wo die G'schicht' mit dem Doktor passiert ist bei den Mannheimers
. . . die Mannheimer selber sollen ja auch Juden sein, getauft natürlich . . . denen merkt man's aber gar nicht an—besonders die Frau
. . . so blond, bildhübsch die Figur . . . War sehr amüsant im ganzen.

If I could only get a good look at that girl in the box! I'd like to borrow the opera glasses from the man next to me, but he's sure to bite my nose off if I disturb him at his devotions . . . In what area is Kopetzky's sister standing? Would I recognize her? I've only seen her two or three times, the last time in the officers' mess . . . I wonder if they're all respectable girls, all hundred of them? Oh, my! . . . "With the cooperation of the Singers' Association"! Singers' Association . . . funny! Actually, I've always thought of that as something like the Vienna Dancing and Singing Girls—of course, I really knew it was something else! . . . Wonderful memories! That time at the Green Gate . . . What *was* her name? And then she once sent me a picture postcard from Belgrade . . . Another nice area! —Kopetzky is having fun, he's been sitting in the tavern for a while now smoking his Virginia cigar! . . .

Why does that guy there keep staring at me? I bet he's noticed that I'm bored and don't fit in here . . . I'd advise you not to make such impudent faces at me, or I'll meet you later on in the foyer! —Now he's looking away! . . . Why is everyone so afraid when I look at them? . . . "You have the most beautiful eyes I've ever come across!" Steffi said recently . . . Oh, Steffi, Steffi, Steffi! —Steffi is really to blame for my sitting here and having people wail at me for hours on end.

Ah, this way Steffi has of always standing me up is really beginning to get on my nerves! How nice this evening could have been. I have a great urge to read Steffi's note. There it is. But if I take out my wallet, the guy next to me will get steamed up! —Of course, I know what it says . . . she can't come because she has to go to supper with "him" . . . Ah, that was funny a week ago, when she was at the "Horticultural Society" with him and I was sitting opposite with Kopetzky; and she kept on signaling to me with her eyes, making a date. He didn't notice a thing—unbelievable! Anyway, he must be a Jew! Sure, he works in a bank, and that black mustache . . . They say he's also a lieutenant in the reserve! Well, he'd better not come to *my* regiment on active duty! And anyway, why do they always make so many Jews officers—all that talk about anti-Semitism is just a story! Lately at the party where that incident with the Doctor occurred, at the Mannheimers' . . . they say the Mannheimers are Jews themselves, converted, of course . . . but you can't tell by looking at *them*—especially the woman . . . so blonde, her figure pretty as a picture . . . It

Famoses Essen, großartige Zigarren . . . Na ja, wer hat's Geld? . . .
Bravo, bravo! Jetzt wird's doch bald aus sein?—Ja, jetzt steht die
ganze G'sellschaft da droben auf . . . sieht sehr gut aus—impo-
sant!—Orgel auch? . . . Orgel hab' ich sehr gern . . . So, das laß' ich
mir g'fall'n—sehr schön! Es ist wirklich wahr, man sollt' öfter in
Konzerte gehen . . . Wunderschön ist's g'wesen, werd' ich dem Kopetzky sagen . . . Werd' ich ihn heut' im Kaffeehaus treffen?—Ah,
ich hab' gar keine Lust, ins Kaffeehaus zu geh'n; hab' mich gestern
so gegiftet! Hundertsechzig Gulden auf einem Sitz verspielt—zu
dumm! Und wer hat alles gewonnen? Der Ballert, grad' der, der's
nicht notwendig hat . . . Der Ballert ist eigentlich schuld, daß ich in
das blöde Konzert hab' geh'n müssen . . . Na ja, sonst hätt' ich heut'
wieder spielen können, vielleicht doch was zurückgewonnen. Aber
es ist ganz gut, daß ich mir selber das Ehrenwort gegeben hab',
einen Monat lang keine Karte anzurühren . . . Die Mama wird wieder ein G'sicht machen, wenn sie meinen Brief bekommt!—
    Ah, sie soll zum Onkel geh'n, der hat Geld wie Mist; auf die paar
hundert Gulden kommt's ihm nicht an. Wenn ich's nur durchsetzen
könnt', daß er mir eine regelmäßige Sustentation gibt . . . aber nein,
um jeden Kreuzer muß man extra betteln. Dann heißt's wieder: Im
vorigen Jahr war die Ernte schlecht! . . . Ob ich heuer im Sommer
wieder zum Onkel fahren soll auf vierzehn Tag'? Eigentlich lang-
weilt man sich dort zum Sterben . . . Wenn ich die . . . wie hat sie
nur geheißen? . . . Es ist merkwürdig, ich kann mir keinen Namen
merken! . . . Ah, ja: Etelka! . . . Kein Wort deutsch hat sie verstanden, aber das war auch nicht notwendig . . . hab' gar nichts zu reden
brauchen! . . . Ja, es wird ganz gut sein, vierzehn Tage Landluft
und vierzehn Nächt' Etelka oder sonstwer . . . Aber acht Tag' sollt'
ich doch auch wieder beim Papa und bei der Mama sein . . . Schlecht
hat sie ausg'seh'n heuer zu Weihnachten . . . Na, jetzt wird die Krän-
kung schon überwunden sein. Ich an ihrer Stelle wär' froh, daß der
Papa in Pension gegangen ist.—Und die Klara wird schon noch
einen Mann kriegen . . . Der Onkel kann schon was hergeben . . .
Achtundzwanzig Jahr', das ist doch nicht so alt . . . Die Steffi ist
sicher nicht jünger . . . Aber es ist merkwürdig: die Frauenzimmer
erhalten sich länger jung. Wenn man so bedenkt: die Maretti neulich in der ›Madame Sans-Gêne‹—siebenunddreißig Jahr' ist sie
sicher, und sieht aus . . . Na, ich hätt' nicht Nein g'sagt!—Schad',
daß sie mich nicht g'fragt hat . . .

was very entertaining, all told. Terrific meal, wonderful cigars . . . So tell me, who's got the money? . . .

Bravo, bravo! It'll surely be over soon now? —Yes, now the whole crowd up there on the stage is standing up . . . they look very good—impressive! —An organ, too? . . . I really like organ music . . . Well, that's my style—very nice! It's really true, I ought to go to concerts more often . . . "It was marvelous," I'll tell Kopetzky . . . Will I meet him in the coffeehouse tonight? Oh, I really don't feel at all like going to the coffeehouse; I got into such a foul mood there last night! A hundred and sixty gulden lost at one card game—what a calamity! And who won the pot? Ballert—just the one who doesn't need it . . . Ballert is actually to blame for my having to go to this stupid concert . . . Sure, otherwise I could have played again tonight, maybe I could have won some of it back. But it's really a good thing that I gave myself my word of honor not to touch a card for a whole month . . . Mama is going to pull a long face again when she gets my letter!—

Oh, she ought to go to Uncle, he's got money to burn; a few hundred gulden wouldn't matter to him. If I could only arrange it for him to give me a regular allowance . . . but no, I've got to beg for each and every additional kreuzer. Then I get the old story: last year the harvest was bad! . . . Should I visit Uncle again this summer for two weeks? To tell the truth, I'm bored to death there . . . But if she . . . what was her name again? . . . It's odd, I can't remember names! . . . Oh, yes: Etelka! She didn't understand a word of German, but that wasn't necessary anyway . . . I didn't need to talk at all! . . . Yes, it'll be fine, fourteen days of country air and fourteen nights of Etelka or whoever . . . But I really ought to spend a week again with Papa and Mama . . . She looked bad this past Christmas . . . Well, by this time she'll be over her ailment. In her place, I'd be glad that Papa retired. —And Klara will still get a husband . . . Uncle can shell out something . . . Twenty-eight, that's not so very old . . . Steffi is certainly no younger . . . But it's odd: *that* kind of female keeps young longer. When you think about it: Maretti, who acted in *Madame Sans-Gêne*[1] lately, is surely thirty-seven, and looks like . . . Well, I wouldn't have said no! —Too bad she didn't ask me . . .

---

[1] A popular play by Victorien Sardou and others, 1893.

Heiß wird's! Noch immer nicht aus? Ah, ich freu' mich so auf die frische Luft! Werd' ein bißl spazieren geh'n, übern Ring . . . Heut' heißt's: früh ins Bett, morgen nachmittag frisch sein! Komisch, wie wenig ich daran denk', so egal ist mir das! Das erstemal hat's mich doch ein bißl aufgeregt. Nicht, daß ich Angst g'habt hätt'; aber nervos bin ich gewesen in der Nacht vorher . . . Freilich, der Oberleutnant Bisanz war ein ernster Gegner.—Und doch, nichts ist mir g'scheh'n! . . . Auch schon anderthalb Jahr' her. Wie die Zeit vergeht! Und wenn mir der Bisanz nichts getan hat, der Doktor wird mir schon gewiß nichts tun! Obzwar, gerade diese ungeschulten Fechter sind manchmal die gefährlichsten. Der Doschintzky hat mir erzählt, daß ihn ein Kerl, der das erstemal einen Säbel in der Hand gehabt hat, auf ein Haar abgestochen hätt'; und der Doschintzky ist heut' Fechtlehrer bei der Landwehr. Freilich—ob er damals schon so viel können hat . . .

Das Wichtigste ist: kaltes Blut. Nicht einmal einen rechten Zorn hab' ich mehr in mir, und es war doch eine Frechheit—unglaublich! Sicher hätt' er sich's nicht getraut, wenn er nicht Champagner getrunken hätt' vorher . . . So eine Frechheit! Gewiß ein Sozialist! Die Rechtsverdreher sind doch heutzutag' alle Sozialisten! Eine Bande . . . am liebsten möchten sie gleich 's ganze Militär abschaffen; aber wer ihnen dann helfen möcht', wenn die Chinesen über sie kommen, daran denken sie nicht. Blödisten!—Man muß gelegentlich ein Exempel statuieren. Ganz recht hab' ich g'habt. Ich bin froh, daß ich ihn nimmer auslassen hab' nach der Bemerkung. Wenn ich dran denk', werd' ich ganz wild! Aber ich hab' mich famos benommen; der Oberst sagt auch, es war absolut korrekt. Wird mir überhaupt nützen, die Sache.

Ich kenn' manche, die den Burschen hätten durchschlüpfen lassen. Der Müller sicher, der wär' wieder objektiv gewesen oder so was. Mit dem Objektivsein hat sich noch jeder blamiert . . . »Herr Leutnant!«. . schon die Art, wie er »Herr Leutnant« gesagt hat, war unverschämt! . . . »Sie werden mir doch zugeben müssen« . . .—Wie sind wir denn nur d'rauf gekommen? Wieso hab' ich mich mit dem Sozialisten in ein Gespräch eingelassen? Wie hat's denn nur angefangen? . . . Mir scheint, die schwarze Frau, die ich zum Büfett geführt hab', ist auch dabei gewesen . . . und dann dieser junge Mensch, der die Jagdbilder malt—wie heißt er denn nur? . . . Meiner Seel', der ist an der ganzen Geschichte schuld gewesen! Der hat von den Manövern geredet; und dann erst ist dieser Doktor dazugekommen und hat irgendwas g'sagt, was mir nicht gepaßt hat, von Kriegsspielerei oder so was—aber wo ich noch

It's getting hot! Not over yet? Oh, how I look forward to the fresh air! I'll take a little walk, across the Ring . . . Motto for tonight: early to bed, be well-rested tomorrow afternoon! Funny how little I think about it, I really couldn't care less about it! Yes, the first time I did get a bit excited. Not that I was afraid; but I *was* nervous the night before . . . Of course, First Lieutenant Bisanz was a serious opponent.—And yet nothing happened to me! . . . And that was a year and a half ago. How time flies! And if Bisanz did nothing to me, the Doctor certainly won't! Although it's just these untrained fencers who are sometimes the most dangerous. Doschintzky told me that a guy who was holding a saber for the first time came within a hair of thrusting him through; and today Doschintzky teaches fencing in the militia. Of course, I wonder if he was already that skilled at the time . . .

The most important thing is to keep cool. I don't even feel rightly angry any more, and it certainly was a piece of insolence—unbelievable! He certainly wouldn't have gone that far if he hadn't been drinking champagne previously . . . What insolence! He must be a socialist! After all, nowadays the pettifoggers are all socialists! A gang . . . what they'd like best of all is to do away with the whole military at once; but they don't stop to think about who would help them then if the Chinese attacked them. Dumbbells! —From time to time a man has to serve as an example. I was completely in the right. I'm glad that I never let him off the hook after that remark. When I think about it, I really get wild! But I behaved terrifically; the Colonel says, too, that I handled myself just as one should. All in all, this affair will help me out.

I know many people who would have let the fellow get away. Müller, surely; he would have been "objective" again or something like that. Everyone who's tried to be objective has made a fool of himself . . . "Lieutenant!" . . . even the way he said "Lieutenant" was brazen! . . . "You will surely have to admit" . . . How did we get into the situation, anyway? Why did I allow myself to get into a conversation with a socialist? How did it start? . . . I think the dark-haired lady I escorted to the buffet was also there . . . and then that youngster who paints hunting scenes—what's his name, now? . . . God bless me, he was to blame for the whole matter! He spoke about maneuvers; and it was only then that this Doctor came by and said something I didn't care for, about playing at war or

nichts hab' reden können . . . Ja, und dann ist von den Kadetten-
schulen gesprochen worden . . . ja, so war's . . . und ich hab' von
einem patriotischen Fest erzählt . . . und dann hat der Doktor gesagt—nicht gleich, aber aus dem Fest hat es sich entwickelt—»Herr
Leutnant, Sie werden mir doch zugeben, daß nicht alle Ihre Kameraden zum Militär gegangen sind, ausschließlich um das Vaterland
zu verteidigen!« So eine Frechheit! Das wagt so ein Mensch einem
Offizier ins Gesicht zu sagen! Wenn ich mich nur erinnern könnt',
was ich d'rauf geantwortet hab'? . . . Ah ja, etwas von Leuten, die
sich in Dinge dreinmengen, von denen sie nichts versteh'n . . . Ja,
richtig . . . und dann war einer da, der hat die Sache gütlich beile-
gen wollen, ein älterer Herr mit einem Stockschnupfen . . . Aber
ich war zu wütend! Der Doktor hat das absolut in dem Ton gesagt,
als wenn er direkt mich gemeint hätt'. Er hätt' nur noch sagen
müssen, daß sie mich aus dem Gymnasium hinausg'schmissen
haben und daß ich deswegen in die Kadettenschul' gesteckt worden
bin . . . Die Leut' können eben unserein'n nicht versteh'n, sie sind
zu dumm dazu . . .

Wenn ich mich so erinner', wie ich das erstemal den Rock angehabt hab', so was erlebt eben nicht ein jeder . . . Im vorigen Jahr'
bei den Manövern—ich hätt' was drum gegeben, wenn's plötzlich
Ernst gewesen wär' . . . Und der Mirovic hat mir g'sagt, es ist ihm
ebenso gegangen. Und dann, wie Seine Hoheit die Front abgeritten
sind, und die Ansprache vom Obersten—da muß einer schon ein
ordentlicher Lump sein, wenn ihm das Herz nicht höher schlägt
. . . Und da kommt so ein Tintenfisch daher, der sein Lebtag nichts
getan hat, als hinter den Büchern gesessen, und erlaubt sich
eine freche Bemerkung! . . . Ah, wart' nur, mein Lieber—bis zur
Kampfunfähigkeit . . . jawohl, du sollst so kampfunfähig werden . . .

Ja, was ist denn? Jetzt muß es doch bald aus sein? . . . »Ihr, seine
Engel, lobet den Herrn« . . .—Freilich, das ist der Schlußchor . . .
Wunderschön, da kann man gar nichts sagen. Wunder-
schön!—Jetzt hab' ich ganz die aus der Loge vergessen, die früher
zu kokettieren angefangen hat. Wo ist sie denn? . . . Schon fortgegangen . . . Die dort scheint auch sehr nett zu sein . . . Zu dumm,
daß ich keinen Operngucker bei mir hab'! Der Brunnthaler ist ganz
gescheit, der hat sein Glas immer im Kaffeehaus bei der Kassa
liegen, da kann einem nichts g'scheh'n . . . Wenn sich die Kleine da
vor mir nur einmal umdreh'n möcht'! So brav sitzt s' alleweil da.
Das neben ihr ist sicher die Mama.

Ob ich nicht doch einmal ernstlich ans Heiraten denken soll? Der
Willy war nicht älter als ich, wie er hineingesprungen ist. Hat schon
was für sich, so immer gleich ein hübsches Weiberl zu Haus vorrätig

something like that—but that was before I was able to say anything . . . Yes, and then they spoke about military academies . . . yes, that's how it was . . . and I told about a patriotic festival . . . and then the Doctor said—not right away, but as a spin-off from that festival—"Lieutenant, you will surely have to admit that not all your comrades joined the service solely to defend their country!" What insolence! A person like that dares to say such a thing to an officer! If I could only remember how I replied to that . . . Oh, yes, something about people who meddle with things they don't understand . . . Yes, that's right . . . and then there was someone there who wanted to settle the matter amicably, an older gentleman with a heavy cold . . . But I was too furious! The Doctor definitely said it as if he meant me personally. All he needed to add was that I was thrown out of high school and that's why I was placed in a military academy . . . People just can't understand our sort, they're too dumb to . . .

When I recall the first time I put on the uniform—that's an experience that not everyone has . . . Last year during maneuvers—what I wouldn't have given if it had suddenly become the real thing . . . And Mirovic told me he felt the same way. And then, when His Highness rode past the front, and the Colonel's speech—a man would have to be a real bum if his heart didn't beat stronger . . . And then an inkslinger like that comes along, who's never done a thing all his life but sit behind books, and feels free to make an insolent remark! . . . Ah, just wait, my good man—till you're put out of action . . . yes, sir, you'll be so far out of action . . .

What's going on? Surely it must be almost over now? . . . "You, His angels, praise the Lord" . . . Of course, that's the closing chorus . . . Very beautiful, you can't deny it. Very beautiful! —Now I've completely forgotten that girl in the box who started to flirt before. Where is she? . . . Gone already . . . That one over there also seems to be very pretty . . . What a nuisance not to have opera glasses with me! Brunnthaler is really clever, he always has his glasses at the cashier's booth in the coffeehouse, that way you can't go wrong . . . If that girl there in front of me would turn around just once! She's been sitting there so well-behaved. The one next to her must be her Mama.

Shouldn't I start to think seriously about getting married? Willy wasn't older than I when he took the plunge. There's something to be said for always having a pretty

zu haben . . . Zu dumm, daß die Steffi grad' heut' keine Zeit hat!
Wenn ich wenigstens wüßte, wo sie ist, möcht' ich mich wieder vis-
à-vis von ihr hinsetzen. Das wär' eine schöne G'schicht', wenn ihr
der draufkommen möcht', da hätt' ich sie am Hals . . . Wenn ich so
denk', was dem Fließ sein Verhältnis mit der Winterfeld kostet!
Und dabei betrügt sie ihn hinten und vorn. Das nimmt noch einmal
ein Ende mit Schrecken . . . Bravo, bravo! Ah, aus! . . . So, das tut
wohl, aufsteh'n können, sich rühren . . . Na, vielleicht! Wie lang'
wird der da noch brauchen, um sein Glas ins Futteral zu stecken?
»Pardon, pardon, wollen mich nicht hinauslassen?« . . .
Ist das ein Gedränge! Lassen wir die Leut' lieber vorbeipassieren
. . . Elegante Person . . . ob das echte Brillanten sind? . . . Die da ist
nett . . . Wie sie mich anschaut! . . . O ja, mein Fräulein, ich möcht'
schon! . . . O, die Nase!—Jüdin . . . Noch eine . . . Es ist doch fabel-
haft, da sind auch die Hälfte Juden . . . nicht einmal ein Oratorium
kann man mehr in Ruhe genießen . . . So, jetzt schließen wir uns
an . . . Warum drängt denn der Idiot hinter mir? Das werd' ich ihm
abgewöhnen . . . Ah, ein älterer Herr! . . . Wer grüßt mich denn
dort von drüben? . . . Habe die Ehre, habe die Ehre! Keine Ahnung
hab' ich, wer das ist . . . Das Einfachste wär', ich ging gleich zum
Leidinger hinüber nachtmahlen . . . oder soll ich in die Gartenbaugesellschaft? Am End' ist die Steffi auch dort? Warum hat sie mir
eigentlich nicht geschrieben, wohin sie mit ihm geht? Sie wird's
selber noch nicht gewußt haben. Eigentlich schrecklich, so eine ab-
hängige Existenz . . . Armes Ding!
So, da ist der Ausgang . . . Ah, die ist aber bildschön! Ganz allein?
Wie sie mich anlacht. Das wär' eine Idee, der geh' ich nach! . . . So,
jetzt die Treppen hinunter: Oh, ein Major von Fünfundneunzig . . .
Sehr liebenswürdig hat er gedankt . . . Bin doch nicht der einzige
Offizier herin gewesen . . . Wo ist denn das hübsche Mädel? Ah,
dort . . . am Geländer steht sie . . . So, jetzt heißt's noch zur Garderobe . . Daß mir die Kleine nicht auskommt . . . Hat ihm schon! So
ein elender Fratz! Laßt sich da von einem Herrn abholen, und jetzt
lacht sie noch auf mich herüber!—Es ist doch keine was wert . . .
Herrgott, ist das ein Gedränge bei der Garderobe! . . . Warten wir
lieber noch ein bisserl . . . So! Ob der Blödist meine Nummer nehmen möcht'? . . .
»Sie, zweihundertvierundzwanzig! Da hängt er! Na, hab'n Sie
keine Augen? Da hängt er! Na, Gott sei Dank! . . . Also bitte! «
. . Der Dicke da verstellt einem schier die ganze Garderobe . . . »Bitte
sehr!« . . .

little wife on hand at home . . . What a shame that Steffi
has no time tonight of all nights! If I at least knew where
she was, I could sit opposite her again. That would be a
fine predicament, if that guy caught on to her, then *I*
would be saddled with her . . . When I think what Fliess's
affair with the Winterfeld woman costs him! And at the
same time she cheats on him left and right. One of these
days it'll end up in a disaster . . . Bravo, bravo! Ah, it's
over! . . . There, that feels good, to be able to stand up, to
move . . . Well, maybe! How long is that guy going to take
to put his glasses into their case?

"Pardon, pardon, would you let me out, please?" . . .

What a crush! Better let the people pass by . . . Elegant
lady . . . I wonder if those are genuine diamonds? . . . That
girl is cute . . . The way she looks at me! . . . Oh, yes, miss,
I'm ready and willing! . . . Oh, her nose!—a Jewess . . .
Another one . . . But this is amazing, half of the audience
are Jews . . . you can't even enjoy an oratorio in peace any
more . . . There, now let's join the procession . . . But why
is that idiot shoving in back of me? I'll teach him better
manners . . . Ah, an older gentleman! . . . And who is
greeting me from up there? . . . Good night, good night!
I have no idea who it is . . . The simplest thing would be
to go right over to Leidinger's for supper . . . or should I
go to the "Horticultural Society"? Maybe Steffi is there
too? Really, why didn't she write to tell me where she was
going with him? She probably didn't know yet herself.
Really awful, such a dependent existence! . . . Poor thing!

Now, there's the exit . . . Ah, but *she* is gorgeous! All
alone? The way she's smiling at me! That's an idea, I'll go
after *her!* . . . There, down the steps now: Oh, a major
of the Ninety-fifth . . . Very charming, the way he returned my salute . . . So I wasn't the only officer here . . .
But where's the pretty girl? Ah, there . . . she's standing
by the balustrade . . . Well, now I just have to get to the
cloakroom . . . I don't want that girl to get away . . . That's
done it! What a miserable brat! She has a man come to
meet her, and now she's still smiling at me!—After all,
not one of them is any good . . . Lord, what a crowd at the
cloakroom! . . . Better wait a little bit longer . . . There! Is
the dumbbell going to take my ticket? . . .

"You there, No. 224! It's hanging *there!* Well, are you
blind? It's hanging *there!* Well, thank God! . . . Come on,
now!" . . . That fat man there is blocking almost the whole
cloakroom . . . "Excuse me, please!" . . .

»Geduld, Geduld! «
Was sagt der Kerl?
»Nur ein bisserl Geduld! «
Dem muß ich doch antworten . . . »Machen Sie doch Platz! «
»Na, Sie werden's auch nicht versäumen! «
Was sagt er da? Sagt er das zu mir? Das ist doch stark! Das kann
ich mir nicht gefallen lassen! »Ruhig! «
»Was meinen Sie? «
Ah, so ein Ton! Da hört sich doch alles auf!
»Stoßen Sie nicht! «
»Sie, halten Sie das Maul! « Das hätt' ich nicht sagen sollen, ich
war zu grob . . . Na, jetzt ist's schon g'scheh'n!
»Wie meinen? «
Jetzt dreht er sich um . . . Den kenn' ich ja!—Donnerwetter, das
ist ja der Bäckermeister, der immer ins Kaffeehaus kommt . . . Was
macht denn der da? Hat sicher auch eine Tochter oder so was bei
der Singakademie . . . Ja, was ist denn das? Ja, was macht er denn?
Mir scheint gar . . . ja, meiner Seel', er hat den Griff von meinem
Säbel in der Hand . . . Ja, ist der Kerl verrückt? . . . »Sie, Herr . . . «
»Sie, Herr Leutnant, sein S' jetzt ganz stad. «
Was sagt er da? Um Gottes willen, es hat's doch keiner gehört?
Nein, er red't ganz leise . . . Ja, warum läßt er denn meinen Säbel
net aus? . . . Herrgott noch einmal . . . Ah, da heißt's rabiat sein . . .
ich bring' seine Hand vom Griff nicht weg . . . nur keinen Skandal
jetzt! . . . Ist nicht am End' der Major hinter mir? . . . Bemerkt's nur
niemand, daß er den Griff von meinem Säbel hält? Er red't ja zu
mir! Was red't er denn?
»Herr Leutnant, wenn Sie das geringste Aufsehen machen, so
zieh' ich den Säbel aus der Scheide, zerbrech' ihn und schick' die
Stück' an Ihr Regimentskommando. Versteh'n Sie mich, Sie dummer Bub? «
Was hat er g'sagt? Mir scheint, ich träum'! Red't er wirklich zu
mir? Ich sollt' was antworten . . . Aber der Kerl macht ja Ernst—der
zieht wirklich den Säbel heraus. Herrgott—er tut's! . . . Ich spür's,
er reißt schon d'ran! Was red't er denn? . . . Um Gottes willen, nur
kein' Skandal——Was red't er denn noch immer?
»Aber ich will Ihnen die Karriere nicht verderben . . . Also, schön
brav sein! . . . So, hab'n S' keine Angst, 's hat niemand was gehört
. . . es ist schon alles gut . . . so! Und damit keiner glaubt, daß wir
uns gestritten haben, werd' ich jetzt sehr freundlich mit Ihnen

"Patience, patience!"

What did the guy say?

"Just have a little patience!"

I just have to answer *him* . . . "Let me through!"

"You're not going to miss anything!"

What did he say? Did he say that to me? That's going too far! I can't put up with that! "Quiet!"

"What do you mean?"

What a tone of voice! That's the limit!

"Don't push!"

"Shut up, you!" I shouldn't have said that, I was too rude . . . Well, what's done is done!

"How was that?"

Now he's turning around . . . I know him! —Damn it, it's the master baker who always comes to the coffeehouse . . . But what is he doing here? He must also have a daughter or something in the chorus . . . But what's this? Yes, what is he doing? It even seems . . . yes, damn me, he's got the hilt of my saber in his hand . . . Is the guy crazy? . . . "You, sir . . ."

"You, Lieutenant, just keep still now."

What did he say? For the love of God, I hope nobody heard! No, he's speaking very low . . . But why doesn't he let go of my saber? . . . Damn it again . . . He's got me raving . . . I can't get his hand off the hilt . . . no uproar now! . . . Could the Major be behind me? . . . Does anyone notice that he's holding the hilt of my saber? But he's talking to me! What is he saying?

"Lieutenant, if you make the slightest disturbance, I'll put your saber out of its scabbard, smash it and send the pieces to your regimental headquarters. Do you understand, you fool?"[2]

What did he say? I must be dreaming! Is he really talking to me? I ought to make some reply . . . But the guy is really serious—he's actually pulling out the saber. Good Lord—he's doing it! . . . I can feel it, he's already tugging at it! What is he saying? For God's sake, no uproar——what does he keep on saying?

"But I don't want to ruin your career . . . So, behave! . . . There, there, don't be afraid, no one heard anything . . . everything's all right now . . . there! And so that no one thinks we had a quarrel, I'll be very friendly to you

---

[2] "Dummer Bub" (more commonly, "dummer Junge") was a standard phrase for a challenge.

sein!—Habe die Ehre, Herr Leutnant, hat mich sehr ge-
freut—habe die Ehre!«
Um Gottes willen, hab' ich geträumt? ... Hat er das wirklich gesagt? ... Wo ist er denn? ... Da geht er ... Ich müßt' ja den Säbel
ziehen und ihn zusammenhauen——Um Gottes willen, es hat's
doch niemand gehört? ... Nein, er hat ja nur ganz leise geredet,
mir ins Ohr ... Warum geh' ich denn nicht hin und hau' ihm
den Schädel auseinander? ... Nein, es geht ja nicht, es geht ja
nicht ... gleich hätt' ich's tun müssen ... Warum hab' ich's denn
nicht gleich getan? ... Ich hab's ja nicht können ... er hat ja den
Griff nicht auslassen, und er ist zehnmal stärker als ich ...
Wenn ich noch ein Wort gesagt hätt', hätt' er mir wirklich den
Säbel zerbrochen ... Ich muß ja noch froh sein, daß er nicht laut
geredet hat! Wenn's ein Mensch gehört hätt', so müßt' ich mich ja
stante pede erschießen ...
Vielleicht ist es doch ein Traum gewesen ... Warum schaut mich
denn der Herr dort an der Säule so an?—Hat der am End' was
gehört? ... Ich werd' ihn fragen ... Fragen?—Ich bin ja verrückt!—Wie schau' ich denn aus?—Merkt man mir was an?—Ich
muß ganz blaß sein.—Wo ist der Hund? ... Ich muß ihn umbringen! ... Fort ist er ... Überhaupt schon ganz leer ... Wo ist denn
mein Mantel? ... Ich hab' ihn ja schon angezogen ... Ich hab's gar
nicht gemerkt ... Wer hat mir denn geholfen? ... Ah, der da ...
dem muß ich ein Sechserl geben ... So! ...
Aber was ist denn das? Ist es denn wirklich gescheh'n? Hat wirklich einer so zu mir geredet? Hat mir wirklich einer »dummer Bub«
gesagt? Und ich hab' ihn nicht auf der Stelle zusammenge-
hauen? ... Aber ich hab' ja nicht können ... er hat ja eine Faust
gehabt wie Eisen ... ich bin ja dagestanden wie angenagelt ...
Nein, ich muß den Verstand verloren gehabt haben, sonst hätt'
ich mit der anderen Hand ... Aber da hätt' er ja meinen Säbel
herausgezogen und zerbrochen, und aus wär's gewesen—Alles
wär' aus gewesen! Und nachher, wie er fortgegangen ist, war's zu
spät ... ich hab' ihm doch nicht den Säbel von hinten in den Leib
rennen können ...
Was, ich bin schon auf der Straße? Wie bin ich denn da herausge-
kommen?—So kühl ist es ... ah, der Wind, der ist gut ... Wer ist
denn das da drüben? Warum schau'n denn die zu mir herüber?
Am End' haben die was gehört ... Nein, es kann niemand was
gehört haben ... ich weiß ja, ich hab' mich gleich nachher umge-
schaut! Keiner hat sich um mich gekümmert, niemand hat was ge-

now!—Good night, Lieutenant, it was a pleasure—good night!"

For God's sake, was I dreaming? . . . Did he really say that? . . . Where is he? . . . There he goes . . . I really ought to have drawn my saber and cut him down——For God's sake, I hope no one heard it . . . No, he was speaking very low, in my ear . . . But why don't I go over and split his skull open? . . . No, that wouldn't do, it wouldn't do . . . I ought to have done it right away . . . Why *didn't* I do it right away? . . . I just wasn't able to . . . he didn't let go of the hilt, and he's ten times stronger than I am . . . If I had said one more word, he would really have broken my saber . . . I ought to be happy that he wasn't speaking out loud! If anyone had heard it, I would have had to shoot myself *stante pede*[3] . . .

Maybe it was a dream after all . . . But why is that man there by the column staring at me like that?—Perhaps he heard something . . . I'll ask him . . . Ask him?—I'm crazy!—How do I look?—Can anyone notice anything from my appearance? I must be very pale.—Where is the dog? . . . I must kill him! . . . He's gone . . . The place is already completely empty . . . But where's my cloak? . . . I've put it on already . . . I didn't even notice . . . Who helped me on with it? . . . Oh, that one . . . I must give him a six-kreuzer piece . . . There! . . .

But what's going on? Did it really happen? Did someone really talk to me that way? Did someone really call me "fool"? And I didn't cut him down on the spot . . . But I wasn't able to . . . he had a fist like iron . . . I stood there as if nailed down . . . No, I must have lost my wits, or else with my other hand I would have . . . But then he would have pulled out my saber and broken it, and it would have been all up with me—I would have been completely finished! And later, when he went away, it was too late . . . after all, I couldn't have run him through from behind with my saber . . .

What, I'm out on the street already? How did I get outside?—It's so cool . . . ah, the breeze, that feels good . . . But who's that over there? Why are they looking my way? Maybe they heard something . . . No, no one could have heard anything . . . I know, because I looked around right away! No one was paying any attention to me, no one

---

[3] Latin for "on the spot." The use of the phrase does not indicate scholarship on Gustl's part.

hört . . . Aber gesagt hat er's, wenn's auch niemand gehört hat; gesagt hat er's doch. Und ich bin dagestanden und hab' mir's gefallen lassen, wie wenn mich einer vor den Kopf geschlagen hätt'! . . . Aber ich hab' ja nichts sagen können, nichts tun können; es war ja noch das einzige, was mir übrig geblieben ist: stad sein, stad sein! . . . 's ist fürchterlich, es ist nicht zum Aushalten; ich muß ihn totschlagen, wo ich ihn treff'! . . .

Mir sagt das einer! Mir sagt das so ein Kerl, so ein Hund! Und er kennt mich . . . Herrgott noch einmal, er kennt mich, er weiß, wer ich bin! . . . Er kann jedem Menschen erzählen, daß er mir das g'sagt hat! . . . Nein, nein, das wird er ja nicht tun, sonst hätt' er auch nicht so leise geredet . . . er hat auch nur wollen, daß ich es allein hör'! . . . Aber wer garantiert mir, daß er's nicht doch erzählt, heut' oder morgen, seiner Frau, seiner Tochter, seinen Bekannten im Kaffeehaus.——Um Gottes willen, morgen seh' ich ihn ja wieder! Wenn ich morgen ins Kaffeehaus komm', sitzt er wieder dort wie alle Tag' und spielt seinen Tapper mit dem Herrn Schlesinger und mit dem Kunstblumenhändler . . . Nein, nein, das geht ja nicht, das geht ja nicht . . . Wenn ich ihn seh', so hau' ich ihn zusammen . . . Nein, das darf ich ja nicht . . . gleich hätt' ich's tun müssen, gleich! . . . Wenn's nur gegangen wär'! . . .

Ich werd' zum Obersten geh'n und ihm die Sache melden . . . ja, zum Obersten . . . Der Oberst ist immer sehr freundlich—und ich werd' ihm sagen: Herr Oberst, ich melde gehorsamst, er hat den Griff gehalten, er hat ihn nicht aus'lassen; es war genau so, als wenn ich ohne Waffe gewesen wäre . . .—Was wird der Oberst sagen?—Was er sagen wird?—Aber da gibt's ja nur eins: quittieren mit Schimpf und Schand'—quittieren! . . .

Sind das Freiwillige da drüben? . . . Ekelhaft, bei der Nacht schau'n sie aus, wie Offiziere . . . sie salutieren!—Wenn die wüßten—wenn die wüßten! . . .—Da ist das Café Hochleitner . . . Sind jetzt gewiß ein paar Kameraden drin . . . vielleicht auch einer oder der andere, den ich kenn' . . . Wenn ich's dem ersten Besten erzählen möcht', aber so, als wär's einem andern passiert? . . .—Ich bin ja schon ganz irrsinnig . . .

Wo lauf' ich denn da herum? Was tu' ich denn auf der Straße?—Ja, aber wo soll ich denn hin? Hab' ich nicht zum Leidinger wollen? Haha, unter Menschen mich niedersetzen . . . ich glaub', ein jeder müßt' mir's anseh'n . . . Ja, aber irgendwas muß doch gescheh'n . . . Was soll denn gescheh'n? . . . Nichts, nichts—es hat ja niemand was gehört . . . es weiß ja niemand was . . . in dem-

heard anything . . . But he did say it even if no one heard it; he did say it. And I stood there and let him, as if I had been hit over the head! . . . But I couldn't say anything or do anything; the only thing left for me to do was to keep still, keep still . . . it's horrible, it's not to be borne; I must kill him whenever I find him! . . .

That someone should talk that way to me! That a guy like that, a dog like that should speak to me like that! And he knows me . . . Lord, oh Lord, he knows me, he knows who I am! . . . He can tell anybody that he said that to me! . . . No, no, he won't do that, otherwise he wouldn't have spoken so low . . . he only wanted *me* to hear! . . . But who can guarantee that he won't eventually tell it, today or tomorrow, to his wife, his daughter, his friends in the coffeehouse?——For God's sake, I'll see him again tomorrow! When I arrive at the coffeehouse tomorrow, he'll be sitting there again, just like every day, playing his game of tarok with Mr. Schlesinger and the artificial-flower dealer . . . No, no, it's no good, it's no good . . . When I see him, I'll cut him down . . . No, I can't . . . I ought to have done it right away, right away! . . . If it had only worked out! . . .

I'll go to the Colonel and report the matter to him . . . yes, to the Colonel . . . The Colonel is always very friendly—and I'll say to him: Colonel, I beg to report, he held on to the hilt, he didn't let go of it; it was exactly as if I were weaponless . . . What will the Colonel say?—What he'll say?—But there's only one thing he can say: resign in disgrace—resign! . . .

Are those volunteers[4] over there? . . . Disgusting! at night they look like officers . . . they're saluting!—If they knew—if they knew! . . . There's the Café Hochleitner . . . There must be a couple of my fellow officers in there now . . . maybe someone or other that I know . . . What if I told it to the first one I meet, but as if it had happened to someone else? . . . I'm completely off my head by now . . .

Where have I got to? What am I doing out on the street?—Yes, but where should I head? Didn't I want to go to Leidinger's? Ha, ha, to sit down among people . . . I'm sure everybody would see it from my face . . . Yes, but *something* has to happen . . . What should happen? . . . Nothing, nothing—because no one heard anything . . . no

---

[4] Men in the service for one year with a certificate of educational proficiency.

Moment weiß niemand was . . . Wenn ich jetzt zu ihm in die Wohnung ginge und ihn beschwören möchte, daß er's niemandem erzählt? . . . —Ah, lieber gleich eine Kugel vor den Kopf, als so
was! . . . Wär' so das Gescheiteste! . . . Das Gescheiteste? Das Gescheiteste?—Gibt ja überhaupt nichts anderes . . . gibt nichts anderes . . . Wenn ich den Oberst fragen möcht', oder den Kopetzky—oder den Blany—oder den Friedmaier:—jeder möcht'
sagen: Es bleibt dir nichts anderes übrig! . . .
   Wie wär's, wenn ich mit dem Kopetzky spräch'? . . . Ja, es wär'
doch das Vernünftigste . . . schon wegen morgen . . . Ja, natürlich—wegen morgen . . . um vier in der Reiterkasern' . . . ich soll
mich ja morgen um vier Uhr schlagen . . . und ich darf's ja nimmer,
ich bin satisfaktionsunfähig . . . Unsinn! Unsinn! Kein Mensch weiß
was, kein Mensch weiß was!—Es laufen viele herum, denen ärgere
Sachen passiert sind, als mir . . . Was hat man nicht alles von dem
Deckener erzählt, wie er sich mit dem Rederow geschossen hat . . .
und der Ehrenrat hat entschieden, das Duell darf stattfinden . . .
Aber wie möcht' der Ehrenrat bei mir entscheiden?—Dummer
Bub—dummer Bub . . . und ich bin dagestanden—!
   Heiliger Himmel, es ist doch ganz egal, ob ein anderer was
weiß! . . . ich weiß es doch, und das ist die Hauptsache! Ich spür',
daß ich jetzt wer anderer bin, als vor einer Stunde—Ich weiß, daß
ich satisfaktionsunfähig bin, und darum muß ich mich totschießen
. . . Keine ruhige Minute hätt' ich mehr im Leben . . . immer hätt'
ich die Angst, daß es doch einer erfahren könnt', so oder so . . .
und daß mir's einer einmal ins Gesicht sagt, was heut' abend gescheh'n ist!
   Was für ein glücklicher Mensch bin ich vor einer Stund' gewesen
. . . Muß mir der Kopetzky die Karte schenken—und die Steffi
muß mir absagen, das Mensch!—Von so was hängt man ab . . .
Nachmittag war noch alles gut und schön, und jetzt bin ich ein
verlorener Mensch und muß mich totschießen . . . Warum renn' ich
denn so? Es lauft mir ja nichts davon . . . Wieviel schlagt's denn? . . .
1, 2, 3, 4, 5, 6, 7, 8, 9, 10, 11 . . . elf, elf . . . ich sollt' doch nachtmahlen geh'n! Irgendwo muß ich doch schließlich hingeh'n . . . ich
könnt' mich ja in irgendein Beisl setzen, wo mich kein Mensch
kennt—schließlich, essen muß der Mensch, auch wenn er sich
nachher gleich totschießt . . . Haha, der Tod ist ja kein Kinderspiel
. . . wer hat das nur neulich gesagt? . . . Aber das ist ja ganz egal . . .
   Ich möcht' wissen, wer sich am meisten kränken möcht'? . . . Die

one knows anything . . . at this moment no one knows anything . . . Should I go to his home now and implore him not to tell anyone about it? . . . Ah, better to blow my brains out at once than do something like that! . . . That would be the most sensible thing! . . . The most sensible? The most sensible?—There just isn't any other way . . . no other way . . . If I were to ask the Colonel, or Kopetz-ky—or Blany—or Friedmaier—everyone would say: There's no other way out for you! . . .

What if I spoke to Kopetzky? . . . Yes, that would be the most rational thing . . . about tomorrow, if for no other reason . . . Yes, of course, about tomorrow . . . at four, in the cavalry barracks . . . yes, I'm to fight a duel tomorrow at four o'clock . . . and I absolutely can't, I'm unqualified to give satisfaction . . . Nonsense! Nonsense! Nobody knows anything, nobody knows anything!—Plenty of men are running around who had worse things happen to them than this . . . All the things they said about Deckener and his pistol fight with Rederow . . . and the court of honor decided the duel ought to take place . . . But how would the court decide in my case?—"Fool—fool" . . . and I stood there—!

God in heaven, it makes no difference if anyone else knows! . . . *I* know, and that's the main thing! *I* realize that I'm not the same man I was an hour ago—*I* know that I'm unfit to fight a duel, and therefore I've got to shoot myself . . . I wouldn't have another peaceful moment in my life . . . I would always be afraid that someone might find out, one way or another . . . and that one day some-one would tell me to my face what happened tonight!

What a fortunate person I was an hour ago . . . Then Kopetzky had to go and give me the ticket—and Steffi had to stand me up, the slut!—Things like that control your fate . . . In the afternoon everything was still per-fectly all right, and now I'm a ruined man and have to shoot myself . . . Why am I dashing along like this? None of my trouble is running away . . . What is the clock strik-ing now? . . . 1, 2, 3, 4, 5, 6, 7, 8, 9, 10, 11 . . . eleven, eleven . . . I really should go to supper! I've got to go somewhere eventually . . . I could sit down in some saloon where no one knows me—after all, a man has to eat, even if he shoots himself immediately afterward . . . Ha, ha, death isn't child's play . . . who was it said that recently? . . . But that makes no difference . . .

I'd like to know who will be most upset? . . . Mama or

Mama, oder die Steffi? . . . Die Steffi . . . Gott, die Steffi . . . die
dürft' sich ja nicht einmal was anmerken lassen, sonst gibt »er« ihr
den Abschied . . . Arme Person!—Beim Regiment—kein Mensch
hätt' eine Ahnung, warum ich's getan hab' . . . sie täten sich alle den
Kopf zerbrechen . . . warum hat sich denn der Gustl umgebracht?—Darauf möcht' keiner kommen, daß ich mich hab' totschießen müssen, weil ein elender Bäckermeister, so ein niederträchtiger, der zufällig stärkere Fäust' hat . . . es ist ja zu dumm, zu
dumm!—Deswegen soll ein Kerl wie ich, so ein junger, fescher
Mensch . . .
   Ja, nachher möchten's gewiß alle sagen: das hätt' er doch nicht
tun müssen, wegen so einer Dummheit; ist doch schad'! . . . Aber
wenn ich jetzt wen immer fragen tät', jeder möcht' mir die gleiche
Antwort geben . . . und ich selber, wenn ich mich frag' . . . das ist
doch zum Teufelholen . . . ganz wehrlos sind wir gegen die Zivili-
sten . . . Da meinen die Leut', wir sind besser dran, weil wir einen
Säbel haben . . . und wenn schon einmal einer von der Waffe Ge-
brauch macht, geht's über uns her, als wenn wir alle die geborenen
Mörder wären . . .
   In der Zeitung möcht's auch steh'n . . . »Selbstmord eines jungen
Offiziers« . . . Wie schreiben sie nur immer? . . . »Die Motive sind
in Dunkel gehüllt« . . . Haha! . . . »An seinem Sarge trauern
. . . «—Aber es ist ja wahr . . . mir ist immer, als wenn ich mir eine
Geschichte erzählen möcht' . . . aber es ist wahr . . . ich muß mich
umbringen, es bleibt mir ja nichts anderes übrig—ich kann's ja
nicht d'rauf ankommen lassen, daß morgen früh der Kopetzky und
der Blany mir ihr Mandat zurückgeben und mir sagen: wir können
dir nicht sekundieren! . . . Ich wär' ja ein Schuft, wenn ich's ihnen
zumuten möcht' . . . So ein Kerl wie ich, der dasteht und sich einen
dummen Buben heißen läßt . . . morgen wissen's ja alle Leut' . . .
das ist zu dumm, daß ich mir einen Moment einbilde, so ein Mensch
erzählt's nicht weiter . . . überall wird er's erzählen . . . seine Frau
weiß's jetzt schon . . . morgen weiß es das ganze Kaffeehaus . . . die
Kellner werd'n's wissen . . . der Herr Schlesinger—die Kassie-
rin——Und selbst, wenn er sich vorgenommen hat, er red't nicht
davon, so sagt er's übermorgen . . . und wenn er's übermorgen
nicht sagt, in einer Woche . . . Und wenn ihn heut' nacht der Schlag
trifft, so weiß ich's . . . ich weiß es . . . und ich bin nicht der Mensch,
der weiter den Rock trägt und den Säbel, wenn ein solcher Schimpf
auf ihm sitzt! . . .
   So, ich muß es tun, und Schluß!—Was ist weiter dabei?—Morgen nachmittag könnt' mich der Doktor mit 'm Säbel erschlagen
. . . so was ist schon einmal dagewesen . . . und der Bauer, der arme
Kerl, der hat eine Gehirnentzündung 'kriegt und war in drei Tagen
hin . . . und der Brenitsch ist vom Pferd gestürzt und hat sich's

Steffi? . . . Steffi . . . God, Steffi . . . she won't even be able
to let anything show, or else "he" will send her packing
. . . Poor girl!—In the regiment—no one would have any
idea why I did it . . . they'd all rack their brains . . . but
why did Gustl kill himself?—No one would guess that I
had to shoot myself because a miserable baker, a low-down
creature like that, who just by chance has stronger fists . . .
it's too bad, too bad! Just for that a fellow like me, such a
young, nice guy . . .

Yes, later on everyone would surely say: he really didn't
have to do that on account of such a trivial incident; it's
really a shame! . . . But if I were to ask anyone at all now,
everyone would give me the same answer . . . and when I
ask myself . . . isn't it the damndest thing? . . . we're completely helpless against civilians . . . People think we're better off because we've got a saber . . . and when an occasion
arises for one of us to use his weapon, we catch hell as if
we were all born murderers . . .

It would be in the paper too . . . "Suicide of a young
officer" . . . How do they always phrase it? . . . "The mo-
tives are veiled in obscurity" . . . Ha, ha! . . . "Mourners
by the grave were . . ."—But it's real . . . I still feel as if I
were telling myself a story . . . but it's real . . . I have to kill
myself, there's no other way out for me—I can't take the
chance that tomorrow morning Kopetzky and Blany will
give me back their commission and say: we can't be your
seconds! . . . I'd really be a blackguard if I expected it of
them . . . A guy like me, who stands there and lets someone call him a fool . . . tomorrow everyone will know about
it . . . it's stupid of me to imagine for a minute that a
person like that isn't going to pass the story along . . . he'll
tell it everywhere . . . his wife knows already . . . tomorrow
the whole coffeehouse will know . . . the waiters will know
. . . Mr. Schlesinger—the lady cashier——And even if he
has made up his mind not to talk about it, he'll come out
with it the day after tomorrow . . . and if he doesn't tell
the day after tomorrow, in a week's time . . . And even if
he were to have a stroke tonight, *I* still know . . . *I* know
. . . and I'm not a man to continue wearing the uniform
and the saber with such a disgrace on his head! . .

There, I must do it, and that's that!—What is there to
it, anyway?—Tomorrow afternoon the Doctor could kill
me with his saber . . . things like that *have* happened . . .
And Bauer, the poor guy, got a brain fever and was gone
in three days . . . and Brenitsch fell off his horse and broke

Genick gebrochen . . . und schließlich und endlich: es gibt nichts anderes—für mich nicht, für mich nicht!—Es gibt ja Leut', die's leichter nähmen . . . Gott, was gibt's für Menschen! . . . Dem Ringeimer hat ein Fleischselcher, wie er ihn mit seiner Frau erwischt hat, eine Ohrfeige gegeben, und er hat quittiert und sitzt irgendwo auf'm Land und hat geheiratet . . . Daß es Weiber gibt, die so einen Menschen heiraten! . . .—Meiner Seel', ich gäb' ihm nicht die Hand, wenn er wieder nach Wien käm' . . .

Also, hast's gehört, Gustl:—aus, aus, abgeschlossen mit dem Leben! Punktum und Streusand d'rauf! . . . So, jetzt weiß ich's, die Geschichte ist ganz einfach . . . So! Ich bin eigentlich ganz ruhig . . . Das hab' ich übrigens immer gewußt: wenn's einmal dazu kommt, werd' ich ruhig sein, ganz ruhig . . . aber daß es so dazu kommt, das hab' ich doch nicht gedacht . . . daß ich mich umbringen muß, weil so ein . . . Vielleicht hab' ich ihn doch nicht recht verstanden . . . am End' hat er ganz was anderes gesagt . . . Ich war ja ganz blöd von der Singerei und der Hitz' . . . vielleicht bin ich verrückt gewesen, und es ist alles gar nicht wahr? . . . Nicht wahr, haha, nicht wahr!—Ich hör's ja noch . . . es klingt mir noch immer im Ohr . . . und ich spür's in den Fingern, wie ich seine Hand vom Säbelgriff hab' wegbringen wollen . . . Ein Kraftmensch ist er, ein Jagendorfer . . . Ich bin doch auch kein Schwächling . . . der Franziski ist der einzige im Regiment, der stärker ist als ich . . .

Die Aspernbrücke . . . Wie weit renn' ich denn noch?—Wenn ich so weiterrenn', bin ich um Mitternacht in Kagran . . .Haha!—Herrgott, froh sind wir gewesen, wie wir im vorigen September dort eingerückt sind. Noch zwei Stunden, und Wien . . . todmüd' war ich, wie wir angekommen sind . . . den ganzen Nachmittag hab' ich geschlafen wie ein Stock, und am Abend waren wir schon beim Ronacher . . . der Kopetzky, der Ladinser und . . . wer war denn nur noch mit uns?—Ja, richtig, der Freiwillige, der uns auf dem Marsch die jüdischen Anekdoten erzählt hat . . . Manchmal sind's ganz nette Burschen, die Einjährigen . . . aber sie sollten alle nur Stellvertreter werden—denn was hat das für einen Sinn? Wir müssen uns jahrelang plagen, und so ein Kerl dient ein Jahr und hat genau dieselbe Distinktion wie wir . . . es ist eine Ungerechtigkeit!—Aber was geht mich denn das alles an?—Was scher' ich mich denn um solche Sachen?—Ein Gemeiner von der Verpflegsbranche ist ja jetzt mehr als ich: ich bin ja überhaupt nicht mehr auf

his neck . . . and finally, once and for all: there's no other way—not for me, not for me!—Of course, there are people who wouldn't take it so hard . . . God, the kinds of people there are! . . . Ringeimer was slapped in the face by a pork butcher who caught him with his wife, and he resigned and is living somewhere in the country and got married . . . To think there are women who would marry such a person! . . . Damn me, I wouldn't shake hands with him if he came back to Vienna . . .

So, you've heard, Gustl:—it's over, over, your life is finished! Totally finished![5]. . . There, now I know, it's quite a simple story . . . There! Now I'm actually quite calm . . . Anyway, I always knew that if it ever came to it, I'd be calm, quite calm . . . but that it would come to it in such a way, *that* I never thought . . . that I'd have to kill myself because such a . . . Maybe I didn't understand him correctly . . . maybe he said something completely different . . . I was all numb from the yowling and the heat . . . maybe I was crazy and none of it is true? . . . Not true, ha, ha, not true!—I can still hear it . . . it's still ringing in my ears . . . and I feel it in my fingers, how I wanted to get his hand off my saber hilt . . . He's a strongman, a Jagendorfer[6] . . . Though I'm no weakling, either . . . Franziski is the only one in the regiment stronger than I am . . .

The Aspern Bridge . . . How far will I keep going?—If I go on like this, I'll be in Kagran around midnight . . . Ha, ha!—Lord God, weren't we happy when we pulled in there last September? Only two more hours, and Vienna . . . I was dead tired when we arrived . . . I slept like a log all afternoon, and in the evening we were already at Ronacher's . . . Kopetzky, Ladinser and . . . who else was with us?—Yes, that's right, the volunteer who told us the Jewish jokes on the march . . . Sometimes they're really fine fellows, the one-year men . . . but they all should become only substitutes—because what's the sense of it? We have to drudge for years, and a guy like that serves for a year and has exactly the same rank as we do . . . it's an injustice!—But what does all that matter to me?—Why should I care about such things? A commissariat private counts more now than I do; I'm no longer in the world at

---

[5] "Punktum und Streusand d'rauf!": literally, "[Write in a] period, and blot it with blotting sand!"

[6] An athlete and wrestler popular in Vienna at the time.

der Welt . . . es ist ja aus mit mir . . . Ehre verloren, alles verloren! . . . Ich hab' ja nichts anderes zu tun, als meinen Revolver zu
laden und . . .

Gustl, Gustl, mir scheint, du glaubst noch immer nicht recht
d'ran? Komm' nur zur Besinnung . . . es gibt nichts anderes . . .
wenn du auch dein Gehirn zermarterst, es gibt nichts anderes!—Jetzt heißt's nur mehr, im letzten Moment sich anständig
benehmen, ein Mann sein, ein Offizier sein, so daß der Oberst
sagt: Er ist ein braver Kerl gewesen, wir werden ihm ein treues
Angedenken bewahren! . . . Wieviel Kompagnien rücken denn aus
beim Leichenbegängnis von einem Leutnant? . . . Das müßt' ich eigentlich wissen . . . Haha! Wenn das ganze Bataillon ausrückt, oder
die ganze Garnison, und sie feuern zwanzig Salven ab, davon wach'
ich doch nimmer auf!

Vor dem Kaffeehaus, da bin ich im vorigen Sommer einmal mit
dem Herrn von Engel gesessen, nach der Armee-Steeple-Chase . . .
Komisch, den Menschen hab' ich seitdem nie wieder geseh'n . . .
Warum hat er denn das linke Aug' verbunden gehabt? Ich hab' ihn
immer d'rum fragen wollen, aber es hätt' sich nicht gehört . . . Da
geh'n zwei Artilleristen . . . die denken gewiß, ich steig' der Person
nach . . . Muß sie mir übrigens anseh'n . . . O schrecklich!—Ich
möcht' nur wissen, wie sich so eine ihr Brot verdient . . . da möcht'
ich doch eher . . . Obzwar, in der Not frißt der Teufel Fliegen . . .
in Przemysl—mir hat's nachher so gegraust, daß ich gemeint hab',
nie wieder rühr' ich ein Frauenzimmer an . . . Das war eine gräßliche Zeit da oben in Galizien . . . eigentlich ein Mordsglück, daß
wir nach Wien gekommen sind. Der Bokorny sitzt noch immer in
Sambor und kann noch zehn Jahr' dort sitzen und alt und grau
werden . . Aber wenn ich dort geblieben wär', wär' mir das nicht
passiert, was mir heut' passiert ist . . . und ich möcht' lieber in Galizien alt und grau werden, als daß . . . als was? Als was?

Ja, was ist denn? Was ist denn?—Bin ich denn wahnsinnig, daß
ich das immer vergeß'?—Ja, meiner Seel', vergessen tu' ich's jeden
Moment . . . ist das schon je erhört worden, daß sich einer in ein
paar Stunden eine Kugel durch'n Kopf jagen muß, und er denkt
an alle möglichen Sachen, die ihn gar nichts mehr angeh'n? Meiner
Seel', mir ist geradeso, als wenn ich einen Rausch hätt'! Haha! Ein
schöner Rausch! Ein Mordsrausch! Ein Selbstmordsrausch!

Ha! Witze mach' ich, das ist sehr gut!—Ja, ganz gut aufgelegt
bin ich—so was muß doch angeboren sein . . . Wahrhaftig, wenn

all . . . I'm over and done with . . . lose honor, lose everything! . . . I have nothing left to do but load my revolver
and . . .

Gustl, Gustl, it seems you still don't seriously believe it?
Come to your senses . . . there's no other way . . . even if
you rack your brains, there's no other way!—Now all that
counts is to behave decently at the end, to be a man, to be
an officer, so that the Colonel will say: He was a brave
fellow, we'll be sure to remember him! . . . Now, how
many companies march out for a lieutenant's funeral? . . .
I really ought to know that . . . Ha, ha! Even if the whole
battalion marches out, or the whole garrison, and they fire
twenty salvos, it'll never wake me up!

In front of the coffeehouse—I was sitting there last
summer with Mr. von Engel, after the army steeplechase
. . . Funny, I've never seen the man since then . . . Why
did he have his left eye bandaged? I kept wanting to ask
him about it, but it wouldn't have been proper . . . There
go two artillerymen . . . they must think I'm following that
tart . . . Anyway, I want to have a look at her . . . Oh,
horrible!—I'd like to know how someone like her makes
a living . . . I'd sooner . . . And yet, any old port in a storm[7]
. . . in Przemysl—I was so disgusted later that I thought
I'd never touch another female . . . That was a ghastly
time up there in Galicia . . . really a great stroke of luck
that we came to Vienna. Bokorny is still in Sambor and
may be there for ten more years and grow old and gray
. . . But if I had stayed there, what happened to me tonight
wouldn't have happened to me . . . and I'd rather grow
old and gray in Galicia than . . . than what? Than what?

Yes, what's going on? What's going on?—Am I crazy
that I keep forgetting?—Yes, damn me, I forget it every
minute . . . has anyone ever heard the like?—that someone has to blow his brains out in a couple of hours and
thinks about all conceivable things that don't concern him
any more! Damn me, I'm acting exactly as if I were drunk!
Ha, ha! Really drunk! Dead drunk! Suicidally drunk![8]

Ha! I'm making jokes, that's just fine!—Yes, I'm in
quite a good mood—something like that surely must be

---

[7] Literally: "When in need, the Devil eats flies."

[8] Untranslatable pun. "Rausch" is a drunken jag; "Mords-" (literally, "murder-") is a slang prefix of intensity (thus: "a colossal jag");
this leads to the joke "Selbstmordsrausch" (literally, "suicide drunk-
en jag").

ich's einem erzählen möcht', er würd' es nicht glauben.—Mir
scheint, wenn ich das Ding bei mir hätt' . . . jetzt würd' ich abdrük-
ken—in einer Sekunde ist alles vorbei . . . Nicht jeder hat's so
gut—andere müssen sich monatelang plagen . . . meine arme Cousin', zwei Jahr' ist sie gelegen, hat sich nicht rühren können, hat die
gräßlichsten Schmerzen g'habt—so ein Jammer! . . . Ist es nicht
besser, wenn man das selber besorgt? Nur Obacht geben heißt's,
gut zielen, daß einem nicht am End' das Malheur passiert, wie dem
Kadett-Stellvertreter im vorigen Jahr . . . Der arme Teufel, gestorben ist er nicht, aber blind ist er geworden . . . Was mit dem nur
geschehen ist? Wo er jetzt lebt?—Schrecklich, so herumlaufen, wie
der—das heißt: herumlaufen kann er nicht, g'führt muß er werden—so ein junger Mensch, kann heut' noch keine Zwanzig sein
. . seine Geliebte hat er besser getroffen . . . gleich war sie tot . . .
   Unglaublich, weswegen sich die Leut' totschießen! Wie kann man
überhaupt nur eifersüchtig sein? . . . Mein Lebtag hab' ich so was
nicht gekannt . . . Die Steffi ist jetzt gemütlich in der Gartenbaugesellschaft; dann geht sie mit »ihm« nach Haus . . . Nichts liegt mir
d'ran, gar nichts! Hübsche Einrichtung hat sie—das kleine Bade-
zimmer mit der roten Latern'.—Wie sie neulich in dem grünseide-
nen Schlafrock hereingekommen ist . . . den grünen Schlafrock
werd' ich auch nimmer seh'n—und die ganze Steffi auch nicht . . .
und die schöne, breite Treppe in der Gußhausstraße werd' ich auch
nimmer hinaufgeh'n . . . Das Fräulein Steffi wird sich weiter amüsie-
ren, als wenn gar nichts gescheh'n wär' . . . nicht einmal erzählen
darf sie's wem, daß ihr lieber Gustl sich umgebracht hat . . . Aber
weinen wirds' schon—ah ja, weinen wirds' . . . Überhaupt, weinen
werden gar viele Leut' . . . Um Gottes willen, die Mama!—Nein,
nein, daran darf ich nicht denken.—Ah, nein, daran darf absolut
nicht gedacht werden . . . An Zuhaus wird nicht gedacht, Gustl,
verstanden?—Nicht mit dem allerleisesten Gedanken . . .
   Das ist nicht schlecht, jetzt bin ich gar im Prater . . . mitten in der
Nacht . . . das hätt' ich mir auch nicht gedacht in der Früh', daß
ich heut' nacht im Prater spazieren geh'n werd' . . . Was sich der
Sicherheitswachmann dort denkt? . . . Na, geh'n wir nur weiter . . .
es ist ganz schön . . . Mit'm Nachtmahlen ist's eh' nichts, mit dem
Kaffeehaus auch nichts; die Luft ist angenehm, und ruhig ist
es . . sehr . . Zwar, ruhig werd' ich's jetzt bald haben, so ruhig, als
ich's mir nur wünschen kann. Haha!—Aber ich bin ja ganz außer
Atem . . . ich bin ja gerannt wie nicht g'scheit . . . langsamer, langsamer, Gustl, versäumst nichts, hast gar nichts mehr zu tun—gar
nichts, aber absolut nichts mehr!—Mir scheint gar, ich frö-

part of your nature . . . Honestly, if I were to tell this to someone, he wouldn't believe it.—I think, if I had the thing with me . . . I'd pull the trigger now—it's all over in a second . . . Not everyone comes off so well—other people have to suffer for months . . . my poor cousin, she was in bed for two years, couldn't move, had the most horrible pains—what a pity! . . . Isn't it better to arrange it by yourself? All that counts is to be careful, to aim well, so no misfortune happens to you, as with that cadet substitute last year . . . Poor devil, he didn't die but went blind . . . I wonder what became of him? Where is he living now? —Terrible, to go around like that—that is: he *can't* go around, he has to be led—such a young man, he can't be twenty yet . . . he took better aim at his sweetheart . . . she was dead on the spot . . .

Unbelievable, the things people shoot themselves over! How can people be jealous, anyhow? . . . I've never had such a feeling in my life . . . Steffi is enjoying herself now at the "Horticultural Society"; then she'll go home with "him" . . . It means nothing to me, nothing! She's got a nicely furnished place—the little bathroom with the red lamp.—The way she came in recently with the green silk robe . . . I'll never see the green robe again, either—nor all of Steffi, either . . . and I'll never again walk up the fine broad stairs on Gusshausstrasse . . . Miss Steffi will go on having good times as if nothing had happened . . . she won't even be able to tell anyone that her dear Gustl killed himself . . . But she *will* cry—oh, yes, she *will* cry . . . All in all, a lot of people will cry . . . For God's sake —Mama!—No, no, I mustn't think of that.—Oh, no, that is definitely not to be thought about . . . No thinking about the family, Gustl, is that understood?—Not the slightest thought . . .

That's not bad, now I'm in the Prater . . . in the middle of the night . . . I wouldn't have imagined this morning that I'd be strolling in the Prater tonight . . . Wonder what that policeman there is thinking? . . . Well, let's keep going . . . it's a lovely night . . . Forget about supper, and about the coffeehouse, too; the air is pleasant and it's quiet . . . very . . . It's true, I'll soon have all the peace and quiet I could ask for. Ha, ha!—But I'm all out of breath . . . I've been walking like a lunatic . . . slower, slower, Gustl, you aren't missing out on anything, you have nothing left to do—nothing, absolutely nothing left!—Is that right, am

stel'?—Es wird halt doch die Aufregung sein . . . dann hab' ich ja
nichts gegessen . . .

Was riecht denn da so eigentümlich? . . . Es kann doch noch
nichts blühen? . . . Was haben wir denn heut'?—Den vierten April
. . . freilich, es hat viel geregnet in den letzten Tagen . . . aber die
Bäume sind beinah' noch ganz kahl . . . und dunkel ist es, hu! Man
könnt' schier Angst kriegen . . . Das ist eigentlich das einzigemal in
meinem Leben, daß ich Furcht gehabt hab', als kleiner Bub, damals
im Wald . . . aber ich war ja gar nicht so klein . . . vierzehn oder
fünfzehn . . . Wie lang' ist das jetzt her?—Neun Jahr' . . . freilich—mit achtzehn war ich Stellvertreter, mit zwanzig Leutnant . . .
und im nächsten Jahr werd' ich . . . Was werd' ich im nächsten Jahr?
Was heißt das überhaupt: nächstes Jahr? Was heißt das: in der
nächsten Woche? Was heißt das: übermorgen? . . . Wie? Zähneklap-
pern? Oho!—Na, lassen wir's nur ein biss'l klappern . . . Herr Leutnant, Sie sind jetzt allein, brauchen niemandem einen Pflanz vorzu-
machen . . . es ist bitter, es ist bitter . . .

Ich will mich auf die Bank setzen . . . Ah!—Wie weit bin ich denn
da?—So eine Dunkelheit! Das da hinter mir, das muß das zweite
Kaffeehaus sein . . bin ich im vorigen Sommer auch einmal gewesen, wie unsere Kapelle konzertiert hat . . . mit'm Kopetzky und
mit'm Rüttner—noch ein paar waren dabei . . .—Ich bin aber müd'
. . . nein, ich bin müd', als wenn ich einen Marsch von zehn Stunden
gemacht hätt' . . . Ja, das wär' sowas, da einschlafen.—Ha! Ein ob-
dachloser Leutnant . . Ja, ich sollt' doch eigentlich nach Haus . . .
was tu' ich denn zu Haus? Aber was tu' ich denn im Prater?—Ah,
mir wär' am liebsten, ich müßt' gar nicht aufsteh'n—da einschlafen
und nimmer aufwachen . . . ja, das wär' halt bequem!—Nein, so
bequem wird's Ihnen nicht gemacht, Herr Leutnant . .

Aber wie und wann?—Jetzt könnt' ich mir doch endlich einmal
die Geschichte ordentlich überlegen . . . überlegt muß ja alles werden . . . so ist es schon einmal im Leben . . . Also überlegen wir . . .
Was denn? . . .—Nein, ist die Luft gut . . . man sollt' öfters bei der
Nacht in' Prater geh'n . . . Ja, das hätt' mir eben früher einfallen
müssen, jetzt ist's aus mit'm Prater, mit der Luft und mit'm Spazie-
rengeh'n . . . Ja, also was ist denn?—Ah, fort mit dem Kappl; mir
scheint, das drückt mir aufs Gehirn . . . ich kann ja gar nicht ordentlich denken . . . Ah . . . so! . . . Also jetzt Verstand zusammenneh-
men, Gustl . . . letzte Verfügungen treffen!

Also morgen früh wird Schluß gemacht . . . morgen früh um
sieben Uhr . . . sieben Uhr ist eine schöne Stund'. Haha!—Also um
acht, wenn die Schul' anfangt, ist alles vorbei . . . der Kopetzky wird

I shivering?—It must be the excitement . . . besides that,
I haven't eaten . . .

What's that unusual smell? . . . Surely, nothing is in blossom . . . What day is today?—April fourth . . . it did rain
a lot the last few days . . . but the trees are still almost
completely bare . . . and it's dark, wow! You could almost
get scared . . . That was really the only time in my life that
I was frightened, as a small boy, in the woods that time
. . . but I wasn't all that small, either . . . fourteen or fifteen
. . . How long ago is that now?—Nine years . . . right—
at eighteen I was a substitute, at twenty a lieutenant . . .
and next year I'll be . . . What will I be next year? What
does that mean, anyway: next year? What does "next
week" mean? What does "the day after tomorrow"
mean? . . . What? Your teeth chattering? Oho!—Well, let
them chatter a little . . . Lieutenant, you're alone now, you
don't need to put on a show for anybody . . . it's bitter, it's
bitter . . .

I'll sit down on this bench . . . Ah!—How far have I
come?—How dark it is! That, behind me there, must be
the "Second Coffeehouse" . . . I was in there once last summer when our band gave a concert . . . with Kopetzky and
with Rüttner—a few more were also there . . .—But I'm
tired . . . no, I'm as tired as if I had put in a ten-hour
march . . . Yes, that would be something, to fall asleep
here.—Ha! A homeless lieutenant . . . Yes, I really should
get back home . . . what will I do at home? But what am I
doing in the Prater?—Ah, what I'd like best is not to have
to get up at all—to fall asleep here and never wake up . . .
yes, that would really be convenient!—No, things aren't
so convenient for you, Lieutenant . . .

But how and when?—Now I could finally think the
matter over properly . . . everything has to be thought
over, you know . . . that's the way life is . . . So, let's think
things over . . . Think what over? . . . No, the air is really
nice . . . I ought to come to the Prater at night more often
. . . Yes, I should have thought of that sooner, now it's all
over with the Prater, with the air and with taking walks
. . . Yes, what's going on? Ah, off with the cap; I feel as if
it's pressing into my brain . . . I can't think straight . . .
Ah . . . there! . . . Now then, pull your thoughts together,
Gustl . . . make your final arrangements!

So, tomorrow morning will be the end . . . tomorrow
morning at seven o'clock . . . seven o'clock is a nice hour.
Ha, ha!—So, at eight, when classes begin, it'll be all over

aber keine Schul' halten können, weil er zu sehr erschüttert sein
wird . . . Aber vielleicht weiß er's noch gar nicht . . . man braucht
ja nichts zu hören . . . Den Max Lippay haben sie auch erst am
Nachmittag gefunden, und in der Früh' hat er sich erschossen, und
kein Mensch hat was davon gehört . . . Aber was geht mich das an,
ob der Kopetzky Schul' halten wird oder nicht? . . . Ha!—Also um
sieben Uhr!—Ja . . . na, was denn noch? . . . Weiter ist ja nichts zu
überlegen. Im Zimmer schieß' ich mich tot, und dann is basta! Mon-
tag ist die Leich' . . . Einen kenn' ich, der wird eine Freud' haben:
das ist der Doktor . . . Duell kann nicht stattfinden wegen Selbstmord des einen Kombattanten . . .
     Was sie bei Mannheimers sagen werden?—Na, er wird sich nicht
viel d'raus machen . . . aber die Frau, die hübsche, blonde . . . mit
der war was zu machen . . . O ja, mir scheint, bei der hätt' ich
Chance gehabt, wenn ich mich nur ein bissl zusammengenommen
hätt' . . . ja, das wär' doch was anders gewesen, als die Steffi, dieses
Mensch . . . Aber faul darf man halt nicht sein . . . da heißt's: Cour
machen, Blumen schicken, vernünftig reden . . . das geht nicht so,
daß man sagt: Komm' morgen nachmittag zu mir in die Kasern'! . . .
Ja, so eine anständige Frau, das wär' halt was g'wesen . . . Die Frau
von meinem Hauptmann in Przemysl, das war ja doch keine anständige Frau . . . ich könnt' schwören: der Libitzky und der Wermutek
und der schäbige Stellvertreter, der hat sie auch g'habt . . . Aber
die Frau Mannheimer . . . ja, das wär' was anders, das wär' doch
auch ein Umgang gewesen, das hätt' einen beinah' zu einem andern
Menschen gemacht—da hätt' man doch noch einen andern Schliff
gekriegt—da hätt' man einen Respekt vor sich selber haben dürfen.——Aber ewig diese Menscher . . . und so jung hab' ich
ang'fangen—ein Bub war ich ja noch, wie ich damals den ersten
Urlaub gehabt hab' und in Graz bei den Eltern zu Haus war . . . der
Riedl war auch dabei—eine Böhmin ist es gewesen . . . die muß
doppelt so alt gewesen sein wie ich—in der Früh bin ich erst nach
Haus gekommen . . . Wie mich der Vater ang'schaut hat . . . und
die Klara . . . Vor der Klara hab' ich mich am meisten g'schämt . . .
Damals war sie verlobt . . . warum ist denn nichts d'raus geworden?
Ich hab' mich eigentlich nicht viel d'rum gekümmert . . . Armes
Hascherl, hat auch nie Glück gehabt—und jetzt verliert sie noch
den einzigen Bruder . . .
     Ja, wirst mich nimmer seh'n, Klara—aus! Was, das hast du dir
nicht gedacht, Schwesterl, wie du mich am Neujahrstag zur Bahn
begleitet hast, daß du mich nie wieder seh'n wirst?—Und die Mama
. . . Herrgott, die Mama . . . nein, ich darf daran nicht denken . . .
wenn ich daran denk', bin ich imstand', eine Gemeinheit zu bege-
hen . . . Ah . . . wenn ich zuerst noch nach Haus fahren möcht' . . .

. . . But Kopetzky won't be able to give classes, because he'll be too broken up . . . But maybe he won't know yet . . . there won't be any need for them to have heard . . . They didn't find Max Lippay till the afternoon, and he shot himself in the morning, and no one heard anything about it . . . But what does it matter to me whether Kopetzky gives classes or not? . . . Ha!—At seven o'clock, then!—Yes . . . well, what else? . . . There's nothing else to think over. I'll shoot myself in my room and that's that! Funeral on Monday . . . I know one person who'll be happy: the Doctor . . . Duel cannot take place owing to suicide of one party . . .

What will they say at the Mannheimers'?—Well, *he* won't be very upset by it . . . but the wife, the pretty blonde . . . I had some hopes for her . . . Oh, yes, I think I would have been lucky with her if I had only concentrated my efforts a bit . . . yes, that would have been a little different than that slut Steffi . . . But you just can't be lazy . . . you've not to flirt, send flowers, talk sensibly . . . you can't come out and say: Come see me in the barracks tomorrow afternoon! . . . Yes, a respectable lady like her, that would have been something . . . My captain's wife in Przemysl, she was no respectable lady . . . I could swear: Libitzky and Wermutek and that shabby substitute, he had her, too . . . But Mrs. Mannheimer . . . yes, that would have been different, that would also have moved me into good society, that could almost have made me a new man—I would have gotten a new polish—I would have gained some respect for myself.——But always these tarts . . . and I started so young—I was still a boy when I had my first leave that time and was home in Graz with my parents . . . Riedl was there, too—it was a Bohemian woman . . . she must have been twice my age—I didn't get home until morning . . . The way my father looked at me . . . and Klara . . . I was ashamed in front of Klara most of all . . . She was engaged at the time . . . why did nothing come of it? To tell the truth, I didn't care very much . . . Poor little thing, she never had any luck—and now, on top of that, she's losing her only brother . . .

Yes, you'll never see me again, Klara—finished! You never imagined, did you, sister, when you accompanied me to the station on New Year's Day, that you would never see me again?—And Mama . . . Lord God, Mama . . . no, I mustn't think about that . . . if I think about it, I'm capable of acting ignobly . . . Ah . . . if I could only go home

sagen, es ist ein Urlaub auf einen Tag . . . noch einmal den Papa,
die Mama, die Klara seh'n, bevor ich einen Schluß mach' . . . Ja, mit
dem ersten Zug um sieben kann ich nach Graz fahren, um eins bin
ich dort . . . Grüß dich Gott, Mama . . . Servus, Klara! Na, wie geht's
euch denn? . . . Nein, das ist eine Überraschung! . . . Aber sie möchten was merken . . . wenn niemand anders . . . die Klara . . . die
Klara gewiß . . . Die Klara ist ein so gescheites Mädel . . .

Wie lieb sie mir neulich geschrieben hat, und ich bin ihr noch
immer die Antwort schuldig—und die guten Ratschläge, die sie
mir immer gibt . . . ein so seelengutes Geschöpf . . . Ob nicht alles
ganz anders geworden wär', wenn ich zu Haus geblieben wär'? Ich
hätt' Ökonomie studiert, wär' zum Onkel gegangen . . . sie haben's
ja alle wollen, wie ich noch ein Bub war . . . Jetzt wär' ich am End'
schon verheiratet, ein liebes, gutes Mädel . . . vielleicht die Anna,
die hat mich so gern gehabt . . . auch jetzt hab' ich's noch gemerkt,
wie ich das letztemal zu Haus war, obzwar sie schon einen Mann
hat und zwei Kinder . . . ich hab's g'seh'n, wie sie mich ang'schaut
hat . . . Und noch immer sagt sie mir »Gustl« wie früher . . . Der
wird's ordentlich in die Glieder fahren, wenn sie erfährt, was es mit
mir für ein End' genommen hat—aber ihr Mann wird sagen: Das
hab' ich vorausgesehen—so ein Lump!

Alle werden meinen, es ist, weil ich Schulden gehabt hab' . . . und
es ist doch gar nicht wahr, es ist doch alles gezahlt . . . nur die letzten
hundertsechzig Gulden—na, und die sind morgen da . . . Ja, dafür
muß ich auch noch sorgen, daß der Ballert die hundertsechzig Gulden kriegt . . . das muß ich niederschreiben, bevor ich mich erschieß' . . . Es ist schrecklich, es ist schrecklich! . . . Wenn ich lieber
auf und davon fahren möcht'—nach Amerika, wo mich niemand
kennt . . . In Amerika weiß kein Mensch davon, was hier heut'
abend gescheh'n ist . . . da kümmert sich kein Mensch d'rum . . .
Neulich ist in der Zeitung gestanden von einem Grafen Runge, der
hat fortmüssen wegen einer schmutzigen Geschichte, und jetzt hat
er drüben ein Hotel und pfeift auf den ganzen Schwindel . . . Und
in ein paar Jahren könnt' man ja wieder zurück . . . nicht nach Wien
natürlich . . . auch nicht nach Graz . . . aber aufs Gut könnt' ich
. . . und der Mama und dem Papa und der Klara möcht's doch
tausendmal lieber sein, wenn ich nur lebendig blieb' . . .

Und was geh'n mich denn die andern Leut' an? Wer meint's denn
sonst gut mit mir?—Außer'm Kopetzky könnt' ich allen gestohlen
werden . . . der Kopetzky ist doch der einzige . . . Und grad der hat
mir heut' das Billett geben müssen . . . und das Billett ist an allem
schuld . . . ohne das Billett wär' ich nicht ins Konzert gegangen,
und alles das wär' nicht passiert . . . Was ist denn nur passiert? . . .
Es ist grad, als wenn hundert Jahr' seitdem vergangen wären, und

first . . . tell them it's a one-day leave . . . see Papa, Mama, Klara again before I sign off . . . Yes, I could take the first train to Graz at seven, I'd be there at one . . . Hello, Mama . . . Hi, Klara! Well, how are things? . . . No, what a surprise! . . . But they might notice something . . . even if no one else does . . . Klara . . . Klara, certainly . . .Klara is such a clever girl . . .

What a nice letter she sent me lately, and I still owe her an answer—and the good advice she always gives me . . . such a truly good creature . . . I wonder whether everything would have been different if I had stayed home? I would have studied agriculture, would have gone to Uncle's . . . that's what they all wanted when I was still a boy . . . Maybe I'd already be married now to some good, sweet girl . . . maybe to Anna, who liked me so much . . . I still noticed it the last time I was home, even though she already has a husband and two children . . . I saw the way she looked at me . . . And she still calls me "Gustl" the way she used to . . . *She'll* get a real shock when she finds out how I came to die—but her husband will say: I always knew it—a bum like that!

Everyone will think it's because I had debts . . . and that's just not true, it's all paid up . . . only the last hundred sixty gulden—yes, and they'll be there tomorrow . . . Yes, I must still arrange for Ballert to get the hundred sixty gulden . . . I must write that down before I shoot myself . . . It's awful, it's awful! . . . If I were to run away instead—to America, where no one knows me . . . In America not a soul knows what happened here tonight . . . not a soul cares about it there . . . Lately there was a bit in the paper about a Count Runge, who had to decamp on account of some unsavory affair, and now he has a hotel there and doesn't give a damn about the whole business . . . And in a few years I could come back . . . not to Vienna, of course . . . and not to Graz . . . but I could go to the farm . . . and Mama and Papa and Klara would prefer it a thousand times if I just stayed alive . . .

And what do the other people matter to me? Who else cares about my welfare?—Outside of Kopetzky, no one would mind if I disappeared . . . Kopetzky is the only one . . . And *he* was the one who had to go and give me the ticket today . . . and the ticket is to blame for everything . . . without the ticket I wouldn't have gone to the concert, and none of this would have happened . . . But what did happen? . . . It's just as if a hundred years had gone by

es kann noch keine zwei Stunden sein ... Vor zwei Stunden hat
mir einer »dummer Bub« gesagt und hat meinen Säbel zerbrechen
wollen ... Herrgott, ich fang' noch zu schreien an mitten in der
Nacht!

Warum ist denn das alles gescheh'n? Hätt' ich nicht länger warten
können, bis's ganz leer wird in der Garderobe? Und warum hab'
ich ihm denn nur gesagt: »Halten Sie's Maul!«? Wie ist mir denn
das nur ausgerutscht? Ich bin doch sonst ein höflicher Mensch ...
nicht einmal mit meinem Burschen bin ich sonst so grob ... aber
natürlich, nervos bin ich gewesen—alle die Sachen, die da zusam-
mengekommen sind ... das Pech im Spiel und die ewige Absagerei
von der Steffi—und das Duell morgen nachmittag—und zu wenig
schlafen tu' ich in der letzten Zeit—und die Rackerei in der Kasern'—das halt't man auf die Dauer nicht aus! ... Ja, über kurz
oder lang wär' ich krank geworden—hätt' um einen Urlaub ein-
kommen müssen ... Jetzt ist es nicht mehr notwendig—jetzt
kommt ein langer Urlaub—mit Karenz der Gebühren—haha! ...

Wie lang werd' ich denn da noch sitzen bleiben? Es muß Mitternacht vorbei sein ... hab' ich's nicht früher schlagen hören?—Was
ist denn das ... ein Wagen fährt da? Um die Zeit? Gummiradl-
ler—kann mir schon denken ... Die haben's besser wie ich—vielleicht ist es der Ballert mit der Bertha ... Warum soll's grad der
Ballert sein?—Fahr' nur zu!—Ein hübsches Zeug'l hat Seine Hoheit in Przemysl gehabt ... mit dem ist er immer in die Stadt hinun-
terg'fahren zu der Rosenberg ... Sehr leutselig war Seine Hoheit—ein echter Kamerad, mit allen auf du und du ... War doch
eine schöne Zeit ... obzwar ... die Gegend war trostlos und im
Sommer zum Verschmachten ... an einem Nachmittag sind einmal
drei vom Sonnenstich getroffen worden ... auch der Korporal von
meinem Zug—ein so verwendbarer Mensch ... Nachmittag haben
wir uns nackt aufs Bett hingelegt.—Einmal ist plötzlich der Wiesner zu mir hereingekommen; ich muß grad geträumt haben und
steh' auf und zieh' den Säbel, der neben mir liegt ... muß gut
ausg'schaut haben ... der Wiesner hat sich halbtot gelacht—der ist
jetzt schon Rittmeister ...—Schad', daß ich nicht zur Kavallerie
gegangen bin ... aber das hat der Alte nicht wollen—wär' ein zu
teurer Spaß gewesen—jetzt ist es ja doch alles eins ... Warum
denn?—Ja, ich weiß schon: sterben muß ich, darum ist es alles
eins—sterben muß ich ...

Also wie?—Schau, Gustl, du bist doch extra da herunter in den
Prater gegangen, mitten in der Nacht, wo dich keine Menschen-
seele stört—jetzt kannst du dir alles ruhig überlegen ... Das ist ja
lauter Unsinn mit Amerika und quittieren, und du bist ja viel zu
dumm, um was anderes anzufangen—und wenn du hundert Jahr'

since then, and it can't be two hours yet . . . Two hours
ago somebody called me a fool and wanted to break my
saber . . . Lord God, on top of everything, I'm starting to
shout in the middle of the night!

Why did this all happen? Couldn't I have waited longer,
until the cloakroom was empty? And why did I tell him to
shut up? How did that slip out of me? After all, I'm usually
a courteous person . . . usually I'm not that rude even to
my orderly . . . but, of course, I was nervous—all those
things combined . . . bad luck at cards and Steffi constantly
standing me up—and the duel tomorrow afternoon
—and I haven't been getting enough sleep lately—
and the drudgery in the barracks—you can't put up with
that forever! . . . Yes, sooner or later I would have gotten
sick—I would have had to apply for a leave . . . Now
it's no longer necessary—a long leave is coming now—
without pay—ha, ha! . . .

How long will I keep sitting here? It must be past midnight . . . didn't I hear it striking before?—What's this . . .
a carriage driving there? At this hour? One with rubber
wheels—I can imagine . . . They're better off than I
am—maybe it's Ballert with his Bertha . . . Why should it
be Ballert of all people?—Drive on!—His Highness had
a nice carriage in Przemysl . . . he always traveled down
into town in it to visit that Rosenberg woman . . . His Highness was very sociable—a real buddy, on close terms with
everybody . . . That *was* a fine time . . . even though . . .
the district was cheerless and you could pass out there in
the summertime . . . once three men got sunstroke on one
afternoon . . . also the corporal of my platoon—such a
useful man . . . Afternoons we would lie down on the bed
naked.—Once Wiesner came into my room suddenly; I
must have been dreaming, and I stood up and drew the
saber, which was lying next to me . . . I must have looked
a sight . . . Wiesner laughed himself half to death—he's a
cavalry captain by now . . . —Too bad I didn't go into the
cavalry . . . but the old man wasn't willing—it would have
been too expensive—but now it's all one . . . Why?—Oh,
yes, now I know: I must die, that's why it's all one—I must
die . . .

So, what then?—Look, Gustl, after all you came down
here to the Prater on purpose, in the middle of the night,
with not a soul to disturb you—now you can think it all
over calmly . . . That's pure nonsense about America and
resigning, and you're much too stupid to make a new

alt wirst, und du denkst d'ran, daß dir einer hat den Säbel zerbrechen wollen und dich einen dummen Buben g'heißen, und du bist
dag'standen und hast nichts tun können—nein, zu überlegen ist
da gar nichts—gescheh'n ist gescheh'n—auch das mit der Mama
und mit der Klara ist ein Unsinn—die werden's schon verschmer-
zen—man verschmerzt alles ... Wie hat die Mama gejammert, wie
ihr Bruder gestorben ist—und nach vier Wochen hat sie kaum
mehr d'ran gedacht ... auf den Friedhof ist sie hinausgefahren
... zuerst alle Wochen, dann alle Monat'—und jetzt nur mehr am
Todestag.——Morgen ist mein Todestag—fünfter April.——Ob
sie mich nach Graz überführen? Haha! Da werden die Würmer in
Graz eine Freud' haben!—Aber das geht mich nichts an—darüber
sollen sich die andern den Kopf zerbrechen ...
   Also, was geht mich denn eigentlich an? ... Ja, die hundertsechzig Gulden für den Ballert—das ist alles—weiter brauch' ich keine
Verfügungen zu treffen.—Briefe schreiben? Wozu denn? An wen
denn? ... Abschied nehmen?—Ja, zum Teufel hinein, das ist doch
deutlich genug, wenn man sich totschießt!—Dann merken's die
andern schon, daß man Abschied genommen hat ... Wenn die
Leut' wüßten, wie egal mir die ganze Geschichte ist, möchten sie
mich gar nicht bedauern—ist eh' nicht schad' um mich ... Und
was hab' ich denn vom ganzen Leben gehabt?—Etwas hätt' ich gern
noch mitgemacht: einen Krieg—aber da hätt ich lang' warten können ... Und alles übrige kenn' ich ... Ob so ein Mensch Steffi
oder Kunigunde heißt, bleibt sich gleich.——Und die schönsten
Operetten kenn' ich auch—und im ›Lohengrin‹ bin ich zwölfmal
d'rin gewesen—und heut' abend war ich sogar bei einem Oratorium—und ein Bäckermeister hat mich einen dummen Buben geheißen—meiner Seel', es ist grad' genug!—Und ich bin gar nimmer neugierig ...—Also geh'n wir nach Haus, langsam, ganz
langsam ... Eile hab' ich ja wirklich keine.—Noch ein paar Minuten ausruhen da im Prater, auf einer Bank—obdachlos.—Ins Bett
leg' ich mich ja doch nimmer—hab' ja genug Zeit zum Ausschla-
fen.——Ah, die Luft!—Die wird mir abgeh'n ...

Was ist denn?—He, Johann, bringen S' mir ein Glas frisches Wasser
... Was ist? ... Wo ... Ja, träum' ich denn? ... Mein Schädel ...
o, Donnerwetter ... Fischamend ... Ich bring' die Augen nicht
auf!—Ich bin ja angezogen!—Wo sitz' ich denn?—Heiliger Himmel, eingeschlafen bin ich! Wie hab' ich denn nur schlafen können;
es dämmert ja schon!—Wie lang' hab' ich denn geschlafen?—Muß
auf die Uhr schau'n ... Ich seh' nichts? ... Wo sind denn meine

start—and if you live to be a hundred and think about
the time when someone wanted to break your saber and
called you a fool, and you stood there unable to do anything—no, there's nothing to think over—what's done is
done—that stuff, too, about Mama and Klara is nonsense—they'll get over it—people get over everything . . .
The way Mama mourned when her brother died—and
four weeks later she hardly thought about it any more . . .
she rode out to the cemetery . . . at first, every week, then
every month—and now only on the anniversary of his
death.——Tomorrow is the date of *my* death—April
fifth.——Will they ship me to Graz? Ha, ha! Then
the worms in Graz will have a treat!—But that doesn't
concern me—other people can rack their brains about
that . . .

So, what *does* really concern me? . . . Yes, the hundred
sixty gulden for Ballert—that's all—I don't need to make
any further dispositions.—Write letters? What for? To
whom? . . . Say goodbye?—Yes, damn it, that's surely
clear enough when you shoot yourself!—Then the others
can't fail to notice that you've said goodbye . . . If people
knew how little I care about the whole matter, they
wouldn't feel sorry for me—I'm not at all to be pitied . . .
And what did I get out of my whole life?—I would gladly
still have done certain things: fight in a war—but I might
have waited a long time . . . And I know all the rest . . .
Whether such and such a tart is named Steffi or Kunigunde is all the same.——And I also know the prettiest
operettas—and I've gone to see *Lohengrin* a dozen
times—and tonight I was even at an oratorio—and a
baker called me a fool—damn me, that's plenty!—And
I'm not inquisitive . . . —So let's go home, slowly, very
slowly . . . I have no reason at all to rush.—Rest here in the
Prater another few minutes, on a bench—homeless.—I
definitely won't go to bed—I have enough time for getting a good sleep.——Ah, the air!—That, I'm going to
miss . . .

What's going on?—Hey, Johann, bring me a glass of
cold water . . . What's this? . . . Where . . . Yes, am I
dreaming? . . . my head . . . damn . . . Fischamend[8A] . . . I
can't open my eyes!—But I'm dressed!—Where am I sitting?—Holy God, I dozed off! How was I able to sleep?
It's dawn already!—How long did I sleep?—I must look
at my watch . . . I don't see anything? . . . Where are my

[8A] A village near Vienna; pun with "Fisch am End"—"a fish at the
end of its rope."

Zündhölzeln? . . . Na, brennt eins an? . . . Drei . . . und ich soll mich um vier duellieren—nein, nicht duellieren—totschießen soll ich mich!—Es ist gar nichts mit dem Duell; ich muß mich totschießen, weil ein Bäckermeister mich einen dummen Buben genannt hat . . . Ja, ist es denn wirklich g'scheh'n?—Mir ist im Kopf so merkwürdig . . . wie in einem Schraubstock ist mein Hals—ich kann mich gar nicht rühren—das rechte Bein ist eingeschlafen. Aufsteh'n! Aufsteh'n! . . . Ah, so ist es besser!—Es wird schon lichter . . . Und die Luft . . . ganz wie damals in der Früh', wie ich auf Vorposten war und im Wald kampiert hab' . . . Das war ein anderes Aufwachen—da war ein anderer Tag vor mir . . Mir scheint, ich glaub's noch nicht recht.—Da liegt die Straße, grau, leer—ich bin jetzt sicher der einzige Mensch im Prater.—Um vier Uhr früh war ich schon einmal herunten, mit'm Pausinger—geritten sind wir—ich auf dem Pferd vom Hauptmann Mirovic und der Pausinger auf seinem eigenen Krampen—das war im Mai, im vorigen Jahr—da hat schon alles geblüht—alles war grün. Jetzt ist's noch kahl—aber der Frühling kommt bald—in ein paar Tagen ist er schon da.—Maiglöckerln, Veigerln—schad', daß ich nichts mehr davon haben werd'—jeder Schubiak hat was davon, und ich muß sterben! Es ist ein Elend! Und die andern werden im Weingartl sitzen beim Nachtmahl, als wenn gar nichts g'wesen wär'—so wie wir alle im Weingartl g'sessen sind, noch am Abend nach dem Tag, wo sie den Lippay hinausgetragen haben . . . Und der Lippay war so beliebt . . . sie haben ihn lieber g'habt, als mich, beim Regiment—warum sollen sie denn nicht im Weingartl sitzen, wenn ich abkratz'?

Ganz warm ist es—viel wärmer als gestern—und so ein Duft—es muß doch schon blühen . . . Ob die Steffi mir Blumen bringen wird?—Aber fallt ihr ja gar nicht ein! Die wird grad hinausfahren . . . Ja, wenn's noch die Adel' wär' . . Nein, die Adel'! Mir scheint, seit zwei Jahren hab' ich an die nicht mehr gedacht . . . Was die für G'schichten gemacht hat, wie's aus war . . . mein Lebtag hab' ich kein Frauenzimmer so weinen geseh'n . . . Das war doch eigentlich das Hübscheste, was ich erlebt hab' . . . So bescheiden, so anspruchslos, wie die war—die hat mich gern gehabt, da könnt' ich d'rauf schwören.—War doch was ganz anderes, als die Steffi . . . Ich möcht' nur wissen, warum ich die aufgegeben hab' . . . so eine Eselei! Zu fad ist es mir geworden, ja, das war das Ganze . . . So jeden Abend mit ein und derselben ausgeh'n . . . Dann hab' ich eine Angst g'habt, daß ich überhaupt nimmer loskomm'—eine solche Raunzen——Na, Gustl, hätt'st schon noch warten können—war doch die einzige, die dich gern gehabt hat . . . Was sie jetzt macht? Na,

matches? . . . Well, is one going to light? . . . Three . . . and
I'm supposed to fight a duel at four—no, not a duel—I'm
supposed to shoot myself!—The duel is nothing any
more; I must shoot myself because a baker called me a
fool . . . Yes, did that really happen?—My head feels so
peculiar . . . my neck seems to be in a vise—I can't move
at all—my right leg has gone to sleep.

Get up! Get up! . . . Ah, that's better!—It's getting
lighter now . . . and the air . . . just like that morning when
I was on outpost duty and camped in the woods . . . that
was a different awakening—I had a different day before
me then . . . I think I still don't completely believe
it.—There is the street, gray, empty—I'm surely the only
human being in the Prater now.—I was down here once
at four in the morning, with Pausinger—we were riding—I was on Captain Mirovic's horse and Pausinger on
his own nag—that was in May, last year—everything was
already in blossom—everything was green. Now it's still
bare—but the spring is coming soon—in a few days it'll
be here.—Lilies of the valley, violets—too bad I'll get
nothing out of it—every rotten fellow will get something
out of it, and I have to die! That's miserable! And the
others will sit at supper in the wine garden as if nothing
had happened—the way we all sat in the wine garden on
the very evening of the day they carried out Lippay . . .
And Lippay was so popular . . . they liked him better than
me in the regiment—why shouldn't they sit in the wine
garden when I snuff it?

It's good and warm—much warmer than yesterday—and so fragrant—there must be some blossoms,
after all . . . Will Steffi bring me flowers?—It will never
occur to her! She'll just take a ride . . . Yes, if it were still
Adele . . . No, Adele! I believe I haven't thought about
her for two years . . . What a fuss she kicked up when it
was over . . . in my whole life I've never seen a broad cry
like that . . . That was really the nicest moment I ever lived
through . . . So modest, so undemanding, as she was—she
loved me, I could swear.—She was altogether different
than Steffi . . . I'd like to know why I gave her up . . . what
a stupid thing to do! It got too monotonous for me, yes,
that was the whole thing . . . To go out with one and the
same girl every night . . . Besides, I was afraid that I'd
never get rid of her—such a crybaby——Well, Gustl, you
could have waited a little longer—she was the only one
who loved you . . . What is she doing now? Well, what

was wird's machen?—Jetzt wird's halt einen andern haben . . . Freilich, das mit der Steffi ist bequemer—wenn man nur gelegentlich engagiert ist und ein anderer hat die ganzen Unannehmlichkeiten, und ich hab' nur das Vergnügen . . . Ja, da kann man auch nicht verlangen, daß sie auf den Friedhof hinauskommt . . Wer ging' denn überhaupt mit, wenn er nicht müßt'!—Vielleicht der Kopetzky, und dann wär' Rest!—Ist doch traurig, so gar niemanden zu haben . . .

Aber so ein Unsinn! Der Papa und die Mama und die Klara . . . Ja, ich bin halt der Sohn, der Bruder . . . aber was ist denn weiter zwischen uns? Gern haben sie mich ja—aber was wissen sie denn von mir?—Daß ich meinen Dienst mach', daß ich Karten spiel' und daß ich mit Menschern herumlauf' . . . aber sonst?—Daß mich manchmal selber vor mir graust, das hab' ich ihnen ja doch nicht geschrieben—na, mir scheint, ich hab's auch selber gar nicht recht gewußt.—Ah was, kommst du jetzt mit solchen Sachen, Gustl? Fehlt nur noch, daß du zum Weinen anfangst . . . pfui Teufel!—Ordentlich Schritt . . . so! Ob man zu einem Rendezvous geht oder auf Posten oder in die Schlacht . . . wer hat das nur gesagt? . . . Ah ja, der Major Lederer, in der Kantin', wie man von dem Wingleder erzählt hat, der so blaß geworden ist vor seinem ersten Duell—und gespieben hat . . . Ja: ob man zu einem Rendezvous geht oder in den sicher'n Tod, am Gang und am G'sicht laßt sich das der richtige Offizier nicht anerkennen!—Also Gustl—der Major Lederer hat's g'sagt! Ha!—

Immer lichter . . . man könnt' schon lesen. . . . Was pfeift denn da? . . . . Ah, drüben ist der Nordbahnhof. . . . Die Tegetthoffsäule . . . so lang' hat sie noch nie ausg'schaut . . . Da drüben stehen Wagen . . . Aber nichts als Straßenkehrer auf der Straße . . . meine letzten Straßenkehrer—ha! Ich muß immer lachen, wenn ich d'ran denk' . . . das versteh' ich gar nicht . . . Ob das bei allen Leuten so ist, wenn sie's einmal ganz sicher wissen? Halb vier auf der Nordbahnuhr . . . jetzt ist nur die Frage, ob ich mich um sieben nach Bahnzeit oder nach Wiener Zeit erschieß? . . . Sieben . . . ja, warum grad' sieben? . . . Als wenn's gar nicht anders sein könnt' . . . Hunger hab' ich—meiner Seel', ich hab' Hunger—kein Wunder . . . seit wann hab' ich denn nichts gegessen? . . . Seit—seit gestern sechs Uhr abends im Kaffeehaus . . . ja! Wie mir der Kopetzky das Billett gegeben hat—eine Melange und zwei Kipfel.

Was der Bäckermeister sagen wird, wenn er's erfahrt? . . . Der verfluchte Hund!—Ah, der wird wissen, warum—dem wird der Knopf aufgeh'n—der wird draufkommen, was es heißt: Offizier!—So ein Kerl kann sich auf offener Straße prügeln lassen, und es hat keine Folgen, und unsereiner wird unter vier Augen

could she be doing?—She must have another man now . . . Really, my arrangement with Steffi is more convenient—if you're tied up only once in a while and someone else has all the unpleasantness and I have only the pleasure . . . Yes, you can't really expect her to come out to the cemetery . . . Anyway, who'd go along if he didn't have to!—Maybe Kopetzky, and that would be all!—-It's sad, after all, not to have anybody . . .

But what nonsense! Papa and Mama and Klara . . . Yes, after all I'm the son, the brother . . . but what more is there between us? Sure, they like me—but what do they know about me?—That I fulfill my military obligations, that I play cards and that I run around with sluts . . . but otherwise?—I've never written them that sometimes I'm disgusted with myself—in fact, I believe I didn't rightly know it myself.—Come now, are you bringing up things like that now, Gustl? All you need now is to start crying . . . Ugh!—Keep in step . . . there! Whether you're going to a rendezvous or on sentry duty or into battle . . . who said that, now? . . . Oh, yes, Major Lederer, in the canteen, when they were talking about Wingleder, who got so pale before his first duel—and threw up . . . Yes: whether you're going to a rendezvous or to certain death, a real officer doesn't let it show in his gait or in his face!—So, Gustl—Major Lederer said so! Ha!—

Lighter all the time . . . by now you could read . . . What's that whistle there? . . . Oh, that's the North Station over there . . . The Tegetthoff Column . . . it never looked so high before . . . There are carriages standing over there . . . But only street cleaners on the street . . . my last street cleaners—ha! I have to laugh when I think of it . . . I don't understand it at all . . . Does this happen to everyone when they finally know for sure? Half-past three by the North Station clock . . . the only question now is, should I shoot myself at seven railroad time or Vienna time? . . . Seven . . . yes, why at seven in particular? . . . As if it couldn't be any other time. . . I'm hungry—damn it, I'm hungry—no wonder . . . how long is it since I ate? . . . Since—since six last evening in the coffeehouse . . . yes! When Kopetzky gave me the ticket—a café au lait and two croissants.

What will the baker say when he hears? . . . The dirty dog!—Oh, *he'll* know why—he'll see the light—he'll find out what it means to be an officer!—A guy like that can let himself be thrashed on the public street and there are no consequences, and one of us is insulted privately and

insultiert und ist ein toter Mann . . . Wenn sich so ein Fallot wenigstens schlagen möcht'—aber nein, da wär' er ja vorsichtiger, da möcht' er sowas nicht riskieren . . . Und der Kerl lebt weiter, ruhig weiter, während ich—krepieren muß!—Der hat mich doch umgebracht . . . Ja, Gustl, merkst d' was?—Der ist es, der dich umbringt! Aber so glatt soll's ihm doch nicht ausgeh'n!—Nein, nein, nein! Ich werd' dem Kopetzky einen Brief schreiben, wo alles drinsteht, die ganze G'schicht' schreib' ich auf . . . oder noch besser: ich schreib's dem Obersten, ich mach' eine Meldung ans Regimentskommando . . . ganz wie eine dienstliche Meldung . . . Ja, wart', du glaubst, daß sowas geheim bleiben kann?—Du irrst dich—aufgeschrieben wird's zum ewigen Gedächtnis, und dann möcht' ich sehen, ob du dich noch ins Kaffeehaus traust!—Ha!—»Das möcht' ich sehen« ist gut! . . . Ich möcht' noch manches gern seh'n, wird nur leider nicht möglich sein—aus is!—

Jetzt kommt der Johann in mein Zimmer, jetzt merkt er, daß der Herr Leutnant nicht zu Haus geschlafen hat.—Na, alles mögliche wird er sich denken; aber daß der Herr Leutnant im Prater übernachtet hat, das, meiner Seel', das nicht . . . Ah, die Vierundvierziger! Zur Schießstätte marschieren s'—lassen wir sie vorübergeh'n . . . so stellen wir uns da her . . .—Da oben wird ein Fenster aufgemacht—hübsche Person—na, ich möcht' mir wenigstens ein Tüchel umnehmen, wenn ich zum Fenster geh' . . . Vorigen Sonntag war's zum letztenmal . . . Daß grad' die Steffi die letzte sein wird, hab' ich mir nicht träumen lassen.—Ach Gott, das ist doch das einzige reelle Vergnügen . . . Na ja, der Herr Oberst wird in zwei Stunden nobel nachreiten . . . die Herren haben's gut—ja, ja, rechts g'schaut!—Ist schon gut . . . Wenn ihr wüßtet, wie ich auf euch pfeif'!

Ah, das ist nicht schlecht: der Katzer . . . seit wann ist denn der zu den Vierundvierzigern übersetzt?—Servus, servus!—Was der für ein G'sicht macht? . . . Warum deut' er denn auf seinen Kopf?—Mein Lieber, dein Schädel interessiert mich sehr wenig . . . Ah, so! Nein, mein Lieber, du irrst dich: im Prater hab' ich übernachtet . . . wirst schon heut' im Abendblatt lesen.—»Nicht möglich!« wird er sagen; »heut' früh, wie wir zur Schießstätte ausgerückt sind, hab' ich ihn noch auf der Praterstraße getroffen!«—Wer wird denn meinen Zug kriegen?—Ob sie ihn dem Walterer geben werden?—Na, da wird was Schönes herauskommen—ein Kerl ohne Schneid, der hätt' auch lieber Schuster werden sollen . . .

Was, geht schon die Sonne auf?—Das wird heut' ein schöner

he's a dead man . . . If a crook like that could fight a duel—but no, then he'd be more careful, then he wouldn't risk anything in that line . . . And the guy goes on living in peace and quiet while I—have to croak!—He's the one who killed me . . . Yes, Gustl, do you get that?—He's the one who's killing you! But he won't get away scot-free!—No, no, no! I'll write a letter to Kopetzky telling him everything, I'll write down the whole story . . . or even better: I'll write it to the Colonel, I'll make a report to regiment headquarters . . . just like an official report . . . Yes, wait, you think something like this can remain secret?—You're wrong—it'll be written down as a permanent record, and then I'd like to see whether you still dare to go to the coffeehouse!—Ha!—"I'd like to see that": that's a good one! . . . There's a lot more I'd like to see, but unfortunately it won't be possible—it's all over!—

At this time Johann must be entering my room, now he notices that the Lieutenant hasn't slept at home.—Well, he'll think of all sorts of things; but that the Lieutenant spent the night in the Prater, damn me, he won't think of that! . . . Ah, the Forty-fourth! They're marching out to the firing range—better let them pass by . . . let's stand over here, then . . . —Someone's opening a window up there—good-looking tart—well, I'd at least wrap something around me if I went to the window . . . This past Sunday was the last time . . . I never dreamed that Steffi, of all women, would be my last.—Oh, God, that's the only real pleasure . . . Yes, the Colonel will ride after them in high style in a couple of hours . . . the fine gentlemen enjoy life—yes, yes, eyes right!—Fine . . . If you knew how little I care about you!

Ah, that's not bad: Katzer . . . since when did he transfer to the Forty-fourth?—Hi, hi!—What a face he's making . . . Why is he pointing to his head?—My good man, I'm not much interested in your cranium . . . Oh, that's it! No, my good man, you're wrong: I spent the night in the Prater . . . You'll read all about it in this evening's paper.— "Impossible!" he'll say; "just this morning when we marched out to the firing range I met him on Prater- strasse!" Who will take over my platoon?—Will they give it to Walterer?—Well, that'll be a fine kettle of fish—a guy with no class, who should have become a shoemaker instead . . .

What, is the sun coming up already?—Today will be a

Tag—so ein rechter Frühlingstag . . . Ist doch eigentlich zum Teufelholen!—Der Komfortabelkutscher wird noch um achte in der
Früh' auf der Welt sein, und ich . . . na, was ist denn das? He,
das wär' sowas—noch im letzten Moment die Contenance verlieren
wegen einem Komfortabelkutscher . . . Was ist denn das, daß ich
auf einmal so ein blödes Herzklopfen krieg'?—Das wird doch nicht
deswegen sein . . . Nein, o nein . . . es ist, weil ich so lang' nichts
gegessen hab'.——Aber Gustl, sei doch aufrichtig mit dir selber:
—Angst hast du—Angst, weil du's noch nie probiert hast . . . Aber
das hilft dir ja nichts, die Angst hat noch keinem was geholfen,
jeder muß es einmal durchmachen, der eine früher, der andere
später, und du kommst halt früher d'ran . . . Viel wert bist du ja
nie gewesen, so benimm dich wenigstens anständig zu guter Letzt,
das verlang' ich von dir!—So, jetzt heißt's nur überlegen—aber
was denn? . . . Immer will ich mir was überlegen . . . ist doch ganz
einfach:—im Nachtkastelladel liegt er, geladen ist er auch, heißt's
nur: losdrucken—das wird doch keine Kunst sein!——
    Die geht schon ins G'schäft . . . die armen Mädeln! Die Adel'
war auch in einem G'schäft—ein paarmal hab' ich sie am Abend
abg'holt . . . Wenn sie in einem G'schäft sind, werd'n sie doch keine
solchen Menscher . . . Wenn die Steffi mir allein g'hören möcht',
ich ließ sie Modistin werden oder sowas . . . Wie wird sie's denn
erfahren?—Aus der Zeitung! . . . Sie wird sich ärgern, daß ich ihr's
nicht geschrieben hab' . . . Mir scheint, ich schnapp' doch noch über
. . . Was geht denn das mich an, ob sie sich ärgert . . . Wie lang' hat
denn die ganze G'schicht gedauert? . . . Seit'm Jänner? . . . Ah nein,
es muß doch schon vor Weihnachten gewesen sein . . . ich hab' ihr
ja aus Graz Zuckerln mitgebracht, und zu Neujahr hat sie mir ein
Brieferl g'schickt . . .
    Richtig, die Briefe, die ich zu Haus hab',—sind keine da, die ich
verbrennen sollt'? . . . Hm, der vom Fallsteiner—wenn man den
Brief findet . . . der Bursch könnt' Unannehmlichkeiten haben . . .
Was mir das schon aufliegt!—Na, es ist ja keine große Anstrengung
. . . aber hervorsuchen kann ich den Wisch nicht . . . Das beste ist,
ich verbrenn' alles zusammen . . . wer braucht's denn? Ist lauter
Makulatur.——Und meine paar Bücher könnt' ich dem Blany ver-
machen.—›Durch Nacht und Eis‹ . . . schad', daß ich's nimmer aus-
lesen kann . . . bin wenig zum Lesen gekommen in der letzten Zeit
. . . Orgel—ah, aus der Kirche . . . Frühmesse—bin schon lang' bei

nice day—a real spring day ... Damn it all again!—At
eight in the morning the cabbies[9] will still be alive, and I
... now, what's all this? Hey, wouldn't that be something—to lose my self-control at the last moment on account of a cabbie ... Now why is my heart starting to
pound so stupidly all at once?—It's surely not because ...
No, oh, no ... it's because I've been without food for so
long. ——But, Gustl, be honest with yourself: you're
afraid—afraid because you've never been through it ...
But that doesn't help you, fear has never done anybody
any good, everyone has to go through it once, one man
sooner, another man later, and it just so happens your
turn is sooner ... You never amounted to much, so at
least behave properly at the very end, that's what I ask of
you!—So, then, what counts now is to think things over—
but what? ... I keep wanting to think something over ...
but it's perfectly simple: it's in the drawer of my night
table, it's loaded also, all I need to do is squeeze—there's
no trick to that!——

She's going to work already ... poor girls! Adele
worked in a shop, too—a couple of times I picked her up
after work in the evening ... When they're in a shop, they
don't become such sluts ... If Steffi belonged to me alone,
I'd make her be a milliner or something like that ... How
is she going to find out?—In the newspaper! ... She'll be
annoyed that I didn't write to her about it ... I think I'll
go crazy yet ... What do I care if she gets annoyed? ...
How long has the whole affair lasted, anyway? ... Since
January? ... Oh, no, it must have been before Christmas
... I brought her back candy from Graz, and at New
Year's she sent me a note ...

That's right, the letters that I have at home—are there
any I should burn? ... Hm, the one from Fallsteiner—
if they find that letter ... it might cause the fellow
some unpleasantness ... But what does that mean to
me?—Well, it takes no great effort ... but I can't go hunting for that one scrap of paper ... The best thing is to
burn up everything ... who needs it? It's nothing but
wastepaper. ———And I could leave my handful of books
to Blany.—*Through Night and Ice* ... too bad, I'll never get
to finish it ... I haven't had much time for reading lately
... an organ—oh, from the church ... early Mass—I

---

[9] "Komfortabelkutscher": driver of a comfortable carriage drawn
by a single horse.

keiner gewesen . . . das letztemal im Feber, wie mein Zug dazu kommandiert war . . . Aber das galt nichts—ich hab' auf meine Leut' aufgepaßt, ob sie andächtig sind und sich ordentlich benehmen . . .—Möcht' in die Kirche hineingeh'n . . . am End' ist doch was d'ran . . .—Na, heut' nach Tisch werd' ich's schon genau wissen . . . Ah, »nach Tisch« ist sehr gut! . . . Also, was ist, soll ich hineingeh'n?—Ich glaub', der Mama wär's ein Trost, wenn sie das wüßt'! . . . Die Klara gibt weniger d'rauf . . . Na, geh'n wir hinein—schaden kann's ja nicht!

Orgel—Gesang—hm!—Was ist denn das?—Mir ist ganz schwindlig . . . O Gott, o Gott, o Gott! Ich möcht' einen Menschen haben, mit dem ich ein Wort reden könnt' vorher!—Das wär' so was—zur Beicht' geh'n! Der möcht' Augen machen, der Pfaff', wenn ich zum Schluß sagen möcht': Habe die Ehre, Hochwürden; jetzt geh' ich mich umbringen! . . .—Am liebsten läg' ich da auf dem Steinboden und tät' heulen . . . Ah nein, das darf man nicht tun! Aber weinen tut manchmal so gut . . . Setzen wir uns einen Moment—aber nicht wieder einschlafen wie im Prater! . . .—Die Leut', die eine Religion haben, sind doch besser d'ran . . . Na, jetzt fangen mir gar die Händ' zu zittern an! . . . Wenn's so weitergeht, werd' ich mir selber auf die Letzt' so ekelhaft, daß ich mich vor lauter Schand' umbring'!—Das alte Weib da—um was betet denn die noch? . . . Wär' eine Idee, wenn ich ihr sagen möcht': Sie, schließen Sie mich auch ein . . . ich hab' das nicht ordentlich gelernt, wie man das macht . . . Ha! Mir scheint, das Sterben macht blöd'!—Aufsteh'n!—Woran erinnert mich denn nur die Melodie?—Heiliger Himmel! Gestern abend!—Fort, fort! Das halt' ich gar nicht aus! . . . Pst! Keinen solchen Lärm, nicht mit dem Säbel scheppern—die Leut' nicht in der Andacht stören—so!—doch besser im Freien . . .

Licht . . . Ah, es kommt immer näher—wenn es lieber schon vorbei wär'!—Ich hätt's gleich tun sollen—im Prater . . . man sollt' nie ohne Revolver ausgeh'n . . . Hätt' ich gestern abend einen gehabt . . . Herrgott noch einmal!—In das Kaffeehaus könnt' ich geh'n frühstücken . . . Hunger hab' ich . . . Früher ist's mir immer sonderbar vorgekommen, daß die Leut', die verurteilt sind, in der Früh' noch ihren Kaffee trinken und ihr Zigarrl rauchen . . . Donnerwetter, geraucht hab' ich gar nicht! Gar keine Lust zum Rauchen!—Es ist komisch: ich hätt' Lust, in mein Kaffeehaus zu geh'n . . . Ja, aufgesperrt ist schon, und von uns ist jetzt doch keiner dort—und wenn schon . . . ist höchstens ein Zeichen von Kaltblütigkeit. »Um sechs hat er noch im Kaffeehaus gefrühstückt, und um sieben hat er sich erschossen« . . .

Ganz ruhig bin ich wieder . . . das Gehen ist so angenehm—und

haven't been to one for a long time . . . the last time was
in February, when my platoon was ordered to go . . . But
that didn't count—I kept an eye on my men to see if they
were attentive and behaved properly . . . —I'd like to go
into the church . . . maybe there's something to it . . .
—Well, after my meal today I'll know exactly . . . Ah,
"after my meal" is a good one! . . . Well, what about it,
should I go in?—I think it would be a comfort to Mama
if she knew! . . . Klara sets less store by it . . . Well, let's go
in—it can't hurt!

Organ music—singing—hm!—What's this?—I'm all
dizzy . . . Oh, God, oh, God, oh, God! I'd like to have a
person to talk to before I die!—That would be something—to go to confession! The priest would be surprised
if at the end I said: Goodbye, Father; now I'm off to kill
myself! . . . —I'd like best of all to lie down here on the
stone floor and cry my heart out . . . Oh, no, that just isn't
done! But crying sometimes helps so much . . . Let's sit
down for a moment—but not fall asleep again as in the
Prater! . . . —People who believe are better off, after all
. . . Say, now even my hands are starting to tremble! . . .
If it keeps on like this, I'll finally become so repulsive to
myself that I'll kill myself purely from shame!—The old
woman there—what can she still be praying for? . . . It
might be an idea if I said to her: You, include me too . . .
I never learned how to do it properly . . . Ha! I think
dying makes you dumb!—Get up!—Now, what does that
melody remind me of?—Holy God! Last night!—Out of
here, out! I can't stand this! . . . Sh! Not so much noise,
don't let your saber rattle—don't disturb the people at
their devotions—there!—it *is* better outdoors . . .

Light . . . Ah, it's getting nearer all the time—if it were
only over already!—I should have done it right away—in
the Prater . . . I should never go out without my revolver
. . . If I had had one last night . . . Damn it again!—I could
go and have breakfast in the coffeehouse . . . I'm hungry
. . . I always used to think it was strange that condemned
prisoners still drank their coffee and smoked their cigar
in the morning . . . Hell, I haven't smoked at all! I don't
feel at all like smoking!—It's funny; I *would* like to go to
my coffeehouse . . . Yes, it's already open, and surely none
of our crowd is there now—and even so . . . at best, it
shows that you kept cool. "At six he still had breakfast in
the coffeehouse, and at seven he shot himself" . . .

I'm completely calm again . . . walking is so pleas-

das Schönste ist, daß mich keiner zwingt.—Wenn ich wollt' könnt'
ich noch immer den ganzen Krempel hinschmeißen ... Amerika
... Was ist das:»Krempel«? Was ist ein »Krempel«? Mir scheint,
ich hab' den Sonnenstich! ... Oho, bin ich vielleicht deshalb so
ruhig, weil ich mir noch immer einbild', ich muß nicht? ... Ich
muß! Ich muß! Nein, ich will!—Kannst du dir denn überhaupt
vorstellen, Gustl, daß du dir die Uniform ausziehst und durch-
gehst? Und der verfluchte Hund lacht sich den Buckel voll—und
der Kopetzky selbst möcht' dir nicht mehr die Hand geben ... Mir
kommt vor, ich bin jetzt ganz rot geworden.

Der Wachmann salutiert mir ... ich muß danken ... »Servus!«—Jetzt hab' ich gar »Servus« gesagt! ... Das freut so einen
armen Teufel immer ... Na, über mich hat sich keiner zu beklagen
gehabt—außer Dienst war ich immer gemütlich.—Wie wir auf Ma-
növer waren, hab' ich den Chargen von der Kompagnie Britannikas
geschenkt;—einmal hab' ich gehört, wie ein Mann hinter mir bei
den Gewehrgriffen was von »verfluchter Rackerei« g'sagt hat, und
ich hab' ihn nicht zum Rapport geschickt—ich hab' ihn nur gesagt:
»Sie, passen S' auf, das könnt' einmal wer anderer hören—da ging's
Ihnen schlecht!« ... Der Burghof ... Wer ist denn heut' auf
Wach'?—Die Bosniaken—schau'n gut aus—der Oberstleutnant
hat neulich g'sagt: Wie wir im 78er Jahr unten waren, hätt' keiner
geglaubt, daß uns die einmal so parieren werden! ... Herrgott, bei
so was hätt' ich dabei sein mögen!—Da steh'n sie alle auf von der
Bank.—Servus, servus!

Das ist halt zuwider, daß unsereiner nicht dazu kommt.—Wär'
doch schöner gewesen, auf dem Feld der Ehre, fürs Vaterland, als
so ... Ja, Herr Doktor, Sie kommen eigentlich gut weg! ... Ob das
nicht einer für mich übernehmen könnt'?—Meiner Seel', das sollt'
ich hinterlassen, daß sich der Kopetzky oder der Wymetal an meiner Statt mit dem Kerl schlagen ... Ah, so leicht sollt' der doch
nicht davonkommen!—Ah, was! Ist das nicht egal, was nachher
geschieht? Ich erfahr's ja doch nimmer!—Da schlagen die Bäume
aus ... Im Volksgarten hab' ich einmal eine angesprochen—ein
rotes Kleid hat sie angehabt—in der Strozzigasse hat sie gewohnt—nachher hat sie der Rochlitz übernommen ... Mir scheint,
er hat sie noch immer, aber er red't nichts mehr davon—er schämt
sich vielleicht ... Jetzt schlaft die Steffi noch ... so lieb sieht sie
aus, wenn sie schlaft ... als wenn sie nicht bis fünf zählen
könnt'!—Na, wenn sie schlafen, schau'n sie alle so aus!—Ich sollt'
ihr doch noch ein Wort schreiben ... warum denn nicht? Es tut's
ja doch ein jeder, daß er vorher noch Briefe schreibt.—Auch der

ant—and the nicest thing about it is that no one is forcing
me.—If I wanted, I could still throw up the whole kit and
caboodle . . . America . . . What is "caboodle"? What's a
"caboodle"? I think I have sunstroke! . . . Oho, can it be
that I'm so calm because I still imagine I don't have to go
through with it? . . . I must! I must! No, I want to!—Anyway, can you picture yourself, Gustl, taking off your uniform and deserting? And that dirty dog would roar with
laughter—and even Kopetzky wouldn't shake hands with
you any more . . . I feel as if I've turned red.

The policeman is saluting me . . . I must return the salute . . . "Hi!" Now I've even said "Hi"! . . . That always
gives pleasure to a poor devil like that . . . Well, no one
has had to complain about me—off duty I was always
friendly.—When we were on maneuvers, I gave Britan-
nika cigars to the company officers and NCOs—I once
heard a man behind me at rifle drill say something about
"damned drudgery," and I didn't report him—I only said
to him: "You, watch out, someone else might hear that
sometime—then you'd be in for it!" . . . The Burghof . . .
Who's on guard today?—The Bosnians—they look
good—the Lieutenant Colonel said lately: When we were
down there in '78, no one thought *they* would ever knuckle
under to us like this! . . . Lord God, I would have liked to
be in on something like that!—Now they're all getting up
from the bench—Hi, hi!

It's really sickening that none of us can see combat.—Surely it would have been finer to die on the field
of honor, for my country, than this way . . . Yes, Doctor,
you're really getting off lightly! . . . Could someone take
over for me?—Damn me, I should leave instructions for
Kopetzky or Wymetal to fight the guy in my place . . . Ha,
he wouldn't get out of it that easily!—What the hell! Isn't
it all the same what happens later on? I'll never find out
about it!—The trees here are in leaf . . . In the Volksgarten I once picked up a tart—she was wearing a red
dress—she lived on Strozzigasse—later Rochlitz took her
over . . . I think he still has her, but he doesn't talk about
it any more—maybe he's ashamed . . . Steffi is still sleeping now . . . she looks so sweet when she sleeps . . . as if
butter wouldn't melt in her mouth![10] —Well, when they
sleep they all look that way!—I really should still write her
a note . . . and why not? Everybody does it—writes letters

---

[10] Literally: "as if she couldn't count up to five."

Klara sollt' ich schreiben, daß sie den Papa und die Mama trö-
stet—und was man halt so schreibt!—und dem Kopetzky doch
auch . . . Meiner Seel', mir kommt vor, es wär' viel leichter, wenn
man ein paar Leuten Adieu gesagt hätt' . . . Und die Anzeige an das
Regimentskommando—und die hundertsechzig Gulden für den
Ballert . . . eigentlich noch viel zu tun . . . Na, es hat's mir ja keiner
g'schafft, daß ich's um sieben tu' . . . von acht an ist noch immer
Zeit genug zum Totsein! . . . Totsein, ja—so heißt's—da kann man
nichts machen . . .
    Ringstraße—jetzt bin ich ja bald in meinem Kaffeehaus . . . Mir
scheint gar, ich freu' mich aufs Frühstück . . . es ist nicht zum glauben.——Ja, nach dem Frühstück zünd' ich mir eine Zigarr' an,
und dann geh' ich nach Haus und schreib' . . . Ja, vor allem mach'
ich die Anzeige ans Kommando; dann kommt der Brief an die
Klara—dann an den Kopetzky—dann an die Steffi . . . Was soll ich
denn dem Luder schreiben . . . »Mein liebes Kind, Du hast wohl
nicht gedacht« . . . Ah, was, Unsinn!—»Mein liebes Kind, ich danke
Dir sehr« . . .—»Mein liebes Kind, bevor ich von hinnen gehe, will
ich es nicht verabsäumen« . . .—Na, Briefschreiben war auch nie
meine starke Seite . . . »Mein liebes Kind, ein letztes Lebewohl von
Deinem Gustl« . . .—Die Augen, die sie machen wird! Ist doch ein
Glück, daß ich nicht in sie verliebt war . . . das muß traurig sein,
wenn man eine gern hat und so . . . Na, Gustl, sei gut: so ist es auch
traurig genug . . . Nach der Steffi wär' ja noch manche andere
gekommen, und am End' auch eine, die was wert ist—junges Mädel
aus guter Familie mit Kaution—es wär' ganz schön gewesen . . .
    Der Klara muß ich ausführlich schreiben, daß ich nicht hab' an-
ders können . . . »Du mußt mir verzeihen, liebe Schwester, und
bitte, tröste auch die lieben Eltern. Ich weiß, daß ich Euch allen
manche Sorge gemacht habe und manchen Schmerz bereitet; aber
glaube mir, ich habe Euch alle immer sehr lieb gehabt, und ich
hoffe, Du wirst noch einmal glücklich werden, meine liebe Klara,
und Deinen unglücklichen Bruder nicht ganz vergessen« . . . Ah,
ich schreib' ihr lieber gar nicht! . . . Nein, da wird mir zum Weinen
. . . es beißt mich ja schon in den Augen, wenn ich d'ran denk' . . .
Höchstens dem Kopetzky schreib' ich—ein kameradschaftliches
Lebewohl, und er soll's den andern ausrichten . . .
    Ist's schon sechs?—Ah, nein: halb—dreiviertel.—Ist das ein lie-
bes G'sichtel! . . . Der kleine Fratz mit den schwarzen Augen, den
ich so oft in der Florianigasse treff'!—Was die sagen wird?—Aber
die weiß ja gar nicht, wer ich bin—die wird sich nur wundern, daß
sie mich nimmer sieht . . . Vorgestern hab' ich mir vorgenommen,

beforehand.—I should write to Klara, too, telling her to console Papa and Mama—and the usual things one writes!—and to Kopetzky, too . . . Damn me, I think it must be much easier if you've said goodbye to a few people . . . And the notification to regiment headquarters—and the hundred sixty gulden for Ballert . . . really still a lot to do . . . Well, nobody made me do it at seven . . . from eight on is still plenty of time to be dead! . . . To be dead, yes—that's what it's called—nothing you can do about it . . .

Ringstrasse—not long now before I'm in my coffee-house . . . I think I'm even looking forward to breakfast . . . it's unbelievable. ——Yes, after breakfast I'll light up a cigar, and then I'll go home and write . . . Yes, first of all I'll do the notification for headquarters; then comes the letter to Klara—then to Kopetzky—then to Steffi . . . but what should I write to that tramp? . . . "My dear child, you probably didn't think" . . . Ah, nonsense!—"My dear child, I thank you very much" . . . —"My dear child, before I depart this life, I do not wish to neglect" . . . —Well, letter writing was never my strong point . . . "My dear child, a last farewell from your Gustl" . . . —What a surprise she'll get! It's really lucky I wasn't in love with her . . . it must be sad to love somebody and then . . . Well, Gustl, behave: even this way it's sad enough . . . After Steffi there would have been many others, you know, and maybe one that was worth something—a young girl from a good family with a dowry—it would have been very nice . . .

I must tell Klara in detail that I had no other way out . . . "You must forgive me, dear sister, and please console our dear parents, too. I know that I gave you all a lot of worries and caused you a lot of pain; but believe me, I always loved you all very much, and I hope you will still be happy some day, my dear Klara, and that you won't altogether forget your unfortunate brother" . . . Oh, it's better if I don't write to her! . . . No, it makes me want to cry . . . my eyes start pricking as soon as I think of it . . . I'll write just to Kopetzky—a chummy farewell, and ask him to give the news to the others . . .

Is it six already?—Oh, no: a half-hour to go—a quarter to. —What a cute face that is! . . . The little charmer with dark eyes I run into so often on the Florianigasse!—What will she say?—But *she* doesn't even know who I am—she'll just be surprised that she never sees me . . . The day be-

das nächstemal sprech' ich sie an.—Kokettiert hat sie genug . . . so
jung war die—am End' war die gar noch eine Unschuld! . . . Ja,
Gustl! Was du heute kannst besorgen, das verschiebe nicht auf morgen! . . . Der da hat sicher auch die ganze Nacht nicht geschlafen.—Na, jetzt wird er schön nach Haus geh'n und sich niederle-
gen—ich auch!—Haha! Jetzt wird's ernst, Gustl, ja! . . . Na, wenn
nicht einmal das biss'l Grausen wär', so wär' ja schon gar nichts
d'ran—und im ganzen, ich muß's schon selber sagen, halt' ich mich
brav . . . Ah, wohin denn noch? Da ist ja schon mein Kaffeehaus
. . . auskehren tun sie noch . . . Na, geh'n wir hinein . . .
  Da hinten ist der Tisch, wo die immer Tarock spielen . . . Merkwürdig, ich kann mir's gar nicht vorstellen, daß der Kerl, der immer
da hinten sitzt an der Wand, derselbe sein soll, der mich . . .—Kein
Mensch ist noch da . . . Wo ist denn der Kellner? . . . He! Da kommt
er aus der Küche . . . er schlieft schnell in den Frack hinein . . . Ist
wirklich nimmer notwendig! . . . Ah, für ihn schon . . . er muß heut'
noch andere Leut' bedienen!—
  »Habe die Ehre, Herr Leutnant!«
  »Guten Morgen.«
  »So früh heute, Herr Leutnant?«
  »Ah, lassen S' nur—ich hab' nicht viel Zeit, ich kann mit'm Man-
tel dasitzen.«
  »Was befehlen Herr Leutnant?«
  »Eine Melange mit Haut.«
  »Bitte gleich, Herr Leutnant!«
  Ah, da liegen ja Zeitungen . . . schon heutige Zeitungen? . . . Ob
schon was drinsteht? . . . Was denn?—Mir scheint, ich will nach-
seh'n, ob drinsteht, daß ich mich umgebracht hab'! Haha!—Warum
steh' ich denn noch immer? . . . Setzen wir uns da zum Fenster . . .
Er hat mir ja schon die Melange hingestellt . . . So, den Vorhang
zieh' ich zu; es ist mir zuwider, wenn die Leut' hereingucken . . . Es
geht zwar noch keiner vorüber . . . Ah, gut schmeckt der Kaffee—doch kein leerer Wahn, das Frühstücken! . . . Ah, ein ganz
anderer Mensch wird man—der ganze Blödsinn ist, daß ich nicht
genachtmahlt hab' . . . Was steht denn der Kerl schon wieder
da?—Ah, die Semmeln hat er mir gebracht . . .
  »Haben Herr Leutnant schon gehört?« . . .
  »Was denn?« Ja, um Gotteswillen, weiß der schon was? . . . Aber,
Unsinn, es ist ja nicht möglich!
  »Den Herrn Habetswallner . . .«
  Was? So heißt ja der Bäckermeister . . . was wird der jetzt
sagen? . . . Ist der am End' schon dagewesen? Ist er am End' gestern

fore yesterday I made up my mind to speak to her
the next time.—She's flirted enough . . . she was so
young—maybe she was even still a virgin! . . . Yes, Gustl!
Don't put off till tomorrow what you can do today! . . . I'm
sure that guy there didn't sleep all night, either. —Well,
now he'll go comfortably home and go to bed—so will
I!—Ha, ha! Now it's getting serious, Gustl, yes! . . . Well,
if it weren't for the little bit of fear, there would be nothing
to it—and all in all, if I say so myself, I'm behaving well
. . . Ah, where to now? That's my coffeehouse . . . they're
still sweeping out . . . Well, let's go in . . .

Back there is the table where they always play tarok.
Strange, I can't get it into my head that the guy who always
sits in back against the wall is the same one who . . . —Not
a soul here yet . . . Where's the waiter? . . . Hey! Here he
comes out of the kitchen . . . he's slipping quickly into his
coat . . . It's really not necessary! . . . Oh, for him it is . . .
he'll have to wait on other people today!—

"How do you do, Lieutenant?"

"Good morning."

"So early today, Lieutenant?"

"Oh, don't bother—I don't have much time, I can sit
with my cloak on."

"What would you like, Lieutenant?"

"Café au lait with a skin of milk."

"Right away, Lieutenant!"

Ah, newspapers are lying there . . . today's papers already? . . . Anything in them yet? . . . What am I
doing?—I think I want to look and see whether they have
the story of my suicide! Ha, ha!—Why am I still standing? . . . Let's sit down there by the window . . . He's already set down my café au lait . . . There, I'll draw the
curtain: I hate it when people look in . . . Not that anyone
is passing by yet . . . Ah, the coffee tastes good—after all,
having breakfast wasn't a foolish idea! . . . Ah, you become
a totally new man—all those muddled thoughts came
from having no supper . . . Why is the fellow already here
again?—Ah, he's brought me the rolls . . .

"Have you heard yet, Lieutenant?" . . .

"What?" For the love of God, does he know something
already? . . . No, nonsense, that's impossible!

"Mr. Habetswallner . . ."

What? That's the name of the baker . . . what will he say
now? . . . Maybe he's already been here. Maybe he was

schon dagewesen und hat's erzählt? . . . Warum red't er denn nicht weiter? . . . Aber er red't ja . . .

» . . .hat heut' nacht um zwölf der Schlag getroffen.«

»Was?« . . . Ich darf nicht so schreien . . . nein, ich darf mir nichts anmerken lassen . . . aber vielleicht träum' ich . . . ich muß ihn noch einmal fragen . . .»Wen hat der Schlag getroffen?«—Famos, famos!—Ganz harmlos hab' ich das gesagt!—

»Den Bäckermeister, Herr Leutnant! . . Herr Leutnant werd'n ihn ja kennen . . . na, den Dicken, der jeden Nachmittag neben die Herren Offiziere seine Tarockpartie hat . . . mit'n Herrn Schlesinger und'n Herrn Wasner von der Kunstblumenhandlung vis-à-vis!«

Ich bin ganz wach—stimmt alles—und doch kann ich's noch nicht recht glauben—ich muß ihn noch einmal fragen . . . aber ganz harmlos . . .

»Der Schlag hat ihn getroffen? . . . Ja, wieso denn? Woher wissen S' denn das?«

»Aber Herr Leutnant, wer soll's denn früher wissen, als unsereiner—die Semmel, die der Herr Leutnant da essen, ist ja auch vom Herrn Habetswallner. Der Bub, der uns das Gebäck um halber fünfe in der Früh bringt, hat's uns erzählt.«

Um Himmelswillen, ich darf mich nicht verraten . . . ich möcht' ja schreien . . . ich möcht' ja lachen . . . ich möcht' ja dem Rudolf ein Bussel geben . . . Aber ich muß ihn noch was fragen! . . . Vom Schlag getroffen werden, heißt noch nicht: tot sein . . . ich muß fragen, ob er tot ist . . . aber ganz ruhig, denn was geht mich der Bäckermeister an—ich muß in die Zeitung schau'n, während ich den Kellner frag' . . .

»Ist er tot?«

»Na, freilich, Herr Leutnant; auf'm Fleck ist er tot geblieben.«

O, herrlich, herrlich!—Am End' ist das alles, weil ich in der Kirchen g'wesen bin . . .

»Er ist am Abend im Theater g'wesen; auf der Stiegen ist er umg'fallen—der Hausmeister hat den Krach gehört . . . na, und dann haben s' ihn in die Wohnung getragen, und wie der Doktor gekommen ist, war's schon lang' aus.«

»Ist aber traurig. Er war doch noch in den besten Jahren.«—Das hab' ich jetzt famos gesagt—kein Mensch könnt' mir was anmerken . . . und ich muß mich wirklich zurückhalten, daß ich nicht schrei' oder aufs Billard spring' . . .

»Ja, Herr Leutnant, sehr traurig; war ein so lieber Herr, und zwanzig Jahr' ist er schon zu uns kommen—war ein guter Freund von unserm Herrn. Und die arme Frau . . .«

Ich glaub', so froh bin ich in meinem ganzen Leben nicht gewesen

already here last night and told the story . . . Why doesn't he continue speaking? . . . But he *is* speaking . . .

". . . had a stroke last night at twelve."

"What?" . . . I shouldn't shout like that . . . no, I shouldn't let anything show . . . but maybe I'm dreaming . . . I must ask him again . . . *"Who* had a stroke?"—Terrific, terrific!—I said that as innocently as possible!—

"The baker, Lieutenant! . . . You must know him, Lieutenant . . . you know, the fat man who plays tarok every afternoon alongside the officers . . . with Mr. Schlesinger and Mr. Wasner from the artificial-flower store sitting opposite!"

I'm fully awake—everything tallies—and yet I still can't quite believe it—I must ask him again . . . but very innocently . . .

"He had a stroke? . . . Yes, but how was it? How do you know?"

"But, Lieutenant, who should know before we do?—the rolls you're eating there were made by Mr. Habetswallner. The boy who brings us the baked goods at half past four in the morning told us."

For the love of God, I mustn't give myself away . . . I'd really like to shout . . . I'd like to laugh . . . I'd like to give Rudolf a kiss . . . But I still must ask him more! . . . To have a stroke doesn't necessarily mean that he's dead . . . I must ask whether he's dead . . . but very calmly, because what's the baker to me?—I must look at the paper while I ask the waiter . . .

"Is he dead?"

"Well, of course, Lieutenant; he was dead on the spot."

Oh, wonderful, wonderful!—maybe all this is because I went to church . . .

"In the evening he was at the theater; he fell over on the stairs—the concierge heard the crash . . . well, and then they carried him into his apartment, and when the doctor got there it was already long over."

"But that's sad. He was still in the prime of life."—It was terrific, the way I just said that—nobody could tell a thing . . . and I really have to restrain myself to keep from shouting or jumping onto the billiard table . . .

"Yes, Lieutenant, very sad; he was such a charming man, and he'd been coming to us for twenty years— he was a good friend of our proprietor. And his poor wife . . ."

I think I've never been so happy in my entire life . . .

... Tot ist er—tot ist er! Keiner weiß was, und nichts ist
g'scheh'n!—Und das Mordsglück, daß ich in das Kaffeehaus gegangen bin ... sonst hätt' ich mich ja ganz umsonst erschossen—es
ist doch wie eine Fügung des Schicksals ... Wo ist denn der Rudolf?—Ah, mit dem Feuerburschen red't er ...—Also, tot ist
er—tot ist er—ich kann's noch gar nicht glauben! Am liebsten
möcht' ich hingeh'n, um's zu seh'n.——Am End' hat ihn der Schlag
getroffen aus Wut, aus verhaltenem Zorn ... Ah, warum, ist mir
ganz egal! Die Hauptsach' ist: er ist tot, und ich darf leben, und
alles g'hört wieder mein! ... Komisch, wie ich mir da immerfort
die Semmel einbrock', die mir der Herr Habetswallner gebacken
hat! Schmeckt mir ganz gut, Herr von Habetswallner! Famos!—So,
jetzt möcht' ich noch ein Zigarrl rauchen ...

»Rudolf! Sie, Rudolf! Sie, lassen S' mir den Feuerburschen dort
in Ruh'!«

»Bitte, Herr Leutnant!«

»Trabucco« ...—Ich bin so froh, so froh! ... Was mach' ich
denn nur? ... Was mach ich denn nur? ... Es muß ja was gescheh'n, sonst trifft mich auch noch der Schlag vor lauter
Freud'! ... In einer Viertelstund' geh' ich hinüber in die Kasern'
und laß mich vom Johann kalt abreiben ... um halb acht sind die
Gewehrgriff', und um halb zehn ist Exerzieren.—Und der Steffi
schreib' ich, sie muß sich für heut' abend frei machen, und wenn's
Graz gilt! Und nachmittag um vier ... na wart', mein Lieber, wart',
mein Lieber! Ich bin grad gut aufgelegt ... Dich hau' ich zu Krenfleisch!

He's dead—he's dead! No one knows a thing, and nothing has happened!—And what a great stroke of luck that I came to the coffeehouse . . . otherwise I would have shot myself for nothing at all—after all, it's like a dispensation of destiny . . . Where is Rudolf?—Ah, he's talking to the furnace man . . . —So he's dead—he's dead—I still can't believe it! I'd really like to go over and see for myself. ——Maybe he had a stroke from rage, from pent-up anger . . . Ah, the reason makes no difference! The main thing is that he's dead, and I can live, and I've got everything back again! . . . Funny how I keep on crumbling the rolls into the coffee—rolls that Mr. Habetswallner baked for me! They taste very good, Mr. von Habetswallner! Terrific!—There, now I'd like to smoke a cigar . . .

"Rudolf! You there, Rudolf! Leave the furnace man there in peace!"

"Yes, Lieutenant?"

"A Trabucco cigar" . . . —I'm so happy, so happy! . . . What shall I do? . . . What shall I do? . . . Something's got to happen, or I'll have a stroke myself from pure happiness! . . . In a quarter of an hour I'll go over to the barracks and get a cold rubdown from Johann . . . half past seven is rifle drill, and half past nine is formation. —And I'll write to Steffi that she must make herself available for tonight, even if all of Graz is at stake! And at four in the afternoon . . . just wait, my good man, just wait, my good man! I happen to be in good form . . . I'll make mincemeat[11] out of you!

---

[11] "Krenfleisch": a pork dish made with vinegar and horseradish.

MANN
AND
"TRISTAN"

THOMAS MANN, winner of the 1929 Nobel Prize for literature, is often considered the greatest twentieth-century writer of German narrative prose. Born in 1875 in Lübeck (the city on the Baltic in "Tristan") into a grain merchant's family (like the Eckhofs and the Klöterjahns in "Tristan"), he lived in Munich, a thriving center of the arts, from 1893 to 1933, when he left Germany out of distaste for Hitler. After five years in Switzerland, he taught and wrote in the United States until 1952, becoming an American citizen in 1944. Returning to Switzerland, he died near Zurich in 1955. His first book of stories appeared in 1898, and two years later he won lasting fame for his first novel, *Buddenbrooks*. Other major novels included *Der Zauberberg* (The Magic Mountain, for which "Tristan," with its sanatorium romance, is to some extent a preliminary sketch), *Joseph und seine Brüder* (Joseph and His Brothers) and *Doktor Faustus*. Other great stories are "Tonio Kröger," "Der Tod in Venedig" (Death in Venice) and "Mario und der Zauberer" (Mario and the Magician). Mann also wrote numerous essays on literature, politics and humanistic subjects.

The writing of "Tristan," Mann's most important story up to that time, extended from the end of 1900 into 1902. It was first published in 1903 by S. Fischer, Berlin, in the volume *Tristan. Sechs Novellen*. In the summer and fall of 1901, Mann, suffering from a gastric complaint (like Mrs. Spatz in the story), visited a health resort and a sanatorium in northern Italy. The setting of "Tristan" may have been inspired by an earlier story by his brother Heinrich.

"Tristan" already features themes and preoccupations that were to be lastingly associated with the author: a traditional German linking of beauty and sex with death (Wagner's opera *Tristan und Isolde* is of course a classic expression of this complex) and a highly personal concern with the role of the artist, who can so easily become a charlatan if he cuts himself off from living reality. Mann's style here is already one of Wagnerian leitmotifs constantly re-echoing and interlacing in meaningful new combinations. Physical traits of the characters, their habits, their catchphrases—all these must be remembered in detail by the reader who wishes to gain full understanding of the author's intent and to appreciate the subtle ironies of the story.

The "plot" can be told in a few words; the form and the painstaking, Byzantinely intricate mosaic of words are what ultimately counts. Even the characters are preternaturally word-conscious, recalling everything that has been said to them and repeating it at crucial moments, even though Mr. Klöterjahn may remember a few of the words incorrectly. In lesser hands, this treatment of characters could lead to bald caricature, but Mann's humanity ultimately prevents this. Nevertheless, this early story comes closer to caricature than Mann's later works, especially with regard to Mr. Spinell, in whose person Mann seems to have pilloried specific Munich acquaintances—and himself as well!

The passage in which Gabriele plays excerpts from *Tristan* on the piano is not only the climactic point of the action—the sacrifice of life to esthetic beauty and to a rather seedy romance—it also contains the most complex and purple writing, consisting largely of direct quotations from, or close paraphrases of, Wagner's libretto. Familiarity with the opera is almost a prerequisite for an exhaustive understanding of Mann's purposes. Incidentally, Mann is very fond of introducing extended verbal descriptions of specific pieces of music that he does not identify immediately or at all; there are further striking instances in *Der Zauberberg* and *Doktor Faustus*.

The proper names in "Tristan" have a significance of their own. Detlev Spinell is somewhat of a hybrid, a north German first name and a family name ultimately derived from Italian; Spinell (spinel in English) is a mineral the red variety of which is the gem known as the spinel ruby. Klöterjahn is a Plattdeutsch (north German) name that can sound bumpkinlike to sophisticated south Germans; it is apparently cognate to "clattering John" in English, and the meaning "testicle John" has also been suggested. Dr. Leander's name is of ancient Greek derivation and is reminiscent of the learned pseudonyms of Renaissance and Baroque scholars and humanists. "Von Osterloh" smacks of Prussian aristocracy. "Spatz" means "sparrow." "Höhlenrauch" means "cavern smoke." Dr. Müller, whose chief role in the sanatorium is to maintain Dr. Leander's reputation for never having lost a patient, is jokingly introduced as being a lowly subordinate *just because* his name is such a dismally common and plebeian one. But the greatest nomenclatural invention in "Tristan" is that of the sanatorium itself, Einfried. Depending on which homonymous German roots one derives it from, one can arrive at meanings like "protective seclusion" or "peace in solitude." There can be little doubt that Mann was also thinking of Wagner's famous villa in Bayreuth called Wahnfried, which connotes "freedom from the world's madness and delusion."

TRISTAN

1

Hier ist ›Einfried‹, das Sanatorium! Weiß und geradlinig liegt es
mit seinem langgestreckten Hauptgebäude und seinem Seitenflügel inmitten des weiten Gartens, der mit Grotten, Laubengängen
und kleinen Pavillons aus Baumrinde ergötzlich ausgestattet ist,
und hinter seinen Schieferdächern ragen tannengrün, massig und
weich zerklüftet die Berge himmelan.

Nach wie vor leitet Doktor Leander die Anstalt. Mit seinem zwei-
spitzigen schwarzen Bart, der hart und kraus ist wie das Roßhaar,
mit dem man die Möbel stopft, seinen dicken, funkelnden Brillengläsern und diesem Aspekt eines Mannes, den die Wissenschaft
gekältet, gehärtet und mit stillem, nachsichtigem Pessimismus erfüllt hat, hält er auf kurz angebundene und verschlossene Art die
Leidenden in seinem Bann,—alle diese Individuen, die, zu
schwach, sich selbst Gesetze zu geben und sie zu halten, ihm ihr
Vermögen ausliefern, um sich von seiner Strenge stützen lassen zu
dürfen.

Was Fräulein von Osterloh betrifft, so steht sie mit unermüdli-
cher Hingabe dem Haushalte vor. Mein Gott, wie tätig sie, treppauf
und treppab, von einem Ende der Anstalt zum anderen eilt! Sie
herrscht in Küche und Vorratskammer, sie klettert in den Wäsche-
schränken umher, sie kommandiert die Dienerschaft und bestellt
unter den Gesichtspunkten der Sparsamkeit, der Hygiene, des
Wohlgeschmacks und der äußeren Anmut den Tisch des Hauses,
sie wirtschaftet mit einer rasenden Umsicht, und in ihrer extremen
Tüchtigkeit liegt ein beständiger Vorwurf für die gesamte Männer-
welt verborgen, von der noch niemand darauf verfallen ist, sie
heimzuführen. Auf ihren Wangen aber glüht in zwei runden, kar-
moisinroten Flecken die unauslöschliche Hoffnung, dereinst Frau
Doktor Leander zu werden . . .

Ozon und stille, stille Luft . . . für Lungenkranke ist ›Einfried‹,
was Doktor Leanders Neider und Rivalen auch sagen mögen, aufs
wärmste zu empfehlen. Aber es halten sich nicht nur Phthisiker, es
halten sich Patienten aller Art, Herren, Damen und sogar Kinder
hier auf: Doktor Leander hat auf den verschiedensten Gebieten
Erfolge aufzuweisen. Es gibt hier gastrisch Leidende, wie die Magistratsrätin Spatz, die überdies an den Ohren krankt, Herrschaften

TRISTAN

1

Here is Einfried, the sanatorium! With its elongated main
building and its lateral wing it lies, white and rectilinear,
in the center of an extensive garden delightfully fitted
out with grottoes, pergolas and small tree-bark pavilions.
Behind its slate roofs the mountains—green with firs,
massive and gently fissured—tower heavenward.

Dr. Leander is still director of the establishment. With
his black beard ending in two points, a beard as tough and
curly as the horsehair used for stuffing furniture, with his
thick, glistening eyeglasses and that look of a man whom
science has cooled, hardened and filled with quiet, for-
bearing pessimism, he holds the patients under his spell
in a brusque and reserved fashion—all those individuals
who, too weak to make their own rules and abide by them,
hand over their fortune to him in return for the privilege
of being shored up by his discipline.

As far as Miss von Osterloh is concerned, she presides
over the housekeeping with tireless devotion. Good heavens, how actively she dashes, upstairs and down, from one
end of the establishment to the other! She governs the
kitchen and pantry; she clambers about in the linen clos-
ets; she bosses the servants and arranges the patients'
menu with a view toward thrift, hygiene, tastiness and
visual appeal; she runs the place with frantic prudence;
and within her extreme capability she conceals a constant
reproach to the entire world of males, none of whom has
yet hit on the idea of making her his bride. But on her
cheeks there glows, in two round crimson spots, the inextinguishable hope of one day becoming Mrs. Leander . . .

Ozone and a perfectly serene atmosphere . . . no matter
what Dr. Leander's rivals or those who envy him may say,
Einfried can be most highly recommended for consump-
tives. Not only tuberculosis victims, however, but patients
of all types stay here, men, women and even children: Dr.
Leander can point to successes in the most diverse areas.
There are gastric patients here, such as Mrs. Spatz, wife
of a town councillor, who has ear trouble besides; well-to-

167

mit Herzfehlern, Paralytiker, Rheumatiker und Nervöse in allen
Zuständen. Ein diabetischer General verzehrt hier unter immerwäh-
rendem Murren seine Pension. Mehrere Herren mit entfleischten
Gesichtern werfen auf jene unbeherrschte Art ihre Beine, die
nichts Gutes bedeutet. Eine fünfzigjährige Dame, die Pastorin Höhlenrauch, die neunzehn Kinder zur Welt gebracht hat und absolut
keines Gedankens mehr fähig ist, gelangt dennoch nicht zum Frie-
den, sondern irrt, von einer blöden Unrast getrieben, seit einem
Jahre bereits am Arm ihrer Privatpflegerin starr und stumm, ziellos
und unheimlich durch das ganze Haus.

Dann und wann stirbt jemand von den ›Schweren‹, die in ihren
Zimmern liegen und nicht zu den Mahlzeiten noch im Konversationszimmer erscheinen, und niemand, selbst der Zimmernachbar
nicht, erfährt etwas davon. In stiller Nacht wird der wächserne Gast
beiseite geschafft, und ungestört nimmt das Treiben in ›Einfried‹
seinen Fortgang, das Massieren, Elektrisieren und Injizieren, das
Duschen, Baden, Turnen, Schwitzen und Inhalieren in den verschiedenen mit allen Errungenschaften der Neuzeit ausgestatteten
Räumlichkeiten . . .

Ja, es geht lebhaft zu hierselbst. Das Institut steht in Flor. Der
Portier, am Eingange des Seitenflügels, rührt die große Glocke,
wenn neue Gäste eintreffen, und in aller Form geleitet Doktor Le-
ander, zusammen mit Fräulein von Osterloh, die Abreisenden zum
Wagen. Was für Existenzen hat ›Einfried‹ nicht schon beherbergt!
Sogar ein Schriftsteller ist da, ein exzentrischer Mensch, der den
Namen irgendeines Minerals oder Edelsteines führt und hier dem
Herrgott die Tage stiehlt . . .

Übrigens ist, neben Herrn Doktor Leander, noch ein zweiter Arzt
vorhanden, für die leichten Fälle und die Hoffnungslosen. Aber er
heißt Müller und ist überhaupt nicht der Rede wert.

2

Anfang Januar brachte Großkaufmann Klöterjahn—in Firma A.
C. Klöterjahn & Comp.—seine Gattin nach ›Einfried‹; der Portier
rührte die Glocke, und Fräulein von Osterloh begrüßte die weither
gereisten Herrschaften im Empfangszimmer zu ebener Erde, das,
wie beinahe das ganze vornehme alte Haus, in wunderbar reinem
Empirestil eingerichtet war. Gleich darauf erschien auch Doktor

do people with heart disease, paralytics, rheumatics and patients with every degree of nervous disorders. A diabetic general is consuming his pension here, grumbling all the while. Several gentlemen with emaciated faces fling about their legs in that uncontrolled manner which means no good. A fifty-year-old lady, Mrs. Höhlenrauch, a pastor's wife who has brought nineteen children into the world and is absolutely incapable of any further thought, nevertheless cannot attain peace, but, driven by an imbecilic restlessness, has for a year now been wandering aimlessly and eerily through the whole house on the arm of her private nurse.

Now and then one of the "serious cases"—those who lie in their rooms and do not show up at meals or in the parlor—dies, and no one, not even their neighbor, finds out anything about it. In the still of the night the waxen guest is removed, and the activities at Einfried proceed without disturbance: the massages, electric shocks, injections, showers, baths, gymnastics, sweat baths and inhalations in the various rooms provided with all the latest technical equipment of the day . . .

Yes, things are lively here. The institution is flourishing. The porter, at the entrance to the lateral wing, rings the big bell when new guests arrive, and Dr. Leander, along with Miss von Osterloh, escorts departing guests to their carriage with great ceremony. What characters has Einfried not already sheltered! There is even a writer here, an eccentric person whose name is that of some mineral or precious stone and who is idling away his time here . . .

Moreover, there is also another doctor on hand in addition to Dr. Leander, for mild cases and for hopeless cases. But his name is Müller and he is hardly worth mentioning at all.

2

At the beginning of January Mr. Klöterjahn, a wholesale merchant—of the firm A. C. Klöterjahn & Co.—brought his wife to Einfried. The porter rang the bell, and Miss von Osterloh greeted the couple, fresh from their long journey, in the first-floor reception room, which, like almost the whole aristocratic old house, was furnished in amazingly pure Empire style. Immediately thereafter Dr. Leander also appeared; he bowed, and an opening con-

Leander; er verbeugte sich, und es entspann sich eine erste, für beide Teile orientierende Konversation.

Draußen lag der winterliche Garten mit Matten über den Beeten, verschneiten Grotten und vereinsamten Tempelchen, und zwei Hausknechte schleppten vom Wagen her, der auf der Chaussee vor der Gatterpforte hielt—denn es führte keine Anfahrt zum Hause—, die Koffer der neuen Gäste herbei.

»Langsam, Gabriele, take care, mein Engel, und halte den Mund zu«, hatte Herr Klöterjahn gesagt, als er seine Frau durch den Garten führte; und in dieses »take care« mußte zärtlichen und zitternden Herzens jedermann innerlich einstimmen, der sie erblickte,—wenn auch nicht zu leugnen ist, daß Herr Klöterjahn es anstandslos auf deutsch hätte sagen können.

Der Kutscher, welcher die Herrschaften von der Station zum Sanatorium gefahren hatte, ein roher, unbewußter Mann ohne Feingefühl, hatte geradezu die Zunge zwischen die Zähne genommen vor ohnmächtiger Behutsamkeit, während der Großkaufmann seiner Gattin beim Aussteigen behilflich war; ja, es hatte ausgesehen, als ob die beiden Braunen, in der stillen Frostluft qualmend, mit rückwärts gerollten Augen angestrengt diesen ängstlichen Vorgang verfolgten, voll Besorgnis für soviel schwache Grazie und zarten Liebreiz.

Die junge Frau litt an der Luftröhre, wie ausdrücklich in dem anmeldenden Schreiben zu lesen stand, das Herr Klöterjahn vom Strande der Ostsee aus an den dirigierenden Arzt von ›Einfried‹ gerichtet hatte, und Gott sei Dank, daß es nicht die Lunge war! Wenn es aber dennoch die Lunge gewesen wäre,—diese neue Patientin hätte keinen holderen und veredelteren, keinen entrückteren und unstofflicheren Anblick gewähren können als jetzt, da sie an der Seite ihres stämmigen Gatten, weich und ermüdet in den weißlackierten, gradlinigen Armsessel zurückgelehnt, dem Gespräche folgte.

Ihre schönen, blassen Hände, ohne Schmuck bis auf den schlichten Ehering, ruhten in den Schoßfalten eines schweren und dunklen Tuchrockes, und sie trug eine silbergraue, anschließende Taille mit festem Stehkragen, die mit hochaufliegenden Sammetarabesken über und über besetzt war. Aber diese gewichtigen und warmen Stoffe ließen die unsägliche Zartheit, Süßigkeit und Mattigkeit des Köpfchens nur noch rührender, unirdischer und lieblicher erscheinen. Ihr lichtbraunes Haar, tief im Nacken zu einem Knoten

versation developed, providing orientation for both parties.

Outdoors was the wintry garden with matting over the flower beds, snow-obstructed grottoes and isolated miniature temples, and two servants were hauling the new guests' luggage over from the carriage, which had stopped on the main road in front of the barred gate, because there was no driveway up to the house.

"Slowly, Gabriele, take care,[1] darling, and keep your mouth closed," Mr. Klöterjahn had said while leading his wife through the garden; and everyone who caught a sight of her had to assent inwardly to that "take care" with a tender, trembling heart—although it cannot be denied that Mr. Klöterjahn could have said it just as well in plain German.

The coachman who had driven the couple from the station to the sanatorium, a rough, insensitive man without finer feelings, had actually put his tongue between his teeth out of helpless cautiousness while the merchant was helping his wife to alight. In fact, it had looked as if the pair of bays, steaming in the calm, frosty air, were observing this painstaking process anxiously with eyes rolled back, full of alarm for so much frail gracefulness and delicate charm.

The young woman had a bad trachea, as was stated expressly in the letter of notification that Mr. Klöterjahn had sent from the shores of the Baltic to the chief physician of Einfried, and thank God it wasn't her lungs! But even if it had been her lungs, this new patient could not have presented a more lovely and refined, a more faraway and immaterial appearance than she did now, as by the side of her robust husband, she leaned back, weak and exhausted, in a white-enameled, rectilinear armchair, paying attention to the conversation.

Her beautiful pale hands, unadorned except for her simple wedding ring, rested on her lap in the pleats of a heavy, dark cloth skirt, and she wore an attached silver-gray bodice that had a stiff stand-up collar and was trimmed all over with velvet arabesques in high relief. But these heavy, warm materials only made the inexpressible delicacy, sweetness and languor of her little head appear even more touching, unearthly and lovable. Her light brown hair, gathered in a bun far down on her neck, was

---

[1] "Take care" is in English in the original.

zusammengefaßt, war glatt zurückgestrichen, und nur in der Nähe der rechten Schläfe fiel eine krause, lose Locke in die Stirn, unfern der Stelle, wo über der markant gezeichneten Braue ein kleines, seltsames Äderchen sich blaßblau und kränklich in der Klarheit und Makellosigkeit dieser wie durchsichtigen Stirn verzweigte. Dies blaue Äderchen über dem Auge beherrschte auf eine beunruhigende Art das ganze feine Oval des Gesichts. Es trat sichtbarer hervor, sobald die Frau zu sprechen begann, ja sobald sie auch nur lächelte, und es gab alsdann dem Gesichtsausdruck etwas Angestrengtes, ja selbst Bedrängtes, was unbestimmte Befürchtungen erweckte. Dennoch sprach sie und lächelte. Sie sprach freimütig und freundlich mit ihrer leicht verschleierten Stimme, und sie lächelte mit ihren Augen, die ein wenig mühsam blickten, ja hie und da eine kleine Neigung zum Verschließen zeigten, und deren Winkel, zu beiden Seiten der schmalen Nasenwurzel, in tiefem Schatten lagen, sowie mit ihrem schönen, breiten Munde, der blaß war und dennoch zu leuchten schien, vielleicht, weil seine Lippen so überaus scharf und deutlich umrissen waren. Manchmal hüstelte sie. Hierbei führte sie ihr Taschentuch zum Munde und betrachtete es alsdann.

»Hüstle nicht, Gabriele«, sagte Herr Klöterjahn. »Du weißt, daß Doktor Hinzpeter zu Hause es dir extra verboten hat, darling, und es ist bloß, daß man sich zusammennimmt, mein Engel. Es ist, wie gesagt, die Luftröhre«, wiederholte er. »Ich glaubte wahrhaftig, es wäre die Lunge, als es losging, und kriegte, weiß Gott, einen Schreck. Aber es ist nicht die Lunge, nee, Deubel noch mal, auf so was lassen wir uns nicht ein, was, Gabriele? hö, hö!«

»Zweifelsohne«, sagte Doktor Leander und funkelte sie mit seinen Brillengläsern an.

Hierauf verlangte Herr Klöterjahn Kaffee,—Kaffee und Buttersemmeln, und er hatte eine anschauliche Art, den K-Laut ganz hinten im Schlunde zu bilden und »Bottersemmeln« zu sagen, daß jedermann Appetit bekommen mußte.

Er bekam, was er wünschte, bekam auch Zimmer für sich und seine Gattin, und man richtete sich ein.

Übrigens übernahm Doktor Leander selbst die Behandlung, ohne Doktor Müller für den Fall in Anspruch zu nehmen.

combed straight back, and only in the vicinity of her right temple a curly loose tress fell upon her forehead, not far from the place where, above her sharply delineated eyebrows, a strange little vein branched out, pale blue and sickly, in the clarity and spotlessness of that seemingly transparent forehead. This little blue vein above her eye dominated the entire fine oval of her face in a disturbing manner. It stood out more visibly as soon as the woman began to speak, indeed as soon as she even merely smiled, and it then gave the expression of her face a strained, yes, even distressed quality that aroused undefined apprehensions. Nevertheless she did speak and smile. She spoke in an open, friendly way with a slightly husky voice, and she smiled just as much with her eyes—which gazed with somewhat of an effort and now and then showed a slight tendency to narrow, and the corners of which, on either side of the narrow bridge of her nose, lay in deep shadow—as with her lovely, wide mouth, which was pale and nevertheless seemed to glow, perhaps because the lips were so very sharply and clearly contoured. From time to time she coughed slightly. When doing so, she put her handkerchief to her mouth and then looked at it.

"Don't cough, Gabriele," said Mr. Klöterjahn. "You know that Dr. Hinzpeter at home specifically forbade that, darling,[2] and you just have to take yourself in hand, sweetheart. As he said, it's the trachea," he repeated. "I really thought it was the lungs when the trouble started, and God knows it gave me a scare. But it isn't the lungs, not by a long shot!—we wouldn't stand for things like that, would we, Gabriele? Ha, ha!"

"Doubtlessly," said Dr. Leander and glistened at them with his eyeglasses.

Next Mr. Klöterjahn requested coffee—coffee and buttered rolls. He had a vivid way of forming the "c" sound far, far back in his throat and saying "buttered rolls" in such a way that everyone had to get an appetite.[3]

He got what he wanted and also got rooms for himself and his wife, and they settled in.

Moreover, Dr. Leander himself undertook the treatment, without calling upon Dr. Müller in this case.

---

[2] "Darling" is in English in the original.
[3] The words "nee," "Deubel" and "Bottersemmeln" indicate a north German dialect (Plattdeutsch).

3

Die Persönlichkeit der neuen Patientin erregte ungewöhnliches
Aufsehen in ›Einfried‹, und Herr Klöterjahn, gewöhnt an solche
Erfolge, nahm jede Huldigung, die man ihr darbrachte, mit Genug-
tuung entgegen. Der diabetische General hörte einen Augenblick
zu murren auf, als er ihrer zum ersten Male ansichtig wurde, die
Herren mit den entfleischten Gesichtern lächelten und versuchten
angestrengt, ihre Beine zu beherrschen, wenn sie in ihre Nähe
kamen, und die Magistratsrätin Spatz schloß sich ihr sofort als ältere
Freundin an. Ja, sie machte Eindruck, die Frau, die Herrn Klöterjahns Namen trug! Ein Schriftsteller, der seit ein paar Wochen in
›Einfried‹ seine Zeit verbrachte, ein befremdender Kauz, dessen
Name wie der eines Edelsteines lautete, verfärbte sich geradezu, als
sie auf dem Korridor an ihm vorüberging, blieb stehen und stand
noch immer wie angewurzelt, als sie schon längst entschwunden
war.

Zwei Tage waren noch nicht vergangen, als die ganze Kurgesellschaft mit ihrer Geschichte vertraut war. Sie war aus Bremen gebürtig, was übrigens, wenn sie sprach, an gewissen liebenswürdigen
Lautverzerrungen zu erkennen war, und hatte dortselbst vor zwie-
facher Jahresfrist dem Großhändler Klöterjahn ihr Jawort fürs
Leben erteilt. Sie war ihm in seine Vaterstadt, dort oben am Ostseestrande, gefolgt und hatte ihm vor nun etwa zehn Monaten
unter ganz außergewöhnlich schweren und gefährlichen Umständen ein Kind, einen bewundernswert lebhaften und wohlgeratenen
Sohn und Erben beschert. Seit diesen furchtbaren Tagen aber war
sie nicht wieder zu Kräften gekommen, gesetzt, daß sie jemals bei
Kräften gewesen war. Sie war kaum vom Wochenbette erstanden,
äußerst erschöpft, äußerst verarmt an Lebenskräften, als sie beim
Husten ein wenig Blut aufgebracht hatte,—oh, nicht viel, ein unbe-
deutendes bißchen Blut; aber es wäre doch besser überhaupt nicht
zum Vorschein gekommen, und das Bedenkliche war, daß derselbe
kleine unheimliche Vorfall sich nach kurzer Zeit wiederholte. Nun,
es gab Mittel hiergegen, und Doktor Hinzpeter, der Hausarzt, be-
diente sich ihrer. Vollständige Ruhe wurde geboten, Eisstückchen
wurden geschluckt, Morphium ward gegen den Hustenreiz verab-
folgt und das Herz nach Möglichkeit beruhigt. Die Genesung aber
wollte sich nicht einstellen, und während das Kind, Anton Klöterjahn der Jüngere, ein Prachtstück von einem Baby, mit ungeheurer
Energie und Rücksichtslosigkeit seinen Platz im Leben eroberte
und behauptete, schien die junge Mutter in einer sanften und stillen Glut dahinzuschwinden . . . Es war, wie gesagt, die Luftröhre,

3

The personality of the new patient created an unusual sensation at Einfried, and Mr. Klöterjahn, accustomed to such successes, received each homage offered to her with satisfaction. The diabetic general stopped grumbling for a moment when he first saw her, the gentlemen with the emaciated faces smiled and tried with a struggle to control their legs when they came near her, and Mrs. Spatz, the town councillor's wife, immediately attached herself to her as an older friend. Yes, she made an impression, the woman who bore Mr. Klöterjahn's name! A writer who had been spending his time at Einfried for a few weeks, an eccentric with strange ways whose name resembled that of a precious stone, actually turned pale when she passed by him in the corridor; he stopped short and was still standing as if rooted to the spot long after she had disappeared.

Not even two days had gone by and the entire patient body was acquainted with her story. She was born in Bremen—and this, by the way, was recognizable when she spoke because of certain endearing distortions of sounds—and it was there that, two years earlier, she had given her lifelong consent to the wholesale merchant Klöterjahn. She had followed him to his hometown, up there on the Baltic coast, and, about ten months previously, in quite unusually difficult and dangerous circumstances, had presented him with a child, an admirably vigorous and finely formed son and heir. But since those frightful days she had never regained her strength, assuming that she had ever had her strength. She had scarcely emerged from confinement, totally exhausted, totally drained of vitality, when she had brought up a little blood upon coughing—oh, not much, an insignificant bit of blood; but still it would have been better had it never showed up, and the serious part was that the same little unsettling incident recurred before very long. Now, there were remedies for this, and Dr. Hinzpeter, the family physician, applied them. Complete rest was prescribed, cracked ice was swallowed, morphine was administered to combat the irritating cough, and her heart was calmed down to the extent possible. But recovery failed to set in, and while the child, Anton Klöterjahn, Jr., a showpiece of a baby, conquered and asserted his place in life with tremendous energy and inconsiderateness, the young mother seemed to be fading away in a gentle, quiet glow . . . It was, as said,

ein Wort, das in Doktor Hinzpeters Munde eine überraschend tröst-
liche, beruhigende, fast erheiternde Wirkung auf alle Gemüter aus-
übte. Aber obgleich es nicht die Lunge war, hatte der Doktor
schließlich den Einfluß eines milderen Klimas und des Aufent-
haltes in einer Kuranstalt zur Beschleunigung der Heilung als dringend wünschenswert erachtet, und der Ruf des Sanatoriums ›Einfried‹ und seines Leiters hatte das übrige getan.

So verhielt es sich; und Herr Klöterjahn selbst erzählte es jedem,
der Interesse dafür an den Tag legte. Er redete laut, salopp und
gutgelaunt, wie ein Mann, dessen Verdauung sich in so guter Ordnung befindet wie seine Börse, mit weit ausladenden Lippenbewe-
gungen, in der breiten und dennoch rapiden Art der Küstenbewoh-
ner vom Norden. Manche Worte schleuderte er hervor, daß jeder
Laut einer kleinen Entladung glich, und lachte darüber wie über
einen gelungenen Spaß.

Er war mittelgroß, breit, stark und kurzbeinig und besaß ein vol-
les, rotes Gesicht mit wasserblauen Augen, die von ganz hellblon-
den Wimpern beschattet waren, geräumigen Nüstern und feuchten
Lippen. Er trug einen englischen Backenbart, war ganz englisch
gekleidet und zeigte sich entzückt, eine englische Familie, Vater,
Mutter und drei hübsche Kinder mit ihrer nurse, in ›Einfried‹ an-
zutreffen, die sich hier aufhielt, einzig und allein, weil sie nicht
wußte, wo sie sich sonst aufhalten sollte, und mit der er morgens
englisch frühstückte. Übrigens liebte er es, viel und gut zu speisen
und zu trinken, zeigte sich als ein wirklicher Kenner von Küche
und Keller und unterhielt die Kurgesellschaft aufs anregendste
von den Diners, die daheim in seinem Bekanntenkreise gegeben
wurden, sowie mit der Schilderung gewisser auserlesener, hier un-
bekannter Platten. Hierbei zogen seine Augen sich mit freundli-
chem Ausdruck zusammen und seine Sprache erhielt etwas Gaumi-
ges und Nasales, indes leicht schmatzende Geräusche im Schlunde
sie begleiteten. Daß er auch anderen irdischen Freuden nicht
grundsätzlich abhold war, bewies er an jenem Abend, als ein Kurgast von ›Einfried‹, ein Schriftsteller von Beruf, ihn auf dem Korridor in ziemlich unerlaubter Weise mit einem Stubenmädchen
scherzen sah,—ein kleiner, humoristischer Vorgang, zu dem der
betreffende Schriftsteller eine lächerlich angeekelte Miene machte.

Was Herrn Klöterjahns Gattin anging, so war klar und deutlich
zu beobachten, daß sie ihm von Herzen zugetan war. Sie folgte
lächelnd seinen Worten und Bewegungen: nicht mit der über-
heblichen Nachsicht, die manche Leidenden den Gesunden entge-

the trachea, a word that on Dr. Hinzpeter's lips exerted a surprisingly consoling, calming, almost cheering effect on everyone's spirits. But even though it was not the lungs, the doctor had finally decided that the influence of a milder climate and a stay in a sanatorium were urgently desirable to speed recovery, and the reputation of the sanatorium Einfried and of its director had done the rest.

That is how things stood; and Mr. Klöterjahn himself told the story to anyone who displayed any interest in it. He spoke loudly, carelessly and good-humoredly, like a man whose digestion is in just as good condition as his pocketbook, pursing his lips far out, in the broad yet rapid style of the northern coast-dwellers. He flung out certain words in such a way that every sound resembled a small explosion, and laughed about it as if it were a well-received joke.

He was of medium height, broad and sturdy, with short legs, and possessed a full, red face with watery blue eyes that were shaded by very light blonde lashes, and with wide nostrils and moist lips. He wore English-style side-whiskers, dressed completely in English fashion and was obviously delighted to meet at Einfried an English family—father, mother and three pretty children with their nursemaid—who were staying here merely because they didn't know where else to stay, and with whom he had an English breakfast every morning. Anyway, he liked to eat and drink plentifully and well, proved to be a real connoisseur of the kitchen and the wine cellar, and entertained the patients in most stimulating fashion with stories of the dinner parties that were given back home among his set of acquaintances, as well as with the description of certain choice dishes unknown here. At such times his eyes partially closed in an expression of friendliness, and his speech took on a palatal and nasal quality, while it was accompanied by quiet smacking noises in his throat. He proved that he was not fundamentally averse to other earthly joys as well on the evening when an Einfried patient, a writer by profession, saw him in the corridor toying with a chambermaid in a rather improper manner—a funny little event that caused the writer in question to grimace with ridiculously exaggerated disgust.

As far as Mr. Klöterjahn's wife was concerned, it was clear and evident to see that she was sincerely devoted to him. She followed his words and gestures with a smile: not with that arrogant forbearance that some sick people

genbringen, sondern mit der liebenswürdigen Freude und Teil-
nahme gutgearteter Kranker an den zuversichtlichen Lebens-
äußerungen von Leuten, die in ihrer Haut sich wohlfühlen.
Herr Klöterjahn verweilte nicht lange in ›Einfried‹. Er hatte seine
Gattin hierher geleitet; nach Verlauf einer Woche aber, als er sie
wohl aufgehoben und in guten Händen wußte, war seines Bleibens
nicht länger. Pflichten von gleicher Wichtigkeit, sein blühendes
Kind, sein ebenfalls blühendes Geschäft, riefen ihn in die Heimat
zurück; sie zwangen ihn, abzureisen und seine Frau im Genusse
der besten Pflege zurückzulassen.

4

Spinell hieß der Schriftsteller, der seit mehreren Wochen in ›Einfried‹ lebte, Detlev Spinell war sein Name, und sein Äußeres war
wunderlich.
Man vergegenwärtige sich einen Brünetten am Anfang der
Dreißiger und von stattlicher Statur, dessen Haar an den Schläfen
schon merklich zu ergrauen beginnt, dessen rundes, weißes, ein
wenig gedunsenes Gesicht aber nicht die Spur irgendeines Bart-
wuchses zeigt. Es war nicht rasiert,—man hätte es gesehen; weich,
verwischt und knabenhaft, war es nur hier und da mit einzelnen
Flaumhärchen besetzt. Und das sah ganz merkwürdig aus. Der
Blick seiner rehbraunen, blanken Augen war von sanftem Ausdruck, die Nase gedrungen und ein wenig zu fleischig. Ferner besaß
Herr Spinell eine gewölbte, poröse Oberlippe römischen Charak-
ters, große, kariöse Zähne und Füße von seltenem Umfang. Einer
der Herren mit den unbeherrschten Beinen, der ein Zyniker und
Witzbold war, hatte ihn hinter seinem Rücken »der verweste Säugling« getauft; aber das war hämisch und wenig zutreffend.—Er
ging gut und modisch gekleidet, in langem schwarzen Rock und
farbig punktierter Weste.
Er war ungesellig und hielt mit keiner Seele Gemeinschaft. Nur
zuweilen konnte eine leutselige, liebevolle und überquellende Stimmung ihn befallen, und das geschah jedesmal, wenn Herr Spinell
in ästhetischen Zustand verfiel, wenn der Anblick von irgend etwas
Schönem, der Zusammenklang zweier Farben, eine Vase von edler
Form, das vom Sonnenuntergang bestrahlte Gebirge ihn zu lauter
Bewunderung hinriß. »Wie schön!« sagte er dann, indem er den
Kopf auf die Seite legte, die Schultern emporzog, die Hände

bestow on the healthy, but with the amiable joy and concern that good-natured patients take in the optimistic manifestations of life of people who are feeling fit and at their ease.

Mr. Klöterjahn did not remain long at Einfried. He had escorted his wife down here; but at the end of a week, when he knew she was well looked after and in good hands, he could stay no longer. Duties of equal importance, his flourishing child, his equally flourishing business, called him back home; they compelled him to depart and leave his wife behind in the enjoyment of the finest care.

4

Spinell was the name of the writer who had been living at Einfried for several weeks; Detlev Spinell was his name, and his appearance was odd.

Picture a dark-haired man in his early thirties, of imposing height, whose hair is already beginning to gray noticeably at the temples, but whose face—round, white and a little puffy—shows no trace of any beard. It wasn't shaven—that could have been detected; soft, blurred and boyish, it was covered only here and there with isolated little downy hairs. And that looked quite peculiar. The gaze of his shiny, fawn-colored eyes had a gentle expression; his nose was short and thick and a little too fleshy. In addition Mr. Spinell possessed an arched, porous upper lip of a Roman type, large, decayed teeth and feet of an unusual size. One of the gentlemen with the uncontrolled legs, who was a cynic and a wag, had dubbed him "the corrupted infant" behind his back; but that was malicious and not too accurate.—He dressed well and fashionably, in a long black frock coat and a waistcoat with colored dots.

He was unsociable and kept company with no one. Only occasionally a companionable, affectionate and effervescent mood might come over him, and this happened each time that Mr. Spinell lapsed into an esthetic frame of mind, when the sight of something beautiful, the harmony of two colors, a vase of noble form, or the mountains in the glow of sunset inspired him with sheer admiration. "How beautiful!" he would then say, tilting his head to one side, raising his shoulders, spreading his hands and

spreizte und Nase und Lippen krauste. »Gott, sehen Sie, wie schön!« Und er war imstande, blindlings die distinguiertesten Herrschaften, ob Mann oder Weib, zu umhalsen in der Bewegung solcher Augenblicke . . .

Beständig lag auf seinem Tische, für jeden sichtbar, der sein Zimmer betrat, das Buch, das er geschrieben hatte. Es war ein Roman von mäßigem Umfange, mit einer vollkommen verwirrenden Umschlagzeichnung versehen und gedruckt auf einer Art von Kaffeesiebpapier mit Buchstaben, von denen ein jeder aussah wie eine gotische Kathedrale. Fräulein von Osterloh hatte es in einer müßigen Viertelstunde gelesen und fand es »raffiniert«, was ihre Form war, das Urteil »unmenschlich langweilig« zu umschreiben. Es spielte in mondänen Salons, in üppigen Frauengemächern, die voller erlesener Gegenstände waren, voll von Gobelins, uralten Meubles, köstlichem Porzellan, unbezahlbaren Stoffen und künstlerischen Kleinodien aller Art. Auf die Schilderung dieser Dinge war der liebevollste Wert gelegt, und beständig sah man dabei Herrn Spinell, wie er die Nase kraus zog und sagte: »Wie schön! Gott, sehen Sie, wie schön!«. . . Übrigens mußte es wundernehmen, daß er noch nicht mehr Bücher verfaßt hatte als dieses eine, denn augenscheinlich schrieb er mit Leidenschaft. Er verbrachte den größeren Teil des Tages schreibend auf seinem Zimmer und ließ außerordentlich viele Briefe zur Post befördern, fast täglich einen oder zwei,—wobei es nur als befremdend und belustigend auffiel, daß er seinerseits höchst selten welche empfing . . .

5

Herr Spinell saß der Gattin Herrn Klöterjahns bei Tische gegenüber. Zur ersten Mahlzeit, an der die Herrschaften teilnahmen, erschien er ein wenig zu spät in dem großen Speisesaal im Erdgeschoß des Seitenflügels, sprach mit weicher Stimme einen an alle gerichteten Gruß und begab sich an seinen Platz, worauf Doktor Leander ihn ohne viel Zeremonie den neu Angekommenen vorstellte. Er verbeugte sich und begann dann, offenbar ein wenig verlegen, zu essen, indem er Messer und Gabel mit seinen großen, weißen und schön geformten Händen, die aus sehr engen Ärmeln hervorsahen, in ziemlich affektierter Weise bewegte. Später ward er frei und betrachtete in Gelassenheit abwechselnd Herrn Klöterjahn und seine Gattin. Auch richtete Herr Klöterjahn im Verlaufe der Mahlzeit einige Fragen und Bemerkungen betreffend die Anlage und das Klima von ›Einfried‹ an ihn, in die seine Frau in ihrer lieblichen Art zwei oder drei Worte einfließen ließ, und die Herr

wrinkling his nose and lips. "God, look, how beautiful!" And he was capable, in the agitation of such moments, of blindly embracing the most distinguished people, whether male or female . . .

There lay constantly on his table, visible to everyone entering his room, the book he had written. It was a novel of moderate length, provided with a totally confusing dust-jacket drawing and printed on a kind of coffee-filter paper in typography every letter of which looked like a Gothic cathedral. Miss von Osterloh had read it in an idle quarter-hour and found it "refined," which was her way of saying that something was horribly boring. It took place in high-society salons, in luxurious boudoirs that were full of rare objects, full of tapestries, very old furniture, expensive porcelain, priceless fabrics and artistic treasures of all sorts. These things were described with the most loving care, and constantly you could see Mr. Spinell there wrinkling up his nose and saying, "How beautiful! God, look how beautiful!" . . . Incidentally, it could not fail to cause surprise that he had not yet written more books than that one, because he was obviously a passionate writer. He spent the greater part of the day writing in his room and sent an extraordinarily great number of letters out to be mailed, one or two almost daily—making it strange and amusing to observe that only extremely rarely did he receive any himself . . .

5

Mr. Spinell sat opposite Mr. Klöterjahn's wife at table. At the first meal at which the couple participated, he arrived a little too late in the large dining room on the first floor of the lateral wing, uttered a general greeting in a low voice and went to his seat, whereupon Dr. Leander introduced him to the newcomers without much ceremony. He bowed and then began to eat, obviously a little embarrassed, handling his knife and fork in a rather affected manner with his large, white and well-formed hands that protruded from very narrow sleeves. Later he became easier and calmly observed Mr. Klöterjahn and his wife in turn. Also, in the course of the meal, Mr. Klöterjahn addressed a few questions and remarks to him concerning the situation and climate of Einfried, his wife interjecting two or three words in her charming manner, and Mr.

Spinell höflich beantwortete. Seine Stimme war mild und recht angenehm; aber er hatte eine etwas behinderte und schlürfende Art zu sprechen, als seien seine Zähne der Zunge im Wege.

Nach Tische, als man ins Konversationszimmer hinübergegangen war und Doktor Leander den neuen Gästen im besonderen eine gesegnete Mahlzeit wünschte, erkundigte sich Herrn Klöterjahns Gattin nach ihrem Gegenüber.

»Wie heißt der Herr?« fragte sie . . . »Spinelli? Ich habe den Namen nich verstanden.«

»Spinell . . . nicht Spinelli, gnädige Frau. Nein, er ist kein Italiener, sondern bloß aus Lemberg gebürtig, soviel ich weiß . . .«

»Was sagten Sie? Er ist Schriftsteller? Oder was?« fragte Herr Klöterjahn; er hielt die Hände in den Taschen seiner bequemen englischen Hose, neigte sein Ohr dem Doktor zu und öffnete, wie manche Leute pflegen, den Mund beim Horchen.

»Ja, ich weiß nicht,—er schreibt . . .«, antwortete Doktor Leander. »Er hat, glaube ich, ein Buch veröffentlicht, eine Art Roman, ich weiß wirklich nicht . . .«

Dieses wiederholte »Ich weiß nicht« deutete an, daß Doktor Leander keine großen Stücke auf den Schriftsteller hielt und jede Verantwortung für ihn ablehnte.

»Aber das ist ja sehr interessant!« sagte Herrn Klöterjahns Gattin. Sie hatte noch nie einen Schriftsteller von Angesicht zu Angesicht gesehen.

»O ja«, erwiderte Doktor Leander entgegenkommend. »Er soll sich eines gewissen Rufes erfreuen . . .« Dann wurde nicht mehr von dem Schriftsteller gesprochen.

Aber ein wenig später, als die neuen Gäste sich zurückgezogen hatten und Doktor Leander ebenfalls das Konversationszimmer verlassen wollte, hielt Herr Spinell ihn zurück und erkundigte sich auch seinerseits.

»Wie ist der Name des Paares?« fragte er . . . »Ich habe natürlich nichts verstanden.«

»Klöterjahn«, antwortete Doktor Leander und ging schon wieder.

»*Wie* heißt der Mann?« fragte Herr Spinell . . .

»*Klöterjahn* heißen sie!« sagte Doktor Leander und ging seiner Wege.—Er hielt gar keine großen Stücke auf den Schriftsteller.

Spinell replying politely. His voice was mild and quite pleasant; but he had a somewhat hampered and slurping manner of talking, as if his teeth were in the way of his tongue.

After eating, when they had moved into the parlor and Dr. Leander was hoping that the new guests in particular had enjoyed their meal,[4] Mr. Klöterjahn's wife inquired about the man who had sat opposite her.

"What is the gentleman's name?" she asked . . . "Spinelli? I didn't get the name."

"Spinell . . . not Spinelli, madam. No, he isn't an Italian, but was merely born in Lemberg,[5] as far as I know . . ."

"What did you say? He's a writer? Or what?" asked Mr. Klöterjahn; his hands in the pockets of his comfortable English trousers, he turned his ear toward the doctor and opened his mouth while listening, as many people do.

"Well, I don't know—he writes . . . ," answered Dr. Leander. "I believe he has published a book, a sort of novel, I really don't know . . ."

This repeated "I don't know" indicated that Dr. Leander had no high opinion of the writer and declined all responsibility for him.

"But that's very interesting!" said Mr. Klöterjahn's wife. She had never yet seen a writer face to face.

"Oh, yes," replied Dr. Leander accommodatingly. "They say he has somewhat of a reputation . . ." Then nothing further was said about the writer.

But a little later, when the new guests had withdrawn and Dr. Leander also wanted to leave the parlor, Mr. Spinell kept him back and made inquiries of his own.

"What is that couple's name?" he asked . . . "Naturally I didn't make it out."

"Klöterjahn," answered Dr. Leander and made as if to go again.

"*What* is the man's name?" asked Mr. Spinell . . .

"Their name is *Klöterjahn!*" said Dr. Leander and went upon his way.—He definitely had no high opinion of the writer.

---

[4] This paraphrases a stereotypical German expression of wishes for good digestion after a meal.

[5] Now Lvov in the Galician part of the Ukraine. Galician origins play no part in the story, however, and Detlev is a north German name. At least one critic has thought that "Lemberg" was a humorous disguise for Lübeck.

6

Waren wir schon soweit, daß Herr Klöterjahn in die Heimat zurück-
gekehrt war? Ja, er weilte wieder am Ostseestrande, bei seinen Geschäften und seinem Kinde, diesem rücksichtslosen und lebensvol-
len kleinen Geschöpf, das seiner Mutter sehr viele Leiden und
einen kleinen Defekt an der Luftröhre gekostet hatte. Sie selbst
aber, die junge Frau, blieb in ›Einfried‹ zurück, und die Magistratsrätin Spatz schloß sich ihr als ältere Freundin an. Das aber hinderte
nicht, daß Herrn Klöterjahns Gattin auch mit den übrigen Kur-
gästen gute Kameradschaft pflegte, zum Beispiel mit Herrn Spinell,
der ihr zum Erstaunen aller (denn er hatte bislang mit keiner Seele
Gemeinschaft gehalten) von Anbeginn eine außerordentliche Erge-
benheit und Dienstfertigkeit entgegenbrachte, und mit dem sie in
den Freistunden, die eine strenge Tagesordnung ihr ließ, nicht
ungern plauderte.

Er näherte sich ihr mit einer ungeheuren Behutsamkeit und Ehr-
erbietung und sprach zu ihr nicht anders als mit sorgfältig gedämpfter Stimme, so daß die Rätin Spatz, die an den Ohren
krankte, meistens überhaupt nichts von dem verstand, was er sagte.
Er trat auf den Spitzen seiner großen Füße zu dem Sessel, in dem
Herrn Klöterjahns Gattin zart und lächelnd lehnte, blieb in einer
Entfernung von zwei Schritten stehen, hielt das eine Bein zurückgestellt und den Oberkörper vorgebeugt und sprach in seiner etwas
behinderten und schlürfenden Art leise, eindringlich und jeden
Augenblick bereit, eilends zurückzutreten und zu verschwinden,
sobald ein Zeichen von Ermüdung und Überdruß sich auf ihrem
Gesicht bemerkbar machen würde. Aber er verdroß sie nicht; sie
forderte ihn auf, sich zu ihr und der Rätin zu setzen, richtete irgendeine Frage an ihn und hörte ihm dann lächelnd und neugierig
zu, denn manchmal ließ er sich so amüsant und seltsam vernehmen,
wie es ihr noch niemals begegnet war.

»Warum sind Sie eigentlich in ›Einfried‹?« fragte sie. »Welche
Kur gebrauchen Sie, Herr Spinell?«

»Kur? . . . Ich werde ein bißchen elektrisiert. Nein, das ist nicht
der Rede wert. Ich werde Ihnen sagen, gnädige Frau, warum ich
hier bin.—Des Stiles wegen.«

»Ah!« sagte Herrn Klöterjahns Gattin, stützte das Kinn in die
Hand und wandte sich ihm mit einem übertriebenen Eifer zu, wie
man ihn Kindern vorspielt, wenn sie etwas erzählen wollen.

6

Had we reached the point where Mr. Klöterjahn returned home? Yes, he abode once again on the Baltic shore, near his business and his child, that inconsiderate and lively little being who had cost his mother much suffering and a little flaw in her trachea. She herself, however, the young woman, stayed behind at Einfried, and Mrs. Spatz, the town councillor's wife, attached herself to her as an older friend. But that did not prevent Mr. Klöterjahn's wife from practicing good fellowship with the other patients as well, for example with Mr. Spinell, who, to everyone's amazement (for up to then he had kept company with no one), from the outset displayed extraordinary devotion and attention toward her, and with whom she was fond of chatting in the free periods permitted her by her rigorous schedule.

He would approach her with tremendous circumspection and respect, and never spoke to her except in carefully lowered tones, so that Mrs. Spatz, who had trouble with her ears, generally understood nothing at all of what he was saying. He would walk on the toe-tips of his large feet to the armchair in which Mr. Klöterjahn's wife was sitting, gentle and smiling, would stop at a distance of two paces away, would place one leg behind him and incline the upper part of his body forward, and, in his somewhat hampered and slurping manner, would speak quietly and emphatically, ready at every instant to withdraw speedily and disappear the moment that a trace of fatigue and weariness might become noticeable in her face. But he did not annoy her; she invited him to sit with her and the councillor's wife, addressed some question or other to him, and then listened to him with smiling curiosity, for sometimes his conversation was more amusing and unusual than anything she had ever come across.

"Why are you really at Einfried?" she asked. "What cure are you taking, Mr. Spinell?"

"Cure? . . . I'm getting a little electric treatment. No, it's not worth mentioning. I'll tell you why I'm here, madam.—Because of the style."

"Oh!" said Mr. Klöterjahn's wife, propping her chin on her hand and turning toward him with that exaggerated eagerness that one simulates with children when they want to tell some story.

»Ja, gnädige Frau. ›Einfried‹ ist ganz empire, es ist ehedem ein Schloß, eine Sommerresidenz gewesen, wie man mir sagt. Dieser Seitenflügel ist ja ein Anbau aus späterer Zeit, aber das Hauptgebäude ist alt und echt. Es gibt Zeiten, in denen ich das empire einfach nicht entbehren kann, in denen es mir, um einen bescheidenen Grad des Wohlbefindens zu erreichen, unbedingt nötig ist. Es ist klar, daß man sich anders befindet zwischen Möbeln weich und bequem bis zur Laszivität, und anders zwischen diesen geradlinigen Tischen, Sesseln und Draperien. . . . Diese Helligkeit und Härte, diese kalte, herbe Einfachheit und reservierte Strenge verleiht mir Haltung und Würde, gnädige Frau, sie hat auf die Dauer eine innere Reinigung und Restaurierung zur Folge, sie hebt mich sittlich, ohne Frage . . .«

»Ja, das ist merkwürdig«, sagte sie. »Übrigens verstehe ich es, wenn ich mir Mühe gebe.«

Hierauf erwiderte er, daß es irgendwelcher Mühe nicht lohne, und dann lachten sie miteinander. Auch die Rätin Spatz lachte und fand es merkwürdig; aber sie sagte nicht, daß sie es verstünde.

Das Konversationszimmer war geräumig und schön. Die hohe, weiße Flügeltür zu dem anstoßenden Billardraume stand weit geöffnet, wo die Herren mit den unbeherrschten Beinen und andere sich vergnügten. Andererseits gewährte eine Glastür den Ausblick auf die breite Terrasse und den Garten. Seitwärts davon stand ein Piano. Ein grünausgeschlagener Spieltisch war vorhanden, an dem der diabetische General mit ein paar anderen Herren Whist spielte. Damen lasen und waren mit Handarbeiten beschäftigt. Ein eiserner Ofen besorgte die Heizung, aber vor dem stilvollen Kamin, in dem nachgeahmte, mit glühroten Papierstreifen beklebte Kohlen lagen, waren behagliche Plauderplätze.

»Sie sind ein Frühaufsteher, Herr Spinell«, sagte Herrn Klöterjahns Gattin. »Zufällig habe ich Sie nun schon zwei- oder dreimal um halb acht Uhr am Morgen das Haus verlassen sehen.«

»Ein Frühaufsteher? Ach, sehr mit Unterschied, gnädige Frau. Die Sache ist die, daß ich früh aufstehe, weil ich eigentlich ein Langschläfer bin.«

»Das müssen Sie nun erklären, Herr Spinell!«—Auch die Rätin Spatz wollte es erklärt haben.

»Nun, . . . ist man ein Frühaufsteher, so hat man es, dünkt mich, nicht nötig, gar so früh aufzustehen. Das Gewissen, gnädige Frau . . . es ist eine schlimme Sache mit dem Gewissen! Ich und meines-

"Yes, madam. Einfried is pure Empire. Formerly it was a palace, a royal summer residence, so they tell me. This lateral wing is of course an addition from a later period, but the main building is old and genuine. There are times at which I simply can't do without Empire, at which I find Empire absolutely necessary in order to attain a modest degree of good health. It is evident that you feel different when in the midst of furniture that is soft and comfortable to the point of lasciviousness than when you are in the midst of these rectilinear tables, armchairs and draperies. . . . This clarity and rigor, this cool, austere simplicity and reserved severity lends me bearing and dignity, madam, in the long run it results in an inner purification and restoration, it improves me morally, no question of it . . ."

"Yes, that is odd," she said. "What's more, I understand it if I make an effort."

Whereupon he replied that it wasn't worth any effort, and then they both laughed. Mrs. Spatz laughed too and found it odd; but she didn't say she understood it.

The parlor was spacious and beautiful. The high, white folding doors to the adjoining billiard room, where the gentlemen with the uncontrolled legs and others amused themselves, were wide open. On another side a glass door afforded a view of the broad terrace and the garden. At an angle to the door stood a piano. There was also a card table with a green cloth top, at which the diabetic general played whist with a few other gentlemen. Ladies were reading or occupied with needlework. An iron stove provided heating, but in front of the tasteful fireplace, in which lay imitation coals with fiery-red strips of paper pasted on them, there were cozy places for conversation.

"You are an early riser, Mr. Spinell," said Mr. Klöterjahn's wife. "I have now happened to see you two or three times leaving the house at half past seven in the morning."

"An early riser? Ah, but with a big difference, madam. The fact is that I get up early because I am actually a late sleeper."

"You must explain that now, Mr. Spinell!"—Mrs. Spatz wanted it explained, too.

"Now . . . if one is an early riser, one need not get up all that early, as I see it. Conscience, madam . . . Conscience is very troublesome! I and those like me struggle with it all

gleichen, wir schlagen uns zeit unseres Lebens damit herum und haben alle Hände voll zu tun, es hier und da zu betrügen und ihm kleine, schlaue Genugtuungen zuteil werden zu lassen. Wir sind unnütze Geschöpfe, ich und meinesgleichen, und abgesehen von wenigen guten Stunden schleppen wir uns an dem Bewußtsein unserer Unnützlichkeit wund und krank. Wir hassen das Nützliche, wir wissen, daß es gemein und unschön ist, und wir verteidigen diese Wahrheit, wie man nur Wahrheiten verteidigt, die man unbedingt nötig hat. Und dennoch sind wir so ganz vom bösen Gewissen zernagt, daß kein heiler Fleck mehr an uns ist. Hinzu kommt, daß die ganze Art unserer inneren Existenz, unsere Weltanschauung, unsere Arbeitsweise . . . von schrecklich ungesunder, unterminierender, aufreibender Wirkung ist, und auch dies verschlimmert die Sache. Da gibt es nun kleine Linderungsmittel, ohne die man es einfach nicht aushielte. Eine gewisse Artigkeit und hygienische Strenge der Lebensführung zum Beispiel ist manchen von uns Bedürfnis. Früh aufstehen, grausam früh, ein kaltes Bad und ein Spaziergang hinaus in den Schnee. . . . Das macht, daß wir vielleicht eine Stunde lang ein wenig zufrieden mit uns sind. Gäbe ich mich, wie ich bin, so würde ich bis in den Nachmittag hinein im Bette liegen, glauben Sie mir. Wenn ich früh aufstehe, so ist das eigentlich Heuchelei.«

»Nein, weshalb, Herr Spinell! Ich nenne das Selbstüberwindung . . . Nicht wahr, Frau Rätin?«—Auch die Rätin Spatz nannte es Selbstüberwindung.

»Heuchelei oder Selbstüberwindung, gnädige Frau! Welches Wort man nun vorzieht. Ich bin so gramvoll ehrlich veranlagt, daß ich . . .«

»Das ist es. Sicher grämen Sie sich zuviel.«

»Ja, gnädige Frau, ich gräme mich viel.«

—Das gute Wetter hielt an. Weiß, hart und sauber, in Windstille und lichtem Frost, in blendender Helle und bläulichem Schatten lag die Gegend, lagen Berge, Haus und Garten, und ein zartblauer Himmel, in dem Myriaden von flimmernden Leuchtkörperchen, von glitzernden Kristallen zu tanzen schienen, wölbte sich makellos über dem Ganzen. Der Gattin Herrn Klöterjahns ging es leidlich in dieser Zeit; sie war fieberfrei, hustete fast gar nicht und aß ohne allzuviel Widerwillen. Oftmals saß sie, wie das ihre Vorschrift war, stundenlang im sonnigen Frost auf der Terrasse. Sie saß im Schnee, ganz in Decken und Pelzwerk verpackt, und atmete hoffnungsvoll die reine, eisige Luft, um ihrer Luftröhre zu dienen. Dann bemerkte sie zuweilen Herrn Spinell, wie er, ebenfalls warm gekleidet und in Pelzschuhen, die seinen Füßen einen phantastischen Um-

our lives, and it's all that we can do to deceive it once in a while and treat it to some small, sly satisfactions. We are useless creatures, I and those like me, and apart from a few good hours, we suffer unbearably from the consciousness of how useless we are. We hate all that is useful, we know that it is vulgar and unlovely, and we defend this truth as people defend truths that they find absolutely essential. And yet we are so gnawed by our bad conscience that there isn't a sound spot left on our bodies. Besides that, the whole manner of our inner existence, our outlook on life, our way of working . . . has a terribly unhealthful, undermining, exhausting effect, and this too makes the situation worse. But there are small palliatives without which we simply wouldn't be able to stand it. A certain neatness and hygienic discipline in our life-style, for example, is a necessity for many of us. Early rising—cruelly early—a cold bath and a walk outside in the snow. . . . That allows us to be a little pleased with ourselves for an hour or so. If I followed my natural bent, I would stay in bed till the afternoon, believe me. If I get up early, it's really hypocrisy."

"No, why do you say that, Mr. Spinell? I call that a victory over oneself . . . Isn't that so, Mrs. Spatz?"—The councillor's wife also called it a victory over oneself.

"Hypocrisy or victory over oneself, madam! Whichever term you happen to prefer. My nature is so fretfully honest that I . . ."

"That's it. You surely fret too much."

"Yes, madam, I fret a great deal."

—The good weather continued. The region, the mountains, house and garden were white, firm and clean, with windless air and light frost, with dazzling daylight and bluish shadows; and a pale blue sky, in which myriads of twinkling particles of light and gleaming crystals seemed to dance, arched spotlessly over the entire ensemble. Mr. Klöterjahn's wife was feeling fairly good during this time; she had no fever, practically never coughed and ate without too much reluctance. She often sat for hours—as had been prescribed for her—in the frosty sunshine on the terrace. She sat amidst the snow, all wrapped up in blankets and furs, and optimistically inhaled the pure, icy air in order to benefit her trachea. Then she would sometimes notice Mr. Spinell, also warmly dressed and wearing fur shoes that made his feet look fantastically large, strolling

fang verliehen, sich im Garten erging. Er ging mit tastenden Schritten und einer gewissen behutsamen und steif-graziösen Armhaltung durch den Schnee, grüßte sie ehrerbietig, wenn er zur
Terrasse kam, und stieg die unteren Stufen hinan, um ein kleines
Gespräch zu beginnen.

»Heute, auf meinem Morgenspaziergang, habe ich eine schöne
Frau gesehen . . . Gott, sie war schön!« sagte er, legte den Kopf auf
die Seite und spreizte die Hände.

»Wirklich, Herr Spinell? Beschreiben Sie sie mir doch!«

»Nein, das kann ich nicht. Oder ich würde Ihnen doch ein un-
richtiges Bild von ihr geben. Ich habe die Dame im Vorübergehen
nur mit einem halben Blicke gestreift, ich habe sie in Wirklichkeit
nicht gesehen. Aber der verwischte Schatten von ihr, den ich empfing, hat genügt, meine Phantasie anzuregen und mich ein Bild mit
fortnehmen lassen, das schön ist . . . Gott, es ist schön!«

Sie lachte. »Ist das Ihre Art, sich schöne Frauen zu betrachten,
Herr Spinell?«

»Ja, gnädige Frau; und es ist eine bessere Art, als wenn ich ihnen
plump und wirklichkeitsgierig ins Gesicht starrte und den Eindruck
einer fehlerhaften Tatsächlichkeit davontrüge . . .«

»Wirklichkeitsgierig . . . Das ist ein sonderbares Wort! Ein richtiges Schriftstellerwort, Herr Spinell! Aber es macht Eindruck auf
mich, will ich Ihnen sagen. Es liegt so manches darin, wovon ich
wenig verstehe, etwas Unabhängiges und Freies, das sogar der
Wirklichkeit die Achtung kündigt, obgleich sie doch das Respekta-
belste ist, was es gibt, ja das Respektable selbst . . . Und dann begreife ich, daß es etwas gibt außer dem Handgreiflichen, etwas Zar-
teres . . .«

»Ich weiß nur ein Gesicht«, sagte er plötzlich mit einer seltsam
freudigen Bewegung in der Stimme, erhob seine geballten Hände
zu den Schultern und ließ in einem exaltierten Lächeln seine kariösen Zähne sehen . . . »Ich weiß nur ein Gesicht, dessen veredelte
Wirklichkeit durch meine Einbildung korrigieren zu wollen sünd-
haft wäre, das ich betrachten, auf dem ich verweilen möchte, nicht
Minuten, nicht Stunden, sondern mein ganzes Leben lang, mich
ganz darin verlieren und alles Irdische darüber vergessen . . .«

»Ja, ja, Herr Spinell. Nur daß Fräulein von Osterloh doch ziemlich abstehende Ohren hat.«

Er schwieg und verbeugte sich tief. Als er wieder aufrecht stand,
ruhten seine Augen mit einem Ausdruck von Verlegenheit und
Schmerz auf dem kleinen, seltsamen Äderchen, das sich blaßblau
und kränklich in der Klarheit ihrer wie durchsichtigen Stirn verzweigte.

in the garden. He walked through the snow with tentative steps and, with his arms in a certain circumspect and stiffly gracious position, greeted her respectfully when he came to the terrace and climbed the lower stairs in order to start a short conversation.

"Today, on my morning walk, I saw a beautiful woman . . . God, she was beautiful!" he said, tilted his head to one side and spread his hands.

"Really, Mr. Spinell? Please describe her to me!"

"No, I can't. Or else I would give you an incorrect picture of her. I merely cast half a glance at the lady as I passed by, I didn't actually see her. But the blurred shadow of her that I perceived was enough to stimulate my imagination and allow me to carry away an image that is beautiful . . . God, it is beautiful!"

She laughed. "Is that your way of looking at beautiful women, Mr. Spinell?"

"Yes, madam; and it is a better way than if I were to stare into their faces crudely, greedy for reality, and were to carry away the impression of a faulty actuality . . ."

"Greedy for reality . . . That's an unusual expression! A real author's expression, Mr. Spinell! But it impresses me, I must say. There's so much in it that I hardly understand, something independent and free, that refuses to allow respect even to reality, even though reality is after all the most respectable thing there is—in fact, respectability itself . . . And then I comprehend that something exists other than the tangible, something more delicate . . ."

"I know only one face," he said suddenly with a strangely joyous agitation in his voice, raised his clenched hands to his shoulders, and exposed his decayed teeth in an overwrought smile . . . "I know only one face whose refined reality it would be sinful to try to improve upon in my imagination, which I would want to observe, dwell upon, not for minutes, not for hours, but my whole life, to lose myself completely in it and forget all earthly things for its sake . . ."

"Yes, yes, Mr. Spinell. It's just that Miss von Osterloh's ears do stick out a bit."

He fell silent and made a low bow. When he stood erect again, his eyes rested with an expression of embarrassment and pain on the small, strange vein that branched out, pale blue and sickly, in the clarity of her seemingly transparent forehead.

7

Ein Kauz, ein ganz wunderlicher Kauz! Herrn Klöterjahns Gattin
dachte zuweilen nach über ihn, denn sie hatte sehr viele Zeit zum
Nachdenken. Sei es, daß der Luftwechsel anfing, die Wirkung zu
versagen, oder daß irgendein positiv schädlicher Einfluß sie berührt hatte: ihr Befinden war schlechter geworden, der Zustand
ihrer Luftröhre schien zu wünschen übrigzulassen, sie fühlte sich
schwach, müde, appetitlos, fieberte nicht selten; und Doktor Leander hatte ihr aufs entschiedenste Ruhe, Stillverhalten und Vorsicht
empfohlen. So saß sie, wenn sie nicht liegen mußte, in Gesellschaft
der Rätin Spatz, verhielt sich still und hing, eine Handarbeit im
Schoße, an der sie nicht arbeitete, diesem oder jenem Gedanken
nach.

Ja, er machte ihr Gedanken, dieser absonderliche Herr Spinell,
und, was das Merkwürdige war, nicht sowohl über seine als über
ihre eigene Person; auf irgendeine Weise rief er in ihr eine seltsame
Neugier, ein nie gekanntes Interesse für ihr eigenes Sein hervor.
Eines Tages hatte er gesprächsweise geäußert:
»Nein, es sind rätselvolle Tatsachen, die Frauen . . . sowenig neu
es ist, sowenig kann man ablassen, davor zu stehen und zu staunen.
Da ist ein wunderbares Geschöpf, eine Sylphe, ein Duftgebild, ein
Märchentraum von einem Wesen. Was tut sie? Sie geht hin und
ergibt sich einem Jahrmarktsherkules oder Schlächterburschen. Sie
kommt an seinem Arme daher, lehnt vielleicht sogar ihren Kopf
an seine Schulter und blickt dabei verschlagen lächelnd um sich
her, als wollte sie sagen: Ja, nun zerbrecht euch die Köpfe über
diese Erscheinung!—Und wir zerbrechen sie uns.«—
Hiermit hatte Herrn Klöterjahns Gattin sich wiederholt beschäftigt.

Eines anderen Tages fand zum Erstaunen der Rätin Spatz fol-
gendes Zwiegespräch zwischen ihnen statt.
»Darf ich einmal fragen, gnädige Frau (aber es ist wohl naseweis),
wie Sie heißen, wie eigentlich Ihr Name ist?«
»Ich heiße doch Klöterjahn, Herr Spinell!«
»Hm.—Das weiß ich. Oder vielmehr: ich leugne es. Ich meine
natürlich Ihren eigenen Namen, Ihren Mädchennamen. Sie werden gerecht sein und einräumen, gnädige Frau, daß, wer Sie ›Frau
Klöterjahn‹ nennen wollte, die Peitsche verdiente.«
Sie lachte so herzlich, daß das blaue Äderchen über ihrer Braue
beängstigend deutlich hervortrat und ihrem zarten, süßen Gesicht
einen Ausdruck von Anstrengung und Bedrängnis verlieh, der tief
beunruhigte.

7

An eccentric, a truly odd eccentric! Mr. Klöterjahn's wife thought about him at times, for she had plenty of time for reflection. Whether it was that the change of air began to lose its effect or that some positively harmful influence had affected her, her health had grown worse, the condition of her trachea apparently left much to be desired, she felt weak and tired, had no appetite and was often feverish; and Dr. Leander had most firmly recommended quiet, inactivity and prudence. And so, when she was not forced to stay in bed, she sat in the company of Mrs. Spatz, kept still and, with needlework in her lap that she didn't work on, pursued this or that thought.

Yes, he gave her food for thought, that strange Mr. Spinell, and, what was peculiar, it was not so much about him as about herself; in some way he aroused a strange curiosity in her, a hitherto unknown interest in her own being. One day, in conversation, he had said:

"No, women are puzzling facts . . . though it's no novelty, still one can't avoid facing it with astonishment. There you see a wonderful being, a sylph, all compounded of fragrance, a fairy-tale dream of a creature. What does she do? She goes out and gives herself to a carnival strongman or a butcher boy. She walks by on his arm, perhaps even leans her head on his shoulder and, as she does so, she artfully looks all around with a smile as if saying: Yes, now rack your brains over this phenomenon!—And we rack them."

Mr. Klöterjahn's wife had repeatedly thought about that.

Another day, to Mrs. Spatz's amazement, the following dialogue took place between them.

"May I ask, madam (but it is surely impudent), what your name is, your real name?"

"But my name is Klöterjahn, Mr. Spinell!"

"Hm.—That I know. Or rather: I deny it. Naturally I mean your own name, your maiden name. You will be just and acknowledge, madam, that anyone who wished to call you 'Mrs. Klöterjahn' would deserve a whipping."

She laughed so heartily that the small blue vein over her eyebrow stood out with alarming clarity and lent her delicate, sweet face an expression of strain and distress that was deeply unsettling.

»Nein! Bewahre, Herr Spinell! Die Peitsche? Ist ›Klöterjahn‹
Ihnen so fürchterlich?«

»Ja, gnädige Frau, ich hasse diesen Namen aus Herzensgrund,
seit ich ihn zum erstenmal vernahm. Er ist komisch und zum Ver-
zweifeln unschön, und es ist Barbarei und Niedertracht, wenn man
die Sitte so weit treibt, auf Sie den Namen Ihres Herrn Gemahls zu
übertragen.«

»Nun, und ›Eckhof‹? Ist Eckhof schöner? Mein Vater heißt
Eckhof.«

»Oh, sehen Sie! ›Eckhof‹ ist etwas ganz anderes! Eckhof hieß
sogar ein großer Schauspieler. Eckhof passiert.—Sie erwähnten
nur Ihres Vaters. Ist Ihre Frau Mutter . . .«

»Ja; meine Mutter starb, als ich noch klein war.«

»Ah.—Sprechen Sie mir doch ein wenig mehr von Ihnen, darf
ich Sie bitten? Wenn es Sie ermüdet, dann nicht. Dann ruhen Sie,
und ich fahre fort, Ihnen von Paris zu erzählen, wie neulich. Aber
Sie könnten ja ganz leise reden, ja, wenn Sie flüstern, so wird das
alles nur schöner machen . . . Sie wurden in Bremen geboren?«
Und diese Frage tat er beinahe tonlos, mit einem ehrfurchtsvollen
und inhaltsschweren Ausdruck, als sei Bremen eine Stadt ohneglei-
chen, eine Stadt voller unnennbarer Abenteuer und verschwiege-
ner Schönheiten, in der geboren zu sein eine geheimnisvolle Hoheit
verleihe.

»Ja, denken Sie!« sagte sie unwillkürlich. »Ich bin aus Bremen.«

»Ich war einmal dort«, bemerkte er nachdenklich.—

»Mein Gott, Sie waren auch *dort*? Nein, hören Sie, Herr Spinell,
zwischen Tunis und Spitzbergen haben Sie, glaube ich, alles gesehen!«

»Ja, ich war einmal dort«, wiederholte er. »Ein paar kurze Abend-
stunden. Ich entsinne mich einer alten, schmalen Straße, über
deren Giebeln schief und seltsam der Mond stand. Dann war ich in
einem Keller, in dem es nach Wein und Moder roch. Das ist eine
durchdringende Erinnerung . . .«

»Wirklich? Wo mag das gewesen sein?—Ja, in solchem grauen
Giebelhause, einem alten Kaufmannshause mit hallender Diele und
weißlackierter Galerie, bin ich geboren.«

»Ihr Herr Vater ist also Kaufmann?« fragte er ein wenig zögernd.

»Ja. Aber außerdem und eigentlich wohl in erster Linie ist er ein
Künstler.«

"No! Heaven forbid, Mr. Spinell! A whipping? Do you find 'Klöterjahn' so frightful?"

"Yes, madam, I have hated that name from the bottom of my heart ever since I first heard it. It is comical and desperately unlovely, and it is barbaric and sordid to carry convention so far as to transfer your husband's name to you."

"Now, what about 'Eckhof'? Is Eckhof lovelier? My father's name is Eckhof."

"Oh, just see! 'Eckhof' is something else altogether! Eckhof was even the name of a great actor.[6] Eckhof will pass.—You mentioned only your father. Is your mother . . ."

"Yes; my mother died when I was still small."

"Ah.—But tell me a little more about yourself, please. It if tires you, don't. Then rest and I shall continue telling you about Paris, as I did recently. But you could speak very quietly; in fact, if you whisper that would make it all even lovelier . . . You were born in Bremen?" And he asked this question almost soundlessly, with a respectful and momentous expression, as if Bremen were a city without equal, a city full of inexpressible adventures and secret beauties, and as if to be born there lent a person some mysterious majesty.

"Yes, just think!" she said involuntarily. "I am from Bremen."

"I was once there," he remarked reflectively.

"Good heavens, you were *there*, too? No, listen, Mr. Spinell, I think you've seen everything between Tunis and Spitzbergen!"

"Yes, I was once there," he repeated. "A few short hours one evening. I recall an old, narrow street with the moon hanging crookedly and oddly over its gables. Then I was in a cellar that smelled of wine and mildew. That is a pungent recollection . . ."

"Really? Where could that have been?—Yes, I was born in just such a gray gabled house, an old merchant's house with an echoing vestibule and a white-painted gallery."

"Then your father is a merchant?" he asked with some hesitation.

"Yes. But in addition, and actually first and foremost, he is an artist."

---

[6] Hans Conrad Dietrich Ekhof (or Eckhof, 1720–1778), "father of the actor's art in Germany."

»Ah! Ah! Inwiefern?«

»Er spielt die Geige . . . Aber das sagt nicht viel. *Wie* er sie spielt, Herr Spinell, das ist die Sache! Einige Töne habe ich niemals hören können, ohne daß mir die Tränen so merkwürdig brennend in die Augen stiegen, wie sonst bei keinem Erlebnis. Sie glauben es nicht . . .«

»Ich glaube es! Ach, ob ich es glaube! . . . Sagen Sie mir, gnädige Frau: Ihre Familie ist wohl alt? Es haben wohl schon viele Generationen in dem grauen Giebelhaus gelebt, gearbeitet und das Zeitliche gesegnet?«

»Ja.—Warum fragen Sie übrigens?«

»Weil es nicht selten geschieht, daß ein Geschlecht mit praktischen, bürgerlichen und trockenen Traditionen sich gegen das Ende seiner Tage noch einmal durch die Kunst verklärt.«

»Ist dem so?—Ja, was meinen Vater betrifft, so ist er sicherlich mehr ein Künstler als mancher, der sich so nennt und vom Ruhme lebt. Ich spiele nur ein bißchen Klavier. Jetzt haben sie es mir ja verboten; aber damals, zu Hause, spielte ich noch. Mein Vater und ich, wir spielten zusammen . . . Ja, ich habe all die Jahre in lieber Erinnerung; besonders den Garten, unseren Garten, hinterm Hause. Er war jämmerlich verwildert und verwuchert und von zerbröckelten, bemoosten Mauern eingeschlossen; aber gerade das gab ihm viel Reiz. In der Mitte war ein Springbrunnen, mit einem dichten Kranz von Schwertlilien umgeben. Im Sommer verbrachte ich dort lange Stunden mit meinen Freundinnen. Wir saßen alle auf kleinen Feldsesseln rund um den Springbrunnen herum . . .«

»Wie schön!« sagte Herr Spinell und zog die Schultern empor. »Saßen Sie und sangen?«

»Nein, wir häkelten meistens.«

»Immerhin . . . Immerhin . . .«

»Ja, wir häkelten und schwatzten, meine sechs Freundinnen und ich . . .«

»Wie schön! Gott, hören Sie, wie schön!« rief Herr Spinell, und sein Gesicht war gänzlich verzerrt.

»Was finden Sie nun *hieran* so besonders schön, Herr Spinell!«

»Oh, dies, daß es sechs außer Ihnen waren, daß Sie nicht in diese Zahl eingeschlossen waren, sondern daß Sie gleichsam als Königin daraus hervortraten . . . Sie waren ausgezeichnet vor Ihren sechs Freundinnen. Eine kleine goldene Krone, ganz unscheinbar, aber bedeutungsvoll, saß in Ihrem Haar und blinkte . . .«

»Nein, Unsinn, nichts von einer Krone . . .«

»Doch, sie blinkte heimlich. Ich hätte sie gesehen, hätte sie deut-

"Ah! Ah! In what way?"

"He plays the violin . . . But that doesn't say much. *How* he plays it, Mr. Spinell, that's what counts! I have never been able to hear certain tones without tears coming to my eyes, such unusually hot tears, as no other experience can cause. You don't believe it . . ."

"I do believe it! Oh, and how I believe it! . . . Tell me, madam: is your family old? No doubt many generations have lived, worked and passed on in that gray gabled house?"

"Yes.—But why do you ask?"

"Because it frequently happens that a family with practical, bourgeois and dry traditions is once more transfigured by art toward the end of its days."

"Is that true?—Yes, as far as my father is concerned, he is surely more of an artist than many a one who calls himself so and lives off his reputation. I merely play a little piano. Now, of course, they have forbidden me to; but at that time, at home, I still played. My father and I would play music together . . . Yes, I hold all those years in fond remembrance; especially the garden, our garden, in back of the house. It was pitifully overgrown and run to seed and was enclosed by crumbling, moss-covered walls; but it was just that that gave it so much charm. In the center was a fountain, surrounded by a dense circle of irises. In the summer I would spend long hours there with my girl friends. We all sat around the fountain on little garden stools . . ."

"How beautiful!" said Mr. Spinell and raised his shoulders. "You would sit and sing?"

"No, we usually crocheted."

"All the same . . . All the same . . ."

"Yes, we would crochet and chatter, my six girl friends and I . . ."

"How beautiful! God, listen, how beautiful!" shouted Mr. Spinell, and his face was completely distorted.

"What do you find so particularly beautiful in *that*, Mr. Spinell?"

"Oh, the fact that there were six besides you, that you weren't included in that number, but stood out as if you were a queen . . . You were set apart from your six friends. A little golden crown, very inconspicuous but significant, rested in your hair and shone . . ."

"No, nonsense! there was nothing like a crown . . ."

"Oh, yes, it was shining secretly. I would have seen it, I

lich in Ihrem Haar gesehen, wenn ich in einer dieser Stunden unvermerkt im Gestrüpp gestanden hätte . . .«

»Gott weiß, was Sie gesehen hätten. Sie standen aber nicht dort,
sondern eines Tages war es mein jetziger Mann, der zusammen mit
meinem Vater aus dem Gebüsch hervortrat. Ich fürchte, sie hatten
sogar allerhand von unserem Geschwätz belauscht . . .«

»Dort war es also, wo Sie Ihren Herrn Gemahl kennenlernten,
gnädige Frau?«

»Ja, dort lernte ich ihn kennen!« sagte sie laut und fröhlich, und
indem sie lächelte, trat das zartblaue Äderchen angestrengt und
seltsam über ihrer Braue hervor. »Er besuchte meinen Vater in
Geschäften, wissen Sie. Am nächsten Tage war er zum Diner geladen, und noch drei Tage später hielt er um meine Hand an.«

»Wirklich! Ging das alles so außerordentlich schnell?«

»Ja . . . Das heißt, von nun an ging es ein wenig langsamer. Denn
mein Vater war der Sache eigentlich gar nicht geneigt, müssen Sie
wissen, und machte eine längere Bedenkzeit zur Bedingung. Erstens wollte er mich lieber bei sich behalten, und dann hatte er noch
andere Skrupel. Aber . . .«

»Aber?«

»Aber ich *wollte* es eben«, sagte sie lächelnd, und wieder beherrschte das blaßblaue Äderchen mit einem bedrängten und
kränklichen Ausdruck ihr ganzes liebliches Gesicht.

»Ah, Sie wollten es.«

»Ja, und ich habe einen ganz festen und respektablen Willen
gezeigt, wie Sie sehen . . .«

»Wie ich es sehe. Ja.«

». . . so daß mein Vater sich schließlich darein ergeben mußte.«

»Und so verließen Sie ihn denn und seine Geige, verließen das
alte Haus, den verwucherten Garten, den Springbrunnen und Ihre
sechs Freundinnen und zogen mit Herrn Klöterjahn.«

»Und zog mit . . . Sie haben eine Ausdrucksweise, Herr Spinell!
Beinahe biblisch!—Ja, ich verließ das alles, denn so will es ja die
Natur.«

»Ja, so will sie es wohl.«

»Und dann handelte es sich ja um mein Glück.«

»Gewiß. Und es kam, das Glück . . .«

»Das kam in der Stunde, Herr Spinell, als man mir zuerst den
kleinen Anton brachte, unseren kleinen Anton, und als er so kräftig
mit seinen kleinen gesunden Lungen schrie, stark und gesund wie
er ist . . .«

»Es ist nicht das erstemal, daß ich Sie von der Gesundheit Ihres

would have seen it clearly in your hair, if I had stood unnoticed in the shrubbery on one of those occasions . . ."

"God knows what you would have seen. You weren't standing there, however, but one day it was my present husband who stepped out of the bushes with my father. I'm afraid that they had even overheard a lot of our chatter . . ."

"So it was there that you met your husband, madam?"

"Yes, I met him there," she said loudly and happily, and as she smiled the little light blue vein stood out over her forehead in a strained, strange way. "He was visiting my father on business, you see. On the next day he was invited to dinner, and just three days later he asked for my hand."

"Really? Did everything go so extraordinarily fast?"

"Yes . . . That is, from then on it went a little more slowly. Because my father wasn't really at all favorable to the matter, you must know, and stipulated a longish period for thinking things over. For one thing, he preferred keeping me at home, and then he had other misgivings as well. But . . ."

"But?"

"But I *wanted* it," she said with a smile, and once again the little pale blue vein dominated her whole lovely face with a distressed and sickly expression.

"Ah, you wanted it."

"Yes, and I displayed some very firm and respectable will power, as you see . . ."

"As I see. Yes."

". . . so that my father finally had to consent."

"And so you then abandoned him and his violin, you abandoned the old house, the overgrown garden, the fountain and your six friends, and wended your way with Mr. Klöterjahn."

"And wended my way with . . . What expressions you use, Mr. Spinell! Almost biblical!—Yes, I abandoned all that, because that's what Nature demands."

"Yes, she does."

"And then it was a question of my happiness."

"Certainly. And your happiness arrived . . ."

"It came, Mr. Spinell, at the moment when they first brought little Anton over to me, our little Anton, and when he yelled so powerfully with his healthy little lungs, strong and healthy as he is . . ."

"This is not the first time I have heard you speak about

kleinen Anton sprechen höre, gnädige Frau. Er muß ganz unge-
wöhnlich gesund sein?«

»Das ist er. Und er sieht meinem Mann so lächerlich ähnlich!«

»Ah!—Ja, so begab es sich also. Und nun heißen Sie nicht mehr
Eckhof, sondern anders, und haben den kleinen gesunden Anton
und leiden ein wenig an der Luftröhre.«

»Ja.—Und *Sie* sind ein durch und durch rätselhafter Mensch,
Herr Spinell, dessen versichere ich Sie . . .«

»Ja, straf' mich Gott, das sind Sie!« sagte die Rätin Spatz, die
übrigens auch noch vorhanden war.

Aber auch mit diesem Gespräch beschäftigte Herrn Klöterjahns
Gattin sich mehrere Male in ihrem Innern. So nichtssagend es war,
barg es doch einiges auf seinem Grunde, was ihren Gedanken über
sich selbst Nahrung gab. War *dies* der schädliche Einfluß, der sie
berührte? Ihre Schwäche nahm zu, und oft stellte Fieber sich ein,
eine stille Glut, in der sie mit einem Gefühle sanfter Gehobenheit
ruhte, der sie sich in einer nachdenklichen, preziösen, selbstgefälli-
gen und ein wenig beleidigten Stimmung überließ. Wenn sie nicht
das Bett hütete und Herr Spinell auf den Spitzen seiner großen
Füße mit ungeheurer Behutsamkeit zu ihr trat, in einer Entfernung
von zwei Schritten stehenblieb und, das eine Bein zurückgestellt
und den Oberkörper vorgebeugt, mit ehrfürchtig gedämpfter
Stimme zu ihr sprach, wie als höbe er sie in scheuer Andacht sanft
und hoch empor und bettete sie auf Wolkenpfühle, woselbst kein
schriller Laut und keine irdische Berührung sie erreichen solle . . .,
so erinnerte sie sich der Art, in der Herr Klöterjahn zu sagen
pflegte: »Vorsichtig, Gabriele, take care, mein Engel, und halte den
Mund zu!«, eine Art, die wirkte, als schlüge er einem hart und
wohlmeinend auf die Schulter. Dann aber wandte sie sich rasch von
dieser Erinnerung ab, um in Schwäche und Gehobenheit auf
den Wolkenpfühlen zu ruhen, die Herr Spinell ihr dienend be-
reitete.

Eines Tages kam sie unvermittelt auf das kleine Gespräch zurück,
das sie mit ihm über ihre Herkunft und Jugend geführt hatte.

»Es ist also wahr«, fragte sie, »Herr Spinell, daß Sie die Krone
gesehen hätten?«

Und obgleich jene Plauderei schon vierzehn Tage zurücklag,
wußte er sofort, um was es sich handelte, und versicherte ihr mit
bewegten Worten, daß er damals am Springbrunnen, als sie unter
ihren sechs Freundinnen saß, die kleine Krone hätte blinken,—sie
heimlich in ihrem Haar hätte blinken sehen.

the good health of your little Anton, madam. He must be quite unusually healthy?"

"He is. And he looks so laughably like my husband!"

"Ah!—Yes, that's how it occurred, then. And now your name is no longer Eckhof, but something else, and you have your healthy little Anton and have a little trouble with your trachea."

"Yes.—And *you* are a thoroughly puzzling person, Mr. Spinell, that I assure you . . ."

"Yes, God punish me, you certainly are!" said Mrs. Spatz, who, incidentally, was still present.

But this conversation, too, occupied the thoughts of Mr. Klöterjahn's wife several times. Inconsequential as it was, it nevertheless contained something deep down that fueled her thoughts about herself. Was *this* the harmful influence that was affecting her? Her weakness increased, and often fever set in, a quiet heat in which she rested with a feeling of gentle elation, and to which she abandoned herself in a reflective, affected, self-indulgent and somewhat offended mood. When she wasn't keeping her bed, and Mr. Spinell advanced toward her with tremendous circumspection on the toe-tips of his large feet, stopped at a distance of two paces and, putting one leg behind him and leaning the upper part of his body forward, spoke to her in respectfully lowered tones, as if he were gently raising her aloft in timid adoration and pillowing her on cushions of clouds, where no shrill sound and no earthly contact could reach her . . . , then she would remember the manner in which Mr. Klöterjahn used to say: "Careful, Gabriele, take care, darling, and keep your mouth closed!," a manner equivalent to his slapping someone on the back hard and benevolently. But then she would quickly turn away from that recollection, in order to rest, weak and elated, on the cushions of cloud that Mr. Spinell was serviceably preparing for her.

One day she abruptly recalled the short conversation she had had with him about her origins and her youth.

"It's true, then, Mr. Spinell," she asked, "that you would have seen the crown?"

And even though that chat had occurred two weeks previously, he immediately knew what she was referring to, and assured her with agitated words that then by the fountain, as she sat among her six friends, he would have seen the little crown shining—would have seen it secretly shining in her hair.

Einige Tage später erkundigte sich ein Kurgast aus Artigkeit bei ihr nach dem Wohlergehen ihres kleinen Anton daheim. Sie ließ zu Herrn Spinell, der sich in der Nähe befand, einen hurtigen Blick hinübergleiten und antwortete ein wenig gelangweilt: »Danke; wie soll es dem wohl gehen?—Ihm und meinem Mann geht es gut.«

8

Ende Februar, an einem Frosttage, reiner und leuchtender als alle, die vorhergegangen waren, herrschte in ›Einfried‹ nichts als Übermut. Die Herrschaften mit den Herzfehlern besprachen sich untereinander mit geröteten Wangen, der diabetische General trällerte wie ein Jüngling, und die Herren mit den unbeherrschten Beinen waren ganz außer Rand und Band. Was ging vor? Nichts Geringeres, als daß eine gemeinsame Ausfahrt unternommen werden sollte, eine Schlittenpartie in mehreren Fuhrwerken mit Schellenklang und Peitschenknall ins Gebirge hinein: Doktor Leander hatte zur Zerstreuung seiner Patienten diesen Beschluß gefaßt.

Natürlich mußten die ›Schweren‹ zu Hause bleiben. Die armen ›Schweren‹! Man nickte sich zu und verabredete sich, sie nichts von dem Ganzen wissen zu lassen; es tat allgemein wohl, ein wenig Mitleid üben und Rücksicht nehmen zu können. Aber auch von denen, die sich an dem Vergnügen sehr wohl hätten beteiligen können, schlossen sich einige aus. Was Fräulein von Osterloh anging, so war sie ohne weiteres entschuldigt. Wer wie sie mit Pflichten überhäuft war, durfte an Schlittenpartien nicht ernstlich denken. Der Hausstand verlangte gebieterisch ihre Anwesenheit, und kurzum: sie blieb in ›Einfried‹. Daß aber auch Herrn Klöterjahns Gattin erklärte, daheim bleiben zu wollen, verstimmte allseitig. Vergebens redete Doktor Leander ihr zu, die frische Fahrt auf sich wirken zu lassen; sie behauptete, nicht aufgelegt zu sein, Migräne zu haben, sich matt zu fühlen, und so mußte man sich fügen. Der Zyniker und Witzbold aber nahm Anlaß zu der Bemerkung:

»Geben Sie acht, nun fährt auch der verweste Säugling nicht mit.«

Und er bekam recht, denn Herr Spinell ließ wissen, daß er heute nachmittag arbeiten wolle;—er gebrauchte sehr gern das Wort ›arbeiten‹ für seine zweifelhafte Tätigkeit. Übrigens beklagte sich keine Seele über sein Fortbleiben, und ebenso leicht verschmerzte

A few days later a patient, out of politeness, asked her about the health of her little Anton at home. She cast a rapid glance at Mr. Spinell, who was close by, and answered with a hint of boredom:

"Thank you; how should he be?—He and my husband are well."

8

On one frosty late February day, purer and more glowing than any that had preceded, nothing but high spirits reigned at Einfried. The people with heart disease conferred with one another with flushed cheeks, the diabetic general hummed like a boy, and the gentlemen with the uncontrolled legs were completely beside themselves. What was going on? Nothing less than this: a general excursion was to take place, a sleigh ride into the mountains in a number of conveyances with jingling bells and cracking whips. Dr. Leander had made this decision for the entertainment of his patients.

Naturally the "serious cases" had to stay home. Poor "serious cases"! People nodded at one another and made a promise not to let them know anything about it; it was generally beneficial to be able to extend a little sympathy and show a little consideration. But even among those who could very well have participated in the festivities, a few absented themselves. As far as Miss von Osterloh was concerned, she was implicitly excused. Anyone so loaded with responsibilities as she was couldn't seriously think about sleigh rides. The housekeeping imperiously demanded her presence, and in short: she stayed at Einfried. But the declaration by Mr. Klöterjahn's wife that she too wanted to stay home caused universal dejection. In vain did Dr. Leander urge her to take advantage of the healthful ride; she claimed that she wasn't in the mood, that she had a migraine, that she felt weak, and so people had to give in. The cynic and wag, however, took the opportunity to remark:

"Watch out, now the corrupted infant won't go along either."

And he proved to be right, for Mr. Spinell let it be known that he wished to work that afternoon—he was very fond of using the word "work" for his dubious activities. Moreover, not a soul lamented his absence, and they

man es, daß die Rätin Spatz sich entschloß, ihrer jüngeren Freundin
Gesellschaft zu leisten, da das Fahren sie seekrank mache.

Gleich nach dem Mittagessen, das heute schon gegen zwölf Uhr
stattgefunden hatte, hielten die Schlitten vor ›Einfried‹, und in lebhaften Gruppen, warm vermummt, neugierig und angeregt, bewegten sich die Gäste durch den Garten. Herrn Klöterjahns Gattin
stand mit der Rätin Spatz an der Glastür, die zur Terrasse führte,
und Herr Spinell am Fenster seines Zimmers, um der Abfahrt zuzu-
sehen. Sie beobachteten, wie unter Scherzen und Gelächter kleine
Kämpfe um die besten Plätze entstanden, wie Fräulein von
Osterloh, eine Pelzboa um den Hals, von einem Gespann zum anderen lief, um Körbe mit Eßwaren unter die Sitze zu schieben, wie
Doktor Leander, die Pelzmütze in der Stirn, mit seinen funkelnden
Brillengläsern noch einmal das Ganze überschaute, dann ebenfalls
Platz nahm und das Zeichen zum Aufbruch gab ... Die Pferde
zogen an, ein paar Damen kreischten und fielen hintüber, die
Schellen klapperten, die kurzstieligen Peitschen knallten und ließen
ihre langen Schnüre im Schnee hinter den Kufen dreinschleppen,
und Fräulein von Osterloh stand an der Gartenpforte und winkte
mit ihrem Schnupftuch, bis an einer Biegung der Landstraße die
gleitenden Gefährte verschwanden, das frohe Geräusch sich verlor.
Dann kehrte sie durch den Garten zurück, um ihren Pflichten nach-
zueilen, die beiden Damen verließen die Glastür, und fast gleichzeitig trat auch Herr Spinell von seinem Aussichtspunkte ab.

Ruhe herrschte in ›Einfried‹. Die Expedition war vor Abend
nicht zurückzuerwarten. Die ›Schweren‹ lagen in ihren Zimmern
und litten. Herrn Klöterjahns Gattin und ihre ältere Freundin un-
ternahmen einen kurzen Spaziergang, worauf sie in ihre Gemächer
zurückkehrten. Auch Herr Spinell befand sich in dem seinen und
beschäftigte sich auf seine Art. Gegen vier Uhr brachte man den
Damen je einen halben Liter Milch, während Herr Spinell seinen
leichten Tee erhielt. Kurze Zeit darauf pochte Herrn Klöterjahns
Gattin an die Wand, die ihr Zimmer von dem der Magistratsrätin
Spatz trennte, und sagte:

»Wollen wir nicht ins Konversationszimmer hinuntergehen, Frau
Rätin? Ich weiß nicht mehr, was ich hier anfangen soll.«

»Sogleich, meine Liebe!« antwortete die Rätin. »Ich ziehe nur
meine Stiefel an, wenn Sie erlauben. Ich habe nämlich auf dem
Bette gelegen, müssen Sie wissen.«

Wie zu erwarten stand, war das Konversationszimmer leer. Die
Damen nahmen am Kamine Platz. Die Rätin Spatz stickte Blumen

found it equally easy to accept the loss of Mrs. Spatz, who decided to keep her younger friend company because riding made her seasick.

Immediately after the midday meal, which had been served early that day, about noon, the sleighs stopped in front of Einfried, and in animated groups, disguised by their bundled warm clothing, curious and excited, the guests passed through the garden. Mr. Klöterjahn's wife stood with Mrs. Spatz by the glass door leading to the terrace, and Mr. Spinell by the window of his room to watch the departure. They observed how, with jokes and laughter, little battles were waged for the best places, how Miss von Osterloh, a fur boa around her neck, ran from one sleigh to the other to shove baskets of food under the seats, how Dr. Leander, his fur cap pulled down over his forehead, surveyed the entire scene once more with his glistening eyeglasses, then took a seat himself and gave the signal for setting out ... The horses began to tug, a few ladies screeched and fell over, the bells jingled, the short-handled whips cracked and let their long cords drag along in the snow behind the runners, and Miss von Osterloh stood at the garden gate and waved with her handkerchief, until the gliding sleighs disappeared at a turn in the highway and the merry noise died away. Then she made her way back through the garden to hasten after her responsibilities; the two ladies left the glass door, and almost simultaneously Mr. Spinell also quitted his observation post.

Calm reigned at Einfried. The expedition could not be expected back before evening. The "serious cases" lay in their rooms and suffered. Mr. Klöterjahn's wife and her older friend took a short walk, then returned to their rooms. Mr. Spinell was also in his, and busied himself after his fashion. About four o'clock the ladies were brought a half liter of milk each, while Mr. Spinell received his weak tea. Shortly thereafter Mr. Klöterjahn's wife knocked on the wall that separated her room from that of Mrs. Spatz, the town councillor's wife, and said:

"Let's go down to the parlor, Mrs. Spatz. I no longer know what to do here."

"Right away, dear!" answered Mrs. Spatz. "I'll just pull on my boots, if you don't mind. You see, I've been lying on the bed."

As was to be expected, the parlor was empty. The ladies sat down by the fireplace. Mrs. Spatz embroidered flowers

auf ein Stück Stramin, und auch Herrn Klöterjahns Gattin tat ein paar Stiche, worauf sie die Handarbeit in den Schoß sinken ließ und über die Armlehne ihres Sessels hinweg ins Leere träumte. Schließlich mache sie eine Bemerkung, die nicht lohnte, daß man ihretwegen die Zähne voneinander tat; da aber die Rätin Spatz trotzdem »Wie?« fragte, so mußte sie zu ihrer Demütigung den ganzen Satz wiederholen. Die Rätin Spatz fragte nochmals »Wie?« In diesem Augenblicke aber wurden auf dem Vorplatze Schritte laut, die Tür öffnete sich, und Herr Spinell trat ein.

»Störe ich?« fragte er noch an der Schwelle mit sanfter Stimme, während er ausschließlich Herrn Klöterjahns Gattin anblickte und den Oberkörper auf eine gewisse zarte und schwebende Art nach vorne beugte ... Die junge Frau antwortete:

»Ei, warum nicht gar? Erstens ist dieses Zimmer doch als Freihafen gedacht, Herr Spinell, und dann: worin sollten Sie uns stören. Ich habe das entschiedene Gefühl, die Rätin zu langweilen ...«

Hierauf wußte er nichts mehr zu erwidern, sondern ließ nur lächelnd seine kariösen Zähne sehen und ging unter den Augen der Damen mit ziemlich unfreien Schritten bis zur Glastür, woselbst er stehen blieb und hinausschaute, indem er in etwas unerzogener Weise den Damen den Rücken zuwandte. Dann machte er eine halbe Wendung rückwärts, fuhr aber fort, in den Garten hinauszublicken, indes er sagte:

»Die Sonne ist fort. Unvermerkt hat der Himmel sich bezogen. Es fängt schon an, dunkel zu werden.«

»Wahrhaftig, ja, alles liegt in Schatten«, antwortete Herrn Klöterjahns Gattin. »Unsere Ausflügler werden doch noch Schnee bekommen, wie es scheint. Gestern war es um diese Zeit noch voller Tag; nun dämmert es schon.«

»Ach«, sagte er, »nach allen diesen überhellen Wochen tut das Dunkel den Augen wohl. Ich bin dieser Sonne, die Schönes und Gemeines mit gleich aufdringlicher Deutlichkeit bestrahlt, geradezu dankbar, daß sie sich endlich ein wenig verhüllt.«

»Lieben Sie die Sonne nicht, Herr Spinell?«

»Da ich kein Maler bin ... Man wird innerlicher ohne Sonne.—Es ist eine dicke, weißgraue Wolkenschicht. Vielleicht bedeutet es Tauwetter für morgen. Übrigens würde ich Ihnen nicht raten, dort hinten noch auf die Handarbeit zu blicken, gnädige Frau.«

»Ach, seien Sie unbesorgt, das tue ich ohnehin nicht. Aber was soll man beginnen?«

Er hatte sich auf den Drehsessel vorm Piano niedergelassen, indem er einen Arm auf den Deckel des Instrumentes stützte.

on a piece of canvas, and Mr. Klöterjahn's wife also sewed a few stitches, then let the needlework drop into her lap and stared dreamily into space over the armrest of her chair. Finally she made some remark that wasn't worth opening one's mouth to reply to; but since Mrs. Spatz nevertheless asked, "What?," she had to repeat the whole sentence, to her mortification. Again Mrs. Spatz asked, "What?" But at that moment footsteps could be heard in the hallway, the door opened and Mr. Spinell entered.

"Am I disturbing you?" he asked quietly while still on the threshold, as he looked solely at Mr. Klöterjahn's wife and leaned the upper part of his body forward in a certain gentle, hovering fashion . . . The young woman answered:

"Indeed, why shouldn't you come in? For one thing, this room is after all intended as an unrestricted area, Mr. Spinell, and then: in what way would you disturb us? I have the decided feeling that I am boring Mrs. Spatz . . ."

Whereupon he could think of no further reply, but merely showed his decayed teeth in a smile and, observed by the ladies, walked with rather constrained steps as far as the glass door, where he stopped and looked out, turning his back to the ladies in somewhat discourteous fashion. Then he made a half turn backwards, but continued to look out into the garden, saying:

"The sun is gone. Without our noticing it, the sky has clouded over. It's already beginning to get dark."

"You're right, yes, everything is in shadow," answered Mr. Klöterjahn's wife. "Our excursionists will get some snow after all, as it seems. Yesterday at this time it was still broad daylight; now it's already twilight."

"Ah," he said, "after all these excessively bright weeks the darkness does one's eyes good. I am actually grateful to this sun, which illuminates the beautiful and the vulgar with equally blatant distinctness, for finally covering itself up a little."

"Don't you like the sun, Mr. Spinell?"

"Since I'm not a painter . . . One feels more deeply when the sun is gone.—There is a thick, gray-white cloud layer. Maybe it means a thaw for tomorrow. At any rate, I wouldn't advise you to keep on looking at your needlework, madam."

"Oh, don't worry, I wasn't doing that anyway. But what should we do now?"

He had sat down on the revolving stool in front of the piano, resting one arm on the lid of the instrument.

»Musik . . .«, sagte er. »Wer jetzt ein bißchen Musik zu hören bekäme! Manchmal singen die englischen Kinder kleine nigger-songs, das ist alles.«

»Und gestern nachmittag hat Fräulein von Osterloh in aller Eile die ›Klosterglocken‹ gespielt«, bemerkte Herrn Klöterjahns Gattin.

»Aber Sie spielen ja, gnädige Frau«, sagte er bittend und stand auf . . . »Sie haben ehemals täglich mit Ihrem Herrn Vater musi-ziert.«

»Ja, Herr Spinell, das war damals! Zur Zeit des Springbrunnens, wissen Sie . . .«

»Tun Sie es heute!« bat er. »Lassen Sie dies eine Mal ein paar Takte hören! Wenn Sie wüßten, wie ich dürste . . .«

»Unser Hausarzt sowohl wie Doktor Leander haben es mir aus-drücklich verboten, Herr Spinell.«

»Sie sind nicht da, weder der eine noch der andere! Wir sind frei . . . Sie sind frei, gnädige Frau! Ein paar armselige Akkorde . . .«

»Nein, Herr Spinell, daraus wird nichts. Wer weiß, was für Wun-derdinge Sie von mir erwarten! Und ich habe alles verlernt, glauben Sie mir. Auswendig kann ich beinahe nichts.«

»Oh, dann spielen Sie dieses Beinahe-nichts! Und zum Überfluß sind hier Noten, hier liegen sie, oben auf dem Klavier. Nein, dies hier ist nichts. Aber hier ist Chopin . . .«

»Chopin?«

»Ja, die Nocturnes. Und nun fehlt nur, daß ich die Kerzen an-zünde . . .«

»Glauben Sie nicht, daß ich spiele, Herr Spinell! Ich darf nicht. Wenn es mir nun schadet?!«—

Er verstummte. Er stand, mit seinen großen Füßen, seinem lan-gen, schwarzen Rock und seinem grauhaarigen, verwischten, bart-losen Kopf, im Lichte der beiden Klavierkerzen und ließ die Hände hinunterhängen.

»Nun bitte ich nicht mehr«, sagte er endlich leise. »Wenn Sie fürchten, sich zu schaden, gnädige Frau, so lassen Sie die Schönheit tot und stumm, die unter ihren Fingern laut werden möchte. Sie waren nicht immer so sehr verständig; wenigstens nicht, als es im Gegenteile galt, sich der Schönheit zu begeben. Sie waren nicht besorgt um Ihren Körper und zeigten einen unbedenklicheren und festeren Willen, als Sie den Springbrunnen verließen und die kleine goldene Krone ablegten . . . Hören Sie«, sagte er nach einer Pause,

"Music . . . ," he said. "If I could only get to hear a little music! Sometimes the English children sing little minstrel songs, that's all."

"And yesterday afternoon Miss von Osterloh played 'The Monastery Bells'[7] at top speed," Mr. Klöterjahn's wife remarked.

"But you play, madam," he said imploringly and stood up. . . ."You used to play music with your father every day."

"Yes, Mr. Spinell, that was long ago! At the time of the fountain, you know . . ."

"Do it today!" he urged. "Let me hear a few bars just this once! If you knew how I thirst for it . . ."

"Our family doctor, and Dr. Leander as well, have expressly forbidden me to, Mr. Spinell."

"They aren't here, neither one nor the other! We are free . . . You are free, madam! A few insignificant chords . . ."

"No, Mr. Spinell, I absolutely refuse. Who knows what kind of wonders you expect from me! And I have forgotten everything, believe me. I know almost nothing by heart."

"Oh, then play that almost nothing! And, what's more, there is sheet music here, here it is on top of the piano. No, this is nothing. But here is Chopin . . ."

"Chopin?"

"Yes, the nocturnes. And now all that we need is for me to light the candles . . ."

"Don't think I'm going to play, Mr. Spinell! I'm not allowed to. What if it did me harm?!"—

He fell silent. With his big feet, his long, black frock coat and his gray-haired, blurred, beardless head, he stood in the light of the two piano candles and let his hands hang down.

"Now I no longer ask you to," he finally said quietly. "If you're afraid of doing yourself harm, madam, then leave the beauty dead and mute that might have found its voice beneath your fingers. You weren't always all that sensible; at least not when, on the contrary, it was a question of renouncing beauty. You weren't concerned about your body and you displayed a more unhesitating and a firmer will when you abandoned the fountain and took off the little golden crown . . . Listen," he said after a pause, and

---

[7] A popular salon piece, the nocturne *Les cloches du monastère* by Louis-James-Alfred Lefébure-Wély (1817–1869).

und seine Stimme senkte sich noch mehr; »wenn Sie jetzt hier nie-
dersitzen und spielen wie einst, als noch Ihr Vater neben Ihnen
stand und seine Geige jene Töne singen ließ, die Sie weinen machten . . ., dann kann es geschehen, daß man sie wieder heimlich in
Ihrem Haare blinken sieht, die kleine, goldene Krone . . .«

»Wirklich?« fragte sie und lächelte . . . Zufällig versagte ihr die
Stimme bei diesem Wort, so daß es zur Hälfte heiser und zur Hälfte
tonlos herauskam. Sie hüstelte und sagte dann:

»Sind es wirklich die Nocturnes von Chopin, die Sie da haben?«

»Gewiß. Sie sind aufgeschlagen, und alles ist bereit.«

»Nun, so will ich denn in Gottes Namen eins davon spielen«,
sagte sie. »Aber nur eines, hören Sie? Dann werden Sie ohnehin
für immer genug haben.«

Damit erhob sie sich, legte ihre Handarbeit beiseite und ging
zum Klavier. Sie nahm auf dem Drehsessel Platz, auf dem ein paar
gebundene Notenbücher lagen, richtete die Leuchter und blätterte
in den Noten. Herr Spinell hatte einen Stuhl an ihre Seite gerückt
und saß neben ihr wie ein Musiklehrer.

Sie spielte das Nocturne in Es-Dur, opus 9, Nummer 2. Wenn
sie wirklich einiges verlernt hatte, so mußte ihr Vortrag ehedem
vollkommen künstlerisch gewesen sein. Das Piano war nur mittel-
mäßig, aber schon nach den ersten Griffen wußte sie es mit siche-
rem Geschmack zu behandeln. Sie zeigte einen nervösen Sinn für
differenzierte Klangfarbe und eine Freude an rhythmischer Be-
weglichkeit, die bis zum Phantastischen ging. Ihr Anschlag war sowohl fest als weich. Unter ihren Händen sang die Melodie ihre
letzte Süßigkeit aus, und mit einer zögernden Grazie schmiegten
sich die Verzierungen um ihre Glieder.

Sie trug das Kleid vom Tage ihrer Ankunft: die dunkle, gewich-
tige Taille mit den plastischen Sammetarabesken, die Haupt und
Hände so unirdisch zart erscheinen ließ. Ihr Gesichtsausdruck verän-
derte sich nicht beim Spiele, aber es schien, als ob die Umrisse ihrer
Lippen noch klarer würden, die Schatten in den Winkeln ihrer
Augen sich vertieften. Als sie geendigt hatte, legte sie die Hände in
den Schoß und fuhr fort, auf die Noten zu blicken. Herr Spinell
blieb ohne Laut und Bewegung sitzen.

Sie spielte noch ein Nocturne, spielte ein zweites und drittes.
Dann erhob sie sich: aber nur, um auf dem oberen Klavierdeckel
nach neuen Noten zu suchen.

his voice became even lower; "if you sit down here now and play as you used to when your father still stood beside you and made his violin sing those tones that made you cry . . . , then it may happen that it will become visible again, secretly shining in your hair, the little golden crown . . ."

"Really?" she asked and smiled . . . Accidentally her voice failed her when speaking that word, so that it emerged half-hoarse and half-soundless. She coughed slightly and then said:

"Is it really Chopin's nocturnes that you have there?"

"Certainly. The music pages are open, and everything is ready."

"Well, in that case, in God's name, I shall play one of them," she said. "But only one, do you hear? That will prove to be enough for you once and for all, anyway."

Thereupon she rose, laid aside her needlework and went to the piano. She sat down on the revolving stool, on which a few bound music volumes lay, arranged the lights and leafed through the music. Mr. Spinell had moved a chair up to her side and sat next to her like a music teacher.

She played the nocturne in E-flat major, opus 9, number 2. If she had really forgotten anything, her former playing must have been artistic in the highest degree. The piano was only mediocre, but even after the first few chords she was able to handle it with a sure taste. She manifested a nervous sense for variation in tone color and a pleasure in rhythmic flexibility that approached the fanciful. Her touch was both firm and soft. Beneath her hands the melody breathed forth its last bit of sweetness, and the ornaments wound about its limbs with a hesitant grace.

She was wearing the same dress as on the day of her arrival: the dark, heavy bodice with the raised velvet arabesques, which lent such unearthly delicacy to her head and hands. Her facial expression did not change while she played, but it seemed as if the contours of her lips became even sharper and the shadows in the corners of her eyes deepened. When she had finished, she put her hands in her lap and continued looking at the music. Mr. Spinell remained sitting without a sound or a movement.

She played another nocturne, played a second and a third. Then she arose: but only to look for more sheet music on the top of the piano.

Herr Spinell hatte den Einfall, die Bände in schwarzen Papp-
deckeln zu untersuchen, die auf dem Drehsessel lagen. Plötzlich
stieß er einen unverständlichen Laut aus, und seine großen, weißen
Hände fingerten leidenschaftlich an einem dieser vernachlässigten
Bücher.

»Nicht möglich! . . . Es ist nicht wahr! . . .«, sagte er . . . »Und
dennoch täusche ich mich nicht! . . . Wissen Sie, was es ist? . . . Was
hier lag? . . . Was ich hier halte? . . .«

»Was ist es?« fragte sie.

Da wies er ihr stumm das Titelblatt. Er war ganz bleich, ließ das
Buch sinken und sah sie mit zitternden Lippen an.

»Wahrhaftig? Wie kommt das hierher? Also geben Sie«, sagte sie
einfach, stellte die Noten aufs Pult, setzte sich und begann nach
einem Augenblick der Stille mit der ersten Seite.

Er saß neben ihr, vornübergebeugt, die Hände zwischen den
Knien gefaltet, mit gesenktem Kopfe. Sie spielte den Anfang mit
einer ausschweifenden und quälenden Langsamkeit, mit beunruhigend gedehnten Pausen zwischen den einzelnen Figuren. Das
Sehnsuchtsmotiv, eine einsame und irrende Stimme in der Nacht,
ließ leise seine bange Frage vernehmen. Eine Stille und ein Warten.
Und siehe, es antwortet: derselbe zage und einsame Klang, nur
heller, nur zarter. Ein neues Schweigen. Da setzte mit jenem ge-
dämpften und wundervollen Sforzato, das ist wie ein Sich-Aufraf-
fen und seliges Aufbegehren der Leidenschaft, das Liebesmotiv
ein, stieg aufwärts, rang sich entzückt empor bis zur süßen Ver-
schlingung, sank, sich lösend, zurück, und mit ihrem tiefen Ge-
sange von schwerer, schmerzlicher Wonne traten die Celli hervor
und führten die Weise fort . . .

Nicht ohne Erfolg versuchte die Spielende, auf dem armseligen
Instrument die Wirkungen des Orchesters anzudeuten. Die Violin-
läufe der großen Steigerung erklangen mit leuchtender Präzision.
Sie spielte mit preziöser Andacht, verharrte gläubig bei jedem Gebilde und hob demütig und demonstrativ das Einzelne hervor, wie
der Priester das Allerheiligste über sein Haupt erhebt. Was geschah? Zwei Kräfte, zwei entrückte Wesen strebten in Leiden und
Seligkeit nacheinander und umarmten sich in dem verzückten und
wahnsinnigen Begehren nach dem Ewigen und Absoluten . . . Das
Vorspiel flammte auf und neigte sich. Sie endigte da, wo der Vorhang sich teilt, und fuhr dann fort, schweigend auf die Noten zu
blicken.

Unterdessen hatte bei der Rätin Spatz die Langeweile jenen Grad
erreicht, wo sie des Menschen Antlitz entstellt, ihm die Augen aus
dem Kopfe treibt und ihm einen leichenhaften und furchteinflößen-

Mr. Spinell got the sudden idea of examining the volumes with black pasteboard covers that were lying on the revolving stool. Suddenly he emitted an unintelligible sound, and his big white hands passionately fingered one of these neglected books.

"Impossible! . . . It can't be true! . . . ," he said . . . "And yet I'm not mistaken! . . . Do you know what it is? . . . What was lying here? . . . What I'm holding here? . . ."

"What is it?" she asked.

Then in silence he showed her the title page. He was quite pale, lowered the book and looked at her with trembling lips.

"Truly? How did that get here? Hand it over, then," she said simply, put the music on the stand, sat down and, after a moment of silence, began on the first page.

He sat next to her, leaning forward, his hands clasped between his knees, with bowed head. She played the opening with excessive and tormenting slowness, with unnervingly protracted pauses between the individual figures. The motif of longing, a lonely, wandering voice in the night, asked its timorous question softly. Silence. Waiting. And see, an answer: the same hesitant and lonely sounds, but clearer, gentler. Another silence. Then, with that softened, marvelous sforzato which is like an awakening and blissful flaring up of passion, the love motif entered, ascended, rapturously struggled upward to the point of sweet intertwining, and sank back, working its way free; and with their deep cantilena of difficult, painful bliss the cellos stood out and continued the melody . . .

The performer attempted, not unsuccessfully, to indicate orchestral effects on the wretched instrument. The violin runs in the great crescendo were heard with gleaming precision. She played with attentive devotion, lingered religiously over every phrase, and humbly and graphically brought out each individual element, like a priest raising the host above his head. What was happening? Two forces, two withdrawn beings were yearning for each other in sorrow and bliss, and embraced each other in their rapturous and mad desire for the eternal and the absolute . . . The prelude flared up and came to rest. She ended at the moment when the curtain rises, and then continued looking at the music in silence.

Meanwhile Mrs. Spatz's boredom had reached the point at which it disfigures people's faces, makes their eyes bulge from their heads and gives them a corpselike and fright-

den Ausdruck verleiht. Außerdem wirkte diese Art von Musik auf
ihre Magennerven, sie versetzte diesen dyspeptischen Organismus
in Angstzustände und machte, daß die Rätin einen Krampfanfall
befürchtete.

»Ich bin genötigt, auf mein Zimmer zu gehen«, sagte sie schwach.
»Leben Sie wohl, ich kehre zurück . . .«

Damit ging sie. Die Dämmerung war weit vorgeschritten.
Draußen sah man dicht und lautlos den Schnee auf die Terrasse
herniedergehen. Die beiden Kerzen gaben ein wankendes und be-
grenztes Licht.

»Den zweiten Aufzug«, flüsterte er; und sie wandte die Seiten
und begann mit dem zweiten Aufzug.

Hörnerschall verlor sich in der Ferne. Wie? oder war es das Säu-
seln des Laubes? Das sanfte Rieseln des Quells? Schon hatte die
Nacht ihr Schweigen durch Hain und Haus gegossen, und kein
flehendes Mahnen vermochte dem Walten der Sehnsucht mehr
Einhalt zu tun. Das heilige Geheimnis vollendete sich. Die Leuchte
erlosch, mit einer seltsamen, plötzlich gedeckten Klangfarbe senkte
das Todesmotiv sich herab, und in jagender Ungeduld ließ die
Sehnsucht ihren weißen Schleier dem Geliebten entgegenflattern,
der ihr mit ausgebreiteten Armen durchs Dunkel nahte.

O überschwenglicher und unersättlicher Jubel der Vereinigung
im ewigen Jenseits der Dinge! Des quälenden Irrtums entledigt,
den Fesseln des Raumes und der Zeit entronnen, verschmolzen das
Du und das Ich, das Dein und Mein sich zu erhabener Wonne.
Trennen konnte sie des Tages tückisches Blendwerk, doch seine
prahlende Lüge vermochte die Nachtsichtigen nicht mehr zu täu-
schen, seit die Kraft des Zaubertrankes ihnen den Blick geweiht.
Wer liebend des Todes Nacht und ihr süßes Geheimnis erschaute,
dem blieb im Wahn des Lichtes ein einzig Sehnen, die Sehnsucht
hin zur heiligen Nacht, der ewigen, wahren, der einsmachen-
den . . .

O sink hernieder, Nacht der Liebe, gib ihnen jenes Vergessen,
das sie ersehnen, umschließe sie ganz mit deiner Wonne und löse
sie los von der Welt des Truges und der Trennung. Siehe, die
letzte Leuchte verlosch! Denken und Dünken versank in heiliger
Dämmerung, die sich welterlösend über des Wahnes Qualen brei-
tet. Dann, wenn das Blendwerk erbleicht, wenn in Entzücken sich
mein Auge bricht: das, wovon die Lüge des Tages mich ausschloß,
was sie zu unstillbarer Qual meiner Sehnsucht täuschend entgegen-
stellte,—*selbst* dann, o Wunder der Erfüllung! selbst dann bin ich

ening expression. Besides that, this kind of music affected her stomach nerves, it drove that dyspeptic organism into states of anxiety and caused the councillor's wife to fear an attack of cramps.

"I am compelled to go to my room," she said feebly. "Goodbye, I'll be back . . ."

Then she left. The twilight had made deep inroads. Outside, the snow could be seen falling on the terrace thickly and soundlessly. The two candles provided a wavering, circumscribed light.

"The second act," he whispered; and she turned the pages and began the second act.

Horn calls were lost in the distance. Is that right? Or was it the rustling of the leaves? The soft murmuring of the brook? Night had already poured its silence upon grove and house, and no imploring warning could any longer impede the surge of longing. The sacred mystery was being accomplished. The torch went out, the death motif descended with a strange, sudden muffling of tone color, and, in driving impatience, longing let its white veil flutter toward the beloved man, who was approaching with outspread arms through the darkness.

O exuberant and insatiable exultation of reunion in the eternity beyond the world! Freed from tormenting error, having escaped from the bonds of space and time, the "you" and the "I," the "yours" and "mine," were blended in sublime bliss. They might be separated by the spiteful dazzle of daylight, but its boastful lies could no long deceive those who saw by night ever since the power of the magic potion had consecrated their vision. Those who, in love, espied the night of death and its sweet mystery had a single longing left to them in the delusion of the light: the longing for holy night, the eternal, true night that would make them one . . .

Oh, descend, night of love, give them that oblivion which they yearn for, surround them completely with your rapture and liberate them from the world of deception and separation. See, the last torch has gone out! Thought and imagination have been submerged in the sacred twilight that is spreading over the pains of delusion and redeeming the world. At the moment when the dazzling deception fades, when my eyes close rapturously in death: that from which the day's lies shut me out, what they deceptively offered my longing, to my unquenchable sorrow—*myself* then, O miracle of fulfillment! I myself

die Welt.—Und es erfolgte zu Brangänens dunklem Habet-Acht-Gesange jener Aufstieg der Violinen, welcher höher ist als alle Vernunft.

»Ich verstehe nicht alles, Herr Spinell; sehr vieles ahne ich nur. Was bedeutet doch dieses ›Selbst—dann bin ich die Welt‹?«

Er erklärte es ihr, leise und kurz.

»Ja, so ist es.—Wie kommt es nur, daß Sie, der Sie es so gut verstehen, es nicht auch spielen können?«

Seltsamerweise vermochte er dieser harmlosen Frage nicht standzuhalten. Er errötete, rang die Hände und versank gleichsam mit seinem Stuhle.

»Das trifft selten zusammen«, sagte er endlich gequält. »Nein, spielen kann ich nicht.—Aber fahren Sie fort.«

Und sie fuhren fort in den trunkenen Gesängen des Mysterienspieles. Starb je die Liebe? Tristans Liebe? Die Liebe deiner und meiner Isolde? Oh, des Todes Streiche erreichen die Ewige nicht! Was stürbe wohl ihm, als was uns stört, was die Einigen täuschend entzweit? Durch ein süßes Und verknüpfte sie beide die Liebe . . . zerriß es der Tod, wie anders, als mit des einen eigenem Leben, wäre dem anderen der Tod gegeben? Und ein geheimnisvoller Zwiegesang vereinigte sie in der namenlosen Hoffnung des Liebestodes, des endlos ungetrennten Umfangenseins im Wunderreiche der Nacht. Süße Nacht! Ewige Liebesnacht! Alles umspannendes Land der Seligkeit! Wer dich ahnend erschaut, wie könnte er ohne Bangen je zum öden Tage zurückerwachen? Banne du das Bangen, holder Tod! Löse du nun die Sehnenden ganz von der Not des Erwachens! O fassungsloser Sturm der Rhythmen! O chromatisch empordrängendes Entzücken der metaphysischen Erkenntnis! Wie sie fassen, wie sie lassen, diese Wonne fern den Trennungsqualen des Lichts? Sanftes Sehnen ohne Trug und Bangen, hehres, leidloses Verlöschen, überseliges Dämmern im Unermeßlichen! Du Isolde, Tristan ich, nicht mehr Tristan, nicht mehr Isolde———

Plötzlich geschah etwas Erschreckendes. Die Spielende brach ab und führte ihre Hand über die Augen, um ins Dunkel zu spähen, und Herr Spinell wandte sich rasch auf seinem Sitze herum. Die Tür dort hinten, die zum Korridor führte, hatte sich geöffnet, und herein kam eine finstere Gestalt, gestützt auf den Arm einer zweiten. Es war ein Gast von ›Einfried‹, der gleichfalls nicht in der Lage gewesen war, an der Schlittenpartie teilzunehmen, sondern diese Abendstunde zu einem seiner instinktiven und traurigen Rund-

then am the world.—And there followed, accompanying Brangäne's dark "Have a care" song, that ascending strain in the violins which is loftier than all human reason.

"I don't understand everything, Mr. Spinell; there's a great deal I only sense. What is the meaning of that 'I myself then am the world'?"

He explained it to her, softly and briefly.

"Yes, that's how it is.—But how is it that you, who understand it so well, can't play it also?"

Oddly, he was unable to hold his own against this harmless question. He blushed, wrung his hands and sank down, as it were, together with his chair.

"The two rarely occur together," he finally said tormentedly. "No, I can't play.—But you continue."

And they continued with the exuberant chants of the mystery play. Did love ever die? Tristan's love? The love of your and my Isolde? Oh, Death's strokes cannot reach the eternal! What would be lost to him by dying, except that which hinders us, that which deceptively keeps the united ones apart? With a sweet "and," love joined them together . . . if Death were to tear it to pieces, how else, except with the very life of one of them, could death be given to the other one? And a mysterious duet united them in the nameless expectation of the love-death, the endlessly inseparable embrace in the wonderland of night. Sweet night! Eternal night of love! All-encompassing land of bliss! How could those who espy you intuitively ever reawaken without anxiety to the dreary day? Exorcise the anxiety, lovely Death! Set the longing ones completely free now from the distress of awakening! O bewildering onslaught of rhythms! O chromatically upward-urging rapture of metaphysical knowledge! How to hold it, how to relinquish it, this bliss far from the separation-pains of the light? Gentle longing without deceit and anxiety, noble, painless extinction, thrice-blissful fading away into the immeasurable! You Isolde, Tristan I, no longer Tristan, no longer Isolde———

Suddenly something frightening happened. The pianist broke off and sheltered her eyes with her hand in order to peer into the darkness, and Mr. Spinell quickly turned around in his chair. The door in the back that led to the corridor had opened, and in came a dark figure leaning on the arm of a second figure. It was another guest of Einfried who had been in no position to participate in the sleigh ride, but was using this evening hour for one of her

gänge durch die Anstalt benutzte, es war jene Kranke, die neunzehn Kinder zur Welt gebracht hatte und keines Gedankens mehr
fähig war, es war die Pastorin Höhlenrauch am Arme ihrer Pflege-
rin. Ohne aufzublicken, durchmaß sie mit tappenden, wandernden
Schritten den Hintergrund des Gemaches und entschwand durch
die entgegengesetzte Tür,—stumm und stier, irrwandelnd und un-
bewußt.—Es herrschte Stille.

»Das war die Pastorin Höhlenrauch«, sagte er.

»Ja, das war die arme Höhlenrauch«, sagte sie. Dann wandte sie
die Blätter und spielte den Schluß des Ganzen, spielte Isoldens
Liebestod.

Wie farblos und klar ihre Lippen waren, und wie die Schatten in
den Winkeln ihrer Augen sich vertieften! Oberhalb der Braue, in
ihrer durchsichtigen Stirn, trat angestrengt und beunruhigend das
blaßblaue Äderchen deutlicher und deutlicher hervor. Unter ihren
arbeitenden Händen vollzog sich die unerhörte Steigerung, zerteilt
von jenem beinahe ruchlosen, plötzlichen Pianissimo, das wie ein
Entgleiten des Bodens unter den Füßen und wie ein Versinken in
sublimer Begierde ist. Der Überschwang einer ungeheuren Lösung
und Erfüllung brach herein, wiederholte sich, ein betäubendes
Brausen maßloser Befriedigung, unersättlich wieder und wieder,
formte sich zurückflutend um, schien verhauchen zu wollen, wob
noch einmal das Sehnsuchtsmotiv in seine Harmonie, atmete aus,
erstarb, verklang, entschwebte. Tiefe Stille.

Sie horchten beide, legten die Köpfe auf die Seite und horchten.

»Das sind Schellen«, sagte sie.

»Es sind die Schlitten«, sagte er. »Ich gehe.«

Er stand auf und ging durch das Zimmer. An der Tür dort hinten
machte er halt, wandte sich um und trat einen Augenblick unruhig
von einem Fuß auf den anderen. Und dann begab es sich, daß er,
fünfzehn oder zwanzig Schritte von ihr entfernt, auf seine Knie
sank, lautlos auf beide Knie. Sein langer, schwarzer Gehrock brei-
tete sich auf dem Boden aus. Er hielt die Hände über seinem
Munde gefaltet, und seine Schultern zuckten.

Sie saß, die Hände im Schoße, vornübergelehnt, vom Klavier
abgewandt, und blickte auf ihn. Ein ungewisses und bedrängtes
Lächeln lag auf ihrem Gesicht, und ihre Augen spähten sinnend
und so mühsam ins Halbdunkel, daß sie eine kleine Neigung zum
Verschließen zeigten.

sad, instinctive walks through the establishment; it was that patient who had brought nineteen children into the world and was incapable of any further thought, it was Mrs. Höhlenrauch, the pastor's wife, on the arm of her nurse. Without looking up she crossed the back of the room with groping, wandering steps and disappeared through the opposite door— mute and stiff, roving and unconscious.—Silence reigned.

"That was Mrs. Höhlenrauch, the pastor's wife," he said.

"Yes, that was poor Mrs. Höhlenrauch," she said. Then she turned the pages and played the end of the whole piece, played Isolde's Love-Death.

How colorless and clear her lips were, and how the shadows in the corners of her eyes deepened! Above her eyebrow, on her transparent forehead, the little pale blue vein, strained and unsettling, stood out more and more distinctly. Under her busy fingers there came to life the wonderful crescendo, cut in two by that almost malicious sudden pianissimo, which is like the dropping away of the ground beneath one's feet and like an immersion in sublime desire. The exuberance of a tremendous liberation and fulfillment broke in and was repeated; a deafening roar of measureless contentment, insatiably again and again, transformed itself into an ebbing flow, seemed as if it would breathe its last, once more wove the motif of longing into its harmony, expired, died away, became silent, drifted off. Deep silence.

They both listened, leaned their heads to one side and listened.

"Those are bells," she said.

"It's the sleighs," he said. "I'm going."

He stood up and walked through the room. At the door in the back he halted, turned around and for a moment restlessly shifted his weight from one foot to the other. And then it happened that, fifteen or twenty paces away from her, he dropped to his knees, soundlessly onto both knees. His long, black frock coat spread out on the floor. He held his hands clasped over his mouth and his shoulders were twitching.

She sat with her hands in her lap, leaning forward, turned away from the piano, and looked at him. An uncertain, distressed smile was on her face, and her eyes peered into the half-darkness thoughtfully and with such an effort that they showed a slight tendency to narrow.

Aus weiter Ferne her näherten sich Schellenklappern, Peitschenknall und das Ineinanderklingen menschlicher Stimmen.

9

Die Schlittenpartie, von der lange noch alle sprachen, hatte am 26.
Februar stattgefunden. Am 27., einem Tauwettertage, an dem alles
sich erweichte, tropfte, plantschte, floß, ging es der Gattin Herrn
Klöterjahns vortrefflich. Am 28. gab sie ein wenig Blut von sich . . .
oh, unbedeutend; aber es war Blut. Zu gleicher Zeit wurde sie von
einer Schwäche befallen, so groß wie noch niemals, und legte sich
nieder. Doktor Leander untersuchte sie, und sein Gesicht war steinkalt
dabei. Dann verordnete er, was die Wissenschaft vorschreibt: Eisstückchen, Morphium, unbedingte Ruhe. Übrigens legte er am folgenden Tage wegen Überbürdung die Behandlung nieder und
übertrug sie an Doktor Müller, der sie pflicht- und kontraktgemäß
in aller Sanftmut übernahm; ein stiller, blasser, unbedeutender und
wehmütiger Mann, dessen bescheidene und ruhmlose Tätigkeit
den beinahe Gesunden und den Hoffnungslosen gewidmet war.
Die Ansicht, der er vor allem Ausdruck gab, war die, daß die
Trennung zwischen dem Klöterjahn'schen Ehepaar nun schon
recht lange währe. Es sei dringend wünschenswert, daß Herr Klöterjahn, wenn anders sein blühendes Geschäft es irgend gestatte, wieder einmal zu Besuch nach ›Einfried‹ käme. Man könne ihm schreiben, ihm vielleicht ein kleines Telegramm zukommen lassen . . .
Und sicherlich werde es die junge Mutter beglücken und stärken,
wenn er den kleinen Anton mitbrächte: abgesehen davon, daß es
für die Ärzte geradezu interessant sein werde, die Bekanntschaft
dieses gesunden kleinen Anton zu machen.
Und siehe, Herr Klöterjahn erschien. Er hatte Doktor Müllers
kleines Telegramm erhalten und kam vom Strande der Ostsee. Er
stieg aus dem Wagen, ließ sich Kaffee und Buttersemmeln geben
und sah sehr verdutzt aus.
»Herr«, sagte er, »was ist? Warum ruft man mich zu ihr?«
»Weil es wünschenswert ist«, antwortete Doktor Müller, »daß Sie
jetzt in der Nähe Ihrer Frau Gemahlin weilen.«
»Wünschenswert . . . Wünschenswert . . . Aber auch notwendig?
Ich sehe auf mein Geld, mein Herr, die Zeiten sind schlecht und
die Eisenbahnen sind teuer. War diese Tagesreise nicht zu umge-

From the far distance there approached the jingling of
bells, the cracking of whips and the confused sound of
human voices.

9

The sleigh ride, which everyone still spoke about long
afterward, had taken place on February 26th. On the
27th, a day of thaw on which everything was softening,
dripping, splashing, flowing, Mr. Klöterjahn's wife felt excellent. On the 28th, she coughed up a little blood . . . oh,
nothing to speak of; but it was blood. At the same time a
weakness came over her that was greater than ever before,
and she took to her bed.

Dr. Leander examined her, and his face was stone-cold
as he did so. Then he prescribed what science calls for in
such cases: cracked ice, morphine, absolute rest. Moreover, on the following day he gave up the treatment because of overwork and passed it on to Dr. Müller, who, in
obedience to his duty and his contract, took it over with
perfect composure; this quiet, pale, insignificant and melancholy man's modest and inglorious activity was devoted
to the nearly healthy and the hopeless.

The view that Dr. Müller particularly expressed was
that the separation between the Klöterjahns had now
lasted for quite some time. He felt it was urgently desirable
for Mr. Klöterjahn, if his flourishing business would at all
permit it, to visit Einfried again. A letter could be sent,
perhaps a little telegram could be sent to him . . . And it
would surely please and strengthen the young mother if
he brought along little Anton: not to mention that it would
be downright interesting for the doctors to make the acquaintance of this healthy little Anton.

And lo, Mr. Klöterjahn appeared. He had received Dr.
Müller's little telegram and came from the shores of the
Baltic. He alighted from the carriage, ordered coffee and
buttered rolls and looked very puzzled.

"Sir," he said, "what is it? Why have I been called to
her?"

"Because it is desirable," answered Dr. Müller, "for you
to remain near your wife now."

"Desirable . . . Desirable . . . But also necessary? I'm considering my money, sir; times are bad and the railroads
are dear. Was this daylong trip unavoidable? I wouldn't

hen? Ich wollte nichts sagen, wenn es beispielsweise die Lunge wäre; aber da es Gott sei Dank die Luftröhre ist . . .«

»Herr Klöterjahn«, sagte Doktor Müller sanft, »erstens ist die Luftröhre ein wichtiges Organ . . .« Er sagte unkorrekterweise »erstens«, obgleich er gar kein »zweitens« darauf folgen ließ.

Gleichzeitig aber mit Herrn Klöterjahn war eine üppige, ganz in Rot, Schottisch und Gold gehüllte Person in ›Einfried‹ eingetroffen, und sie war es, die auf ihrem Arme Anton Klöterjahn den Jüngeren, den kleinen gesunden Anton trug. Ja, er war da, und niemand konnte leugnen, daß er in der Tat von einer exzessiven Gesundheit war. Rosig und weiß, sauber und frisch gekleidet, dick und duftig lastete er auf dem nackten, roten Arm seiner betreßten Dienerin, verschlang gewaltige Mengen von Milch und gehacktem Fleisch, schrie und überließ sich in jeder Beziehung seinen Instinkten.

Vom Fenster seines Zimmers aus hatte der Schriftsteller Spinell die Ankunft des jungen Klöterjahn beobachtet. Mit einem seltsamen, verschleierten und dennoch scharfen Blick hatte er ihn ins Auge gefaßt, während er vom Wagen ins Haus getragen wurde, und war dann noch längere Zeit mit demselben Gesichtsausdruck an seinem Platze verharrt.

Von da an mied er das Zusammentreffen mit Anton Klöterjahn dem Jüngeren so weit als tunlich.—

10

Herr Spinell saß in seinem Zimmer und ›arbeitete‹.

Es war ein Zimmer wie alle in ›Einfried‹: altmodisch, einfach und distinguiert. Die massige Kommode war mit metallenen Löwenköpfen beschlagen, der hohe Wandspiegel war keine glatte Fläche, sondern aus vielen kleinen quadratischen, in Blei gefaßten Scherben zusammengesetzt, kein Teppich bedeckte den bläulich lackierten Estrich, in dem die steifen Beine der Meubles als klare Schatten sich fortsetzten. Ein geräumiger Schreibtisch stand in der Nähe des Fensters, vor welches der Romancier einen gelben Vorhang gezogen hatte, wahrscheinlich, um sich innerlicher zu machen.

In gelblicher Dämmerung saß er über die Platte des Sekretärs gebeugt und schrieb,—schrieb an einem jener zahlreichen Briefe, die er allwöchentlich zur Post befördern ließ, und auf die er belustigenderweise meistens gar keine Antwort erhielt. Ein großer, starker Bogen lag vor ihm, in dessen linkem oberen Winkel unter einer verzwickt gezeichneten Landschaft der Name Detlev Spinell in völ-

say anything if it were the lungs, for example; but since, thank God, it's the trachea . . ."

"Mr. Klöterjahn," said Dr. Müller gently, "in the first place the trachea is an important organ . . ." He incorrectly said "in the first place" even though he didn't follow it up with any "in the second place."

But when Mr. Klöterjahn had arrived at Einfried, so had a buxom person, all dressed in red, plaid and gold, and it was she who carried in her arms Anton Klöterjahn, Jr., the little healthy Anton. Yes, he was there, and no one could deny that he was truly endowed with excessively good health. Pink and white, clean and dressed in fresh clothing, chubby and fragrant, he weighed down the bare red arms of his galloon-adorned servant woman, swallowed enormous amounts of milk and chopped meat, yelled, and abandoned himself to his instincts in all ways.

From the window of his room the writer Spinell had observed the arrival of young Klöterjahn. With a strange, veiled and yet sharp glance he had eyed him while he was being carried from the carriage into the house, and then had lingered on the same spot for a considerable time with the same expression on his face.

From then on he avoided all encounters with Anton Klöterjahn, Jr., as much as possible.

10

Mr. Spinell was sitting in his room and "working."

It was a room like all of those at Einfried: old-fashioned, simple and distinguished. The voluminous commode had metal lion-head mounts; the high wall mirror did not have a smooth surface, but was composed of a number of small square panes in lead compartments; no carpet covered the plastered stone flooring, painted light blue, in which the stiff legs of the furniture were prolonged as clear reflections. A spacious desk stood in the vicinity of the window, in front of which the novelist had drawn a yellow curtain, probably to achieve greater "inwardness."

In the yellowish twilight he sat bowed over the flap of the secretary and was writing—writing one of those numerous letters that he sent weekly to be mailed and to which, amusingly, he received hardly any replies. A large, thick sheet of paper lay before him, in the upper left corner of which, under an intricately drawn landscape, could

lig neuartigen Lettern zu lesen war, und den er mit einer kleinen, sorgfältig gemalten und überaus reinlichen Handschrift bedeckte. »Mein Herr!« stand dort. »Ich richte die folgenden Zeilen an Sie, weil ich nicht anders kann, weil das, was ich Ihnen zu sagen habe, mich erfüllt, mich quält und zittern macht, weil mir die Worte mit einer solchen Heftigkeit zuströmen, daß ich an ihnen ersticken würde, dürfte ich mich ihrer nicht in diesem Briefe entlasten . . .«

Der Wahrheit die Ehre zu geben, so war dies mit dem »Zuströmen« ganz einfach nicht der Fall, und Gott wußte, aus was für eitlen Gründen Herr Spinell es behauptete. Die Worte schienen ihm durchaus nicht zuzuströmen; für einen, dessen bürgerlicher Beruf das Schreiben ist, kam er jämmerlich langsam von der Stelle, und wer ihn sah, mußte zu der Anschauung gelangen, daß ein Schriftsteller ein Mann ist, dem das Schreiben schwerer fällt als allen anderen Leuten.

Mit zwei Fingerspitzen hielt er eins der sonderbaren Flaumhärchen an seiner Wange erfaßt und drehte Viertelstunden lang daran, indem er ins Leere starrte und nicht um eine Zeile vorwärtsrückte, schrieb dann ein paar zierliche Wörter und stockte aufs neue. Andererseits muß man zugeben, daß das, was schließlich zustande kam, den Eindruck der Glätte und Lebhaftigkeit erweckte, wenn es auch inhaltlich einen wunderlichen, fragwürdigen und oft sogar unverständlichen Charakter trug.

»Es ist«, so setzte der Brief sich fort, »das unabweisliche Bedürfnis, das, was ich sehe, was seit Wochen als eine unauslöschliche Vision vor meinen Augen steht, auch Sie sehen zu machen, es Sie mit meinen Augen, in derjenigen sprachlichen Beleuchtung schauen zu lassen, in der es vor meinem inneren Blicke steht. Ich bin gewohnt, diesem Drange zu weichen, der mich zwingt, in unvergeßlich und flammend richtig an ihrem Platze stehenden Worten meine Erlebnisse zu denen der Welt zu machen. Und darum hören Sie mich an.

Ich will nichts als sagen, was war und ist, ich erzähle lediglich eine Geschichte, eine ganz kurze, unsäglich empörende Geschichte, erzähle sie ohne Kommentar, ohne Anklage und Urteil, nur mit meinen Worten. Es ist die Geschichte Gabriele Eckhofs, mein Herr, der Frau, die Sie die Ihrige nennen . . . und merken Sie wohl! Sie waren es, der sie erlebte; und dennoch bin ich es, dessen Worte sie Ihnen erst in Wahrheit zur Bedeutung eines Erlebnisses erheben wird.

Erinnern Sie sich des Gartens, mein Herr, des alten, verwucherten Gartens hinter dem grauen Patrizierhause? Das grüne Moos sproß in den Fugen der verwitterten Mauern, die seine verträumte Wildnis umschlossen. Erinnern Sie sich auch des Springbrunnens

be read the name "Detlev Spinell" in completely original lettering, and which he was covering with small, carefully formed and extremely neat handwriting.

"Sir!" it said. "I am addressing the following lines to you because I cannot help myself, because what I have to say to you fills me, torments me and makes me tremble, because the words come to me in such a violent flood that I would choke on them if I could not unburden myself of them in this letter . . ."

To be strictly truthful, the "violent flood" was quite simply not the case, and only God knew for what reasons of vanity Mr. Spinell claimed that it was. The words by no means seemed to come to him in a flood; for someone whose profession in life was writing, he was proceeding with pitiful slowness, and anyone who saw him would have had to reach the conclusion that a writer is a man who finds writing more difficult than anybody else does.

With the tips of two fingers he clutched one of the odd little downy hairs on his cheek and twisted it for quarter-hours at a time while he stared into space and didn't add a single line, then wrote a few decorative words and stopped short again. On the other hand, it must be admitted that what he finally produced gave the impression of smoothness and vivacity, although its contents were of a peculiar, questionable and often incomprehensible nature.

"It is," the letter continued, "the imperative necessity to make you too see what I see, what has stood before my eyes for weeks as an inextinguishable vision, to make you look at it with my eyes, in that verbal illumination in which it stands before my inner vision. I am accustomed to yield to the urge that forces me to make my experiences those of the world, by means of phrases that are unforgettably and blazingly well expressed. And therefore listen to me.

"I wish only to say what was and is, I am merely telling a story, a very short, unspeakably infuriating story; I tell it without commentary, without accusations or judgments, only with my words. It is the story of Gabriele Eckhof, sir, the woman you call your own . . . and note this well! it was you who lived it; and yet it is I whose words will for the first time truly raise the story to the significance of an experience for you.

"Do you remember the garden, sir, the old overgrown garden in back of the gray patrician house? Green moss sprouted in the cracks of the decaying walls that enclosed its dreamy wilderness. Do you also remember the fountain

in seiner Mitte? Lilafarbene Lilien neigten sich über sein morsches
Rund, und sein weißer Strahl plauderte geheimnisvoll auf das zer-
klüftete Gestein hinab. Der Sommertag neigte sich.

Sieben Jungfrauen saßen im Kreis um den Brunnen; in das Haar
der Siebenten aber, der Ersten, der Einen, schien die sinkende
Sonne heimlich ein schimmerndes Abzeichen der Oberhoheit zu
weben. Ihre Augen waren wie ängstliche Träume, und dennoch
lächelten ihre klaren Lippen . . .

Sie sangen. Sie hielten ihre schmalen Gesichter zur Höhe des
Springstrahles emporgewandt, dorthin, wo er in müder und edler
Rundung sich zum Falle neigte, und ihre leisen, hellen Stimmen
umschwebten seinen schlanken Tanz. Vielleicht hielten sie ihre zarten Hände um ihre Knie gefaltet, indes sie sangen . . .

Entsinnen Sie sich des Bildes, mein Herr? Sahen Sie es? Sie sahen
es nicht. Ihre Augen waren nicht geschaffen dafür, und Ihre Ohren
nicht, die keusche Süßigkeit seiner Melodie zu vernehmen. Sahen
Sie es—Sie durften nicht wagen, zu atmen, Sie mußten Ihrem Herzen zu schlagen verwehren. Sie mußten gehen, zurück ins Leben,
in Ihr Leben, und für den Rest Ihres Erdendaseins das Geschaute
als ein unantastbares und unverletzliches Heiligtum in Ihrer Seele
bewahren. Was aber taten Sie?

Dies Bild war ein Ende, mein Herr; mußten Sie kommen und
es zerstören, um ihm eine Fortsetzung der Gemeinheit und des
häßlichen Leidens zu geben? Es war eine rührende und friedevolle
Apotheose, getaucht in die abendliche Verklärung des Verfalles,
der Auflösung und des Verlöschens. Ein altes Geschlecht, zu müde
bereits und zu edel zur Tat und zum Leben, steht am Ende seiner
Tage, und seine letzten Äußerungen sind Laute der Kunst, ein paar
Geigentöne, voll von der wissenden Wehmut der Sterbensreife . . .
Sahen Sie die Augen, denen diese Töne Tränen entlockten? Vielleicht, daß die Seelen der sechs Gespielinnen dem Leben gehörten;
diejenige aber ihrer schwesterlichen Herrin gehörte der Schönheit
und dem Tode.

Sie sahen sie, diese Todesschönheit: sahen sie an, um ihrer zu
begehren. Nichts von Ehrfurcht, nichts von Scheu berührte Ihr
Herz gegenüber ihrer rührenden Heiligkeit. Es genügte Ihnen
nicht, zu schauen; Sie mußten besitzen, ausnützen, entweihen . . .
Wie fein Sie Ihre Wahl trafen! Sie sind ein Gourmand, mein Herr,
ein plebejischer Gourmand, ein Bauer mit Geschmack.

Ich bitte Sie, zu bemerken, daß ich keineswegs den Wunsch hege,
Sie zu kränken. Was ich sage, ist kein Schimpf, sondern die Formel,
die einfache psychologische Formel für Ihre einfache, literarisch

in its center? Lilac-colored lilies bent over its brittle rim, and its white jet chattered mysteriously as it fell on the cleft stones. The summer day was drawing to a close.

"Seven maidens sat in a circle around the fountain; but into the hair of the seventh, the first, the only one, the setting sun seemed secretly to weave a glittering token of supreme majesty. Her eyes were like uneasy dreams, and yet her clearly formed lips were smiling . . .

"They were singing. Their narrow faces were turned upward toward the level of the fountain jet, at the point where it inclined downward in a weary and noble curve, and their quiet, bright voices hovered about its slender dance. Perhaps their delicate hands were clasped around their knees as they sang . . .

"Do you recall the picture, sir? Did you see it? You didn't see it. Your eyes were not made for it, nor were your ears made to perceive the chaste sweetness of its melody. If you *had* seen it—you would not have dared to breathe, you would have had to forbid your heart to beat. You would have had to leave, to go back to life, to *your* life, and for the rest of your earthly existence to retain that vision in your soul as a sacred and inviolable relic. But what did you do?

"That picture was a full close, sir; did you have to come and destroy it in order to give it a prolongation of vulgarity and ugly suffering? It was a touching and peaceful apotheosis, tinged with the crepuscular transfiguration of decay, decomposition and extinction. An old family, already too weary and too noble for action and for life, is at the end of its days, and its last utterances are sounds of art, a few violin tones, full of the knowing melancholy of ripeness for death . . . Did you see the eyes from which those tones elicited tears? It may be that the souls of the six playmates belonged to life; but that of their sisterly mistress belonged to beauty and death.

"You saw it, that death-destined beauty; you looked at it to desire it. No particle of respect, no particle of awe touched your heart when faced with its touching sacredness. You were not satisfied to gaze; you had to possess, exploit, profane . . . With what nicety you made your choice! You are a gourmand, sir, a plebeian gourmand, a peasant with taste.

"Please notice that I by no means harbor the wish to offend you. What I am saying is no insult, but the formula, the simple psychological formula for your simple, literar-

gänzlich uninteressante Persönlichkeit, und ich spreche sie aus, nur
weil es mich treibt, Ihnen Ihr eigenes Tun und Wesen ein wenig
zu erhellen, weil es auf Erden mein unausweichlicher Beruf ist,
die Dinge bei Namen zu nennen, sie reden zu machen, und das
Unbewußte zu durchleuchten. Die Welt ist voll von dem, was ich
den ›unbewußten Typus‹ nenne: und ich ertrage sie nicht, alle diese
unbewußten Typen! Ich ertrage es nicht, all dies dumpfe, unwissende und erkenntnislose Leben und Handeln, diese Welt von auf-
reizender Naivität um mich her! Es treibt mich mit qualvoller Unwi-
derstehlichkeit, alles Sein in der Runde—so weit meine Kräfte
reichen—zu erläutern, auszusprechen und zum Bewußtsein zu
bringen,—unbekümmert darum, ob dies eine fördernde oder
hemmende Wirkung nach sich zieht, ob es Trost und Linderung
bringt oder Schmerz zufügt.

Sie sind, mein Herr, wie ich sagte, ein plebejischer Gourmand,
ein Bauer mit Geschmack. Eigentlich von plumper Konstitution
und auf einer äußerst niedrigen Entwicklungsstufe befindlich, sind
Sie durch Reichtum und sitzende Lebensweise zu einer plötzlichen,
unhistorischen und barbarischen Korruption des Nervensystems
gelangt, die eine gewisse lüsterne Verfeinerung des Genußbedürf-
nisses nach sich zieht. Wohl möglich, daß die Muskeln Ihres Schlun-
des in eine schmatzende Bewegung gerieten, wie angesichts einer
köstlichen Suppe oder seltenen Platte, als Sie beschlossen, Gabriele
Eckhof zu eigen zu nehmen . . .

In der Tat, Sie lenken ihren verträumten Willen in die Irre, Sie
führen sie aus dem verwucherten Garten in das Leben und in die
Häßlichkeit, Sie geben ihr Ihren ordinären Namen und machen sie
zum Eheweibe, zur Hausfrau, machen sie zur Mutter. Sie erniedri-
gen die müde, scheue und in erhabener Unbrauchbarkeit blühende
Schönheit des Todes in den Dienst des gemeinen Alltags und jenes
blöden, ungefügen und verächtlichen Götzen, den man die Natur
nennt, und nicht eine Ahnung von der tiefen Niedertracht dieses
Beginnens regt sich in Ihrem bäuerischen Gewissen.

Nochmals: Was geschieht? Sie, mit den Augen, die wie ängstliche
Träume sind, schenkt Ihnen ein Kind; sie gibt diesem Wesen, das
eine Fortsetzung der niedrigen Existenz seines Erzeugers ist, alles
mit, was sie an Blut und Lebensmöglichkeit besitzt, und stirbt. Sie
stirbt, mein Herr! Und wenn sie nicht in Gemeinheit dahinfährt,
wenn sie dennoch zuletzt sich aus den Tiefen ihrer Erniedrigung
erhob und stolz und selig unter dem tödlichen Kusse der Schönheit
vergeht, so ist das *meine* Sorge gewesen. Die Ihrige war es wohl
unterdessen, sich auf verschwiegenen Korridoren mit Stubenmädchen die Zeit zu verkürzen.

Ihr Kind aber, Gabriele Eckhofs Sohn, gedeiht, lebt und trium-
phiert. Vielleicht wird er das Leben seines Vaters fortführen, ein

ily quite uninteresting personality, and I pronounce it merely because I have the urge to enlighten you to some extent as to your own actions and essence, because it is my inescapable vocation on earth to call things by their name, to lend them a voice, and to illuminate the unconscious. The world is full of what I call 'the unconscious type': and I cannot abide them, all these unconscious types! I cannot abide all this dull, unknowing and ignorant life and behavior, this world of provoking naïveté all around me! I have the painfully irresistible urge to explain, expound and bring to the level of consciousness all existence round about me—to the limits of my strength—regardless whether this will produce a positive or a negative effect, whether it results in comfort and relief or in pain.

"You, sir, are, as I said, a plebeian gourmand, a peasant with taste. Though in reality you have a coarse constitution and are situated at an extremely low stage of development, through wealth and a sedentary life-style you have attained a sudden, unhistoric and barbaric corruption of the nervous system that entails a certain lascivious refinement of the sensual urges. Possibly the muscles of your throat initiated a smacking motion, as if you had caught sight of a tasty soup or unusual dish, when you decided to make Gabriele Eckhof your own . . .

"In point of fact, you lead astray her dreaming will, you escort her out of the overgrown garden into life and ugliness, you give her your base name and make her a wife, a housewife, you make her a mother. You degrade the weary, timid beauty of death, blooming in sublime uselessness, forcing it into the service of everyday vulgarity and of that stupid, awkward and contemptible idol called Nature, and not a notion of the low vileness of this procedure stirs in your peasant conscience.

"Once again: What happens? She, with the eyes that are like uneasy dreams, gives you a child; she bestows upon this creature, which is a prolongation of the vile existence of its begetter, all she possesses of blood and vitality, and dies. She is dying, sir! And if she is not departing in vulgarity, if she has nevertheless at the end raised herself from the depths of her degradation and is perishing proudly and happily beneath the fatal kiss of beauty, that was thanks to *my* cares. *Yours,* meanwhile, no doubt consisted of passing the time with chambermaids in secluded corridors.

"But your child, Gabriele Eckhof's son, thrives, lives and triumphs. Perhaps he will continue his father's life, and

handeltreibender, Steuern zahlender und gut speisender Bürger werden; vielleicht ein Soldat oder Beamter, eine unwissende und tüchtige Stütze des Staates; in jedem Falle ein amusisches, normal funktionierendes Geschöpf, skrupellos und zuversichtlich, stark und dumm.

Nehmen Sie das Geständnis, mein Herr, daß ich Sie hasse, Sie und Ihr Kind, wie ich das Leben selbst hasse, das gemeine, das lächerliche und dennoch triumphierende Leben, das Sie darstellen, den ewigen Gegensatz und Todfeind der Schönheit. Ich darf nicht sagen, daß ich Sie verachte. Ich kann es nicht. Ich bin ehrlich. Sie sind der Stärkere. Ich habe Ihnen im Kampfe nur eines entgegenzustellen, das erhabene Gewaffen und Rachewerkzeug der Schwachen: Geist und Wort. Heute habe ich mich seiner bedient. Denn dieser Brief—auch darin bin ich ehrlich, mein Herr—ist nichts als ein Racheakt, und ist nur ein einziges Wort darin scharf, glänzend und schön genug, Sie betroffen zu machen, Sie eine fremde Macht spüren zu lassen, Ihren robusten Gleichmut einen Augenblick ins Wanken zu bringen, so will ich frohlocken.

Detlev Spinell.«

Und dieses Schriftstück kuvertierte und frankierte Herr Spinell, versah es mit einer zierlichen Adresse und überlieferte es der Post.

11

Herr Klöterjahn pochte an Herrn Spinells Stubentür; er hielt einen großen, reinlich beschriebenen Bogen in der Hand und sah aus wie ein Mann, der entschlossen ist, energisch vorzugehen. Die Post hatte ihre Pflicht getan, der Brief war seinen Weg gegangen, er hatte die wunderliche Reise von ›Einfried‹ nach ›Einfried‹ gemacht und war richtig in die Hände des Adressaten gelangt. Es war vier Uhr am Nachmittage.

Als Herr Klöterjahn eintrat, saß Herr Spinell auf dem Sofa und las in seinem eigenen Roman mit der verwirrenden Umschlagzeichnung. Er stand auf und sah den Besucher überrascht und fragend an, obgleich er deutlich errötete.

»Guten Tag«, sagte Herr Klöterjahn.»Entschuldigen Sie, daß ich Sie in Ihren Beschäftigungen störe. Aber darf ich fragen, ob Sie dies geschrieben haben?« Damit hielt er den großen, reinlich beschriebenen Bogen mit der linken Hand empor und schlug mit dem Rücken der Rechten darauf, so daß es heftig knisterte. Hierauf schob er die Rechte in die Tasche seines weiten, bequemen Bein-

become a businessman, taxpayer and well-fed bourgeois; perhaps a soldier or bureaucrat, an ignorant and solid pillar of the state; in any case, an unintellectual, normally functioning creature, without scruples, self-assured, strong and stupid.

"Receive this confession, sir, that I hate you, you and your child, as I hate life itself, the vulgar, ridiculous and yet triumphant life that you represent, the eternal opposite and mortal enemy of beauty. I must not say that I despise you. I cannot. I am honest. You are the stronger. I have only one thing to oppose you with in battle, the sublime weaponry and instrument of revenge of the weak: intellect and words. Today I have used them. For this letter—and here, too, I am honest, sir—is nothing but an act of vengeance, and if only a single word in it is sharp, shining and beautiful enough to confound you, to make you feel the presence of another power, to shake your robust equanimity for a moment, then I shall exult.

Detlev Spinell."

And this letter Mr. Spinell placed in an envelope and stamped, provided it with a decorative address and put it into the mail.

11

Mr. Klöterjahn knocked at the door of Mr. Spinell's room; he was holding in his hand a large sheet of paper covered with neat writing, and looked like a man determined to act energetically. The postal service had done its duty, the letter had gone on its way, it had made the odd journey from Einfried to Einfried and had reached the hands of its proper addressee. It was four o'clock in the afternoon.

When Mr. Klöterjahn entered, Mr. Spinell was sitting on the sofa and reading his own novel with the confusing dust-jacket drawing. He stood up and looked at his visitor in a surprised and questioning manner, although he distinctly blushed.

"Good day," said Mr. Klöterjahn. "Excuse me for disturbing you while you're busy. But may I ask whether you wrote this?" As he spoke these words, he held up the large sheet with the neat writing in his left hand and struck it with the back of his right hand, so that it crackled loudly. Then he thrust his right hand into the pocket of his wide,

kleides, legte den Kopf auf die Seite und öffnete, wie manche
Leute pflegen, den Mund zum Horchen.

Sonderbarerweise lächelte Herr Spinell; er lächelte zuvorkom-
mend, ein wenig verwirrt und halb entschuldigend, führte die
Hand zum Kopfe, als besänne er sich, und sagte:
»Ah, richtig ... ja ... ich erlaubte mir ...«
Die Sache war die, daß er sich heute gegeben hatte, wie er war,
und bis gegen Mittag geschlafen hatte. Infolge hiervon litt er an
schlimmem Gewissen und blödem Kopfe, fühlte er sich nervös und
wenig widerstandsfähig. Hinzu kam, daß die Frühlingsluft, die ein-
getreten war, ihn matt und zur Verzweiflung geneigt machte. Dies
alles muß erwähnt werden als Erklärung dafür, daß er sich während
dieser Szene so äußerst albern benahm.

»So! Aha! Schön!« sagte Herr Klöterjahn, indem er das Kinn auf
die Brust drückte, die Brauen emporzog, die Arme reckte und eine
Menge ähnlicher Anstalten traf, nach Erledigung dieser Formfrage
ohne Erbarmen zur Sache zu kommen. Aus Freude an seiner Person ging er ein wenig zu weit in diesen Anstalten; was schließlich
erfolgte, entsprach nicht völlig der drohenden Umständlichkeit
dieser mimischen Vorbereitungen. Aber Herr Spinell war ziemlich
bleich.

»Sehr schön!« wiederholte Herr Klöterjahn.»Dann lassen Sie
sich die Antwort mündlich geben, mein Lieber, und zwar in Anbe-
tracht des Umstandes, daß ich es für blödsinnig halte, jeman-
dem, den man stündlich sprechen kann, seitenlange Briefe zu
schreiben ...«

»Nun ... blödsinnig ...«, sagte Herr Spinell lächelnd, entschuldigend und beinahe demütig ...

»Blödsinnig!« wiederholte Herr Klöterjahn und schüttelte heftig
den Kopf, um zu zeigen, wie unangreifbar sicher er seiner Sache
sei.»Und ich würde dies Geschreibsel nicht eines Wortes würdigen,
es wäre mir, offen gestanden, ganz einfach als Butterbrotpapier zu
schlecht, wenn es mich nicht über gewisse Dinge aufklärte, die ich
bis dahin nicht begriff, gewisse Veränderungen ... Übrigens geht
Sie das nichts an und gehört nicht zur Sache. Ich bin ein tätiger
Mann, ich habe Besseres zu bedenken als Ihre unaussprechlichen
Visionen ...«

»Ich habe ›unauslöschliche Vision‹ geschrieben«, sagte Herr Spinell und richtete sich auf. Es war der einzige Moment dieses Auftrit-
tes, in dem er ein wenig Würde an den Tag legte.

»Unauslöschlich ... unaussprechlich ...!« entgegnete Herr Klöterjahn und blickte ins Manuskript.»Sie schreiben eine Hand, die
miserabel ist, mein Lieber; ich möchte Sie nicht in meinem Kontor

comfortable trousers, leaned his head to one side and, as many people do, opened his mouth while he listened.

Strange to say, Mr. Spinell smiled; he smiled accommodatingly, a little confusedly and half-apologetically, raised his hand to his head, as if he were reflecting, and said:

"Ah, that's right . . . yes . . . I took the liberty . . ."

The truth of the matter was that today he had followed his bent and had slept till about noon. As a result he was suffering from a bad conscience and a weak head; he was feeling nervous and incapable of much resistance. Besides that, the spring air that had set in made him languid and inclined toward despair. All this must be mentioned as an explanation for his extremely stupid behavior during this scene.

"So! Aha! Fine!" said Mr. Klöterjahn, pressing his chin onto his breast, raising his eyebrows, stretching his arms and making numerous similar preparations for coming to the point implacably, now that the formality of his opening question had been disposed of. Out of pleasure in his own body he went a little too far with these preparations; what finally followed did not fully correspond to the menacing circumstantiality of these mimed preliminaries. But Mr. Spinell was rather pale.

"Very fine!" repeated Mr. Klöterjahn. "Then let me give you the answer in person, my good man, particularly in view of the circumstance that I consider it idiotic to write letters pages and pages long to someone you can talk to at any time . . ."

"Now . . . idiotic . . . ," said Mr. Spinell with a smile, apologetically and almost humbly.

"Idiotic!" repeated Mr. Klöterjahn and shook his head violently to show how unassailably sure of his position he was. "And I wouldn't honor this scribble with a single word—to be candid, I wouldn't even use it to wrap a sandwich—if it didn't enlighten me about certain things that I hadn't understood until then, certain changes . . . Anyway, that's none of your business and it's beside the point. I am a busy man, I have better things to think about than your inexpressible visions . . ."

"I wrote 'inextinguishable vision,'" said Mr. Spinell and drew himself up. It was the only moment in this scene in which he displayed a little dignity.

"Inextinguishable . . . inexpressible . . . !" countered Mr. Klöterjahn and looked at the manuscript. "You write a miserable hand, my good man; I wouldn't want to em-

beschäftigen. Auf den ersten Blick scheint es ganz sauber, aber bei Licht besehen ist es voller Lücken und Zittrigkeiten. Aber das ist Ihre Sache und geht mich nichts an. Ich bin gekommen, um Ihnen zu sagen, daß Sie erstens ein Hanswurst sind—, nun, das ist Ihnen hoffentlich bekannt. Außerdem aber sind Sie ein großer Feigling, und auch das brauche ich Ihnen wohl nicht ausführlich zu beweisen. Meine Frau hat mir einmal geschrieben, Sie sähen den Weibspersonen, denen Sie begegnen, nicht ins Gesicht, sondern schielten nur so hin, um eine schöne Ahnung davonzutragen, aus Angst vor der Wirklichkeit. Leider hat sie später aufgehört, in ihren Briefen von Ihnen zu erzählen; sonst wüßte ich noch mehr Geschichten von Ihnen. Aber so sind Sie. ›Schönheiten‹ ist Ihr drittes Wort, aber im Grunde ist es nichts als Bangebüchsigkeit und Duckmäuserei und Neid, und daher wohl auch Ihre unverschämte Bemerkung von den ›verschwiegenen Korridoren‹, die mich wahrscheinlich so recht durchbohren sollte und mir doch bloß Spaß gemacht hat. Spaß hat sie mir gemacht! Aber wissen Sie nun Bescheid? Habe ich Ihnen Ihr ... Ihr ›Tun und Wesen‹ nun ›ein wenig erhellt‹, Sie Jammermensch? Obgleich es nicht mein ›unausbleiblicher Beruf‹ ist, hö, hö! ...«

»Ich habe ›unausweichlicher Beruf‹ geschrieben«, sagte Herr Spinell; aber er gab es gleich wieder auf. Er stand da, hilflos und abgekanzelt, wie ein großer, kläglicher, grauhaariger Schuljunge.

»Unausweichlich ... unausbleiblich ... Ein niederträchtiger Feigling sind Sie, sage ich Ihnen. Täglich sehen Sie mich bei Tische. Sie grüßen mich und lächeln, Sie reichen mir Schüsseln und lächeln, Sie wünschen mir gesegnete Mahlzeit und lächeln. Und eines Tages schicken Sie mir solch einen Wisch voll blödsinniger Injurien auf den Hals. Hö, ja, schriftlich haben Sie Mut! Und wenn es bloß dieser lachhafte Brief wäre. Aber Sie haben gegen mich intrigiert, hinter meinem Rücken gegen mich intrigiert, ich begreife es jetzt sehr wohl ... obgleich Sie sich nicht einzubilden brauchen, daß es Ihnen etwas genützt hat! Wenn Sie sich etwa der Hoffnung hingeben, meiner Frau Grillen in den Kopf gesetzt zu haben, so befinden Sie sich auf dem Holzwege, mein wertgeschätzter Herr, dazu ist sie ein zu vernünftiger Mensch! Oder wenn Sie am Ende gar glauben, daß sie mich irgendwie anders als sonst empfangen hat, mich und das Kind, als wir kamen, so setzten Sie Ihrer Abgeschmacktheit die

ploy you in my office. At first glance it looks quite neat, but on closer inspection it's full of holes and trembles. But that's your business and doesn't concern me. I came to tell you that first of all you're a buffoon—now, I hope you know that. But in addition you're a big coward, and that, too, I probably don't need to prove to you in detail. My wife wrote me once that you don't look the women you meet in the face but just squint at them, in order to come away with a beautiful impression, out of fear of reality. Unfortunately she later stopped talking about you in her letters; otherwise I would know even more stories on your account. But that's the way you are. Every other word with you is 'beauties,' but at the bottom it's nothing but chickenheartedness, hypocrisy and envy, and that's probably why you made that fresh remark about the 'secluded corridors,' which was probably intended to pulverize me, but just handed me a laugh. It handed me a laugh! But are you in the know now? Have I now 'enlightened you to some extent as to your actions and essence,' you pathetic character? Although it isn't my 'inevitable vocation,' ha, ha! . . ."

"I wrote 'inescapable vocation,'" said Mr. Spinell; but he immediately gave up again.[8] He stood there, helpless and reprimanded, like a big, pitiful, gray-haired schoolboy.

"Inescapable . . . inevitable . . . You're a low-down coward, I tell you. You see me at meals every day. You say hello to me and smile, you pass plates to me and smile, you wish me good digestion and smile. And one day you send me a rag like this full of idiotic insults. Ha, yes, when you write you have courage. And if it were only this ludicrous letter. But you have plotted against me, plotted against me behind my back, now I understand it very well . . . although you needn't imagine that it has done you any good! If you perhaps cherish the hope that you put crazy ideas in my wife's head, you're barking up the wrong tree, my dear sir, she's too sensible a person for that! Or if after all this you even think that she welcomed me any differently than she used to, me and the child, when we came, you would be putting the final touch to your absur-

---

[8] "Inescapable" vs. "inevitable": it is difficult to render Mr. Klöterjahn's distortion of Mr. Spinell's adjective with single-word English equivalents. "Unausweichlich" connotes the irresistibility of a powerful force, whereas "unausbleiblich" connotes a consequence that cannot fail to occur as the result of some prior action.

Krone auf! Wenn sie dem Kleinen keinen Kuß gegeben hat, so geschah es aus Vorsicht, weil neuerdings die Hypothese aufgetaucht ist, daß es nicht die Luftröhre, sondern die Lunge ist, und man in diesem Falle nicht wissen kann ... obgleich es übrigens noch sehr zu beweisen ist, das mit der Lunge, und Sie mit Ihrem ›sie stirbt, mein Herr!‹ Sie sind ein Esel!«

Hier suchte Herr Klöterjahn seine Atmung ein wenig zu regeln. Er war nun sehr in Zorn geraten, stach beständig mit dem rechten Zeigefinger in die Luft und richtete das Manuskript in seiner Linken aufs übelste zu. Sein Gesicht, zwischen dem blonden englischen Backenbart, war furchtbar rot, und seine umwölkte Stirn war von geschwollenen Adern zerrissen wie von Zornesblitzen.

»Sie hassen mich«, fuhr er fort, »und Sie würden mich verachten, wenn ich nicht der Stärkere wäre ... Ja, das bin ich, zum Teufel, ich habe das Herz auf dem rechten Fleck, während Sie das Ihre wohl meistens in den Hosen haben, und ich würde Sie in die Pfanne hauen mitsamt Ihrem ›Geist und Wort‹, Sie hinterlistiger Idiot, wenn das nicht verboten wäre. Aber damit ist nicht gesagt, mein Lieber, daß ich mir Ihre Invektiven so ohne weiteres gefallen lasse, und wenn ich das mit dem ›ordinären Namen‹ zu Haus meinem Anwalt zeige, so wollen wir sehen, ob Sie nicht Ihr blaues Wunder erleben. Mein Name ist gut, mein Herr, und zwar durch mein Verdienst. Ob Ihnen jemand auf den Ihren auch nur einen Silbergroschen borgt, diese Frage mögen Sie mit sich selbst erörtern, Sie hergelaufener Bummler! Gegen Sie muß man gesetzlich vorgehen! Sie sind gemeingefährlich! Sie machen die Leute verrückt! ... Obgleich Sie sich nicht einzubilden brauchen, daß es Ihnen diesmal gelungen ist, Sie heimtückischer Patron! Von Individuen, wie Sie eins sind, lasse ich mich denn doch nicht aus dem Felde schlagen. Ich habe das Herz auf dem rechten Fleck ...«

Herr Klöterjahn war nun wirklich äußerst erregt. Er schrie und sagte wiederholt, daß er das Herz auf dem rechten Fleck habe.

» ›Sie sangen.‹ Punkt. Sie sangen gar nicht! Sie strickten. Außerdem sprachen sie, soviel ich verstanden habe, von einem Rezept für Kartoffelpuffer, und wenn ich das mit dem ›Verfall‹ und der ›Auflösung‹ meinem Schwiegervater sage, so belangt er Sie gleichfalls von Rechts wegen, da können Sie sicher sein! ... ›Sahen Sie das Bild, sahen Sie es?‹ Natürlich sah ich es, aber ich begreife nicht, warum ich deshalb den Atem anhalten und davonlaufen sollte. Ich schiele den Weibern nicht am Gesicht vorbei, ich sehe sie mir an, und wenn sie mir gefallen, und wenn sie mich wollen, so nehme ich sie mir. Ich habe das Herz auf dem rechten Fl ...«

dity! If she didn't give the little one a kiss, that was out of cautiousness, because lately the hypothesis has surfaced that it isn't the trachea but the lungs, and in that case you can never know . . . although it still remains to be proved, that business about the lungs, and you, with your 'She is dying, sir!' You're a jackass!'"

At this point Mr. Klöterjahn attempted to regulate his breathing somewhat. He had now worked himself up into a real rage, was repeatedly stabbing the air with his right index finger and was mangling the manuscript in his left hand. His face, framed by the blonde English side-whiskers, was terribly red, and his clouded brow was cleft with swollen veins as if with angry lightning flashes.

"You hate me," he continued, "and you would despise me if I weren't the stronger . . . Yes, that I am, damn it, I have my heart in the right place, while you, most likely, usually have yours in your boots, and I'd beat you to a pulp together with your 'intellect and words,' you back-stabbing idiot, if it weren't prohibited. But that doesn't mean to say, my good man, that I'm just going to put up with your insults, and when I show my lawyer at home that part about my 'base name,' we'll see if you don't get the surprise of your life! My name is good, sir, and that's because I made it so. Whether anyone would even lend you a red cent on yours, you can think that over on your own, you worthless loafer! The law ought to protect people from you! You're a danger to the community! You drive people crazy! . . . Although you have no call to imagine that you succeeded this time, you underhanded character! I don't let shady customers like you get the better of me. I have my heart in the right place . . ."

Mr. Klöterjahn was now really extremely excited. He yelled and said repeatedly that he had his heart in the right place.

"'They were singing.' Period. They were not singing! They were knitting. Besides, as far as I could understand, they were talking about a recipe for potato pancakes, and when I tell my father-in-law the part about the 'decay' and 'decomposition,' he'll take legal proceedings against you too, you can be sure of it! . . . 'Did you see the picture, did you see it?' Of course I saw it, but I don't understand why it should have made me hold my breath and run away. I don't squint into women's faces as I pass by, I take a real look at them, and if I like them, and if they want me, I take them. I have my heart in the right pl . . ."

Es pochte. — Es pochte gleich neun- oder zehnmal ganz rasch hintereinander an die Stubentür, ein kleiner, heftiger, ängstlicher Wirbel, der Herrn Klöterjahn verstummen machte, und eine Stimme, die gar keinen Halt hatte, sondern vor Bedrängnis fortwährend aus den Fugen ging, sagte in größter Hast:

»Herr Klöterjahn, Herr Klöterjahn, ach, ist Herr Klöterjahn da?«

»Draußen bleiben«, sagte Herr Klöterjahn unwirsch . . . »Was ist? Ich habe hier zu reden.«

»Herr Klöterjahn«, sagte die schwankende und sich brechende Stimme, »Sie müssen kommen . . . auch die Ärzte sind da . . . oh, es ist so entsetzlich traurig . . .«

Da war er mit einem Schritt an der Tür und riß sie auf. Die Rätin Spatz stand draußen. Sie hielt ihr Schnupftuch vor den Mund, und große, längliche Tränen rollten paarweise in dieses Tuch hinein.

»Herr Klöterjahn«, brachte sie hervor . . . , »es ist so entsetzlich traurig . . . Sie hat so viel Blut aufgebracht, so fürchterlich viel . . . Sie saß ganz ruhig im Bette und summte ein Stückchen Musik vor sich hin, und da kam es, lieber Gott, so übermäßig viel . . .«

»Ist sie tot?« schrie Herr Klöterjahn . . . Dabei packte er die Rätin am Oberarm und zog sie auf der Schwelle hin und her. »Nein, nicht ganz, wie? Noch nicht ganz, sie kann mich noch sehen . . . Hat sie wieder ein bißchen Blut aufgebracht? Aus der Lunge, wie? Ich gebe zu, daß es vielleicht aus der Lunge kommt . . . Gabriele!« sagte er plötzlich, indem die Augen ihm übergingen, und man sah, wie ein warmes, gutes, menschliches und redliches Gefühl aus ihm hervorbrach. »Ja, ich komme!« sagte er, und mit langen Schritten schleppte er die Rätin aus dem Zimmer hinaus und über den Korridor davon. Von einem entlegenen Teile des Wandelganges her vernahm man noch immer sein rasch sich entfernendes »Nicht ganz, wie? . . . Aus der Lunge, was? . . .«

12

Herr Spinell stand auf dem Fleck, wo er während Herrn Klöterjahns so jäh unterbrochener Visite gestanden hatte, und blickte auf die offene Tür. Endlich tat er ein paar Schritte vorwärts und horchte ins Weite. Aber alles war still, und so schloß er die Tür und kehrte ins Zimmer zurück.

There was a knock.—About nine or ten knocks in very
rapid succession were struck on the room door, a violent,
nervous little drumroll that silenced Mr. Klöterjahn; and
a voice devoid of all composure and constantly cracking
with anguish said in great haste:
"Mr. Klöterjahn, Mr. Klöterjahn, oh, is Mr. Klöterjahn
there?"
"Stay outside," said Mr. Klöterjahn rudely . . . "What is
it? I have things to say here."
"Mr. Klöterjahn," said the wavering and breaking voice,
"you must come . . . the doctors are there too . . . oh, it's
so awfully sad . . ."
Then he was at the door in one stride and pulled it
open. Mrs. Spatz stood outside. She was holding her handkerchief in front of her mouth, and big long tears were
rolling into that cloth in pairs.
"Mr. Klöterjahn," she managed to say . . . , "it's so awfully sad . . . She coughed up so much blood, so terribly
much . . . She was sitting up in bed quite calmly and was
humming a piece of music to herself, and then it came,
dear God, so very, very much . . ."
"Is she dead?" cried Mr. Klöterjahn . . . As he shouted,
he seized the councillor's wife by the upper arm and
pulled her to and fro on the threshold. "No, not altogether, right? Not yet altogether, she can still see me . . .
Did she cough up a bit of blood again? From the lungs,
right? I admit that it may be coming from the lungs . . .
Gabriele!" he suddenly said, bursting into tears, and
warm, kindly, human and sincere feelings could be seen
breaking forth from him. "Yes, I'm coming!" he said, and
with long strides he dragged the councillor's wife out of
the room and away down the corridor. From a remote
part of the hallway his voice could still be constantly heard
rapidly moving away: "Not altogether, right? . . . From
the lungs, right?"

12

Mr. Spinell stood on the spot where he had stood during
Mr. Klöterjahn's so abruptly interrupted visit, and looked
at the open door. Finally he took a few steps forward and
listened for distant sounds. But all was still, so he closed
the door and returned to the room.

Eine Weile betrachtete er sich im Spiegel. Hierauf ging er zum
Schreibtisch, holte ein kleines Flakon und ein Gläschen aus einem
Fache hervor und nahm einen Kognak zu sich, was kein Mensch
ihm verdenken konnte. Dann streckte er sich auf dem Sofa aus und
schloß die Augen.

Die obere Klappe des Fensters stand offen. Draußen im Garten
von ›Einfried‹ zwitscherten die Vögel, und in diesen kleinen, zarten
und kecken Lauten lag fein und durchdringend der ganze Frühling
ausgedrückt. Einmal sagte Herr Spinell leise vor sich hin: »Unausbleiblicher Beruf . . .« Dann bewegte er den Kopf hin und her und
zog die Luft durch die Zähne ein wie bei einem heftigen Nerven-
schmerz.

Es war unmöglich, zur Ruhe und Sammlung zu gelangen. Man
ist nicht geschaffen für so plumpe Erlebnisse wie dieses da!
—Durch einen seelischen Vorgang, dessen Analyse zu weit führen
würde, gelangte Herr Spinell zu dem Entschlusse, sich zu erheben
und sich ein wenig Bewegung zu machen, sich ein wenig im Freien
zu ergehen. So nahm er den Hut und verließ das Zimmer.

Als er aus dem Hause trat und die milde, würzige Luft ihn um-
fing, wandte er das Haupt und ließ seine Augen langsam an dem
Gebäude empor bis zu einem Fenster gleiten, einem verhängten
Fenster, an dem sein Blick eine Weile ernst, fest und dunkel haftete.
Dann legte er die Hände auf den Rücken und schritt über die
Kieswege dahin. Er schritt in tiefem Sinnen.

Noch waren die Beete mit Matten bedeckt, und Bäume und Sträu-
cher waren noch nackt; aber der Schnee war fort, und die Wege
zeigten nur hier und da noch feuchte Spuren. Der weite Garten
mit seinen Grotten, Laubengängen und kleinen Pavillons lag in
prächtig farbiger Nachmittagsbeleuchtung, mit kräftigen Schatten
und sattem, goldigem Licht, und das dunkle Geäst der Bäume stand
scharf und zart gegliedert gegen den hellen Himmel.

Es war um die Stunde, da die Sonne Gestalt annimmt, da die
formlose Lichtmasse zur sichtbar sinkenden Scheibe wird, deren
sattere, mildere Glut das Auge duldet. Herr Spinell sah die Sonne
nicht; sein Weg führte ihn so, daß sie ihm verdeckt und verborgen
war. Er ging gesenkten Hauptes und summte ein Stückchen Musik
vor sich hin, ein kurzes Gebild, eine bang und klagend aufwärtssteig-
gende Figur, das Sehnsuchtsmotiv . . . Plötzlich aber, mit einem
Ruck, einem kurzen, krampfhaften Aufatmen, blieb er gefesselt
stehen, und unter heftig zusammengezogenen Brauen starrten
seine erweiterten Augen mit dem Ausdruck entsetzter Abwehr ge-
radeaus . . .

For a while he observed himself in the mirror. Then he went to the desk, fetched a little bottle and a liqueur glass from a drawer and drank a cognac, something that no one could hold against him. Then he stretched out on the sofa and closed his eyes.

The upper section of the window was open. Outside in Einfried's garden the birds were twittering, and in those small, delicate and pert sounds all of springtime was subtly and penetratingly expressed. Once Mr. Spinell said quietly to himself: "Inevitable vocation . . ." Then he shook his head back and forth and drew in air between his teeth as if suffering from a violent attack of nerves.

It was impossible to achieve rest and composure. People aren't made for such gross experiences as that one! —Through a psychic process, the analysis of which would lead us too far from the topic, Mr. Spinell arrived at the decision to get up and take a little exercise, to take a short stroll outside. So he took his hat and left the room.

When he stepped out of the house and the mild, spicy air encircled him, he turned his head and let his eyes glide slowly up the building until reaching a window, a curtained window, on which his gaze fastened awhile, earnestly, steadily and darkly. Then he put his hands behind his back and strode off over the gravel paths. He strode in deep meditation.

The flower beds were still covered with matting, and trees and bushes were still bare; but the snow was gone, and there were only occasional damp traces on the paths. The extensive garden with its grottoes, pergolas and small pavilions lay in splendidly colorful afternoon light, with strong shadows and a rich golden glow, and the dark boughs of the trees were sharply and delicately articulated against the bright sky.

It was about that time of day when the sun assumes a shape, when the formless mass of light becomes a visibly sinking disk whose richer, milder beams can be tolerated by the eye. Mr. Spinell did not see the sun; his path led him in such a way that it was covered and hidden from him. He walked with bowed head and hummed a little piece of music to himself, a brief phrase, a timorous and plangent rising figure, the motif of longing . . . But suddenly, with a jerk, a brief, convulsive intake of breath, he stood stock still, and beneath his violently contracted eyebrows his wide-open eyes stared straight ahead with an expression of horrified repulsion . . .

Der Weg wandte sich; er führte der sinkenden Sonne entgegen. Durchzogen von zwei schmalen, erleuchteten Wolkenstreifen mit vergoldeten Rändern stand sie groß und schräge am Himmel, setzte die Wipfel der Bäume in Glut und goß ihren gelbrötlichen Glanz über den Garten hin. Und inmitten dieser goldigen Verklärung, die gewaltige Gloriole der Sonnenscheibe zu Häupten, stand hochaufgerichtet im Wege eine üppige, ganz in Rot, Gold und Schottisch gekleidete Person, die ihre Rechte in die schwellende Hüfte stemmte und mit der Linken ein grazil geformtes Wägelchen leicht vor sich hin und her bewegte. In diesem Wägelchen aber saß das Kind, saß Anton Klöterjahn der Jüngere, saß Gabriele Eckhofs dicker Sohn!

Er saß, bekleidet mit einer weißen Flausjacke und einem großen weißen Hut, pausbäckig, prächtig und wohlgeraten in den Kissen, und sein Blick begegnete lustig und unbeirrbar demjenigen Herrn Spinells. Der Romancier war im Begriffe, sich aufzuraffen, er war ein Mann, er hätte die Kraft besessen, an dieser unerwarteten, in Glanz getauchten Erscheinung vorüberzuschreiten und seinen Spaziergang fortzusetzen. Da aber geschah das Gräßliche, daß Anton Klöterjahn zu lachen und jubeln begann, er kreischte vor unerklärlicher Lust, es konnte einem unheimlich zu Sinne werden.

Gott weiß, was ihn anfocht, ob die schwarze Gestalt ihm gegenüber ihn in diese wilde Heiterkeit versetzte oder was für ein Anfall von animalischem Wohlbefinden ihn packte. Er hielt in der einen Hand einen knöchernen Beißring und in der anderen eine blecherne Klapperbüchse. Diese beiden Gegenstände reckte er jauchzend in den Sonnenschein empor, schüttelte sie und schlug sie zusammen, als wollte er jemanden spottend verscheuchen. Seine Augen waren beinahe geschlossen vor Vergnügen, und sein Mund war so klaffend aufgerissen, daß man seinen ganzen rosigen Gaumen sah. Er warf sogar seinen Kopf hin und her, indes er jauchzte.

Da machte Herr Spinell kehrt und ging von dannen. Er ging, gefolgt von dem Jubilieren des kleinen Klöterjahn, mit einer gewissen behutsamen und steif-graziösen Armhaltung über den Kies, mit den gewaltsam zögernden Schritten jemandes, der verbergen will, daß er innerlich davonläuft.

The path turned; it led toward the setting sun. Traversed by two narrow, illuminated bands of cloud with gilded edges, it hung in the sky, large and oblique, set fire to the treetops and poured its yellow-red glow over the garden. And in the midst of this golden transfiguration, with the mighty gloriole of the solar disk at her head, there stood tall and erect in the path a buxom person dressed all in red, gold and plaid; her right hand was pressed into her distended hip and with her left hand she was lightly pushing a daintily built little carriage to and fro in front of her. In that carriage, however, sat the child, sat Anton Klöterjahn, Jr., sat Gabriele Eckhof's plump son!

He sat on the cushions, dressed in a white fleecy jacket and a large white hat, chubby-cheeked, splendid and well-formed, and his glance, merry and unruffled, met that of Mr. Spinell. The novelist was on the point of pulling himself together, he was a man, he would have possessed the strength to walk past this unexpected, sunlight-bathed phenomenon, and to continue his walk. But then the ghastly thing occurred: Anton Klöterjahn began to laugh and shout with joy, he screeched with inexplicable pleasure, so powerfully as to be unnerving.

God knows what got into him, whether the black-clad figure facing him reduced him to that state of wild hilarity, or what sort of attack of animal good spirits took hold of him. In one hand he held a bone teething ring and in the other a tin rattle. He jubilantly stretched these two objects upward into the sunshine, shook them and banged them together as if he wanted to scare someone away with mockery. His eyes were nearly closed with pleasure, and his mouth was pulled open in such a wide gape that his whole pink palate could be seen. He even tossed his head back and forth as he exulted.

Then Mr. Spinell did an about-face and departed. Followed by the merry shouts of young Klöterjahn, he walked over the gravel with his arms in a certain circumspect and stiffly graceful position, with the forcefully hesitant steps of a man who wants to hide the fact that inwardly he is running away.

KAFKA
AND
"THE JUDGMENT"

PROBABLY THE most influential German-language author of the twentieth century, Kafka was a Bohemian Jew, born into a merchant family in Prague in 1883. He studied law, receiving his degree in 1906, then worked for an insurance firm for almost the rest of his life, doing his writing chiefly at night. In his last years he suffered from tuberculosis; he died near Vienna in 1924. Only a handful of his works were published in his lifetime, and many of his writings, such as his great novels *Der Prozess* (The Trial) and *Das Schloss* (The Castle), were left incomplete. But his friend Max Brod arranged for posthumous publication of his papers, and now his diaries and letters are read as avidly as his fiction. Other major short stories by Kafka are "Die Verwandlung" (The Metamorphosis), "Ein Landarzt" (A Country Doctor), "In der Strafkolonie" (In the Penal Colony) and "Ein Hungerkünstler" (A Hunger Artist). He is recognized as a supreme spokesman of modern man's anguish and perplexity.

Kafka's diary reveals that he wrote "The Judgment" in one sitting between ten o'clock on the night of September 22, 1912, and six the following morning. He realized at once that it was his best work to date, and the confirmation of his vocation as a writer. The year 1912 was especially fruitful for him, inspired as he was by his engagement (ultimately broken, like the others) to Felice Bauer, to whom he dedicated "The Judgment." In his diary and his letters to Felice, he discusses the meaning of the story (the father-son conflict in which "possession" of the friend in Russia is the immediate stake), and indicates the close identification of two of the characters with himself and Felice: "Georg" has the same number of letters as "Franz"; "Bendemann," stripped of the "-mann," has the same number of letters as "Kafka" with a repeated vowel in the same places; "Frieda" has the same number of letters and the same initial as "Felice," and connotes "peace"; while the "-feld" part of "Brandenfeld" is a field, the realm of activity of a "Bauer" (farmer). The story was first published in 1913 in Max Brod's journal *Arkadia. Ein Jahrbuch für Dichtkunst*, published by Kurt Wolff in Leipzig.

"The Judgment" is heavily autobiographical. The continuous confrontation between Kafka and his father is completely spelled out in a long letter ("Brief an den Vater") written in 1919, in which

244

Kafka accuses his father of thwarting his attempts at marriage and of permanently crippling him emotionally by his tyrannical, overbearing manner and egotistic, know-it-all behavior; in this letter, his father's approval is said to be the chief goal of the author's existence, and their hostility the ultimate source of all his literary production. Certainly, Kafka had imbibed many of his father's views, such as the distaste for physical sex evident in "The Judgment" and other stories.

"The Judgment" is typical of Kafka's mature style: very lucid, everyday language (the strangeness is all "between the lines"); words and phrases artistically placed without calling undue attention to the skill and craftsmanship involved; random colloquialisms spicing the diction, sometimes in an unsettling way (the father's first use of double meanings and colorful language serves as the surprise turning point in the story).

The present translator would much prefer to render the title "Das Urteil" as "The Sentence," but has retained the version "The Judgment" for recognition value, the story being so well known by that name to English-language readers.

DAS URTEIL

Es war an einem Sonntagvormittag im schönsten Frühjahr. Georg Bendemann, ein junger Kaufmann, saß in seinem Privatzimmer im ersten Stock eines der niedrigen, leichtgebauten Häuser, die entlang des Flusses in einer langen Reihe, fast nur in der Höhe und Färbung unterschieden, sich hinzogen. Er hatte gerade einen Brief an einen sich im Ausland befindenden Jugendfreund beendet, verschloß ihn in spielerischer Langsamkeit und sah dann, den Ellbogen auf den Schreibtisch gestützt, aus dem Fenster auf den Fluß, die Brücke und die Anhöhen am anderen Ufer mit ihrem schwachen Grün.

Er dachte darüber nach, wie dieser Freund, mit seinem Fortkommen zu Hause unzufrieden, vor Jahren schon nach Rußland sich förmlich geflüchtet hatte. Nun betrieb er ein Geschäft in Petersburg, das anfangs sich sehr gut angelassen hatte, seit langem aber schon zu stocken schien, wie der Freund bei seinen immer seltener werdenden Besuchen klagte. So arbeitete er sich in der Fremde nutzlos ab, der fremdartige Vollbart verdeckte nur schlecht das seit den Kinderjahren wohlbekannte Gesicht, dessen gelbe Hautfarbe auf eine sich entwickelnde Krankheit hinzudeuten schien. Wie er erzählte, hatte er keine rechte Verbindung mit der dortigen Kolonie seiner Landsleute, aber auch fast keinen gesellschaftlichen Verkehr mit einheimischen Familien und richtete sich so für ein endgültiges Junggesellentum ein.

Was sollte man einem solchen Manne schreiben, der sich offenbar verrannt hatte, den man bedauern, dem man aber nicht helfen konnte. Sollte man ihm vielleicht raten, wieder nach Hause zu kommen, seine Existenz hierher zu verlegen, alle die alten freundschaftlichen Beziehungen wieder aufzunehmen—wofür ja kein Hindernis bestand—und im übrigen auf die Hilfe der Freunde zu vertrauen? Das bedeutete aber nichts anderes, als daß man ihm gleichzeitig, je schonender, desto kränkender, sagte, daß seine bisherigen Versuche mißlungen seien, daß er endlich von ihnen ablassen solle, daß er zurückkehren und sich als ein für immer Zurückgekehrter von allen mit großen Augen anstaunen lassen müsse, daß nur seine Freunde etwas verstünden und daß er ein altes Kind sei, das den erfolgreichen, zu Hause gebliebenen Freunden einfach zu

THE JUDGMENT

It was on a Sunday morning in the loveliest part of the spring. Georg Bendemann, a young merchant, sat in his room on the second floor of one of the low, lightly built houses that extended along the river in a long line, differing, if at all, only in height and coloration. He had just finished a letter to a childhood friend who was living abroad; he sealed the letter with playful slowness and then, leaning his elbow on the desk, looked out the window at the river, the bridge and the pale-green hills on the far bank.

He thought about how this friend, dissatisfied with his advancement at home, had, years ago now, literally fled to Russia. Now this friend was running a business in St. Petersburg that had been very promising at the start, but for a long time now seemed to be at a standstill, as he complained during his increasingly infrequent visits to Georg. And so he was wearing himself out uselessly far from home; his foreign-style beard failed to disguise the face Georg had known so well since they were children, a face whose yellow complexion was apparently the sign of a developing illness. As he told Georg, he had no close relations with the colony of his compatriots in that place, but, in addition, practically no social intercourse with native families, and thus was in a fair way to remain a bachelor always.

What was one to write to a man like that, who had obviously taken a wrong course, whom one could pity but not help? Should one perhaps advise him to come home, resume his life back here, restore all his old friendships (there was no obstacle to this) and, for all the rest, rely on his friends' assistance? But that would mean nothing less than to tell him at the same time—hurting him more, the more one wished to spare his feelings—that his efforts up to now had been unsuccessful, that he should finally abandon them, that he had to return and be gaped at by everyone as a man who had come back as a failure. It would mean telling him that his friends were the only ones with any sense, and that he was just a grown-up child who should merely obey his successful friends that had stayed

folgen habe. Und war es dann noch sicher, daß alle die Plage, die man ihm antun müßte, einen Zweck hätte? Vielleicht gelang es nicht einmal, ihn überhaupt nach Hause zu bringen—er sagte ja selbst, daß er die Verhältnisse in der Heimat nicht mehr verstünde—und so bliebe er dann trotz allem in seiner Fremde, verbittert durch die Ratschläge und den Freunden noch ein Stück mehr entfremdet. Folgte er aber wirklich dem Rat und würde hier—natürlich nicht mit Absicht, aber durch die Tatsachen—niedergedrückt, fände sich nicht in seinen Freunden und nicht ohne sie zurecht, litte an Beschämung, hätte jetzt wirklich keine Heimat und keine Freunde mehr, war es da nicht viel besser für ihn, er blieb in der Fremde, so wie er war? Konnte man denn bei solchen Umständen daran denken, daß er es hier tatsächlich vorwärts bringen würde?

Aus diesen Gründen konnte man ihm, wenn man noch überhaupt die briefliche Verbindung aufrecht erhalten wollte, keine eigentlichen Mitteilungen machen, wie man sie ohne Scheu auch den entferntesten Bekannten machen würde. Der Freund war nun schon über drei Jahre nicht in der Heimat gewesen und erklärte dies sehr notdürftig mit der Unsicherheit der politischen Verhältnisse in Rußland, die demnach also auch die kürzeste Abwesenheit eines kleinen Geschäftsmannes nicht zuließen, während hunderttausende Russen ruhig in der Welt herumfuhren. Im Laufe dieser drei Jahre hatte sich aber gerade für Georg vieles verändert. Von dem Todesfall von Georgs Mutter, der vor etwa zwei Jahren erfolgt war und seit welchem Georg mit seinem alten Vater in gemeinsamer Wirtschaft lebte, hatte der Freund wohl noch erfahren und sein Beileid in einem Brief mit einer Trockenheit ausgedrückt, die ihren Grund nur darin haben konnte, daß die Trauer über ein solches Ereignis in der Fremde ganz unvorstellbar wird. Nun hatte aber Georg seit jener Zeit, so wie alles andere, auch sein Geschäft mit größerer Entschlossenheit angepackt. Vielleicht hatte ihn der Vater bei Lebzeiten der Mutter dadurch, daß er im Geschäft nur seine Ansicht gelten lassen wollte, an einer wirklichen eigenen Tätigkeit gehindert, vielleicht war der Vater seit dem Tode der Mutter, trotzdem er noch immer im Geschäfte arbeitete, zurückhaltender geworden, vielleicht spielten—was sogar sehr wahrscheinlich war—glückliche Zufälle eine weit wichtigere Rolle, jedenfalls aber hatte sich das Geschäft in diesen zwei Jahren ganz unerwartet entwickelt, das Personal hatte man verdoppeln müssen, der Umsatz

at home. And was it even certain that all the pain that would have to be inflicted on him would be to any purpose? Maybe they wouldn't even succeed in bringing him home at all—for he himself said that he no longer understood the conditions back home—and so he would remain abroad in spite of everything, embittered by their suggestions and all the more alienated from his friends. But if he actually followed their advice and were to come to grief here—not intentionally, of course, but through circumstances—if he failed to find a proper footing either with or without his friends, if he suffered humiliation, if he then really had no home or friends left, wasn't it much better for him to remain abroad just as he was? In such circumstances, was it possible to believe that he would actually make a go of it here?

For these reasons, if one was to maintain communication by letter at all, one could not send him any real news, as one would unhesitatingly do even to the most casual acquaintances. Now, it was more than three years since Georg's friend had been home, giving as a quite flimsy excuse for his absence the instability of political conditions in Russia, which according to him did not allow a small businessman to leave his work for even the briefest period—while hundreds of thousands of Russians were calmly traveling all over. In the course of those three years, however, much had changed for Georg in particular. The death of Georg's mother, which had occurred about two years earlier, since which time Georg had been sharing the household with his old father, had, of course, still been communicated to his friend. The friend had expressed his sympathy in a letter so dry that the only possible explanation for it was that mourning over such an event becomes quite unimaginable when one is abroad. But, in addition, since that time Georg had taken charge of the family business with greater decisiveness, as he had done with everything else. Perhaps, while his mother was alive, his father had hindered Georg from taking a really active part in the business by insisting that only *his* views were valid; perhaps, since the death of Georg's mother, his father, while still working in the business, had become more withdrawn; perhaps—and this was extremely probable—lucky accidents played a far more important role. But at any rate, in these two years the business had grown at a quite unexpected rate, they had had to double their

hatte sich verfünffacht, ein weiterer Fortschritt stand zweifellos bevor.

Der Freund aber hatte keine Ahnung von dieser Veränderung. Früher, zum letztenmal vielleicht in jenem Beileidsbrief, hatte er Georg zur Auswanderung nach Rußland überreden wollen und sich über die Aussichten verbreitet, die gerade für Georgs Geschäftszweig in Petersburg bestanden. Die Ziffern waren verschwindend gegenüber dem Umfang, den Georgs Geschäft jetzt angenommen hatte. Georg aber hatte keine Lust gehabt, dem Freund von seinen geschäftlichen Erfolgen zu schreiben, und hätte er es jetzt nachträglich getan, es hätte wirklich einen merkwürdigen Anschein gehabt.

So beschränkte sich Georg darauf, dem Freund immer nur über bedeutungslose Vorfälle zu schreiben, wie sie sich, wenn man an einem ruhigen Sonntag nachdenkt, in der Erinnerung ungeordnet aufhäufen. Er wollte nichts anderes, als die Vorstellung ungestört lassen, die sich der Freund von der Heimatstadt in der langen Zwischenzeit wohl gemacht und mit welcher er sich abgefunden hatte. So geschah es Georg, daß er dem Freund die Verlobung eines gleichgültigen Menschen mit einem ebenso gleichgültigen Mädchen dreimal in ziemlich weit auseinanderliegenden Briefen anzeigte, bis sich dann allerdings der Freund, ganz gegen Georgs Absicht, für diese Merkwürdigkeit zu interessieren begann.

Georg schrieb ihm aber solche Dinge viel lieber, als daß er zugestanden hätte, daß er selbst vor einem Monat mit einem Fräulein Frieda Brandenfeld, einem Mädchen aus wohlhabender Familie, sich verlobt hatte. Oft sprach er mit seiner Braut über diesen Freund und das besondere Korrespondenzverhältnis, in welchem er zu ihm stand. »Da wird er gar nicht zu unserer Hochzeit kommen«, sagte sie, »und ich habe doch das Recht, alle deine Freunde kennen zu lernen.« »Ich will ihn nicht stören«, antwortete Georg, »verstehe mich recht, er würde wahrscheinlich kommen, wenigstens glaube ich es, aber er würde sich gezwungen und geschädigt fühlen, vielleicht mich beneiden und sicher unzufrieden und unfähig, diese Unzufriedenheit jemals zu beseitigen, allein wieder zurückfahren. Allein—weißt du, was das ist?« »Ja, kann er denn von unserer Heirat nicht auch auf andere Weise erfahren?« »Das kann ich allerdings nicht verhindern, aber es ist bei seiner Lebensweise unwahrscheinlich.« »Wenn du solche Freunde hast, Georg, hättest du dich überhaupt nicht verloben sollen.« »Ja, das ist unser beider Schuld; aber ich wollte es auch jetzt nicht anders haben.« Und wenn sie dann, rasch atmend unter seinen Küssen, noch vorbrachte: »Eigentlich kränkt es mich doch«, hielt er es wirklich für unverfänglich, dem Freund alles zu schreiben. »So bin ich und so hat er mich

personnel, the returns had increased fivefold, and further expansion was undoubtedly due in the future.

But Georg's friend had no idea of this change. Earlier, perhaps most recently in that letter of sympathy, he had tried to persuade Georg to emigrate to Russia and had expatiated on the prospects in St. Petersburg for Georg's line of business in particular. The figures he quoted were infinitesimal compared with the volume of business Georg was now doing. But Georg had not felt like writing his friend about his business successes, and if he were to have done so belatedly now, it would really have looked odd.

And so Georg confined himself to continually writing his friend about nothing but insignificant events, as they accumulate disorderedly in one's memory when one thinks back on a quiet Sunday. His only wish was to leave undisturbed the mental picture of his hometown that his friend must have created during the long interval, a picture he could live with. And so it happened that three times, in letters written fairly far apart, Georg informed his friend of the engagement of a man of no consequence to an equally inconsequential girl, until his friend, quite contrary to Georg's intentions, really began to be interested in this curious fact.

But Georg far preferred to write him about things like that than to admit that he himself, a month earlier, had become engaged to a Miss Frieda Brandenfeld, a girl from a well-to-do family. He often spoke to his fiancée about that friend and their special relationship as correspondents. "Now, he won't come to our wedding," she said, "and I do have the right to meet all your friends." "I don't want to bother him," Georg replied; "mind you, he probably would come—at least, I think so—but he would feel constrained and injured; perhaps he would envy me, and he would surely go back again alone, discontented and incapable of ever overcoming that discontentment. Alone—do you know what that means?" "Yes, but couldn't he come to hear about our marriage in some other way?" "Naturally I can't prevent that, but, given his mode of life, it's not likely." "If you have friends like that, Georg, you shouldn't have become engaged at all." "Yes, that's the fault of both of us; but even so I wouldn't have wanted it any other way." And when she then, breathing rapidly as he kissed her, still managed to say: "And yet it does really make me sad," he decided it would really do no harm to write his friend about everything. "That's how

hinzunehmen«, sagte er sich, »Ich kann nicht aus mir einen Menschen herausschneiden, der vielleicht für die Freundschaft mit ihm geeigneter wäre, als ich es bin.«

Und tatsächlich berichtete er seinem Freunde in dem langen Brief, den er an diesem Sonntagvormittag schrieb, die erfolgte Verlobung mit folgenden Worten: »Die beste Neuigkeit habe ich mir bis zum Schluß aufgespart. Ich habe mich mit einem Fräulein Frieda Brandenfeld verlobt, einem Mädchen aus einer wohlhabenden Familie, die sich hier erst lange nach Deiner Abreise angesiedelt hat, die Du also kaum kennen dürftest. Es wird sich noch Gelegenheit finden, Dir Näheres über meine Braut mitzuteilen, heute genüge Dir, daß ich recht glücklich bin und daß sich in unserem gegenseitigen Verhältnis nur insofern etwas geändert hat, als Du jetzt in mir statt eines ganz gewöhnlichen Freundes einen glücklichen Freund haben wirst. Außerdem bekommst Du in meiner Braut, die Dich herzlich grüßen läßt, und die Dir nächstens selbst schreiben wird, eine aufrichtige Freundin, was für einen Junggesellen nicht ganz ohne Bedeutung ist. Ich weiß, es hält Dich vielerlei von einem Besuche bei uns zurück, wäre aber nicht gerade meine Hochzeit die richtige Gelegenheit, einmal alle Hindernisse über den Haufen zu werfen? Aber wie dies auch sein mag, handle ohne alle Rücksicht und nur nach Deiner Wohlmeinung.«

Mit diesem Brief in der Hand war Georg lange, das Gesicht dem Fenster zugekehrt, an seinem Schreibtisch gesessen. Einem Bekannten, der ihn im Vorübergehen von der Gasse aus gegrüßt hatte, hatte er kaum mit einem abwesenden Lächeln geantwortet.

Endlich steckte er den Brief in die Tasche und ging aus seinem Zimmer quer durch einen kleinen Gang in das Zimmer seines Vaters, in dem er schon seit Monaten nicht gewesen war. Es bestand auch sonst keine Nötigung dazu, denn er verkehrte mit seinem Vater ständig im Geschäft, das Mittagessen nahmen sie gleichzeitig in einem Speisehaus ein, abends versorgte sich zwar jeder nach Belieben, doch saßen sie dann meistens, wenn nicht Georg, wie es am häufigsten geschah, mit Freunden beisammen war oder jetzt seine Braut besuchte, noch ein Weilchen, jeder mit seiner Zeitung, im gemeinsamen Wohnzimmer.

Georg staunte darüber, wie dunkel das Zimmer des Vaters selbst an diesem sonnigen Vormittag war. Einen solchen Schatten warf also die hohe Mauer, die sich jenseits des schmalen Hofes erhob. Der Vater saß beim Fenster in einer Ecke, die mit verschiedenen Andenken an die selige Mutter ausgeschmückt war, und las die Zeitung, die er seitlich vor die Augen hielt, wodurch er irgendeine

I am and that's how he's got to accept me," he said to himself; "I can't remake myself into a person who might be more suited to be his friend than I am."

And, in fact, in the long letter he composed on that Sunday morning he informed his friend of the engagement that had taken place, writing as follows: "I have saved the best news for the end. I have become engaged to a Miss Frieda Brandenfeld, a girl from a well-to-do family that did not move here until long after your departure, and whom you thus can hardly be expected to know. There will be further opportunities to tell you details about my fiancée; let it suffice for today that I am very happy and that the only change in the relationship between you and me is that, in place of a very ordinary friend, you will now have in me a happy friend. In addition, in my fiancée, who sends warmest regards and who will soon write to you herself, you are acquiring a sincere female friend, which is not totally insignificant for a bachelor. I know that all sorts of things prevent you from visiting us, but wouldn't my wedding, of all things, be the right occasion for you to cast all obstacles to the winds? However that may be, though, don't make any special allowances but act only as you see fit."

With this letter in his hand Georg had sat at his desk for a long time, his face turned toward the window. When an acquaintance had greeted him from the street passing by, he had barely responded with an absent smile.

Finally he put the letter in his pocket and stepped from his room across a small corridor into his father's room, which he had not been in for months. Nor was there any particular need for him to go there, because he saw his father constantly in their office and they took their lunch in a restaurant at the same hour; in the evening, to be sure, each of them saw to his own needs as he wished, but then usually (unless Georg, as happened most often, was together with friends or, as things were now, visited his fiancée) each would sit with his newspaper for another little while in the living room that they shared.

Georg was surprised at how dark his father's room was even on this sunny morning. So the high wall that rose beyond the narrow yard cast such a great shadow! His father was sitting by the window in a corner that was decorated with various mementos of his late mother, and was reading the newspaper, which he held off to one side in front of his face, attempting to correct some eye condition.

Augenschwäche auszugleichen suchte. Auf dem Tisch standen die Reste des Frühstücks, von dem nicht viel verzehrt zu sein schien. »Ah, Georg!« sagte der Vater und ging ihm gleich entgegen. Sein schwerer Schlafrock öffnete sich im Gehen, die Enden umflatterten ihn—»mein Vater ist noch immer ein Riese«, sagte sich Georg. »Hier ist es ja unerträglich dunkel«, sagte er dann. »Ja, dunkel ist es schon«, antwortete der Vater. »Das Fenster hast du auch geschlossen?« »Ich habe es lieber so.« »Es ist ja ganz warm draußen«, sagte Georg, wie im Nachhang zu dem Früheren, und setzte sich.

Der Vater räumte das Frühstücksgeschirr ab und stellte es auf einen Kasten.

»Ich wollte dir eigentlich nur sagen«, fuhr Georg fort, der den Bewegungen des alten Mannes ganz verloren folgte, »daß ich nun doch nach Petersburg meine Verlobung angezeigt habe.« Er zog den Brief ein wenig aus der Tasche und ließ ihn wieder zurückfallen.

»Wieso nach Petersburg?« fragte der Vater.

»Meinem Freunde doch«, sagte Georg und suchte des Vaters Augen.—»Im Geschäft ist er doch ganz anders«, dachte er, »wie er hier breit sitzt und die Arme über der Brust kreuzt.«

»Ja. Deinem Freunde«, sagte der Vater mit Betonung.

»Du weißt doch, Vater, daß ich ihm meine Verlobung zuerst verschweigen wollte. Aus Rücksichtnahme, aus keinem anderen Grunde sonst. Du weißt selbst, er ist ein schwieriger Mensch. Ich sagte mir, von anderer Seite kann er von meiner Verlobung wohl erfahren, wenn das auch bei seiner einsamen Lebensweise kaum wahrscheinlich ist—das kann ich nicht hindern—, aber von mir selbst soll er es nun einmal nicht erfahren.«

»Und jetzt hast du es dir wieder anders überlegt?« fragte der Vater, legte die große Zeitung auf den Fensterbord und auf die Zeitung die Brille, die er mit der Hand bedeckte.

»Ja, jetzt habe ich es mir wieder überlegt. Wenn er mein guter Freund ist, sagte ich mir, dann ist meine glückliche Verlobung auch für ihn ein Glück. Und deshalb habe ich nicht mehr gezögert, es ihm anzuzeigen. Ehe ich jedoch den Brief einwarf, wollte ich es dir sagen.«

»Georg«, sagte der Vater und zog den zahnlosen Mund in die

On the table were the leftovers of his breakfast, not much of which seemed to have been eaten.

"Ah, Georg!" said his father and walked right over to him. His heavy bathrobe opened as he walked, the tails flapping around him—"My father is *still* a giant," Georg said to himself.

"But it's unbearably dark here," he said then.

"Yes, it is dark, isn't it?" his father answered.

"You shut the window, too?"

"I like it better this way."

"But it's quite warm outside," said Georg, as an addition to his earlier remark, and sat down.

His father cleared away the breakfast dishes and put them on a chest.

"All that I really wanted to tell you," continued Georg, who was following the old man's movements in great perplexity, "is that, after all, I have written to St. Petersburg announcing my engagement." He drew the letter a little way out of his pocket and let it slide back.

"What do you mean, to St. Petersburg?" asked his father.

"To my friend, of course," said Georg and tried to meet his father's eyes.—"At work he's quite different," he thought; "the way he sits here, filling out the chair, with his arms folded over his chest!"

"Yes. To your friend," said his father with a special emphasis.

"You know, of course, Father, that at first I wanted to keep my engagement a secret from him. Out of consideration for his feelings, for no other reason. You know yourself, he's a difficult man. I said to myself that he could find out about my engagement in some other way, even though, given his lonely way of life, that's hardly likely—I couldn't prevent that—but that he definitely wasn't going to find out about it from me."

"And now you've changed your mind?" asked his father, laid his voluminous paper down on the windowsill and put his glasses, which he covered with his hand, on top of the paper.

"Yes, now I have changed my mind. If he is a good friend of mine, I said to myself, then my happy engagement is a bit of happiness for him too. And therefore I no longer hesitated to tell him about it. But before I mailed the letter I wanted to tell you."

"Georg," said his father and drew the corners of his

Breite, »hör' einmal! Du bist wegen dieser Sache zu mir gekommen, um dich mit mir zu beraten. Das ehrt dich ohne Zweifel. Aber es ist nichts, es ist ärger als nichts, wenn du mir jetzt nicht die volle Wahrheit sagst. Ich will nicht Dinge aufrühren, die nicht hierher gehören. Seit dem Tode unserer teuren Mutter sind gewisse unschöne Dinge vorgegangen. Vielleicht kommt auch für sie die Zeit und vielleicht kommt sie früher, als wir denken. Im Geschäft entgeht mir manches, es wird mir vielleicht nicht verborgen—ich will jetzt gar nicht die Annahme machen, daß es mir verborgen wird—, ich bin nicht mehr kräftig genug, mein Gedächtnis läßt nach, ich habe nicht mehr den Blick für alle die vielen Sachen. Das ist erstens der Ablauf der Natur, und zweitens hat mich der Tod unseres Mütterchens viel mehr niedergeschlagen als dich.—Aber weil wir gerade bei dieser Sache halten, bei diesem Brief, so bitte ich dich, Georg, täusche mich nicht. Es ist eine Kleinigkeit, es ist nicht des Atems wert, also täusche mich nicht. Hast du wirklich diesen Freund in Petersburg?«

Georg stand verlegen auf. »Lassen wir meine Freunde sein. Tausend Freunde ersetzen mir nicht meinen Vater. Weißt du, was ich glaube? Du schonst dich nicht genug. Aber das Alter verlangt seine Rechte. Du bist mir im Geschäft unentbehrlich, das weißt du ja sehr genau, aber wenn das Geschäft deine Gesundheit bedrohen sollte, sperre ich es noch morgen für immer. Das geht nicht. Wir müssen da eine andere Lebensweise für dich einführen. Aber von Grund aus. Du sitzt hier im Dunkel und im Wohnzimmer hättest du schönes Licht. Du nippst vom Frühstück, statt dich ordentlich zu stärken. Du sitzt bei geschlossenem Fenster und die Luft würde dir so gut tun. Nein, mein Vater! Ich werde den Arzt holen und seinen Vorschriften werden wir folgen. Die Zimmer werden wir wechseln, du wirst ins Vorderzimmer ziehen, ich hierher. Es wird keine Veränderung für dich sein, alles wird mit übertragen werden. Aber das alles hat Zeit, jetzt lege dich noch ein wenig ins Bett, du brauchst unbedingt Ruhe. Komm, ich werde dir beim Ausziehn helfen, du wirst sehn, ich kann es. Oder willst du gleich ins Vorderzimmer gehn, dann legst du dich vorläufig in mein Bett. Das wäre übrigens sehr vernünftig.«

Georg stand knapp neben seinem Vater, der den Kopf mit dem struppigen weißen Haar auf die Brust hatte sinken lassen.

»Georg«, sagte der Vater leise, ohne Bewegung.

Georg kniete sofort neben dem Vater nieder, er sah die Pupillen

toothless mouth out wide, "listen! You came to me with this matter to consult with me. That doubtless does you honor. But it is meaningless, it is worse than meaningless, if you don't tell me the whole truth now. I don't wish to stir up matters that don't pertain to this. Since the death of your dear mother, certain unpleasant things have occurred. Perhaps the time is coming for them, too, and perhaps it is coming sooner than we think. At work a lot escapes me; perhaps it isn't intentionally hidden from me—for the moment I shall definitely assume that it is not hidden from me—I am no longer strong enough, my memory is going, I can no longer keep up with all the particulars. For one thing, that is perfectly natural for my age, and, for another, your mother's death took a much greater toll of me than of you.—But since we are discussing this matter, this letter, I implore you, Georg, don't deceive me. It's a trifle, it's not worth mentioning, so don't deceive me. Do you really have this friend in St. Petersburg?"

Georg stood up in embarrassment. "Let's forget about my friends. A thousand friends are no substitute for my father. Do you know what I think? You don't take good enough care of yourself. But old age demands its due. I can't do without you in the business, you know that very well, but if the business were to threaten your health, I would shut it down forever tomorrow. This is no good. We must institute a new way of life for you. And thoroughly. You sit here in the dark while you would have fine light in the living room. You nibble at your breakfast instead of nourishing yourself properly. You sit by a closed window while the air would do you so much good. No, Father! I am going to get the doctor and we'll follow his advice. We'll exchange rooms; you'll move into the front room, I'll move in here. It won't mean any change for you, all your possessions will be brought in with you. But there's time for all that; for the moment do lie down in bed for a while, you definitely need rest. Come, I'll help you undress; you'll see, I can. Or if you want to go to the front room at once, then you can lie down on my bed for the time being. In fact, that would be very sensible."

Georg was standing close by his father, who had let his head, with its disheveled white hair, drop onto his breast.

"Georg," said his father quietly, without moving.

Georg immediately knelt down beside his father; in his

in dem müden Gesicht des Vaters übergroß in den Winkeln der Augen auf sich gerichtet.

»Du hast keinen Freund in Petersburg. Du bist immer ein Spaß-macher gewesen und hast dich auch mir gegenüber nicht zurückge-halten. Wie solltest du denn gerade dort einen Freund haben! Das kann ich gar nicht glauben.«

»Denk doch noch einmal nach, Vater«, sagte Georg, hob den Vater vom Sessel und zog ihm, wie er nun doch recht schwach dastand, den Schlafrock aus, »jetzt wird es bald drei Jahre her sein, da war ja mein Freund bei uns zu Besuch. Ich erinnere mich noch, daß du ihn nicht besonders gern hattest. Wenigstens zweimal habe ich ihn vor dir verleugnet, trotzdem er gerade bei mir im Zimmer saß. Ich konnte ja deine Abneigung gegen ihn ganz gut verstehn, mein Freund hat seine Eigentümlichkeiten. Aber dann hast du dich doch auch wieder ganz gut mit ihm unterhalten. Ich war damals noch so stolz darauf, daß du ihm zuhörtest, nicktest und fragtest. Wenn du nachdenkst, mußt du dich erinnern. Er erzählte damals unglaubliche Geschichten von der russischen Revolution. Wie er z. B. auf einer Geschäftsreise in Kiew bei einem Tumult einen Geist-lichen auf einem Balkon gesehen hatte, der sich ein breites Blut-kreuz in die flache Hand schnitt, diese Hand erhob und die Menge anrief. Du hast ja selbst diese Geschichte hie und da wiedererzählt.«

Währenddessen war es Georg gelungen, den Vater wieder nie-derzusetzen und ihm die Trikothose, die er über den Leinenun-terhosen trug, sowie die Socken vorsichtig auszuziehn. Beim An-blick der nicht besonders reinen Wäsche machte er sich Vorwürfe, den Vater vernachlässigt zu haben. Es wäre sicherlich auch seine Pflicht gewesen, über den Wäschewechsel seines Vaters zu wachen. Er hatte mit seiner Braut darüber, wie sie die Zukunft des Vaters einrichten wollten, noch nicht ausdrücklich gesprochen, denn sie hatten stillschweigend vorausgesetzt, daß der Vater allein in der alten Wohnung bleiben würde. Doch jetzt entschloß er sich kurz mit aller Bestimmtheit, den Vater in seinen künftigen Haushalt mitzunehmen. Es schien ja fast, wenn man genauer zusah, daß die Pflege, die dort dem Vater bereitet werden sollte, zu spät kommen könnte.

Auf seinen Armen trug er den Vater ins Bett. Ein schreckliches Gefühl hatte er, als er während der paar Schritte zum Bett hin merkte, daß an seiner Brust der Vater mit seiner Uhrkette spiele. Er konnte ihn nicht gleich ins Bett legen, so fest hielt er sich an dieser Uhrkette.

Kaum war er aber im Bett, schien alles gut. Er deckte sich selbst

father's weary face he saw that the unnaturally large pupils in the corners of the eyes were directed at himself.

"You have no friend in St. Petersburg. You've always been a practical joker and you haven't spared even me. How could you have a friend there, of all places! I can't believe that at all."

"Just try to remember, Father," said Georg, lifting his father from the armchair and drawing off his bathrobe as the old man now stood there in great debility; "it's now almost three years ago that my friend was here on a visit. I still recall that you didn't particularly like him. At least twice I told you that he wasn't here, although he was sitting in my room at the moment. Of course, I could understand your dislike of him very well: my friend does have his peculiarities. But then after all you got along very well with him again. I was still so proud at the time that you listened to him, nodded and asked him questions. If you think about it, you must remember. At the time he told us unbelievable stories about the Russian revolution. For example, how, on a business trip to Kiev, during a riot he had seen a priest on a balcony cutting a wide bloody cross into the palm of his hand, raising that hand and addressing the crowd. You yourself repeated that story from time to time."

Meanwhile Georg had succeeded in sitting his father down again and carefully pulling off the long knitted drawers he wore over his linen underpants, as well as his socks. At sight of the not especially clean underwear, he reproached himself for having neglected his father. It surely would also have been his duty to watch over his father's changes of underwear. He had not yet spoken expressly with his fiancée about how they wished to arrange his father's future, for they had tacitly presupposed that his father would remain alone in the old house. But now he quickly decided, with full determination, to take his father along into his future household. Indeed, it almost seemed, upon examining the situation more closely, that the care that would be given his father there might come too late.

He carried his father to bed in his arms. He had a frightening feeling when he noticed, during the few paces over to the bed, that his father was playing with the watch chain on his chest. He couldn't put him right into bed because he was holding onto that watch chain so tightly.

But scarcely was he in bed when all seemed well. He

zu und zog dann die Bettdecke noch besonders weit über die Schulter. Er sah nicht unfreundlich zu Georg hinauf.

»Nicht wahr, du erinnerst dich schon an ihn?« fragte Georg und nickte ihm aufmunternd zu.

»Bin ich jetzt gut zugedeckt?« fragte der Vater, als könne er nicht nachschauen, ob die Füße genug bedeckt seien.

»Es gefällt dir also schon im Bett«, sagte Georg und legte das Deckzeug besser um ihn.

»Bin ich gut zugedeckt?« fragte der Vater noch einmal und schien auf die Antwort besonders aufzupassen.

»Sei nur ruhig, du bist gut zugedeckt.«

»Nein!« rief der Vater, daß die Antwort an die Frage stieß, warf die Decke zurück mit einer Kraft, daß sie einen Augenblick im Fluge sich ganz entfaltete, und stand aufrecht im Bett. Nur eine Hand hielt er leicht an den Plafond. »Du wolltest mich zudecken, das weiß ich, mein Früchtchen, aber zugedeckt bin ich noch nicht. Und ist es auch die letzte Kraft, genug für dich, zuviel für dich. Wohl kenne ich deinen Freund. Er wäre ein Sohn nach meinem Herzen. Darum hast du ihn auch betrogen die ganzen Jahre lang. Warum sonst? Glaubst du, ich habe nicht um ihn geweint? Darum doch sperrst du dich in dein Bureau, niemand soll stören, der Chef ist beschäftigt—nur damit du deine falschen Briefchen nach Rußland schreiben kannst. Aber den Vater muß glücklicherweise niemand lehren, den Sohn zu durchschauen. Wie du jetzt geglaubt hast, du hättest ihn untergekriegt, so untergekriegt, daß du dich mit deinem Hintern auf ihn setzen kannst und er rührt sich nicht, da hat sich mein Herr Sohn zum Heiraten entschlossen!«

Georg sah zum Schreckbild seines Vaters auf. Der Petersburger Freund, den der Vater plötzlich so gut kannte, ergriff ihn, wie noch nie. Verloren im weiten Rußland sah er ihn. An der Türe des leeren, ausgeraubten Geschäftes sah er ihn. Zwischen den Trümmern der Regale, den zerfetzten Waren, den fallenden Gasarmen stand er gerade noch. Warum hatte er so weit wegfahren müssen!

»Aber schau mich an!« rief der Vater, und Georg lief, fast zerstreut, zum Bett, um alles zu fassen, stockte aber in der Mitte des Weges.

»Weil sie die Röcke gehoben hat«, fing der Vater zu flöten an,

covered himself and then pulled the blanket extremely far up over his shoulders. He looked up at Georg in a not unfriendly way.

"Then, you remember him now?" asked Georg and nodded to him encouragingly.

"Am I completely covered up now?" asked his father, as if he couldn't see whether his feet were sufficiently covered.

"So you're already pleased to be in bed," said Georg and tucked him in more thoroughly.

"Am I completely covered up?" asked his father again, and seemed to wait for the answer with particular attention.

"Relax, you're all covered up."

"No!" shouted his father, running his reply into his preceding remark, then threw the blanket back with such force that it completely unfolded for a moment as it flew through the air, and stood upright on the bed. He merely touched the ceiling lightly with one hand. "You wanted to cover me up, I know, offspring of mine, but I'm not covered up yet. And even if I am doing this with my last strength, it is enough for you—too much for you. Of course I know your friend. He would have been a son after my own heart. And that's why you have cheated him all these years. Why else? Do you think I haven't wept over him? Isn't that why you lock yourself into your office, so no one will disturb you—'the boss is busy'—just so you can write your treacherous little letters to Russia. But fortunately no one needs to teach a father how to see through his son. Now that you believed you had got the better of him, got the better of him to such an extent that you can seat yourself on him with your backside and he won't move, this fine son of mine has decided to get married!"

Georg looked up at the frightening image his father presented. His St. Petersburg friend, whom his father suddenly knew so well, stirred his emotions as never before. He saw him lost in far-off Russia. He saw him at the door of his empty, plundered establishment. He was still standing amid the ruins of the shelves, the mangled merchandise, the falling gas brackets. Why did he have to travel so far away!

"But look at me!" shouted his father, and Georg ran almost absentmindedly toward the bed, in order to grasp everything, but came to a sudden halt midway.

"Because she lifted her skirts," his father began to pipe,

»weil sie die Röcke so gehoben hat, die widerliche Gans«, und er
hob, um das darzustellen, sein Hemd so hoch, daß man auf seinem
Oberschenkel die Narbe aus seinen Kriegsjahren sah, »weil sie die
Röcke so und so und so gehoben hat, hast du dich an sie herange-
macht, und damit du an ihr ohne Störung dich befriedigen kannst,
hast du unserer Mutter Andenken geschändet, den Freund verraten und deinen Vater ins Bett gesteckt, damit er sich nicht rühren
kann. Aber kann er sich rühren oder nicht?«
    Und er stand vollkommen frei und warf die Beine. Er strahlte
vor Einsicht.
    Georg stand in einem Winkel, möglichst weit vom Vater. Vor
einer langen Weile hatte er sich fest entschlossen, alles vollkommen
genau zu beobachten, damit er nicht irgendwie auf Umwegen, von
hinten her, von oben herab überrascht werden könne. Jetzt erinnerte er sich wieder an den längst vergessenen Entschluß und
vergaß ihn, wie man einen kurzen Faden durch ein Nadelöhr zieht.
    »Aber der Freund ist nun doch nicht verraten!« rief der Vater,
und sein hin- und herbewegter Zeigefinger bekräftigte es. »Ich war
sein Vertreter hier am Ort.«
    »Komödiant!« konnte sich Georg zu rufen nicht enthalten, er-
kannte sofort den Schaden und biß, nur zu spät,—die Augen erstarrt—in seine Zunge, daß er vor Schmerz einknickte.
    »Ja, freilich habe ich Komödie gespielt! Komödie! Gutes Wort!
Welcher andere Trost blieb dem alten verwitweten Vater?
Sag'—und für den Augenblick der Antwort sei du noch mein le-
bender Sohn—, was blieb mir übrig, in meinem Hinterzimmer,
verfolgt vom ungetreuen Personal, alt bis in die Knochen? Und
mein Sohn ging im Jubel durch die Welt, schloß Geschäfte ab, die
ich vorbereitet hatte, überpurzelte sich vor Vergnügen und ging
vor seinem Vater mit dem verschlossenen Gesicht eines Ehrenman-
nes davon! Glaubst du, ich hätte dich nicht geliebt, ich, von dem du
ausgingst?«
    »Jetzt wird er sich vorbeugen«, dachte Georg, »wenn er fiele und
zerschmetterte!« Dieses Wort durchzischte seinen Kopf.
    Der Vater beugte sich vor, fiel aber nicht. Da Georg sich nicht
näherte, wie er erwartet hatte, erhob er sich wieder.
    »Bleib', wo du bist, ich brauche dich nicht! Du denkst, du hast
noch die Kraft, hierher zu kommen und hältst dich bloß zurück,
weil du so willst. Daß du dich nicht irrst! Ich bin noch immer der
viel Stärkere. Allein hätte ich vielleicht zurückweichen müssen, aber

"because she lifted her skirts that way, the disgusting ninny," and, in order to depict this, he lifted his nightshirt so high that the scar from his war years could be seen on his upper thigh; "because she lifted her skirts so and so and so, you went for her, and in order to satisfy yourself with her without being disturbed, you profaned your mother's memory, betrayed your friend and stuck your father in bed so he couldn't move. But can he move or can't he?"

And he stood completely unsupported and flung out his legs. He was radiant with insight.

Georg stood in a corner, as far from his father as possible. A long time ago he had firmly decided to observe everything with complete thoroughness, so that he might not be somehow taken by surprise in a roundabout way, from behind, from above. Now he once more remembered that long-forgotten decision and forgot it, as one draws a short thread through the eye of a needle.

"But my friend is *not* betrayed!" shouted his father, and his index finger, moving to and fro, confirmed this. "I was his local representative here."

"Play actor!" Georg could not help calling out, immediately recognized the harm he had done himself, and, with staring eyes—but too late—bit his tongue so hard that he doubled up with pain.

"Yes, of course I was playing a part! Play actor! What a good expression! What other comfort remained for an old, bereaved father? Tell me—and, for the moment that it takes you to reply, be my living son yet—what else could I do, in my back room, persecuted by my faithless staff, old to my very bones? And my son went everywhere exultantly, closed business deals that I had set up, turned somersaults from joy, and moved about in front of his father with the poker face of a man of honor! Do you think I wouldn't have loved you, I who gave you your being?"

"Now he'll lean forward," thought Georg; "if he would only fall and smash himself!" This sentence hissed through his mind.

His father leaned forward, but did not fall. Since Georg did not come closer, as he had expected, he straightened up again.

"Stay where you are, I don't need you! You think you still have the strength to come over here, and are merely hanging back because you want to. Don't make a mistake! I am still by far the stronger. On my own I might have

so hat mir die Mutter ihre Kraft abgegeben, mit deinem Freund
habe ich mich herrlich verbunden, deine Kundschaft habe ich hier
in der Tasche!«

»Sogar im Hemd hat er Taschen!« sagte sich Georg und glaubte,
er könne ihn mit dieser Bemerkung in der ganzen Welt unmöglich
machen. Nur einen Augenblick dachte er das, denn immerfort
vergaß er alles.

»Häng' dich nur in deine Braut ein und komm' mir entgegen!
Ich fege sie dir von der Seite weg, du weißt nicht wie!«

Georg machte Grimassen, als glaube er das nicht. Der Vater
nickte bloß, die Wahrheit dessen, was er sagte, beteuernd, in Georgs
Ecke hin.

»Wie hast du mich doch heute unterhalten, als du kamst und
fragtest, ob du deinem Freund von der Verlobung schreiben sollst.
Er weiß doch alles, dummer Junge, er weiß doch alles! Ich schrieb
ihm doch, weil du vergessen hast, mir das Schreibzeug wegzuneh-
men. Darum kommt er schon seit Jahren nicht, er weiß ja alles
hundertmal besser als du selbst, deine Briefe zerknüllt er ungelesen
in der linken Hand, während er in der Rechten meine Briefe zum
Lesen sich vorhält!«

Seinen Arm schwang er vor Begeisterung über dem Kopf. »Er
weiß alles tausendmal besser!« rief er.

»Zehntausendmal!« sagte Georg, um den Vater zu verlachen,
aber noch in seinem Munde bekam das Wort einen toternsten
Klang.

»Seit Jahren passe ich schon auf, daß du mit dieser Frage kämest!
Glaubst du, mich kümmert etwas anderes? Glaubst du, ich lese Zeitungen? Da!« und er warf Georg ein Zeitungsblatt, das irgendwie
mit ins Bett getragen worden war, zu. Eine alte Zeitung, mit einem
Georg schon ganz unbekannten Namen.

»Wie lange hast du gezögert, ehe du reif geworden bist! Die Mutter mußte sterben, sie konnte den Freudentag nicht erleben, der
Freund geht zugrunde in seinem Rußland, schon vor drei Jahren
war er gelb zum Wegwerfen, und ich, du siehst ja, wie es mit mir
steht. Dafür hast du doch Augen!«

»Du hast mir also aufgelauert!« rief Georg.

Mitleidig sagte der Vater nebenbei: »Das wolltest du wahrscheinlich früher sagen. Jetzt paßt es ja gar nicht mehr.«

Und lauter: »Jetzt weißt du also, was es noch außer dir gab, bisher
wußtest du nur von dir! Ein unschuldiges Kind warst du ja eigent-

had to retreat, but your mother passed her strength along to me, I made a wonderful alliance with your friend, I have your clientele here in my pocket!"

"He even has pockets in his nightshirt!" Georg said to himself, and thought that he could obliterate him with that remark. He thought so only for a moment, because he kept forgetting everything.

"Just lock arms with your fiancée and come over to me. I'll sweep her away from your side before you know it!"

Georg made grimaces as if he didn't believe that. His father merely nodded toward Georg's corner, in asseveration of the truth of what he said.

"How you did amuse me today when you came and asked whether you should write your friend about your engagement. He knows everything, foolish boy, he knows everything! I wrote to him because you forgot to take away my writing supplies. That's why he hasn't come for years now, he knows everything a hundred times better than you do; he crumples up your letters in his left hand without reading them, while he holds my letters in front of him in his right hand to read them!"

In his enthusiasm he swung his arm above his head. "He knows everything a thousand times better!" he shouted.

"Ten thousand times!" said Georg, meaning to mock his father, but while still on his lips the words took on a deadly serious tone.

"For years I've been watching and waiting for you to come along with that question! Do you think I care about anything else? Do you think I read newspapers? There!" and he threw over to Georg a sheet of the newspaper that had somehow been carried into the bed along with him. An old paper, with a name now completely unknown to Georg.

"How long you hesitated before your time was ripe! Mother had to die, she couldn't live until the happy day; your friend is going to ruin in his Russia, even three years ago his face was yellow enough to throw away; and I—well, you see how things stand with me. That you have eyes for!"

"So you were lying in wait for me!" shouted Georg.

In a sympathetic tone his father said parenthetically: "You probably wanted to say that before. Now it's no longer fitting."

And in a louder voice: "So now you know what existed outside yourself; up to now you knew only about yourself!

lich, aber noch eigentlicher warst du ein teuflischer Mensch!—Und darum wisse: Ich verurteile dich jetzt zum Tode des Ertrinkens!«

Georg fühlte sich aus dem Zimmer gejagt, den Schlag, mit dem der Vater hinter ihm aufs Bett stürzte, trug er noch in den Ohren davon. Auf der Treppe, über deren Stufen er wie über eine schiefe Fläche eilte, überrumpelte er seine Bedienerin, die im Begriffe war heraufzugehen, um die Wohnung nach der Nacht aufzuräumen. »Jesus!« rief sie und verdeckte mit der Schürze das Gesicht, aber er war schon davon. Aus dem Tor sprang er, über die Fahrbahn zum Wasser trieb es ihn. Schon hielt er das Geländer fest, wie ein Hungriger die Nahrung. Er schwang sich über, als der ausgezeichnete Turner, der er in seinen Jugendjahren zum Stolz seiner Eltern gewesen war. Noch hielt er sich mit schwächer werdenden Händen fest, erspähte zwischen den Geländerstangen einen Autoomnibus, der mit Leichtigkeit seinen Fall übertönen würde, rief leise: »Liebe Eltern, ich habe euch doch immer geliebt«, und ließ sich hinfallen.

In diesem Augenblick ging über die Brücke ein geradezu unendlicher Verkehr.

You were truly an innocent child, but even more truly you were a fiendish person!—And therefore know this: I now condemn you to death by drowning!"

Georg felt himself driven from the room; the crash with which his father collapsed onto the bed behind him was still in his ears as he went. On the staircase, as he dashed down the steps as if down an inclined plane, he knocked over his maid, who was about to go upstairs to tidy up the house after the night. "Jesus!" she cried and covered her face with her apron, but he was already gone. He leapt past the gate and across the roadway, impelled to reach the water. Now he clutched the railing as a hungry man clutches food. He vaulted over like the accomplished gymnast he had been in his youth, to his parents' pride. He was still holding tight with hands that were growing weaker; between the bars of the railing he caught sight of a bus that would easily smother the noise of his fall; he called softly: "Dear parents, I *did* always love you," and let himself fall.

At that moment a simply endless stream of traffic was passing over the bridge.

A CATALOG OF SELECTED
DOVER BOOKS
IN ALL FIELDS OF INTEREST

A CATALOG OF SELECTED DOVER BOOKS IN ALL FIELDS OF INTEREST

CONCERNING THE SPIRITUAL IN ART, Wassily Kandinsky. Pioneering work by father of abstract art. Thoughts on color theory, nature of art. Analysis of earlier masters. 12 illustrations. 80pp. of text. 5⅜ x 8½. 0-486-23411-8

CELTIC ART: The Methods of Construction, George Bain. Simple geometric techniques for making Celtic interlacements, spirals, Kells-type initials, animals, humans, etc. Over 500 illustrations. 160pp. 9 x 12. (Available in U.S. only.) 0-486-22923-8

AN ATLAS OF ANATOMY FOR ARTISTS, Fritz Schider. Most thorough reference work on art anatomy in the world. Hundreds of illustrations, including selections from works by Vesalius, Leonardo, Goya, Ingres, Michelangelo, others. 593 illustrations. 192pp. 7⅛ x 10¼. 0-486-20241-0

CELTIC HAND STROKE-BY-STROKE (Irish Half-Uncial from "The Book of Kells"): An Arthur Baker Calligraphy Manual, Arthur Baker. Complete guide to creating each letter of the alphabet in distinctive Celtic manner. Covers hand position, strokes, pens, inks, paper, more. Illustrated. 48pp. 8¼ x 11. 0-486-24336-2

EASY ORIGAMI, John Montroll. Charming collection of 32 projects (hat, cup, pelican, piano, swan, many more) specially designed for the novice origami hobbyist. Clearly illustrated easy-to-follow instructions insure that even beginning papercrafters will achieve successful results. 48pp. 8¼ x 11. 0-486-27298-2

BLOOMINGDALE'S ILLUSTRATED 1886 CATALOG: Fashions, Dry Goods and Housewares, Bloomingdale Brothers. Famed merchants' extremely rare catalog depicting about 1,700 products: clothing, housewares, firearms, dry goods, jewelry, more. Invaluable for dating, identifying vintage items. Also, copyright-free graphics for artists, designers. Co-published with Henry Ford Museum & Greenfield Village. 160pp. 8¼ x 11. 0-486-25780-0

THE ART OF WORLDLY WISDOM, Baltasar Gracian. "Think with the few and speak with the many," "Friends are a second existence," and "Be able to forget" are among this 1637 volume's 300 pithy maxims. A perfect source of mental and spiritual refreshment, it can be opened at random and appreciated either in brief or at length. 128pp. 5⅜ x 8½. 0-486-44034-6

JOHNSON'S DICTIONARY: A Modern Selection, Samuel Johnson (E. L. McAdam and George Milne, eds.). This modern version reduces the original 1755 edition's 2,300 pages of definitions and literary examples to a more manageable length, retaining the verbal pleasure and historical curiosity of the original. 480pp. 5³⁄₁₆ x 8¼. 0-486-44089-3

ADVENTURES OF HUCKLEBERRY FINN, Mark Twain, Illustrated by E. W. Kemble. A work of eternal richness and complexity, a source of ongoing critical debate, and a literary landmark, Twain's 1885 masterpiece about a barefoot boy's journey of self-discovery has enthralled readers around the world. This handsome clothbound reproduction of the first edition features all 174 of the original black-and-white illustrations. 368pp. 5⅜ x 8½. 0-486-44322-1

THE CLARINET AND CLARINET PLAYING, David Pino. Lively, comprehensive work features suggestions about technique, musicianship, and musical interpretation, as well as guidelines for teaching, making your own reeds, and preparing for public performance. Includes an intriguing look at clarinet history. "A godsend," *The Clarinet*, Journal of the International Clarinet Society. Appendixes. 7 illus. 320pp. 5⅜ x 8½. 0-486-40270-3

HOLLYWOOD GLAMOR PORTRAITS, John Kobal (ed.). 145 photos from 1926-49. Harlow, Gable, Bogart, Bacall; 94 stars in all. Full background on photographers, technical aspects. 160pp. 8⅜ x 11¼. 0-486-23352-9

THE RAVEN AND OTHER FAVORITE POEMS, Edgar Allan Poe. Over 40 of the author's most memorable poems: "The Bells," "Ulalume," "Israfel," "To Helen," "The Conqueror Worm," "Eldorado," "Annabel Lee," many more. Alphabetic lists of titles and first lines. 64pp. 5$^{3}/_{16}$ x 8¼. 0-486-26685-0

PERSONAL MEMOIRS OF U. S. GRANT, Ulysses Simpson Grant. Intelligent, deeply moving firsthand account of Civil War campaigns, considered by many the finest military memoirs ever written. Includes letters, historic photographs, maps and more. 528pp. 6⅛ x 9¼. 0-486-28587-1

ANCIENT EGYPTIAN MATERIALS AND INDUSTRIES, A. Lucas and J. Harris. Fascinating, comprehensive, thoroughly documented text describes this ancient civilization's vast resources and the processes that incorporated them in daily life, including the use of animal products, building materials, cosmetics, perfumes and incense, fibers, glazed ware, glass and its manufacture, materials used in the mummification process, and much more. 544pp. 6⅛ x 9¼. (Available in U.S. only.) 0-486-40446-3

RUSSIAN STORIES/RUSSKIE RASSKAZY: A Dual-Language Book, edited by Gleb Struve. Twelve tales by such masters as Chekhov, Tolstoy, Dostoevsky, Pushkin, others. Excellent word-for-word English translations on facing pages, plus teaching and study aids, Russian/English vocabulary, biographical/critical introductions, more. 416pp. 5⅜ x 8½. 0-486-26244-8

PHILADELPHIA THEN AND NOW: 60 Sites Photographed in the Past and Present, Kenneth Finkel and Susan Oyama. Rare photographs of City Hall, Logan Square, Independence Hall, Betsy Ross House, other landmarks juxtaposed with contemporary views. Captures changing face of historic city. Introduction. Captions. 128pp. 8¼ x 11. 0-486-25790-8

NORTH AMERICAN INDIAN LIFE: Customs and Traditions of 23 Tribes, Elsie Clews Parsons (ed.). 27 fictionalized essays by noted anthropologists examine religion, customs, government, additional facets of life among the Winnebago, Crow, Zuni, Eskimo, other tribes. 480pp. 6⅛ x 9¼. 0-486-27377-6

TECHNICAL MANUAL AND DICTIONARY OF CLASSICAL BALLET, Gail Grant. Defines, explains, comments on steps, movements, poses and concepts. 15-page pictorial section. Basic book for student, viewer. 127pp. 5⅜ x 8½. 0-486-21843-0

THE MALE AND FEMALE FIGURE IN MOTION: 60 Classic Photographic Sequences, Eadweard Muybridge. 60 true-action photographs of men and women walking, running, climbing, bending, turning, etc., reproduced from rare 19th-century masterpiece. vi + 121pp. 9 x 12. 0-486-24745-7

ANIMALS: 1,419 Copyright-Free Illustrations of Mammals, Birds, Fish, Insects, etc., Jim Harter (ed.). Clear wood engravings present, in extremely lifelike poses, over 1,000 species of animals. One of the most extensive pictorial sourcebooks of its kind. Captions. Index. 284pp. 9 x 12.   0-486-23766-4

1001 QUESTIONS ANSWERED ABOUT THE SEASHORE, N. J. Berrill and Jacquelyn Berrill. Queries answered about dolphins, sea snails, sponges, starfish, fishes, shore birds, many others. Covers appearance, breeding, growth, feeding, much more. 305pp. 5¼ x 8¼.   0-486-23366-9

ATTRACTING BIRDS TO YOUR YARD, William J. Weber. Easy-to-follow guide offers advice on how to attract the greatest diversity of birds: birdhouses, feeders, water and waterers, much more. 96pp. 5³⁄₁₆ x 8¼.   0-486-28927-3

MEDICINAL AND OTHER USES OF NORTH AMERICAN PLANTS: A Historical Survey with Special Reference to the Eastern Indian Tribes, Charlotte Erichsen-Brown. Chronological historical citations document 500 years of usage of plants, trees, shrubs native to eastern Canada, northeastern U.S. Also complete identifying information. 343 illustrations. 544pp. 6½ x 9¼.   0-486-25951-X

STORYBOOK MAZES, Dave Phillips. 23 stories and mazes on two-page spreads: Wizard of Oz, Treasure Island, Robin Hood, etc. Solutions. 64pp. 8¼ x 11.
0-486-23628-5

AMERICAN NEGRO SONGS: 230 Folk Songs and Spirituals, Religious and Secular, John W. Work. This authoritative study traces the African influences of songs sung and played by black Americans at work, in church, and as entertainment. The author discusses the lyric significance of such songs as "Swing Low, Sweet Chariot," "John Henry," and others and offers the words and music for 230 songs. Bibliography. Index of Song Titles. 272pp. 6½ x 9¼.   0-486-40271-1

MOVIE-STAR PORTRAITS OF THE FORTIES, John Kobal (ed.). 163 glamor, studio photos of 106 stars of the 1940s: Rita Hayworth, Ava Gardner, Marlon Brando, Clark Gable, many more. 176pp. 8⅜ x 11¼.   0-486-23546-7

YEKL and THE IMPORTED BRIDEGROOM AND OTHER STORIES OF YIDDISH NEW YORK, Abraham Cahan. Film Hester Street based on *Yekl* (1896). Novel, other stories among first about Jewish immigrants on N.Y.'s East Side. 240pp. 5⅜ x 8½.   0-486-22427-9

SELECTED POEMS, Walt Whitman. Generous sampling from *Leaves of Grass*. Twenty-four poems include "I Hear America Singing," "Song of the Open Road," "I Sing the Body Electric," "When Lilacs Last in the Dooryard Bloom'd," "O Captain! My Captain!"–all reprinted from an authoritative edition. Lists of titles and first lines. 128pp. 5³⁄₁₆ x 8¼.   0-486-26878-0

SONGS OF EXPERIENCE: Facsimile Reproduction with 26 Plates in Full Color, William Blake. 26 full-color plates from a rare 1826 edition. Includes "The Tyger," "London," "Holy Thursday," and other poems. Printed text of poems. 48pp. 5¼ x 7.
0-486-24636-1

THE BEST TALES OF HOFFMANN, E. T. A. Hoffmann. 10 of Hoffmann's most important stories: "Nutcracker and the King of Mice," "The Golden Flowerpot," etc. 458pp. 5⅜ x 8½.   0-486-21793-0

THE BOOK OF TEA, Kakuzo Okakura. Minor classic of the Orient: entertaining, charming explanation, interpretation of traditional Japanese culture in terms of tea ceremony. 94pp. 5⅜ x 8½.   0-486-20070-1

FRENCH STORIES/CONTES FRANÇAIS: A Dual-Language Book, Wallace Fowlie. Ten stories by French masters, Voltaire to Camus: "Micromegas" by Voltaire; "The Atheist's Mass" by Balzac; "Minuet" by de Maupassant; "The Guest" by Camus, six more. Excellent English translations on facing pages. Also French-English vocabulary list, exercises, more. 352pp. 5⅜ x 8½. 0-486-26443-2

CHICAGO AT THE TURN OF THE CENTURY IN PHOTOGRAPHS: 122 Historic Views from the Collections of the Chicago Historical Society, Larry A. Viskochil. Rare large-format prints offer detailed views of City Hall, State Street, the Loop, Hull House, Union Station, many other landmarks, circa 1904-1913. Introduction. Captions. Maps. 144pp. 9⅜ x 12¼. 0-486-24656-6

OLD BROOKLYN IN EARLY PHOTOGRAPHS, 1865-1929, William Lee Younger. Luna Park, Gravesend race track, construction of Grand Army Plaza, moving of Hotel Brighton, etc. 157 previously unpublished photographs. 165pp. 8⅞ x 11¾. 0-486-23587-4

THE MYTHS OF THE NORTH AMERICAN INDIANS, Lewis Spence. Rich anthology of the myths and legends of the Algonquins, Iroquois, Pawnees and Sioux, prefaced by an extensive historical and ethnological commentary. 36 illustrations. 480pp. 5⅜ x 8½. 0-486-25967-6

AN ENCYCLOPEDIA OF BATTLES: Accounts of Over 1,560 Battles from 1479 B.C. to the Present, David Eggenberger. Essential details of every major battle in recorded history from the first battle of Megiddo in 1479 B.C. to Grenada in 1984. List of Battle Maps. New Appendix covering the years 1967-1984. Index. 99 illustrations. 544pp. 6½ x 9¼. 0-486-24913-1

SAILING ALONE AROUND THE WORLD, Captain Joshua Slocum. First man to sail around the world, alone, in small boat. One of great feats of seamanship told in delightful manner. 67 illustrations. 294pp. 5⅜ x 8½. 0-486-20326-3

ANARCHISM AND OTHER ESSAYS, Emma Goldman. Powerful, penetrating, prophetic essays on direct action, role of minorities, prison reform, puritan hypocrisy, violence, etc. 271pp. 5⅜ x 8½. 0-486-22484-8

MYTHS OF THE HINDUS AND BUDDHISTS, Ananda K. Coomaraswamy and Sister Nivedita. Great stories of the epics; deeds of Krishna, Shiva, taken from puranas, Vedas, folk tales; etc. 32 illustrations. 400pp. 5⅜ x 8½. 0-486-21759-0

MY BONDAGE AND MY FREEDOM, Frederick Douglass. Born a slave, Douglass became outspoken force in antislavery movement. The best of Douglass' autobiographies. Graphic description of slave life. 464pp. 5⅜ x 8½. 0-486-22457-0

FOLLOWING THE EQUATOR: A Journey Around the World, Mark Twain. Fascinating humorous account of 1897 voyage to Hawaii, Australia, India, New Zealand, etc. Ironic, bemused reports on peoples, customs, climate, flora and fauna, politics, much more. 197 illustrations. 720pp. 5⅜ x 8½. 0-486-26113-1

THE PEOPLE CALLED SHAKERS, Edward D. Andrews. Definitive study of Shakers: origins, beliefs, practices, dances, social organization, furniture and crafts, etc. 33 illustrations. 351pp. 5⅜ x 8½. 0-486-21081-2

THE MYTHS OF GREECE AND ROME, H. A. Guerber. A classic of mythology, generously illustrated, long prized for its simple, graphic, accurate retelling of the principal myths of Greece and Rome, and for its commentary on their origins and significance. With 64 illustrations by Michelangelo, Raphael, Titian, Rubens, Canova, Bernini and others. 480pp. 5⅜ x 8½. 0-486-27584-1

THE MALLEUS MALEFICARUM OF KRAMER AND SPRENGER, translated by Montague Summers. Full text of most important witchhunter's "bible," used by both Catholics and Protestants. 278pp. 6⅝ x 10. 0-486-22802-9

SPANISH STORIES/CUENTOS ESPAÑOLES: A Dual-Language Book, Angel Flores (ed.). Unique format offers 13 great stories in Spanish by Cervantes, Borges, others. Faithful English translations on facing pages. 352pp. 5⅜ x 8½. 0-486-25399-6

GARDEN CITY, LONG ISLAND, IN EARLY PHOTOGRAPHS, 1869–1919, Mildred H. Smith. Handsome treasury of 118 vintage pictures, accompanied by carefully researched captions, document the Garden City Hotel fire (1899), the Vanderbilt Cup Race (1908), the first airmail flight departing from the Nassau Boulevard Aerodrome (1911), and much more. 96pp. 8⅞ x 11¾. 0-486-40669-5

OLD QUEENS, N.Y., IN EARLY PHOTOGRAPHS, Vincent F. Seyfried and William Asadorian. Over 160 rare photographs of Maspeth, Jamaica, Jackson Heights, and other areas. Vintage views of DeWitt Clinton mansion, 1939 World's Fair and more. Captions. 192pp. 8⅞ x 11. 0-486-26358-4

CAPTURED BY THE INDIANS: 15 Firsthand Accounts, 1750-1870, Frederick Drimmer. Astounding true historical accounts of grisly torture, bloody conflicts, relentless pursuits, miraculous escapes and more, by people who lived to tell the tale. 384pp. 5⅜ x 8½. 0-486-24901-8

THE WORLD'S GREAT SPEECHES (Fourth Enlarged Edition), Lewis Copeland, Lawrence W. Lamm, and Stephen J. McKenna. Nearly 300 speeches provide public speakers with a wealth of updated quotes and inspiration–from Pericles' funeral oration and William Jennings Bryan's "Cross of Gold Speech" to Malcolm X's powerful words on the Black Revolution and Earl of Spenser's tribute to his sister, Diana, Princess of Wales. 944pp. 5⅜ x 8⅜. 0-486-40903-1

THE BOOK OF THE SWORD, Sir Richard F. Burton. Great Victorian scholar/adventurer's eloquent, erudite history of the "queen of weapons"–from prehistory to early Roman Empire. Evolution and development of early swords, variations (sabre, broadsword, cutlass, scimitar, etc.), much more. 336pp. 6⅛ x 9¼. 0-486-25434-8

AUTOBIOGRAPHY: The Story of My Experiments with Truth, Mohandas K. Gandhi. Boyhood, legal studies, purification, the growth of the Satyagraha (nonviolent protest) movement. Critical, inspiring work of the man responsible for the freedom of India. 480pp. 5⅜ x 8½. (Available in U.S. only.) 0-486-24593-4

CELTIC MYTHS AND LEGENDS, T. W. Rolleston. Masterful retelling of Irish and Welsh stories and tales. Cuchulain, King Arthur, Deirdre, the Grail, many more. First paperback edition. 58 full-page illustrations. 512pp. 5⅜ x 8½. 0-486-26507-2

THE PRINCIPLES OF PSYCHOLOGY, William James. Famous long course complete, unabridged. Stream of thought, time perception, memory, experimental methods; great work decades ahead of its time. 94 figures. 1,391pp. 5⅜ x 8½. 2-vol. set. Vol. I: 0-486-20381-6 Vol. II: 0-486-20382-4

THE WORLD AS WILL AND REPRESENTATION, Arthur Schopenhauer. Definitive English translation of Schopenhauer's life work, correcting more than 1,000 errors, omissions in earlier translations. Translated by E. F. J. Payne. Total of 1,269pp. 5⅜ x 8½. 2-vol. set. Vol. 1: 0-486-21761-2 Vol. 2: 0-486-21762-0

LIGHT AND SHADE: A Classic Approach to Three-Dimensional Drawing, Mrs. Mary P. Merrifield. Handy reference clearly demonstrates principles of light and shade by revealing effects of common daylight, sunshine, and candle or artificial light on geometrical solids. 13 plates. 64pp. 5⅜ x 8½. 0-486-44143-1

ASTROLOGY AND ASTRONOMY: A Pictorial Archive of Signs and Symbols, Ernst and Johanna Lehner. Treasure trove of stories, lore, and myth, accompanied by more than 300 rare illustrations of planets, the Milky Way, signs of the zodiac, comets, meteors, and other astronomical phenomena. 192pp. 8⅜ x 11.
0-486-43981-X

JEWELRY MAKING: Techniques for Metal, Tim McCreight. Easy-to-follow instructions and carefully executed illustrations describe tools and techniques, use of gems and enamels, wire inlay, casting, and other topics. 72 line illustrations and diagrams. 176pp. 8¼ x 10⅞. 0-486-44043-5

MAKING BIRDHOUSES: Easy and Advanced Projects, Gladstone Califf. Easy-to-follow instructions include diagrams for everything from a one-room house for bluebirds to a forty-two-room structure for purple martins. 56 plates; 4 figures. 80pp. 8¾ x 6⅜. 0-486-44183-0

LITTLE BOOK OF LOG CABINS: How to Build and Furnish Them, William S. Wicks. Handy how-to manual, with instructions and illustrations for building cabins in the Adirondack style, fireplaces, stairways, furniture, beamed ceilings, and more. 102 line drawings. 96pp. 8¾ x 6⅜. 0-486-44259-4

THE SEASONS OF AMERICA PAST, Eric Sloane. From "sugaring time" and strawberry picking to Indian summer and fall harvest, a whole year's activities described in charming prose and enhanced with 79 of the author's own illustrations. 160pp. 8¼ x 11. 0-486-44220-9

THE METROPOLIS OF TOMORROW, Hugh Ferriss. Generous, prophetic vision of the metropolis of the future, as perceived in 1929. Powerful illustrations of towering structures, wide avenues, and rooftop parks—all features in many of today's modern cities. 59 illustrations. 144pp. 8¼ x 11. 0-486-43727-2

THE PATH TO ROME, Hilaire Belloc. This 1902 memoir abounds in lively vignettes from a vanished time, recounting a pilgrimage on foot across the Alps and Apennines in order to "see all Europe which the Christian Faith has saved." 77 of the author's original line drawings complement his sparkling prose. 272pp. 5⅜ x 8½.
0-486-44001-X

THE HISTORY OF RASSELAS: Prince of Abissinia, Samuel Johnson. Distinguished English writer attacks eighteenth-century optimism and man's unrealistic estimates of what life has to offer. 112pp. 5⅜ x 8½. 0-486-44094-X

A VOYAGE TO ARCTURUS, David Lindsay. A brilliant flight of pure fancy, where wild creatures crowd the fantastic landscape and demented torturers dominate victims with their bizarre mental powers. 272pp. 5⅜ x 8½. 0-486-44198-9

Paperbound unless otherwise indicated. Available at your book dealer, online at www.doverpublications.com, or by writing to Dept. GI, Dover Publications, Inc., 31 East 2nd Street, Mineola, NY 11501. For current price information or for free catalogs (please indicate field of interest), write to Dover Publications or log on to www.doverpublications.com and see every Dover book in print. Dover publishes more than 500 books each year on science, elementary and advanced mathematics, biology, music, art, literary history, social sciences, and other areas.